RURAL DEVELOPMENT IN INDIA

By the same Author

—Village Development in North East India: New Approaches
—Rural Development in North East India
—Economy of A Primitive Tribal Village in Manipur

About the Editor

Komol Singha (1972) is a Senior Faculty in the Department of Economics, Gaeddu College of Business Studies, Royal University of Bhutan. Earlier, he was a faculty in Economics at Don Bosco College in Manipur and St. Joseph's College in Nagaland. He has to his credit a book entitled: *Village Development in North-East India* (ed. 2009) and a good number of research papers published in national and international journals of repute. He has also participated in various seminars. His research interests include the study of Human Resource Development, Social Capital and Social Sector. He is also a life member of North-East Economic Association.

Rural Development in India

Retrospect and Prospects

Edited by

Komol Singha

CONCEPT PUBLISHING COMPANY PVT. LTD.
NEW DELHI-110 059

ISBN-13: 978-81-8069-704-3

First Published 2010

Published and Printed by

Concept Publishing Company, Pvt. Ltd.
Regd. Office:
A/15-16, Commercial Block, Mohan Garden
New Delhi-110059 (India)
Phones : 25351460, 25351794, *Fax* : 091-11-25357109
Email : publishing@conceptpub.com,
Website: www.conceptpub.com

Editorial Office:
H-13, Bali Nagar, New Delhi-110 015, India.

Cataloging in Publication Data--*Courtesy:* D.K. Agencies (P) Ltd. <docinfo@dkagencies.com>

Rural development in India : retrospect and prospects / edited by Komol Singha.
p. cm.
Contributed articles.
Includes bibliographical references and index.
ISBN 9788180697043

1. Rural development--India, Northeastern. 2. Rural development--India--Nāgāland. 3. Rural development--India. 4. Agriculture--Economic aspects--India. I. Singha, Komol, 1972-

DDC 307.1409541 22

Preface

India, from the point of social, economic and political perspectives, the study of rural development is very relevant today. Around 70 per cent of the country's population is living in rural areas. Further, there are cascading effects of poverty, unemployment, poor and inadequate infrastructure in rural areas. During recent past, Indian economy has witnessed spectacular success in terms of achieving a higher growth rate. However, the benefits of the same have not percolated and shared by the poor masses. The process of growth, therefore, has not been inclusive. Knowing this, the Eleventh Five Year Plan (2007-12) lays emphasis on providing basic facilities, especially, education and health, to masses of our people to enable them to avail of the benefits of growth.

Still, the situation remains more or less same in the rural areas of the country, or pace of development is very slow. Relook to our past mistakes has become need of the hour and from the experiences, we have to remodel future strategies for a strong and sustainable rural India with better access to services, technology, education and health-care will reduce inequality and alleviate poverty for hundreds of millions of its citizens. The prime goal of rural development is to improve the quality of life of the rural people by alleviating poverty through various approaches.

Keeping all these in mind, the present volume attempts to explore ways and means for the development of rural India. It contains twenty (20) articles, based on the theme of rural development contributed by the renowned scholars of the country. They tried to exhibit the problems and possibilities of rural development of the country in different approaches. The contributors also have analyzed the past experiences, present scenario and recommend future policies accordingly. To achieve the goal of rural development, valuable contributors of this volume have tried their level best and shown various possible ways for rural development. For their contribution, I would like to extend my heartfelt gratitude and credit to all the valuable contributors. Last, but not the least; I would like to thank Mr. Ashok Kumar Mittal of Concept Publishing Company Pvt. Ltd., New Delhi for his effort to bring out this volume on time.

22 March, 2009 **Komol Singha**

Introduction

Rural India is currently the home to approximately 70 per cent of country's population. The country from the social, economic and political perspectives, the study and the analysis of rural sector is very significant today. There are cascading effects of poverty, unemployment, poor and inadequate infrastructure in rural areas. The prime goal of rural development is to improve the quality of life of the rural people by alleviating poverty through the instrument of self-employment and wage employment programmes. This process can be accelerated by providing community infrastructure facilities such as drinking water, electricity, road connectivity, health facilities, rural housing and education and promoting decentralization of powers to strengthen the Panchayati Raj institutions, and empowerment of village community and women, etc.

During recent past, Indian economy has witnessed spectacular success in terms of achieving a higher growth rate. Especially, since Independence and inception of plan periods, huge amounts have been spent for the rural development in the country. The Eleventh Five Year Plan (2007-12) also lays emphasis on providing basic facilities, especially education and health, to masses of our people to enable them to avail the benefits of growth. However, the benefits of the same have not percolated and shared by the rural masses. The process of growth, therefore, has not been inclusive. Still, it remains an illusive goal.

Despite concerted efforts, the rural populace remains poor in the midst of abundant resources. The Government of India's programme to assist the rural poor could not do much to alleviate the sufferings of the poor. In spite of the schemes' commendable objectives, the projects fell short of providing accessibility to education, health, infrastructure, electricity, water supply, telecommunication, employment, etc. to the rural masses. Even the most flagship rural development programme of the UPA-led Coalition Government, National Rural Employment Guarantee Scheme (NREGS) has turned out to be an elite-biased programme (as reported by *Social Audit* of the renowned economist, Prof. Jean Dreze of Delhi School of Economics). Many poor farmers have been thrown out of their own lands in the name of urbanization and industrialization. The country became the fifth largest economy and the home to Asia's biggest club of billionaires on the one side, and on the other side, the country became the home to half of the world's poor. Most of the infrastructure projects are formulated and undertaken for execution not based on their technical and economic superiority but on extraneous considerations.

Now the question that arises is whether the failure is due to the lack of initiatives on the part of the Government or the lack of support from the people. Whatsoever the reason, rural masses still remains poor and the pace of development is comparatively very slow. So, re-look to past mistakes has become need of the hour and from the experiences, we have to redesign our future plans for strong and sustainable rural India with better access to services, technology, education and health-care which will reduce inequality and alleviate poverty for hundreds of millions of its citizens.

Chapter Scheme

The primary objective of this volume is to provide readers with case studies and empirical insights into the structure of rural India. For the convenience and easy indexing, this volume is broadly divided into three sections and contains twenty (20) essays on various aspects and approaches of rural development in the country.

Section I : Development, especially the Rural Sector is a very complex and dynamic process which transforms an economy and society from a relatively backward State to a more advanced State. For a sustainable rural development, the evaluation of past experience is necessary. So, this section is named as *Past Lesson and New Approaches to Rural Development* and contains seven essays. At the very outset, M.P. Bezbaruah, in his essay entitled on *Rural Development in India : The Past Experience and a Future Perspective* portrays the difficulties of implementing agencies to meet huge investment of rural sector in the country. From the past experiences, he further cautions the proper implementation and transparency of projects sanctioned under different schemes in the rural areas. The same idea is also highlighted by Ratan Kaurinta, in his essay (fourth essay of the volume) entitled *VDB and Rural Development : A Case Study of Paren District in Nagaland.* The Second essay of the book by Raj Kumar Sen, entitled *Rural Development in India in the Post-Reform Era* explains the changes that are taking place since the initiation of economic reforms in 1991 and the impacts they have on the agricultural sector. His essay further discusses the rural and agricultural development in the pre-reform decades, the impacts of the economic reforms and the WTO agreements, debatable issues like SEZ and agri-business, food security and hunger of the Indian economy and the present situation. The third essay of this volume is about shifting cultivation, entitled *Cognitive Frame and Occupational Opportunity : A Study of Jhum Cultivators in Nagaland* jointly contributed by Saradindu Bhaduri and Abhinandan Saikia. In their words, occupational opportunities are important for reducing poverty not only by generating income, but also by raising human capability to choose an appropriate living condition. Further, they discuss why people only accept 'changes' selectively in the process of economic adjustment. Limited alternative avenues due to basic physical infrastructures, *jhum* cultivation remains significant for the Naga community. Slightly similar to this essay, Amod Sharma, K.K. Jha and D.S. Dhakre together in the seventh essay of the volume *Harnessing Agricultural Resources for Socio-economic Development of North-East India* have highlighted the importance of infrastructure for agricultural development. Agricultural potentials have not been explored fully in NEI due to the lack of necessary infrastructure in the region. In the sixth essay of this volume, J.U. Ahmed, in his essay on *Rural Transformation in India : A Study on the Efficiency of DWCRA* also portrays the difficulties faced by the rural women-folk. The rural women hesitate to undertake non-traditional trade due to lack of marketing opportunities. There is an undue delay in the delivery of assistance because of lack of functional coordination among banks, DRDA and the beneficiaries. The potentiality of the programme as a result nipped in the bud due to its non-implementation in the grassroot level. In the fifth essay entitled *Hedonic Demand for Rented House in Kohima, Nagaland,* S.K. Mishra and M.L. Ngullie try to show how the demand for a rentable house can be quantitatively expressed. It further draws on the theory of consumer's demand from Kelvin Lancaster who suggested that a commodity may be considered as a bundle of numerous characteristics and consumers are willing to pay for those characteristics.

Section II : The essays in this section basically deal with the problems of unemployment, population, poverty and various primary sectors in rural India. The subtitle of this section is given as *Population, Migration and Sectoral Development* and contains seven essays. To begin with, the eighth essay of this volume on *Mining along Indo-Bangla Border : A Study of State Politics, Migrant Labour and Land Relations in Meghalaya,* contributed by Debojyoti Das, tries to analyse the nexus between coal mining and environment policies on the one hand, and the land ownership conflict among the tribal communities on the other in rural Meghalaya. He further attempts to ethnographically tell the life stories of mine workers and draw upon the colonial and post colonial articulation of local politics that have shaped contemporary anxiety on how to regulate informal coal mining in the hill State of Meghalaya. In a slightly similar idea, Mahmood Ansari, in his chapter entitled *Agricultural Functions in Purnia : A Study of North Bihar,* the fourteenth chapter of this volume also analyses the policies of different classes of agricultural farmers in Bihar. He further discusses the peasant-operators are not uniformly profit-maximizers and a uniform technology is not accessible to all classes of peasantry, particularly in North Bihar. It is, therefore, posited that there are bound to be logically a hierarchy of production functions rather than a unique aggregate function in agriculture. A unique production function is best suitable for a cross-section of uniformly controlled experimental farms, but not the diverse class of actually existing farms owned and operated by differentiated peasantry. In such a differentiated agricultural milieu, a uniform rural development policy would be self-defeating. The ninth essay of the volume is contributed jointly by D.P. Pal and Debottam Chakraborty entitled *Levels of Living, Demographic Changes and Growth Divergence : A Study of North-East India.* The chapter tries to examine the levels of living of the people in NEI during 1993-2004 in the context of demographic changes and economic growth. Further in their chapter, they found that irrespective of the regions in the North-East India, the level of living has been improving since 1993. In case of rural areas, inter-State disparity in consumption and hence well-being among the region has been declining, and in case of urban areas, it tends to be increasing. Similarly, in the tenth essay of this volume on *Rural Poverty and Rural Non-farm Employment in India : An Inter-State Analysis* contributed by Prankrishna Pal also highlighted the different aspects of rural poverty and rural non-farm employment in India during 1973-74 to 2004-05. Further, he tries to portray how development of the rural economy occurs when dependence on farm activities decreases and non-farm activities increases. The thirteenth essay entitled *Employment, Well-being and Growth in Rural India : An Inter-State Comparison* contributed by Gunendra Prasad Pal also gives the same idea. In his chapter, he concluded that the level of rural poverty will be reduced if rural labour force is engaged intensively in rural alternative activities as scheduled in the rural development programmes of the Government. In the eleventh chapter entitled *Sericulture in Assam : Problems and Prospects* contributed jointly by P.C. Dutta and A. Kherkatary has explored the potentials of Sericulture in Assam. Despite the opportunities, the sector cannot uplift the living standard of rural masses in the State. They further draw the attention of Government to fill the development gaps. The twelfth essay of the volume entitled *Agriculture and Forestry : A Road Map to Rural Development* jointly contributed by K.C. Kabra and R.K.P.G. Singha tries to identify the opportunities of self-employment opportunities to educated youths in rural Mizoram. The chapter gives courage to the rural unemployed to start non-traditional farm activities. Success will not be there if there is no failure.

Section III : The study of rural development without some basic infrastructures and peoples' support is incomplete. So, this section covers some core issues of rural development, consisting of six essays named as *Infrastructure, Education and Participation.* The basic physical infrastructure is concerned, the fifteenth essay of the volume entitled *Infrastructure Development in Coastal Kkarnataka : Major Challenges and Key Policy Issues* jointly contributed by V. Sham Bhat and Musthaf depicts a brief profile of coastal Karnataka and highlights the major challenges and key policy issues with respect to infrastructure. The chapter further elaborates that the low level of human development is both a cause and consequence of inadequate and insufficient infrastructure. Thus, they caution that most of the infrastructure projects in the coastal Karnataka are formulated and undertaken for execution sake not based on their technical and economic superiority but on extraneous considerations. In many cases, premature investments are made in infrastructure capacity creation entailing enormous resources that could otherwise have been devoted to maintenance, modernization or improvements in service quality. Again, infrastructure investments have often been misallocated. The situation is not different in NEI too. The same is also highlighted in the twentieth chapter of this volume by Gautam Patikar in *Rural Transport Development in Nagaland.* It portrays the road transport system of Nagaland and how the State of Nagaland is neglected in this direction without which, the development of rural sector is like a boat without radar. Similarly, the seventeenth and nineteenth essay of this volume have also highlighted the need of infrastructure in the rural development. Sudipta Sarkar and Priyam Kumar Roy in their article entitled *Bilateral Relation with Myanmar : Its Influence on Rural Development in Nagaland* has given the importance of transportation in border trade with Myanmar. The NEI, especially rural Nagaland can be developed much faster if the basic road communication is developed. D.S. Dhakre and Amod Sharma also together in their chapter on *Inter-district Disparities in Socio-economic Development in Nagaland* also try to evaluate the imbalances of development in the State by using some socio-economic indicators. The study also throws light on the relationships of socio-economic development with the agricultural development and infrastructural facilities. The sixteenth and the eighteenth chapter of this volume deal with the education system. How the education takes care of the development process in an economy, especially in the rural sector is discussed. Komol Singha in his article on *English Education and Rural Development : A North-East Perspective* discusses the importance of English education especially in the primary level. Primary education is the foundation of a strong society. How the English education uplifts the tribal region in NEI is discussed on one hand, and the development pace of regional medium educational system in the rural NEI is much slower than the former. Similarly, G.V. Chalam; C. Suresh Babu; and J. Sucharitha together in their chaper on *Rural Development in India : The Strategic Leadership Model of an Education Enterprise* lamented the degrading quality of education in India. It is due to the commercialization of education system in the country. It explains educational scenario of the country and tries to expose the defects in the system in a satirical way.

Thus, this volume has touched upon almost all the components needed for the development of rural sector in India. Though the contributors have given insights and their approaches differently, all of them have highlighted the role of physical infrastructure with institutional supports, social sector, sectoral development, trade and industry, the people's involvement, etc. in the development process of rural sector. They have focused to a common objective, *i.e.* 'Development of Rural Sector of the Country'. It is believed that the volume will contribute positively to plan and execute policies, projects and programmes for the development of country's rural sector, one of the resource-rich but underdeveloped sectors.

Komol Singha

Contents

SECTION II

POPULATION, MIGRATION AND SECTORAL DEVELOPMENT

SECTION III

INFRASTRUCTURE, EDUCATION AND PARTICIPATION

List of Contributors

Ahmed, J.U., Faculty, Department of Management, North Eastern Hill University, Tura Campus, Meghalaya.

Ansari, Mahmood, Faculty, Department of Economics, Assam University, Silchar, Assam.

Bezbaruah, M.P., Faculty, Department of Economics, Guwahati University, Guwahati, Assam.

Babu, C. Suresh, Faculty, Department of Management Studies, Madanapalle Institute of Technology and Science, Madanapalle, Andhra Pradesh.

Bhat, V. Sham, Faculty and Head, Department of Economics, Sacred Heart College, Madanthyar, Karnataka.

Bhaduri, Saradindu, Faculty, Centre for Studies in Science Policy, Jawaharlal Nehru University, New Delhi.

Chalam, G.V., Faculty, Department of Commerce and Business Administration, Acharya Nagarjuna University, Guntur, Andhra Pradesh.

Chakraborty, Debottam, Research Scholar, Department of Economics, University of Kalyani, Nadia, West Bengal.

Das, Debojyoti, Research Scholar, School of Oriental and African Studies (SoAS), University of London, Russell Square, London.

Dhakre, D.S., Faculty, Department of Agricultural Economics, School of Agricultural Science and Rural Development, Nagaland University, Medziphema, Nagaland.

Dutta, P.C., Faculty and Head, Department of Statistics, S.S. College, Hailakandi, Assam.

Jha, K.K., Faculty, Department of Agricultural Economics, School of Agricultural Science and Rural Development, Nagaland University, Medziphema, Nagaland.

Kabra, K.C., Faculty, Department of Commerce, North-Eastern Hill University, Shillong, Meghalaya.

Kherkatary, A., Faculty, Department of Economics, S.S. College, Hailakandi, Assam.

Kaurinta, Ratan, Faculty, Department of Commerce, Nagaland University, Kohima, Nagaland.

Musthaf, Research Scholar and Project Fellow, Department of Economics, Mangalore University, Mangalore, Karnataka.

Mishra, S.K., Faculty, Department of Economics, North Eastern Hill University, Shillong, Meghalaya.

Ngullie, M.L., Faculty, Department of Economics, Dimapur Government College, Dimapur, Nagaland.

Pal, D.P., Faculty, Department of Economics, University of Kalyani, Nadia, West Bengal.

Pal, Prankrishna, Faculty, Department of Economics, Rabindra Bharati University, Kolkata, West Bengal.

Pal, Gunendra Prasad, Faculty, Department of Economics, Umes Chandra College, Kolkata, West Bengal.

Patikar, Gautam, Faculty, Department of Commerce, Nagaland University, Kohima, Nagaland.

Roy, Priyam Kumar, Faculty, Department of History, Kalyani Mahavidyalaya, Kalyani, Nadia, West Bengal.

Sarkar, Sudipta, Faculty, Department of Commerce, Kalyani Mahavidyalaya, Kalyani, Nadia, West Bengal.

Sen, Raj Kumar, Faculty, Department of Economics and Director, Centre for Studies on Environment and Sustainable Development, Rabindra Bharati University, Kolkata, West Bengal and Former President, Indian Economic Association.

Saikia, Abhinandan, Research Scholar, Centre for Studies in Science Policy, Jawaharlal Nehru University, New Delhi.

Sucharitha, J., Faculty, Department of Management Studies, Madanapalle Institute of Technology and Science, Madanapalle, Andhra Pradesh.

Singha, R.K.P.G., Faculty and Head, Department of Commerce, Pachhunga University College, Mizoram University, Aizawl, Mizoram.

Singha, Komol, Faculty, Department of Economics, Royal University of Bhutan, Gaeddu College of Business Studies, Gedu, Bhutan.

Sharma, Amod, Faculty, Department of Agricultural Economics, School of Agricultural Science and Rural Development, Nagaland University, Medziphema, Nagaland.

SECTION I

Past Lessons and New Approaches to Rural Development

1

Rural Development in India

The Past Experience and a Future Perspective

M.P. BEZBARUAH

Development and Rural Development

Development essentially is a dynamic process which transforms an economy and society from a relatively backward state to a more advanced state. The transition encompasses several dimensions such as growth in productivity and income, structural change in the economy and the society, institutional changes, changes in attitudes and values of people and even in customs and social practices. However, the bottom line of the process is an improvement of the quality of life of the people at large. In other words, the process of change will qualify as development only if it results into an improvement in the quality of life of the people reflected in better nutrition and health standard, greater opportunity to be educated and elimination of deprivation from participation in social and economic life.

The focus on rural development over and above the concern for overall economic development has arisen from two lines of reasoning. The first and the more obvious one, especially for a country like India, arises from the fact that a large majority of the population say around, 70 to 80 per cent for most States in India, live in rural areas among which the incidence and intensity of poverty is relatively higher. Interestingly, the widespread poverty and hunger in rural areas arise not so much from open unemployment as from low intensity of employment and general low productivity of resources. Though in the peak agricultural seasons village communities often experience labour shortage, for the better part of the year agricultural workers find it hard to get paying work. The general deficiency of basic facilities such as roads, communication, power, education, health care and even sanitation and drinking water, not only contributes to and compounds low productivity and intensity of employment but also has a general depressing effect in the quality of life. Obviously special attention is required to address the problem of development of rural areas and the people living there.

The other and somewhat less obvious line of reasoning, which calls for special focus on rural development, arises from disparities in the distribution of opportunities between urban and rural areas. With concentration of industrial, commercial, financial and administrative set-ups in the urban centres, in a modernizing economy, socio-economic prospect and opportunities are usually disproportionately concentrated in town and cities. This naturally pulls immigrants in pursuit of better opportunities. But in most third world countries, the stagnancy in the neglected rural sector pushes far too many immigrants from villages to cities to be absorbed in the organized sector. While the surplus immigrants wait in the informal sector swelling the ranks of urban unemployed or semi-employed, the slums and squatter population expands. Urban poverty surfaces, civic facilities and basic infrastructure are strained and urban environment gets degraded. Thus developing urban oriented islands of growth without concomitant improvement of opportunities in rural areas has landed up many developing countries in a dualistic structure not conducive to sustainable and overall progress of the economy and the society. Hence, greater attention, efforts and resources for expediting rural development have become an imperative not only for improving the quality of lives of people in the villages but also for ensuring that the metropolitan centres of industry, commerce and administration take strides towards prosperity with less congestion and better socio-economic and physical environment.

Evolution of Rural Development Policy in India

The Approach in India during Early Plans

As India launched serious planned development efforts with the Second Five Year-Plan starting in 1956, rural development did not receive enough attention (as also in case of many of the contemporary developing countries). Instead of the Gandhian idea of village based economies, the official line of Nehru-Mahalanobis strategy of planning opted for catching up with the developed countries through rapid industrialization. From the supply side this necessitates setting up of capital goods industries requiring lumpy investments with long gestation. Socialistic ideology and a lack of confidence on the private sector prompted the policy-makers to deploy those investments in the public sector leaving out insufficient resources with the State for developing the rest of the economy. The initiatives towards rural development in early planning era were confined to land reforms, setting up community development blocks and promotion of cooperatives. Besides elimination of *zamindary*, the land reform legislations were not fully implemented in most parts of the country. Cooperatives were generally promoted and pursued as government agencies and failed to deliver the goods, notwithstanding some significant exceptions. The community development blocks sprang up as mediums of implementation of government programmes at the grassroots. But the blocks remained as implementing units of programmes dictated from above, rather than institutions for securing community participation for formulation and implementation of their own development programmes.

In the late 1960s, the introduction of new agriculture technology led to 'green revolution' in parts of rural India. But income gains from this development, for quite some time, remained confined to a small section of rural society because of slow diffusion of new technology to rest of the country and across to the smaller size class of farmers. Hence, in spite of the advent of the green revolution, poverty in rural India remains so widespread and acute that even official statistics recorded that in the late 1970s a half of India's rural population lived below the poverty line.

Specific Programmes since the Sixth Plan

The dismal state of affairs led to some rethinking on the overall strategy of development in general and the initiatives for rural development in particular. With the overall growth rate showing no tendency to step up from the so-called 'Hindu rate' of 3.6 per cent, the trickle down effect of growth could at best be extremely weak. It was realized that reduction of poverty could not be left to the trickle down effect alone and special programmes would have to be taken to attack poverty directly. Meanwhile positive feedbacks from localised experiments like 'food for work' and 'employment guarantee programme' in Maharashtra encouraged policy-makers to formulate similar programmes at nation-wide scale. The Sixth Plan launched in 1980 accordingly came up with two important programmes aimed at alleviating people in rural areas from below poverty line. The Integrated Rural Development Programme (IRDP) was targeted for those rural poors such as marginal farmers and village artisans who had some, though insufficient, resource base. Under the programme the beneficiaries were provided with such assets which they could combine with their resource for enhancing productivity and their income. The target beneficiaries of National Rural Employment Programme (NREP) were such rural poors as landless agricultural workers who could not get employment usually in off peak agricultural season and in bad agricultural years virtually throughout the year. Under this programme construction work of social capital goods such as village roads, school and community buildings, tanks etc., were to be taken up which would provide additional employment to the target beneficiaries. Apart from directly reducing poverty for the seasonally unemployed worker in the rural areas, the programme was to use the surplus foodgrains stock arising from the success of green revolution and create productive and useful assets for the rural society.

Disappointing Impacts and Yearning for Genuine Decentralisation

The experiences with these programmes in different parts of the country have been varied. However, the impacts by and large have been found to be disappointing. While the employment generation programme has been found to be useful in situations of draught affected bad agricultural years, the Integrated Rural Development Programme did not have much success in reducing poverty. The reasons for this unsatisfactory impact of this programme are many. But the most important factor has been the leakage of fund in the channel from central allocation to the beneficiaries in the grassroots, which prompted no less a person than the then Prime Minister of India Late Rajiv Gandhi to publicly state that of every rupee spent on rural development, only 15 paise percolated down to the actual beneficiary. The other problems with these programmes have been found to be their irrelevance in many situations and poor implementation in general. The irrelevance of the programmes arises because these are usually formulated by the bureaucrats and there is no participation of people in the grassroots in the formulation process. Moreover programme formulated at the central level many a time did not take into account the diversity in socio-economic and environmental conditions through the length and breadth of the country. In implementation too the communities at the grassroots were not adequately involved and bureaucrats in charge of implementation had been found to finish off the job by fulfilling the required targets. Though such programmes have been modified from time to time and more frequently the nomenclatures of the programmes changed, there has been no major changes in the content of the programme. But during the 1980s itself a realization had sunk in that it would be difficult to achieve broad-based and robust rural development without adequately involving the people at the grassroots in formulation and implementation of the programmes for their own economic uplift. The top down approach of formulating programmes and allocating funds from the top for target groups at the bottom had been beset with problems at both formulation and implementation stages. The need for replacing this by bottom-up approach through genuine decentralization of the planning process and involvement of people and communities at the grassroots in both formulation and implementation of the programmes came to be increasingly recognized. Though the talk of decentralized planning had been going on for quite some time, it came to be recognized that genuine decentralization could not come about without adequate decentralization of political power to the grassroots. In a bid to empower the communities at the grassroots, in the year 1992 the Constitution of India was amended for the 73rd time. The 73rd Constitution Amendment Act was aimed at extension of institutionalised democratisation of the Indian society to the grassroots level. This was to be achieved by setting up 'Panchayat's as statutory local self-governing institutions in rural areas of the country.'

The New Panchayati Raj Institutions

Incidentally the term and idea of Panchayat is not a new one. Indeed Panchayats had been traditionally existing in rural society and used to perform the role of local governments. However traditional Panchayats often reflected the traditional hierarchical structure of the rural society and were perhaps not conducive to socio-economic progress of the villages in the modern context. In post-independent India, Panchayati Raj institutions were set up and functioned in the States even prior to the 73rd Amendment Act of 1992. Sometimes the Panchayats were elected and at other times bodies were simply nominated by State governments. But except in a few States like West Bengal the Panchayati Raj institutions were nowhere adequately empowered. So even when they functioned they operated merely as implementing agencies of programmes formulated from the top. The radical nature of the 73rd Amendment Act lies in its provisions to give Panchayats constitutional status and model them as truly self-governing institutions in the villages so as to adequately empower the people at the grassroots.

The basic provisions of the Act specifying the structure and compositions of the Panchayati Raj Institutions (PRI) are the following :

- Setting up of *gram sabha* in which all adults of the village are constituents.
- Establishment of a three-tier Panchayat system and stipulation of direct elections at each level.
- Reservation of 33 per cent of the seats in Panchayat bodies for scheduled castes/tribes.
- Reservation of 33 per cent of the seats in Panchayat bodies for women.
- A five-year term for PRIs with provision for election within six months if a Panchayat is superseded midway.
- Setting up of State-level Election Commission for conduct and superintendence of elections to PRIs.

As for powers and authority of the PRIs, the Act further enjoins the States to "endow Panchayats with such powers and authority as may be necessary to enable them to function as institutions of self-government". To that end, it devolves on Panchayats power to prepare plans for economic development and social justice in respect of territories falling under their respective jurisdictions. The functional jurisdiction of Panchayats regarding the above is identified in the Eleventh Schedule, which lists 29 specific items to indicate the nature and scope of their work. Since the paucity of financial resources had been a serious bottleneck in the functioning of PRIs, the Act incorporates specific provisions to address the problem. Panchayats have been empowered to levy, collect and appropriate taxes, duties, tolls and fees. They are additionally entitled to grant-in-aid from Consolidated Fund of the state. The Act further stipulates the appointment of the State-level Finance Commission to undertake a quinquennial review of the financial position of the Panchayats and to make recommendations to the Governor in their behalf.

Progress in Empowerment

Thus it appears that the 73rd Constitution Amendment Act has instituted wide-ranging provisions to secure genuine decentralisation of power and concomitant empowerment of masses at the grassroots. Now that a decade and a half has passed since the Act came into being, it is worthwhile to have a look at the progress in implementation of the Act and its impact in actual field. In this context it is a little disappointing to note that not all State governments have yet adequately empowered the PRIs (Pal 2004). Most State governments did not show much urgency in implementing the Act that would require them to shed quite a bit of power they currently enjoy. Subsequently linking of central allocations for rural developmental programmes to setting up of elected PRIs finally induced them to start the process. Meanwhile reports on experiences in States, which took a lead in implementing the amendment, have come out. Kerala for instance, has gone all the way by handing over 40 per cent of the State's fiscal resource to the PRIs. As mentioned above West Bengal has had empowered elected PRIs from even before the 73rd Amendment Act. The impressive stride of West Bengal in rural development in general and reduction of rural poverty and growth in agricultural production in particular, is attributed by many to empowerment at the grassroots through strengthening of the PRIs. As Pillai (2001: 620) puts it, "a notable feature of West Bengal success story is that this (the success in rural development and agricultural productivity growth) was preceded by a series of institutional reforms. Limited redistribution of surplus land to poor and small farmers, strengthening the rights of the tenants and successful implementation of Panchayat system at the grassroots level are some of the changes that marked a clear shift in the agrarian policy in West Bengal during the late (nineteen) 70s and 80s. Panchayats were involved in various developmental activities such as planning of tube-well development at the local level, management of minor irrigation schemes, agricultural extension work etc...." However a fallout of this decentralization process in West Bengal has also been observed in the form of excessive politicisation along party lines of a section of the rural population and, according to Acharya (2002), the process contributed significantly to the decline in primary school education in certain regions of West Bengal. Another State, which has made considerable headway in instituting the PRIs as per the 73rd Constitution Amendment Act, is Madhya Pradesh. However, the experience there in achieving empowerment at the grassroots has reportedly not been dramatic (Subramoniam: 2002). For instance, reservation of 33 per cent of membership for disadvantaged groups (SC/ST) have not resulted in proportionate empowerment of such group in many areas and the old power structure seems to persist in these new elected bodies. This has been possible because the existing influential persons have been able to get their servants and loyalists belonging to SC/STs elected in these reserve seats. Similarly many women members elected on reserve seats meant for empowerment of women merely sign for decisions taken by males. Fortunately, however, the experience is not uniformly bad throughout and in some pockets there has been significant progress.

In the light of such mixed experiences the conclusion of Sharma (1999: 68) sounds very instructive. She points out, "Legislation can only create a basis for action. They cannot enforce themselves. Action does not follow automatically from legislation. Legislation acquires a meaning and teeth from action." She further elaborates, "Laws, which are on the side of poors and the disadvantaged—whether it is the land reform laws or the minimum wages legislations—remain unenforced because that will hurt the powerful vested interests and the mafia, who virtually run a parallel government. Under the circumstances, the success which may be achieved in promoting peoples participation would in the ultimate analysis appear to be directly contingent upon the possibility of organizing the rural poors, organizing them for securing the execution of the existing laws, organizing them to break the resistance of the vested interests and organizing them eventually for a role in local governance." "This", she adds "will largely be an NGO-social activist sponsored initiative, which could draw a heavy support from press and the electronic media".

Institutional Framework for Rural Grassroots Empowerment in Northeast India

At this stage a slight detour for a closer look at the institutional framework for grassroots empowerment in Northeast India will not be totally out of context as the paradigm emerging in the region bears marked distinctions from the broad all-India pattern.

The institutional frameworks that exist in different areas within the region display considerable diversity keeping in tune with the physiographic and ethnic variations within the region. The 73rd Amendment Act is not applicable in many predominantly tribal inhabited area of the region. For many such areas various Autonomous Councils are provided by the Constitution. Originally constituted under the provisions of the Sixth Schedule of the Constitution, these councils enjoy considerable power and autonomy in administrative, judicial and legislative matters. Indeed some of them, like the Karbi Anglong Autonomous Council and more recently constituted Bodoland Territorial Council, enjoy more power than the others and virtually enjoy the status of a State within the State. However there are no bindings on these councils to share the power they command with the people at the grassroots. In fact as Datta Ray (1999) comments the council have been designed more to 'provide autonomy in social and cultural spheres to the areas which are inhabited by fairly homogeneous ethnic groups' than as 'organisations for promoting participatory processes for formulation and execution of programmes for social and economic development'. Not surprisingly, therefore, their track record in mobilising widely shared development impetus has not been notable.

One form of social capital that exists in good measure among the tribal population in the region but has been rarely harnessed for development oriented activities, is the traditional tribal institutions of self governance such as the village council. Though the traditional institutions have weakened and faded away in some areas, in others they still command legitimacy and authority. In such areas, taking the traditional community bonds as the nucleus development oriented grassroots level institutions can be engineered. In attempting to do so, it would however be necessary to keep in mind both the strengths and the limitations of the traditional institutions in the context of requirements of forward looking social transformation. Not all such institutions are based on democratic norms. In particular women are virtually deprived of participation in the affairs of virtually all such institutions (Goswami 2002). Economically these institutions have been effectively performing the static role of allocating and regulating access of individual members/families to land and other community resources. But their capability in formulating and implementing programmes for dynamic change has been rarely tested.

In this context the Village Development Boards of Nagaland should serve as an inspiring example. These are village level institutions with a modern, development oriented outlook which derive popular confidence on them from their blending with the traditional community-based institutions (Singh, 2004). The success in implementing rural developmental programmes in that State, in spite of host of other difficulties, is attributed by many to the strength of the VDBs. But in most other tribal areas impositions of statutory institutions without cognizance to traditional institutions has resulted in conflict and confusion of authorities of the two forms of institutions and consequent loss of development opportunities. In the rest of the region, comprised of most of the plains of Assam, Manipur and Tripura and also the State of Arunachal Pradesh, setting up PRIs is provided by the 73rd Constitution Amendment Act 1992. However taking advantage of the flexibility provided in the Act to the States in drawing the details of these institutions keeping in view the local conditions, for quite some time the State governments in the region avoided taking any initiative towards implementing the Act. Even after when they finally had to move, their reluctance to shed power to PRIs has been apparent from the slow progress in instituting and empowering the institutions as per the spirit of the Act (Pal 2004). Notable exception in this regard is Tripura. Recent surge in agricultural production, rural development and overall economic growth in the State has taken place concomitantly with institution of PRIs empowered in the spirit of the 73rd Constitution Amendment Act.

Meanwhile another category of grassroots level social institutions, which are neither statutory nor traditional, is becoming increasingly visible as development agents. These are the Non Governmental Organisations (NGO) and other micro organisation of people such as the self-help groups (SHG). Partly inspired by success elsewhere and partly encouraged and induced by policy-makers and funding agencies, the NGO and SHG movement has caught up in this region too. Such forces have the potential of organising people at the micro level for gearing themselves up in a development oriented mode. Unfortunately such groups are sometimes started out of mere short-term lure of grants from government and other donor agencies under different developmental and welfare scheme. In fact the policy of routing fund and other resources through NGOs and SHGs has led to proliferation of such groups and organisations, many of which lack long-term vision and commitment, close bonding among members, transparency and discipline—ingredients essential for their sustainability. While there is much to gain from the growth of the SHG movement, overenthusiastic replication and multiplication of groups through short-term doles and incentives can be self-defeating.

A Vision and Strategy for Rural Development

The Vision

Starting at the present base, a realistic vision for rural development to be achieved say by 2020 may include the following components :

- Deprivation of all rural households from the basic needs of drinking water, shelter and sanitations is eliminated.
- Access to primary health care is achieved for all.
- All children acquire functional literacy and get the basic and quality education to be able to access opportunities in the increasingly knowledge-based economy of the future.
- All villages get connected to communication network and remain accessible throughout the year.
- All villages not only get electrified but also benefited from uninterrupted power supply in adequate voltage.
- Farm production takes place at near potential levels. Rural employment not only expands in volume but also diversifies with agro processing, trading and catering various productive services to the modernised farm sector emerging as important economic activities. With increased affluences of the rural population, consumption related services also take a boost and add to the growth and diversification of rural employment.
- With widespread participation in the upswing of the rural economy, disparities across gender and groups, such as castes and tribes, get markedly reduced.

The Strategy

In essence the strategy for realisation of the vision can be a simple two pronged approach comprised of (a) acceleration of income and employment growth through facilitation of fuller utilisation of production potentials, and (b) elimination of deprivation of people from the basic facilities of drinking water, shelter, sanitation, elementary education and primary health care by directly providing these services.

The income and employment generation process will be spearheaded by farm sector growth which can arise from fuller exploitation of technical possibilities in combination with better use of the natural resource base. Apart from direct employment in the farms, increased farm production will generate income and employment in related activities through backward and forward linkages. Backward linkages will force higher activity levels in provision of sectoral infrastructure like irrigation and services like input supply, extension and repair and maintenance of farm equipment. Forward linkages will induce growth in storage, processing and trading of farm products. Thus farm sector growth will lead to mutually reinforcing growth in income and employment in both farm and non-farm economic activities in rural areas.

However, the above-mentioned farm-sector-led growth will critically depend on improved rural connectivity through quantitative and qualitative expansion of road and telecommunication network. Without improved connectivity rural markets will remain fragmented and increased farm production will be a bane rather than a boon for the farmers as prices of the products are likely to collapse from over supply. The farm-sector-led growth strategy thus presupposes that rural markets are integrated to the regional, national and global markets so that farmers need not produce only that which will be absorbed in the local market but can specialise in such production activities for which his resource base is most suited and for which he is adequately rewarded.

Direct action will have to be taken to eliminate people's deprivation from such basic amenities as drinking water, shelter, sanitation, primary health care and elementary education. Special delivery mechanisms will have to be designed for encompassing people in special problem sectors such as flood-prone areas, interior hills and also for such sections of population as those internally displaced due to violence and women and children in the fringes of the society. Action in this area will help directly in achieving the goals of development by mitigating human misery arising from deprivation from these basic facilities. Moreover by building human capabilities, such action will also enable the masses to be more productive players in the dynamics of growth. This in turn will not only enhance long-term growth prospect of the economy but will ensure wider diffusion of gains of the growth process among different sections of the society.

Implementation Mechanism

In the implementation of the above-mentioned strategy of rural development, specific roles have been envisaged for the different agents such as individuals and households, the community, the Non Governmental Organizations (NGOs) and the State and the Central Governments.

The State Government will have to directly intervene to put the necessary institutions and basic infrastructure in place. The *Panchayati Raj* will have to be instituted in full spirit. Besides accomplishing grassroots level empowerment, establishing roads and telecommunication systems linking villages to the broader network will have to be direct responsibility of the State Government. Power connection to each village will also have to be provided. These critical areas will remain deficient without active State Government initiatives. In most other spheres of the rural economy the State Government's role will be of that of a facilitator.

Community action has to be channelised through elected *Panchayats* or similar other village level institutions. These bodies will have to be empowered and entrusted to oversee all village level community based developmental activities such as construction and maintenance of intra-village roads, management of village primary schools and health centres, management of other common resources like forest, wasteland, water bodies, execution of specific rural developmental programmes right from selection of beneficiaries to completion of the tasks and so on.

Production activities will be organized in a market oriented manner. Households and individuals will operate as individual market agents. Market forces will guide their production and consumption decisions and buying and selling operations. But co-ordination and co-operation between these operators may be required in many areas for their mutual benefit. Farmers may be encouraged to form their co-operatives and peer societies to address their common problems and exploit the advantages from co-ordination and co-operation. Such bodies should be allowed to come up as spontaneous peer organization and should not be led into existence by government over-enthusiasm.

NGOs are/may be operating in many different specific areas. Their role in the developmental process can be broadly viewed as one of enabling people through spread of awareness, networking among social activists for greater leverage and inducement to initiate actions socio-economically beneficial to the rural community.

Financing of the Strategy

The necessary financial resources for implementing the above laid out strategy for rural development will have to be harnessed from a variety of sources such as governments, international donor agencies, financial institutions and private savings.

Funds for public investments in rural infrastructure and provisions of basic facilities can be sourced from the growing central allocations for rural developmental programmes and infrastructure projects. For instance, funds can be obtained for construction and maintenance of rural roads under *Pradhan Mantri Gram Sadak Yojana*. Many of these schemes are centrally sponsored, though some of the schemes require certain amount of matching grant from the State governments. But what is of great importance is proper implementation of projects under these schemes. While faltering in implementation may lead to drying up of funds from such sources, successful and timely implementation is likely to ensure renewed flow of funds under such programmes.

The international donor/funding agencies can also be roped into meet shortfall of funds, especially for delivery of basic services. For instance, programmes in which the target beneficiary segments are children and women, organizations like UNICEF can be approached for funding.

Since the production activities in both farm and non-farm sectors will be carried out primarily by market-oriented agents, private investments along commercial lines will have a significant role to play in successful implementation of the strategy. However, funding of private investment in the rural sector will perhaps be more difficult to organize, at least in the initial stages in which investment requirements will be large and the households in general will not have enough internal resources to fund them. The credit institutions need to step up their operations in rural areas so as to meet the various types of credit needs of the rural farm and non-farm production units. But even if the delivery of institutional credit picks up, the credit institutions are unlikely to be able to cater to the entire credit needs of the rural society. A large number of rural households often require small to medium credit for both production and consumption purposes which the bank may find expensive and imprudent to cater to. In the absence of suitable credit institutions in this segment, households are often left with no choice but to depend on non-institutional sources such as money-lenders who usually charge extremely high interest rates. While the non-institutional credit market may be meeting the immediate credit need of rural households, in the longer run the high cost of such credit aggravates poverty and reduces investment capabilities of households. For the cause of rural development, financial institutions can intervene in this segment by setting up their own micro-finance credit schemes and/or by supporting other micro-finance credit schemes to operate effectively.

REFERENCES

Acharya, Poromesh (2002), 'Education: Panchayat and Decentralisation, Myths and Reality', *Economic and Political Weekly*, February 23, 2002.

Goswami, Atul (2002), 'Introduction' in Goswami, Atul (ed.) *Traditional Self-Governing Institutions among the Hill Tribes of North-East India*, Akansha Publishing House, New Delhi.

Government of India, (2001) *Approach Paper to the Tenth Five Year Plan (2002–2007)*. Planning Commission, New Delhi.

Pal, Mani (2004), 'Panchayati Raj and Rural Governance: Experience of a Decade', *Economic and Political Weekly*, January 10, 2004.

Pillai, Renuka (2001), 'An Analysis on Paddy Productivity Growth in West Bengal and Orissa', *Indian Journal of Agricultural Economics*, Vol. 56, No. 4, October-December.

Ray, B. Datta (1999), 'Autonomous District Councils and the Strategy of Development in North-East India' in Banerjee, A. and Kar, B.(ed), *Economic Planning and Development of North-Eastern States,* Kanishka Publishers, New Delhi.

Sharma, Bharati (1999), 'People's Participation and its Relevance to Development', *Dialogue,* Vol. 1, No. 2, Oct.-Dec., 1999.

Singh, Chandrika (2004), 'Functioning of the Village Development Boards (VDBs) in Nagaland', Dialogue, Vol. 5, No. 3.

Subramaniam, P.N. (2002), 'Observations on New Panchayati Raj Experiences in Madhya Pradesh', *Economic and Political Weekly.*

2

Rural Development in India in the Post-Reform Era

RAJ KUMAR SEN

Introduction

The Economic Survey 2007-08 has stated that 'Agriculture is the mainstay of the Indian economy because of its high share in employment and livelihood creation'. Though its share in the GDP continuously declined as expected in a developing economy from 55 per cent in 1950-51 to 31 per cent in 1990-91 and to 18.5 per cent in 2006-07, yet it supports more than half a billion people providing employment to 52 per cent of the workforce declining from 70 per cent in 1951. Thus it is clear that there has been an imbalance in the pattern of decline of these two rates and the people depending on the agricultural sector are to share a rapidly shrinking part of the GDP leading to an increasingly falling standard of living. Thus while the Indian production structure exhibits the more or less the text-book pattern of a developing economy, her occupational structure is still left with the characteristics of a backward country. Naturally, as an occupation, farm employment is no longer attractive and the farmers are unhappy as they think that they are not getting the right price for their products. This has been also hinted in the Survey, when it states that 'there has been a loss of dynamism in the agriculture and allied sectors in recent years'. Perhaps as a cause, it has blamed the degrading quality of the soil and other natural resources due to overuse and inappropriate use of chemical fertilizers leading to stagnation in the yield levels. Besides, this sector could not attract the required investment from the private sector at a time when the public sector investment is falling. The limited success of the new extension of the irrigation system and the failure of the agricultural extension system are also mentioned in this context. Though all these features are highlighted only recently at the official level, the genesis of the crisis may be traced since the beginning of India's path of planned economic development in 1951 though it has been accelerated due to various factors initiated since the days of economic reforms started in 1991.

If we concentrate on the Indian agriculture under the Five Year Plans, we note that the priority of the planning authorities was always on industry and not agriculture as the planners wanted to convert the Indian economy to a developed one through the path of planned industrialization. This was due to the dominance of the Nehruvian ideas influenced by the Soviet success stories about the development model based on centralized planning promoting heavy industrialization. The implementation of this strategy was facilitated by the martyrdom of Gandhi in 1948 as Gandhi favoured village-based decentralized development pattern emphasizing production by masses through employment-oriented small and cottage industries leading to a self-sufficient economy as far as possible. He was in favour of 'village republics' as to him India lived in her villages. The Indian authorities depended on the Mahalanobis-Feldman model to formulate the second plan and relied on the trickle down of benefits theory for removal of poverty, which was a perennial problem of the Indian economy. This model put the maximum emphasis on the growth of the GDP at the maximum possible rate and expected that the growing GDP will take care of everything including employment generation. In the words of Charan Singh, former Prime Minister of India, "neglect of agriculture is so to set the 'original sin' of the planners of India's destiny." Criticising Nehru's preference of the Soviet model he went further to say that "in the communist jargon, it is the peasantry which must act as the 'nutrient base' for the non-agricultural sector or pay for economic growth" (Datt and Sundharam, 2007).

Before we move to the discussion of plan-wise investment pattern, the official version of the agricultural sector may be briefly mentioned. This sector, under the first three plans, was composed of agriculture and allied sectors (horticulture, animal husbandry and fisheries) and irrigation and flood control. In the next plan rural development and special area programmes were added to this list but irrigation and flood control were omitted. Then from the Fifth Plan rural development was omitted and research and education were included. Again from the Sixth Plan animal husbandry was included in agriculture. Thus under the official concept with changing concept of the terminology, it is difficult to compare between different plans in the strict sense. It is also difficult to distinguish between the rural sector and agricultural sector and for our purpose we shall put emphasis on the agricultural development especially when the development of the non-farm sector in the rural areas in the form of setting up of agro-based industries, promotion of rural transport etc., has been only marginal.

In absolute terms, the plan outlay in successive plans increased considerably, but the percentage of it on agriculture remained more or less stable at a low but declining level of 14.9 to 12.3 per cent during the First to the Fifth Plans. During this period, steps were adopted to solve the problems that this sector faced during the time of independence and immediately after. These include shortage of food and agricultural raw materials like cotton and jute. With the fulfilment of the target of food production emphasised in the First Plan, the focus shifted to large scale industrialization from the Second Plan. But the experience in this Plan highlighted the crucial role of the development of the agricultural sector in the successful implementation of the Plan. The Government initiated the process of introduction of the High Yielding Variety (HYV) seeds in the Third Plan but due to two external aggressions in 1962 and 1965, the Plan itself suffered a setback and in the last year of this Plan due to extreme drought a near famine situation prevailed which compelled the authorities to declare a Plan holiday for three years. In the meantime, India had to import wheat from the USA under the ignonimous PL 480 scheme but at the same time the green revolution in wheat and rice started with the introduction of the Mexican wheat and dwarf rice varieties. As the green revolution could ensure a quantum jump in the cereal production, India could stop wheat import and build up a buffer stock of surplus foodgrains. However, the food production target in the Fourth Plan could not be fulfilled and the Fifth Plan suffered a setback due to serious inflationary pressure. Moreover due to political changes this Plan was terminated one year before its completion and was followed by the rolling plan system of the Janata Government. The Sixth Plan (1980-85) started after two years and it was perhaps the most successful Plan in the agricultural sector with a growth rate of 4.3 per cent. In 1983-84, the second green revolution was started as hailed by the government and it was due to the expansion in supplies of the inputs and services to the farmers, agricultural extensions and better management. While the first green revolution was confined mainly to Punjab, Haryana and Western U.P., the second green revolution had spread to eastern and central States including West Bengal, Bihar, Orissa, M.P. and Western U.P. But the percentage of outlay for agriculture to total plan outlay was drastically reduced and it is continuing in the range of 5.8-5.2 per cent only. The Seventh Plan was actually the last Plan in the pre-reform period and all Plans from the Eighth Plan were formulated after the initiation of the economic reform process. Of course, it is a peculiar mixture of economic planning with market mechanism and till now both of them are continuing side by side.

Rural Development in India in the Post-Reform Era

When India adopted the reform process in 1991 the economy took a U-turn and undertook reform policies mainly targeted at the opening of the external trade sector following a serious balance of payment crisis and to obtain loan from the international credit agencies. Though there was no explicit mention about the reforms in agriculture, a number of policy reforms addressed to this sector were initiated specially since the mid 1990s when India signed the WTO agreement. Some of the important measures of economic liberalization in Indian agriculture may be enlisted in this context (Radhakrishna 2008). So far as the internal market liberalization is concerned we note that in the case of seeds, not only there were more liberalized import of seeds but also cent per cent foreign equity was allowed in seeds industry since 1991. In the case of fertilizers there was gradual reduction of subsidies from the very beginning. In case of agricultural marketing there were changes in the provisions of the Essential Commodity Act and a Model Agricultural Marketing Act was formulated to facilitate the entry of the corporate sector in the market of agro products. There has been also relaxation of restrictions on the inter-State movement of farm produces. The system of contract farming was encouraged and already several MNCs (like ITC, Kargil, Pepsi Foods, Kellog and many others) have entered in this area. At the same time agricultural commodity forward markets are introduced and according to many this has been one of the main reasons of the steep food price rise in recent years and still the government did not revoke this provision nor has amended it as per the recommendations of the 1993 Report of the Kabra Committee.

Another important area has been the provision of institutional credit where the Khusro Committee and the Narasimham Committee II (1992) have undermined the importance of targeted priority sector lending by commercial banks. At the same time the objectives of the regional rural banks' priority to lending to weaker sections in rural areas were diluted since 1997. It may be mentioned in this context the major portion of the Indian agriculture is based on the activities of the small farms. As per NSS 59th round survey in 2003 we find that still now only one and five per cent farmer households are respectively large (more than 10 ha) and medium (4-10 ha) so far as the size of land possessed by them is concerned. On the other hand the remaining 94 per cent of the households may be termed as small consisting of 11 per cent, semi-medium (2-4 ha), 18 per cent small (1-2 ha), 64 per cent marginal (0.1-1 ha) and 1 per cent near landless (less than 0.1 ha). Alongwith them we can add the increasing number of agricultural labourers and together we may call them as rural under class. Since the days of radical banking reforms in the 1960s in the form of social control and later by bank nationalization, a rapid expansion of banking took place in the rural areas. But since 1991 the situation has changed and in fact the number of rural bank branches has reduced from more than 34,000 to 32,000 during the period 1990-2003. This constraint on bank credit to agriculture has led to disastrous consequences. At the same time the regional rural banks also started to function on commercial principles with hike in interest rates.

Among the infrastructures crucial for agriculture we may mention about the irrigation and power. In case of irrigation water rates are increased in some States, and participatory water management was sought to be introduced through water users' associations. In State like Andhra Pradesh new large irrigation projects were made conditional on stakeholder contribution to part of investment. In the State of Madhya Pradesh even rivers are being leased out to private companies as a part of the privatization drive under economic reforms by displacing the fishermen and all other people dependent on the river. In case of the power sector the private sector was allowed to invest in it. Since 1997, power sector reforms were introduced in a number of States like Andhra Pradesh with increase in power charges as a part of World Bank conditions. Under the fiscal reforms there was an emphasis on reduction of tax and public expenditure with great consequences for public investment in agriculture and rural infrastructure. In the external trade sector we find that all Indian products are placed under generalized system of preferences since 1997 according to the WTO agreement. In 1998 quantitative restrictions for 470 agricultural products were dismantled and in 1999 another 1400 products were brought under the open general licensing and canalization of external trade in agriculture was almost reversed. The average tariffs on agricultural imports were reduced from 100 per cent in 1990 to 30 per cent in 1997. Though India is still in principle against Minimum Common Access yet actually she is already importing 2 per cent of her food requirements.

In addition to all these policy reforms, it is observed that the Gross Fixed Capital Formation (GFCF) in Indian agriculture has declined drastically. The ratio of the GFCF in agriculture as percentage of total GFCF came down from 9.6 per cent in the Seventh Plan (1985-92) to 7.4 per cent in the Ninth Plan (1997-2002). Contrary to expectation, the private investment also did not increase. In this period expenditure on agriculture as percentage of total plan expenditure declined from 5.9 to 4.5. The number of agricultural loan accounts in scheduled commercial banks declined from 27.7 million in 1992 to 20.3 million in 2002. Mostly small farmers suffered as a consequence of it. Their share in bank credit declined steeply from 21.9 per cent in 1992 to 7 per cent in 2001. It means that the small farmers were compelled to go back to non-institutional sources and became exploited by the village money-lenders. Naturally the farmer indebtedness has gone up under economic reforms. It has been observed that this proportion is higher in State like Andhra Pradesh where the borrowing for investment in agriculture is also higher. The share of institutional sources is lower also in such States while the rate of farmer suicides is higher in them. One may try to find out, quite naturally some correlation between them. The impact of reforms on the health conditions of the farming community is difficult to estimate due to lack of sufficient data but it is clear that while the extent of poverty declined from 39.5 million in 1993-94 to 36.5 million in 1999-2000, the number of undernourished people in the same period has gone up from 39.2 million to 42.8 million.

As a result of increase in input prices the cost of farming has gone up throughout the country due to the reforms. The agricultural trade liberalization was expected to provide higher prices prevailing in the global markets to the cultivators. But in reality there has been some decline for some commodities like rice and cotton. The growth of farm business income started declining in the 1990s. The widening of the disparities between agricultural and non-agricultural income also put the farmers in distress in this period. Of course there is wide inter-State variation and in the hilly States like Himachal Pradesh, Jammu & Kashmir, the North-Eastern States, the share of expenses to the value of output is less where the dependence on market-based inputs is low.

Inspite of all these negative impacts of the economic reforms on agricultural sector there was no sign of any crisis in the food production throughout the 1990s. The benefit of green revolution on the production front could sustain the growth of food production in this decade. Perhaps the roots of the present crisis in Indian agriculture can be traced back to the official complacency about the self sufficiency in foodgrain products. Even in 2005 the Government claimed about the self sufficiency in wheat though the overall growth of crop production declined from 3.7 per cent to 2.3 per cent and productivity declined from nearly 3 per cent to 1.2 per cent. On the other hand the government was worried about the huge stocks of surplus food grains in government godowns. The buffer stock of 60 million tonnes built up over the years was frittered away within a period of three years through exports and by other means even when there were famine deaths in different corners of the country.

It is only when during the last 2-3 years when steep rise in food prices with lean agricultural production coupled with growing farmer suicides engulfed the whole country, there was a sense of panic among the authorities. An idea of the severity of the farmer suicide can be observed when the crude death rate declined from 9.8 in 1991 to 8.0 in 2003; the suicide mortality rate has gone up in the same period from 9.3 to 10.4. It has been further observed that farmer suicides are higher in areas with predominance of small holdings and low share of priority sector advance to agriculture. As a consequence the government had to import five million tonnes of wheat for the first time in three decades. This looming agricultural crisis is marked by several danger symptoms viz., annual production of foodgrains has declined since 2001-02, with mild trend of recovery in recent years and prime agricultural lands are being diverted in the name of development by the government to powerful promoters and builders. Thus the manufacturing and service sectors are growing and financial markets are booming and on the other hand the agricultural sector is in darkness and could not sustain itself any more. The subsistence farming of India dominated by small and marginal farmers cannot be sustainable without official infrastructure support and social security measures.

The question of food security and hunger has also cropped up in this context. The Challenge of Hunger 2008 Report has constructed the Global Hunger Index (GHI) on the basis of 2006 data. It has noted that hunger is the major threat to as many as 33 countries. It has divided 88 countries into five groups and placed India in the 66th place with an index of 23.7. India is placed in the fourth group called 'alarming' with the range of index 20 to 29.9 with countries like Pakistan, Nepal and Bangladesh in the same group. The other groups are low (GHI less or equal to 4.9), moderate (GHI 5.0 to 9.9), serious (GHI 10.0 to 19.9) and extremely alarming (GHI greater or equal to 30.0). The state of Food Insecurity in the World 2006 is a FAO report to take stock after 10 years of the World Food Summit and with the objective of eradicating world hunger. This has also created categories on the basis of percentage of undernourished people in total population during 2001-03 like less than 5 per cent, 5 to 9 per cent, 10 to 19 per cent, 20 to 34 per cent and 35 per cent or more. Here also India is placed in the fourth group indicating the vulnerable position of food insecurity, hunger and undernourishment for a major portion of her population.

Another issue figuring in discussion on food security is the debate over Special Economic Zones (SEZs). The Ministry of Commerce has suggested that it will lead to high growth in the economy, industrialization, more jobs and high exports. However, those who will benefit and lose from SEZs will be different set of people. The more important objection to the SEZs is that these are creating spaces within a country which will be free from all restrictions imposed by the labour laws, environmental rules and other rules of the land. The amount of displacement that will take place in these zones will be a new set of development out sees over and above the existing army of displaced people due to development activities. The present official policy of growth at any cost will lead to more inequality in the population as the benefits will be cornered by the better off sections of the society while the cost will fall on deprived and marginalized people. The growing areas under the SEZs will gradually take away the agricultural land and will lead to food insecurity in the long run. It is high time that the appropriate regulations are formulated to protect the agricultural lands from the onslaught of the creation of the SEZs.

A Note on the Agricultural Sustainability of the North-Eastern States

Much of the North-East India is hilly and the majority of the population consists of tribal people and shifting agriculture and forest resources play a major role in their life. The incidence of poverty is high. Travel in this region is slow and difficult as this region is deeply dissected by rivers and streams. The traditional shifting agriculture is gradually becoming unsustainable in the hilly areas of the region. Per capita income of North-East are still low but not always below the overall income levels of other parts of India. The rate of population growth is rapid in this region though population densities are low. However, population density is rising rapidly and continuing to affect the region's natural environment. Income aspirations are rising. Shifting agriculture or *jhum* cultivation practiced by a number of tribal groups is becoming less sustainable as cultivation cycles are shortened due to population pressure. The length of this cycle when less than 10 to 12 years is not considered as economic form of agriculture compared to possible types of settled agriculture.

In North-East India large scale disturbance of the rain forest eco-system has resulted in various levels of degraded bamboo forests. Large scale timber extraction for industrial purposes has cleared vast areas of land limiting the *jhum* farmer further. Consequently the *jhum* cycles have become very short and the system operates below subsistence level causing further environmental degradation. The situation may call for promotion of relatively sustainable forms of settled agriculture. Agro-forestry and food trees may be other alternatives. However, changing to settled agriculture involves substantial alteration in the social system which may be quite difficult.

The analysis of agricultural development in the North-Eastern India is limited by the lack of data and its integration with the main line academic research. A number of features which are unique to agriculture in this region require extensive field study to derive their own conclusions. The North-Eastern States can evolve their own criteria to analyze various economic indicators and may not depend on others (e.g., the poverty line of Assam is used for other States in this region).

Conclusion and Policy Prescriptions

The various impacts of economic reforms on the agricultural sector clearly show that the small firm based rural economy of India is still not prepared to adopt the neo-liberal capitalistic farming under market mechanism where public subsidy and livelihood support are gradually taken away. A proper crop insurance system coupled with measures to enhance agricultural productivity, restoration of the indigenous irrigation system, proper rehabilitation and compensation of the people displaced due to industrial and other developmental activities are some of the policy prescriptions which can uplift the agricultural sector from its present crisis. The reform process has continued for nearly two decades but the majority of the population is in a distressed position not to speak of sharing the prosperity that is enjoyed by the shining India. In countries like India the role of the State should increase to protect the weaker sections and should not decrease following the neo-liberal philosophy.

REFERENCES

Alternative Survey Group (2005): *Alternative Economic Survey, India 2004-05. Disequalising Growth*. Daanish Books, Delhi.

Do (2006): *Alternative Economic Survey, India, 2005-06. Disempowering Masses*. Daanish Books, Delhi.

Do (2007): *Alternative Economic Survey, India 2006-07. Pauperizing Masses*. Daanish Books, Delhi.

Datt, R. and K.P.M. Sundharam (2007): *Indian Economy*, 55th Ed. S. Chand & Co. Ltd. New Delhi.

Datta Ray and Athparia (1999 eds.): 'Use of Water Resource for Agricultural Production in North-East India'. *Water and Water Resource Management*. Omsons Publications, New Delhi.

FAO (2006): *The State of Food Insecurity in the World 2006*. FAO. Rome.

Govt. of India (2008): *Economic Survey 2007-08*. Oxford, New Delhi.

Hindu, The. (2008): *Survey of Indian Agriculture 2008. India and Global Food Security*, Chennai.

IFPRI *et al.* (2008): *Global Hunger Index. The Challenge of Hunger. 2008*. IFPRI *et al*. Bonn, Dublin, New York.

Kurukshetra (2007): Annual Issue. Changing Face of Rural India. Vol. 55, No. 12. October.

Patnaik, Utsa (2007): 'Neoliberalism and Rural Poverty in India'. *Economic and Political Weekly*, July 28.

Radhakrishna (ed.) (2008): *India Development Report 2008*. Oxford, New Delhi.

Shiva, V. and G. Bedi (eds.)(2007): *Sustainable Agriculture and Food Security. The Impact of Globalization*. Sage Publications, New Delhi.

USDA (2008): *Food Security Assessment 2007. Agriculture and Trade Report*. Washington.

World Bank (2007): *World Development Report 2008. Agriculture for Development*. IBRD/World Bank, Washington.

3

Cognitive Frame and Occupational 'Opportunity'

The Case of Jhum Cultivators in Nagaland

SARADINDU BHADURI and ABHINANDAN SAIKIA

Introduction

Occupational opportunities are important for reducing poverty not only by generating income, but also by raising human capability to choose an appropriate living condition. Prevalence of poverty and unemployment has often been attributed to physical factors like infrastructural bottlenecks, lack of opportunities, social constraints like social division of labour, or individual constraints like lack of education and human capital. The case of the Jhumia families in Nagaland is an interesting case in hand. Although they have demonstrated a high level of adaptive and innovative capability by sustaining and enriching the oldest form of agricultural practice called shifting cultivation, their adaptive ability to conform to the requirement of alternative employment opportunities have not been satisfactory. In fact, it is now common knowledge that *jhum* replacing employment opportunities provided by the Government have only met with limited success. This chapter explores the reason for this limited success in that governmental attempt to provide employment to (erstwhile) shifting cultivators. Going beyond usual explanations, this chapter argues that the reason for the failures of many of those employment opportunities requires a detail analysis of human cognitive process regarding identification and recognition of opportunity. The branch in economics, which has, of late, paid adequate attention to understanding the cognitive dimensions of economic behaviour seems to be the literature on entrepreneurship (see, for instance, Bhaduri and Worch 2008). This literature points out that "opportunities" are not objectively given, but is rather constructed or identified by individuals through a complex cognitive process. We draw upon this literature alongwith the literature on cognitive science to argue that the reservations of erstwhile *jhumia* families in Nagaland to accept some of the employment schemes offered by the Government lie in their schematic representation of what occupation means. After a brief overview of the literature on cognitive science in the next section, we discuss the principal characteristics of shifting cultivation and attempt to construct the so-called, "occupational frame" of shifting cultivators in section 3. Section 4 takes the case of terrace cultivation compares the differences and similarities in the principal cognitive features of this scheme with those of shifting cultivation. Section 5 draws broad policy implications.

Methodological Framework

The cognitive science literature points out that the human beings are boundedly rational (Simon 1948). The idea of bounded rationality refers to human limitation to process information. Under the assumption of bounded rationality, past experience influences the processing of incoming information. Consequently, activities like goal formulation, opportunity identification, and interpretation of environment—all would depend on existing knowledge and experience of the decision-maker (Simon, 1978). This insight has important implications for economic behaviour (Simon, 1947, ch. 5; March and Simon, 1958; Cyert and March, 1963).

More recent research in cognitive science and social psychology has explained the process in greater detail. It is emphasized that human cognitive capacity can respond to incoming sensory experiences and information only in a limited manner (e.g., Devetag, 1999). As a result, human memory pays attention to new incoming information only in a discriminatory manner. The pieces of incoming information which can be associated with the existing pattern in the memory are favoured over the rest. Incoming information are ignored when some similar pattern cannot be identified in the memory. This systems of cognitive patterns are called cognitive frame (Anderson, 2000). Associative cognitive cues are thus important to help enrich long-term memories. These associative cognitive cues play the central role in restricting or guiding the memory structure to interpret new information. In this sense, a cognitive frame is a schematic representation of an individual's perception of the environment built through prior learning and adaptation (Witt, 1998, 2000).

Schemas represent categorical knowledge, pertaining to an object or an event, according to a 'slot' structure (Anderson, 2000: 155). Values in these slots or attributes are, often, assigned on the basis of past experience with the event. Since prior learning and adaptation is a social process, these schemas or frames can be assumed to function as socially shaped filters (Bandura, 1986).[1] Note that it is precisely this influence of past experience on the subjective memory structure that makes cognitive processes central to the concept of bounded rationality (Loasby, 2001, 2002).

Subjectivity in perceiving and making sense of environment provides an explanation why past experience has a significant influence on learning, decision-making and economic behaviour. Cognitive frames are, therefore, central to understand why individuals might stick to a particular mode of perceiving the environment and are often unable to switch into another mode, even in the medium run (Bhaduri and Worch 2008). Individuals can develop a shared cognitive frame about an event through interpersonal communication and exchange of views (Witt 1998).

Jhum Cultivation and the Associated "occupational frame"

Shifting cultivation is the dominant land-use system and mainstay of economy for hill people in the South and Southeast

Asia, including India's North-eastern region (Darlong, 2004). The method of cultivation has been called by different names locally in different countries or states (Borthakur, 2002). For the Northeast India, it is locally known as ***'jhum'*** meaning **cultivation in hill slopes by the use of hoe,** which is widely prevalent in all the States of the region (Dev Varman, 1971). *Jhum,* which is slash and burn agriculture is a traditional practice over generations. Though reliable figures about the exact extent of *jhum* land and other related practices are not available, broad estimates indicate that out of the total area of 25.5 million ha of land in North-East, about 3 million ha is under settled agriculture and about 2.7 million ha is under *jhum.* At any given time roughly about one-sixth of the total *jhum* land is under current *jhum.* It is the tribal population that practices shifting cultivation and which comprises 80 per cent and more of the total population in the States of Arunachal Pradesh, Manipur, Mizoram and Nagaland.

The basic principle of *jhum* cultivation is the alteration of short crop phases (usually one or two years of cropping) with phases of natural (or slightly modified) vegetational fallow. It is argued that such a system can be called a temporally separated agro-forestry system, where mixed cropping is done during the cropping phase, and perennial shrubs and trees are confined to the fallow regenerative phase of the forest. The duration of fallow cycle, therefore, have important bearing on the sustainability of the system. Tiwari (2005) divides *jhum* into four categories. They are—Traditional *jhum,* (ii) Distorted *jhum* (having shorter fallow cycle), (iii) Improvised *jhum* (cash crops), (iv) Modified *jhum* (mainly the NEPED project). While extremely useful, this classification does not throw adequate light on innovative and adaptive behaviour of the indigenous communities. Indeed, the fascinating diversity observed in the method of *jhum* cultivation across the north-eastern States reflect that *jhum* cultivation has not remained static over time, but have responded to the changing need of economy and environment through various adaptive and innovative changes (See Ramakrishnan 2001; Tiwari 2003)[2].

Jhum in Nagaland

Located in north-eastern part of India, this hilly State has 16 tribes and sub-tribes. Each tribe can be easily distinguished by the colourful and intricately designed costumes, jewellery and beads they adorn. Nagaland has special provisions provided under Article 371A of the Constitution of India. The provisions bars the application of all acts of Indian Parliament dealing with "religious or social practices of the Nagas; Naga customary law and procedure; administration of civil and criminal justice involving decisions according to Naga customary law; ownership and transfer of land and its resources unless approved by the State legislature to the entire State of Nagaland". Nagaland is the State where the number of *jhumia* families is the largest. About 72 per cent of the population in the State depends on agriculture. *Jhum* covers about 37 per cent of the State's total geographical area and is followed by about 85 per cent farming families in Nagaland[3].

Jhum has evolved through the years and is rooted in customs, beliefs and folklore. It influences the cultural ethos and social fabric of these agrarian societies. Besides it is a complex agricultural system that is well adapted under certain conditions, which require exhaustive comprehension of the environment to succeed. In a nutshell, it is a time-tested system of cultivation, drawing upon traditional knowledge and indigenous practices.[4] Some salient features of *jhum* cultivation can be summarised as follows :

- *Jhum* lands are commonly owned and distributed by the Village Council, only for temporary occupation during *jhum*. Agricultural lands, therefore, are neither privately owned nor meant for permanent holding.
- Unlike permanent or terrace cultivation shifting cultivation is almost entirely dependent on human labour. Numerous forms of co-operative labour arrangements exist to draw labour outside the family.
- Due to the dependence on family labour the size of *jhum* depends mainly on the number of able-bodied

members in a *jhumia* family. Marriage is an important source of procuring more working hands. Among the *jhumias,* the institution of marriage requires the prospective groom to stay in his in-law's house for a period of three to five years. It is an important source of labour supply.

- Fertiliser is natural, and derived from the slash and burn activities.
- One also observes the oldest form of division of labour, namely social division of labour (Polanyi, 1944). Men participate in *jhum* cutting operations and clearance of fields. Women take up the jobs of sowing, watching and harvesting which spread over the longer part of the year.
- Mostly the economy of the shifting cultivators has been found to be self-sufficient in nature. Usually there is little marketable surplus with the shifting cultivators. Their marketing façilities are limited and the extent of monetisation is restricted. The surplus produce is exchanged with traditional goods such as brass bells, beads and in some cases salt, utensils, dry fish and clothes.

In a nutshell, the practice of *jhum* can be regarded as the science of long-resident peoples, which differs considerably from group to group depending on locale where knowledge is built up through generations of living in close contact with the land.[5] "It is culturally bounded with ethos, which represents a hard epistemological core, reflecting upon unique mix of practices, methods, beliefs, institutional framework of communities, which defend and protect the scientific temper associated with the practice".[6]

In terms of cognitive frame, the perception of *jhum* cultivators about what an occupation consisting of following slots would mean (not exhaustive) :

(a) whether the knowledge required to carry out this job is locally developed,

(b) whether local people can undertake necessary innovative/adaptive steps,
(c) whether the practice is embedded in local institutional norms and social framework.

Policies towards Jhum

Ironically, however, policy-makers since the British period, has looked at *jhum* as a prodigal child in the field of agriculture. Despite its deep-rooted history associated with local knowledge and customary values, the qualities embedded within are often underestimated in the policy framework of India since the days of the British Raj. In the words of Baden Powell, a British policy-maker (in 1883) "...... this (*jhum*) cultivation is so wasteful that somehow or the other it must be put to a stop, just like *settee* or any great evil. It consists of destroying a large and valuable capital (forest cover and environment) to produce a miserable and temporary return."[7] The observation finally led a strong advocacy towards absolution of *jhum* which later found a place in the National Forest Policy of 1894.[8] The post-independence India following the colonial legacy tried to maintain a policy which was stereotype and often based on hard core reductionist science. The overriding principle and spirit of policy intervention on *jhum* cultivation had been to wean away the *jhumias* to settled agriculture and to gradually reduce the areas under *jhum*. Policy-makers, Governments, and analysts have often assumed that *jhum* cultivation is universally unsustainable and destructive of forests and wildlife and have failed to recognise the great variety of land-use types involved, to understand the cultural knowledge of the indigenous peoples. Timely intervention of efforts made through the work of Elwin[9], Chaturvedi and others[10] also didn't help much in opening up a humanist approach towards *jhum*. Rather, it opened up a path for alternative models that could replace *jhum*. The National Forest Policy, 1988, for instance, emphasised on the alternative avenues of income, suitably harmonised with the right land-use practices. It was devised to discourage *jhum* where efforts had been made for propagating "improved" agricultural practices like social forestry and energy plantations. Over time, what has changed in the policy arena is perhaps an increased attempt to make this replacement "participatory" in nature. However, when we compare the perspectives of the policy-makers with that of the framers it becomes clear that factors like deforestation due to *jhum* are clearly not perceived by the latter as problems worth taking note of.

Studies by Jodha (1997), ICAR (1985), Maithani (2005) have pointed out various reasons for the failures of certain employment schemes to meet the requirement of these people. Although factors like "trust", "psychology" appear in their reasoning, the main emphasis of these studies remain on physical and socio-cultural factors alongwith the most commonly observed reason for any policy failure, namely, "bad implementation". However, it is always difficult to ascertain the meaning of "good implementation". The use of socio-cultural factor is also vague, and devoid of any clear theoretical underpinning. Moreover, recent literature also suggests that culture is not a rigid framework, but rather loosely organised schematic structure, rooted in cognitive belief system of the individuals. Thus, genesis of cultural change may also be assumed to lie in the way human cognitive system unfolds and works (DiMaggio 1997).

Shifting Cultivation and Terrace Cultivation : Similarities and Differences in "Occupational Frame"

In the following Table 3.1 we highlight some of the key differences between shifting cultivation and terrace cultivation. These differences are structured in terms of a few important slots, which, in our view, constitute the slots of one's "occupational frame".

Table 3.1: Shifting Cultivation vis-à-vis Terrace Cultivation

Slot		*Shifting Cultivation*	*Terrace Cultivation*
Nature of Knowledge		Locally developed	Brought from outside
Type of Land Use		Temporary	Permanent
Nature of Cropping		Many at a time	One/few at a time
Role of Technology		Minimum, mostly human labour	Use of livestock, Mechanisation also present.
Labour arrangement/ management		Family labour	Wage labour
Decision Making	Land allocation	Village council	
	Labour arrangement	Village council	Individual
	Nature of crops	Village council	Individual
Property rights of land		Community owned	Individual rights
Gender specific division of labour		Present	Absent
Links with social events		Present	Absent
Primary objective		Consumption/social exchange	Consumption/sale

To elaborate, these two systems of agriculture differ not only with respect to physical factors, knowledge source, inputs and type of raw materials, but also they rely on two different kinds of relations between human beings and its surrounding norms and conventions (gender relations, relationship with technology, institution of property rights, role of traditional governance, end use of their produce, social obligation). As a result, these two systems lead to two very different ways of perceiving the environment. At the cognitive level, all these relations shape the way their brain interprets the surrounding environment related to their occupation, and, hence, develop their "occupational frame".

Conclusion : Broad Policy Implications

We argue that the inability to accept new form of employment (or occupation) may lie in people's cognitive limitation to forge new connection between various associated norms of the new occupation. This mechanism can provide an interesting insight to understand why people only accept 'changes' selectively in the process of economic adjustment.

One must, however, not be allowed to portray a picture that everything is going well with *jhum* cultivation. Besides policy interventions, people in many tribes, especially belonging to younger generations, do tend to avoid participating in *jhum* cultivation. Growing movement towards urban places has become a common feature in many parts of this region. So, how can one provide a cognitive level explanation for these behavioural changes among younger generation? Indeed, it remains to be looked into in detail. Theories of social-cognitive learning (Bandura 1986) often emphasise that indirect vicarious learning can lead to behavioural change at a faster rate. In a nutshell, when people observe behavioural change by individuals with high social status, they follow suit. It would be interesting to study whether the differences in the rate and extent of adopting 'modern' livelihood among groups in Nagaland can be explained in this manner. However, one explanation of such behaviour of Nagamese people may not be difficult to think of its tryst with modern education. In the appendix we have elaborated on how modern system of education introduced by the missionaries has shaped their aspiration for modern livelihood and employment profile. Note that education begins at an early age, and influences the way new incoming information and sensory experiences are handled by the brain. Education, therefore, plays an important role on shaping human perception about environment.

To conclude, therefore, we argue that short-run policies are more successful when it calls for minimal change among people in the way they perceive the 'environment'. In the long-run, however, individuals can be encouraged to change their perception about an environment through mechanisms which alter the way they handle information and develop connections in their cognitive system.

Acknowledgement

We had helpful discussions with Arunim Bandyopadhyay, Sabari Mitra and Sabyasachi Saha while developing the central argument of the paper. The paper was presented in the national seminar at St. Joseph College, Jakhama. Many students and research scholars gave useful comments. Usual disclaimer applies.

NOTES

1. Cognitive learning can be of two types, namely learning through own experiences and vicarious learning by observing others. Our conceptualization of past experience encapsulates both these forms of learning. For details on vicarious learning see Bandura (1986, ch. 2).
2. In a pattern called *'Alda'* in Nagaland the tribes cut but do not burn at the time of shifting cultivation. Thus the cut plants and undergrowth grow very quickly the next year with fresh leaves and thus prevent soil erosion and also preserve soil fertility. In many areas in Nagaland tree trunks are used across the slope so as to check the velocity of water. In some areas where the slopes are covered with grass and bamboo groves; pegs, bamboo pieces and grass are fixed across the slope to prevent soil erosion. Through the deposition of washed down soil along the tree trunk or bamboo and grass barriers, a sort of rudimentary terrace develops in the course of time.
3. *Nagaland State Human Development Report* 2004.
4. NEPED and IIRR (1999).
5. See, Berkes (1993).
6. See Ramakrishnan (1992).
7. See Peel (1983).
8. "A system of shifting cultivation ...costs more to the community than it is worth and can only be permitted under due regulation".
9. Verrier Elwin, an expert in anthropology was appointed by Pt. Jawahar Lal Nehru as an advisor for tribal affairs in the North Eastern Frontier Agency (NEFA), present day Arunachal Pradesh in the early 1950s. Elwin emphasized upon the importance of local knowledge and tribal customs that is entrenched in *jhum*.
10. "The motion widely held that shifting cultivation was responsible in the main for large scale soil erosion need to be effectively dispelled. The correct approach to the problem lies in accepting it not as a necessary evil, but recognising it as a way of life."

(Chaturvedi and Uppal, 1953) "It is a mistake to assume that shifting cultivation in itself is unscientific land-use.... In most of the interior areas where communication is not developed and sufficient land suitable for terracing is not available, shifting cultivation alone can be done for the present and as such very effort should be made to improve the fertility of such land" (Sivaraman, 1953).

REFERENCES

Anderson, J.R., (2000): *Cognitive Psychology and Its Implications.* W.H. Freeman, New York.

Bandura, A., (1986): *Social Foundations of Thought and Action: A Social Cognitive Theory*. Prentice-Hall, Englewood Cliffs, N.J.

Bendangnagshi (1976): *Glimpses of Naga History*, Saraighat, Guwahati, pp. 18-19.

Berkes, F. (1993): *Traditional Ecological Knowledge in Perspective,* in J.T. Inglir (ed.) 'Traditional Ecological Knowledge: Concepts and Cases', International Development Research Centre, Ottawa, Ontario, 1-9.

Bhaduri, S. and Worch, H. (2008): 'Past Experience, Cognitive Frame and Entrepreneurship: Some Evidence from Indian Pharmaceutical Small Scale Enterprises'. Papers on Economics and Evolution.

Borthakur, D.N. (2002): 'Shifting Cultivation in North-East India: An Approach towards Control', in Bimal J. Deb (ed.), *Development Priorities in North-East India.* New Delhi: Concept Publishing Company.

Cyert, R.M. and March, J.G. (1963): *'A Behavioral Theory of the Firm'.* Prentice-Hall, Inc., Englewood Cliffs, New Jersey.

Darlong, V.T. (2004): *To Jhum Or Not To Jhum*—Policy Perspectives on Shifting Cultivation, The Missing Link—Society for Environment and Communication, Guwahati, Assam.

Dev Varman, S.B.K. (1971): *A Study over the Jhum and Jhumia Rehabilitation in the Union Territory of Tripura,* Directorate of Research, Government of Tripura, Agartala.

Devetag, M.G. (1999): *From Utilities to Mental Models: A Critical Survey on Decision Rules and Cognition in Consumer Choice.* Industrial and Corporate Change, 8(2), 289-351.

DiMaggio, P. (1997); 'Culture and Cognition' *American Review of Sociology.* Vol. 23, 263-87.

Jodha, N.S. (1997): 'Mountain Agriculture', in B. Messerli and J.D. Ives (eds.) *Mountains of the World, A Global Priority,* The Parthenon Publishing Group, London. pp. 313-35.

Loasby, B.J. (2001): 'Time, Knowledge and Evolutionary Dynamics: Why Connections Matter'. *Journal of Evolutionary Economics*, 11(4), 393-412.

Loasby, B.J. (2002): 'The Organizational Basis of Cognition and the Cognitive Basis of Organization', in M. Augier and J.G. March (Eds.), *The Economics of Choice, Change and Organization : Essays in Memory of Richard M. Cyert Edward Elgar*, Cheltenham, UK and Northampton, MA, USA.

Maithani, B.P. (2005): *'Shifting Cultivation in North-East India*—Policy Issues and Options'. Mittal Publications, New Delhi.

March, J.G. and Simon, H.A. (1958): *Organizations*. Wiley, New York.

Mills, J.P (1973): *The Ao Nagas*, Oxford University Press, London, pp. 97-98.

Nagaland State Human Development Report 2004, Department of Planning and Coordination, Government of Nagaland.

NEPED and IIRR (1999). *Building upon Traditional Agriculture in Nagaland*, India. NEPED and IIRR, Philippines.

Polanyi, K. (1944): *The Great Transformation*. Beacon Press. Boston.

Ramakrishnan, P.S. (1992): 'Tropical Forest: Exploitation, Conservation and Management', *Impact of Science on Society*, 42 (No. 166): 149-162.

Ramakrishnan, P.S. (2001): *Ecology and Sustainable Development*. National Book Trust of India, New Delhi.

Simon, H.A. (1947): *Administrative Behaviour : A Study of Decision-Making Processes in Administrative Organizations*. Macmillan, Chicago, IL.

Simon, H.A. (1978): *'Rational Decision-Making in Business Organizations'*, Nobel Memorial Lecture, December 8, 1978.

Singh, Chandrika (2008): *The Naga Society*, Manas Publications, New Delhi.

Tiwari, B.K. (2005): 'Shifting Agriculture in North-Eastern India: Some Insights in Spatiotemporal Patterns and Processes'. Paper presented in *Workshop on Shifting Agriculture, Environmental Conservation and Sustainable Livelihoods of Marginal Mountain Societies*, 6-10 October 2005, NIRD, Guwahati.

Tiwari, B.K. (2003). "Chapter-6: Innovations in Shifting Cultivation, Land Use and Land Cover Change in Higher Elevations of Meghalaya, India." in P.S. Ramakrishnan, *et al.* (Eds.) *Methodological Issues in Mountain Research-A Socio-ecological Systems Approach*. UNESCO.

Witt, U. (1998): 'Imagination and Leadership—The Neglected Dimension of an Evolutionary Theory of the Firm. *Journal of Economic Behaviour and Organization*, 35(2), 161-177.

Witt, U. (2000): 'Changing Cognitive Frames—Changing Organizational Forms: An Entrepreneurial Theory of Organizational Development', *Industrial and Corporate Change*, 9(4), 733-755.

4

VDB and Rural Development
A Case Study of Peren District in Nagaland

RATAN KAURINTA

Introduction

Rural Development Programme in India started as an all-inclusive development effort to rebuild rural life and their livelihood. Of late, the main programme of rural development has been the Community Development until the Third Five-Year Plan when it became a package with special focus on poverty alleviation.

India is a vast country with over 300 million poor people, a number that has hardly declined over the last decades of development. About 50 per cent of the villages have very poor socio-economic conditions. Since the dawn of Independence, efforts were on to improve the living standard of rural masses. Therefore, rural development became an integrated concept of growth and poverty elimination and has been a vital concern in all the subsequent Five-Year plans. It covers provision of basic infrastructural facilities in the rural areas, like schools, health facilities, roads, drinking water, electrification etc., in improving agricultural productivity, provision of social services, like health and education for socio-economic development, implementing scheme for the promotion of rural industry, increasing agricultural productivity, providing rural employment and assistance to individual families and their Self-Help Groups (SHGs) living below poverty line by providing productive resources through credit and subsidy.

The Community Development Programme was started in the State since the early fifties. However, the concept of Rural Development through active participation of the village community took shape only during the Seventh Plan period and the idea of grassroot level planning and development became a reality in 1980-81 with the constitution of the Village Development Boards (VDBs) in all the recognized villages in the State. Since then, the Department of Rural Development has been involving in the activities of development of rural areas through the implementation of various programmes and schemes with the objective of improving socio-economic standard of the rural poor, employment generation and infrastructural development programmes etc. All activities of the Department are implemented through the grassroot level organizations, the Village Development Boards (VDBs), which has been active since its inception, to mobilize resources and implement the scheme through the involvement of village community, the activity of which are determined and selected on the basis of their felt need.

VDB is an attempt to benefit from the strength of traditional tribal institutions or village community. With 1083 villages now having a VDB, Nagaland has put in place, over the last 28 years, a structure that has the potential to solve many of the State's developmental problems such as lack of accountability, corruption and inadequate resources.

A linkage to the grassroots through the VDBs is for delivering the rural developmental inputs. These linkages have become vital for decentralizing governance and decision-making in the post-independence era especially in the statehood period.

The VDB consists of members representing all clans (*khels*) of the village including a women member chosen by the Village Council and one member as the Secretary. The VDB formulates their own schemes for the development of the village as well as for individuals and a cluster living in the village.

The organization of VDBs possessed distinctive features. As a matter of fact, Nagaland is the only State in the Indian sub-continent to have followed the traditional system of rural development through recognized VDBs. The VDBs are comparable to the more popular Panchayati Raj System prevailing elsewhere in the country. The VDBs are the developmental wing and the effective body entrusted with the responsibility for developmental work in the village.

Objectives of the Study

The study has been undertaken with the overall objective of evaluating the role and impact of VDBs as an institution for rural development in Peren district. It can be a replica in other rural based communities in the country.

The specific objectives of the study are:

- to study the working mechanism of VDB and its performance in rural development,
- to evaluate the existing schemes and programmes undertaken by VDB in Peren district,
- to assess the people's participation in preparation of the Village Plan through VDB,
- to study the utilization pattern of VDB fund,
- to identify the difficulties and problems faced by the VDB in the village, and
- to suggest suitable measures for improving the performance of VDB.

Methodology

The present study was conducted by taking a sample of five villages drawn from each block in Peren district in Nagaland. A total of 10 (ten) respondents from each identified 5 (five) villages and block were interviewed. The data on financial achievements, works implemented and undergoing were collected from the Secretary of the respective VDBs by administering a well structured questionnaires schedule. Two schedules were used, viz. schedule-I for collection of data from the VDB Secretary and Schedule-II for collection of data from the common villagers. The secondary data were also collected from the department of Rural Development, Government of Nagaland; District Rural Development Agency (DRDA), Peren;

Block Development Officers of three blocks; Deputy Commissioner Office, Peren; and other Reports from periodicals and journals.

Organization and Plan of the Study

For the convenient of the understanding, the entire chapter is broadly classified into twelfth sections. They are as follows :

The section 5 deals with the Structure and Scenario of VDB in Nagaland, followed by VDB as an institution for Rural Development in the section 6. The section 7 deals with the socio-economic profile of the district. Achievement and performance of the VDB in the district is illustrated in the section 8. In the section 9, implementation of developmental programmes of the villages through VDBs are incorporated. Section 10 analyses the Issues and Challenges of VDBs are discussed and some possible suggestions are recommended in the section 11, and followed by concluding remarks in the last section.

Organizational Structure of RD/VDB

Effective organization and programme designing is very critical and it helps in successful implementation of rural development programmes in the State. Rural development programmes can have impact only when they are implemented with clarity of purpose and a commitment to the task. Therefore, to have an effective delivery agency, the rural development department are organised into a four-tier agency.

(a) State Level : At the State level, the Rural Development Department is the sanctioning authority and the main agency to control the Village Development Board Programmes in the State. The main function is to prepare plan, release fund, frame policy, and co-ordinate with Government of India for general matters and fund release. The Department of Rural Development has been involved in the developmental activities of the rural areas of Nagaland through the implementation of various programmes and schemes with the objective of improving the economic and social living standard of the rural poors through employment generation and infrastructural development programmes. All the activities of the department are implemented through the grassroot level organization "The Village Development Boards (VDBs)" which has been active since its inception in 1980.

(b) District Level : The District Rural Development Agency (DRDA) as the principal organ at the district level to oversees the implementation of different anti-poverty programmes of the Rural Development Department. The DRDA looks after the rural development programme of the State Government as well as the Centrally Sponsored Schemes.

(c) Block Level : The Block Development Officers is the overall incharge at the Block Level. The BDO guides and assists the villagers in the preparation of Village Plans till the completion of the scheme, visit and supervise the work done by the villagers from time to time, submit tentative Village Plan as well as the complete report of the project to the Chairman of the VDB for necessary approval. The works done by the VDB are supervised and certified by the BDO.

(d) Village Level : At the village level, the Village Development Board (VDB) prepares a tentative Village Plan every year within the allocated fund. The VDB after putting in their own priority prepare Village Plan according to the model schemes prepared by the Rural Development Department. The VDB participates in the implementation of the schemes by providing help and assistance to prospective Self Help Groups (SHGs) and other beneficiaries. The Deputy Commissioner is the Ex-officio Chairman of Village Development Boards.

The Centrally and State sponsored schemes launched by the Government of India and Nagaland are implemented by the DRDAs through the Block Development Officers, as per guidelines prescribed by the Government of India and Nagaland. The programmes that the DRDA deals with at present are as follows :

Swarnjayanti Gram Swarozgar Yojana (SGSY)

As a National Policy, the SGSY programme was launched in the State during the year 1999-2000 with the objective of bringing every assisted poor family above the poverty line within a period of 3 (three) years through the implementation of micro-enterprises. The scheme emphasises on cluster and group approach. Under the programme, Self-Help Group (SHG) consisting of 10-20 members are formed and provided a maximum subsidy of Rs. 1.25 lakh. For individual beneficiaries, they are provided a maximum subsidy of Rs. 10,000. The balance investment cost of the key activities as approved by the NABARD is provided as bank loan. Of the total resources available in a DRDA, a minimum of 55 per cent is provided as subsidy component; upto 25 per cent is earmarked for infrastructural development to meet the critical gap; upto 10 per cent as revolving fund and 10 per cent for training purposes. The total fund for this programme is shared between Centre and State in the ratio of 75 : 25.

Indira Awaas Yojana (IAY)

IAY programme was introduced with the objective of providing dwelling houses to the rural poors. This is a Centrally Sponsored Programme where funding is shared between the Centre and State on 75 : 25 basis. Under the Programme, the Department provides roofing materials to the beneficiaries for construction of their houses at 5 bundles per unit. Other requirements like bally posts, timber, nails are to be arranged by the beneficiaries themselves. The labour will be contributed by the community free of cost at the time of construction.

Sampoorna Grameen Rozgar Yojana (SGRY)

Following the merger of the erstwhile JGSY and EAS, the Ministry of Rural Development announced the launching of the Sampoorna Grameen Rozgar Yojana (SGRY) with effect from October 2002. This is funded on 75 : 25 ratios between the Centre and State. The objective of the programme is to generate employment to the rural labourers by providing foodgrains as wages per manday. The department has been implementing this scheme with emphasis on agricultural related activities to supplement the production and economic activities of the rural people.

National Rural Employment Guarantee Scheme (NREGS)

This is a Centrally Sponsored Employment Generation Scheme, implemented in consonance with the enforcement of the Section IV of the National Rural Employment Guarantee Act 2005 (NREGA). The scheme is funded on the basis of 90 : 10 between the Centre and the State. The NREGS was launched in the State in Mon district on 2nd February 2006 and currently implemented in the districts of Mon, Kohima, Tuensang, Wokha and Mokokchung. The objectives of this scheme are (i) to provide 100 days of guaranteed employment in a financial year to every household in the rural areas notified by the Central Government under section 3 (1) of the NREGA and whose adult member, by application, are willing to work: (ii) to create durable assets in rural areas; and (iii) to strengthen the livelihood security to the rural households as per the provisions made in the guidelines.

Grants-in-Aid to the VDBs

Grant-in-aid to the VDBs is a State Sponsored Scheme which is under implementation since 1980-81. The fund under this programme is allocated to all the recognized villages on the basis of number of tax-paying households for implementation of developmental schemes. This is the only programme, which ensures the participation of the women in the activities of the VDBs through earmarking of 25 per cent of the fund allocated to the VDB. Another 20 per cent of the fund is also earmarked for Youth Programme in all the villages. This scheme ensures the active participation of all sections of the rural people in their developmental activities.

Matching Cash Grants (MCG)

This programme was introduced in the later part of the Fifth Five-Year Plan with a view to encourage the VDBs to raise their own resources either through household contribution or by implementation of projects through community participation and other innovative means. The fund is deposited in the VDB

Fixed Deposit account for an initial period of 5 years which is renewed on maturity. As an incentive, the State Government provides matching grant to the VDBs with a maximum ceiling limit of Rs. 2.50 lakh for each VDB. This amount is utilized as collateral for the VDB to obtain loans from financial institutions to supplement developmental activities. A sum of Rs. 20 lakh has been kept as budget provision during the current financial year for providing matching grants to the VDBs.

Backward Region Grant Fund (BRGF)

The Backward Region Grant Fund is a cent per cent centrally sponsored programme. It is designed to redress regional imbalances in development. The fund will provide financial resources for supplementing and converging existing developmental inflows into identified districts. This programme will be implemented in the selected districts on the same four-tier of the VDB Grants-in-Aid Programme and thus the fund meant for Rural Development of rural areas will be allocated through VDBs on the basis of household. This fund will be released to VDB's savings accounts by District Planning Committee (VDP/DRDA). A portion of the fund under the programme will be allocated to the urban local bodies i.e. Municipal Town Councils. Fund allocation between VDB and Town Councils will be calculated on the basis of population as per 2001 Census. During 2007-08, the Government of India has given fund provision of Rs. 10 crore each for Mon, Tuensang and Wokha District. Another sum of Rs. 250 crore is made available for use of building capacity in planning implementation, monitoring and accounting and improving accountability and transparency.

VDB as Micro Financing : To promote Micro Financing Activities

During 2004-05, the Rural Development Department had selected 25 VDBs as Financial Intermediaries as a pilot project in the State. A Corpus Fund of Rs. 1 lakh was created through the contribution of VDBs, State Government, Central Government and NABARD at the rate of 40 : 20 : 20 : 20. By experiencing the successful implementation of the Pilot Project, the department had selected 406 VDBs during 2006-07 and 2007-08 in the 21 unbanked blocks. Under Micro-Financing, the Corpus Fund of Rs. 2.40 lakh had been created with the contribution of VDBs Rs, 40,000, State Government Rs.1,00,000 and Government of India Rs.1,00,000 (Yet to be released). This innovative venture will go a long way in providing credit facilities to the rural people.

VDB as an Institution for Rural Development

The VDB is a statutory body, functioning under the primary village authority known as Village Council. The institution of the VDBs are synonymous with the concept of decentralized grassroot level planning in Nagaland, was first set up in 1976 in Ketsapo village in Phek district on an experimental basis. The success of the Ketsapo VDB led to launching of a mass campaign since 1980 to expand the coverage of this unique institution through the State. Thereafter, VDBs were gradually constituted in the remaining parts of the State and the concept institutionalized with the enactment of VDB Model Rules in 1980.

The initial allocation of Rs. 5000 per VDB was provided by the Government under what was known as common funds, which later was termed as matching cash grant scheme. The VDBs were advised to open account in the local State Bank of India and commercial banks for deposit of this fund, which provided for the registration of the VDBs.

The VDBs are involved in all phases of developmental activities as a part of their responsibilities. These include receipt of allocation of funds, selection of beneficiaries or schemes, monitoring of progress of works and expenditure and completion of schemes. They are responsible organization, where book keeping of accounts is mandatory, open and subject to any audit of its account.

Funds are available in the form of grants to all 1089 recognized villages through the VDBs. The allocation is made on the basis of number of households of every village in proportion to the size of each village to ensure that each citizen of the State is equally involved and provided for in all rural development activities. The funds released are being collectively pooled for implementation of the schemes for the benefit of the entire community. Through the involvement of VDBs, several major schemes have been successfully implemented. This has been made possible by way of contribution of free community labour organized by VDBs to ensure that schemes are completed.

Nagaland is characterised by 90 per cent of its geographical area under the rural category with 80 per cent of the State population residing in 1128 recognized villages and other settlements. At present, there are around 2,63,129 rural household in the State. Nagaland is exempted from the purview of the 73rd Constitutional Amendment due to the existence of the traditional Local Self-Government bodies like Village Council and VDBs for its Rural Development activities.

There are around 1,63,786 rural families in the State still living Below Poverty Line (BPL). The BPL percentage in the State is 62.24 per cent, which is very high, as compared to the national level. Therefore, to alleviate the status of this staggering percentage of families living BPL in the State, many new schemes and programmes were started in the State. Village Development Board (VDB) is a distinctive institution which formed in line with the originality of the Naga traditional village administration with the concept of grassroots planning to give greater focus on rural areas and its population.

At present, there are 1089 VDBs formed in the State to undertake developmental activities in the village. The VDB aims at removing the existing gap between rural and urban areas through the creation of basic infrastructure as well as by undertaking employment generation programmes. For this a discretionary fund at the disposal of the VDB is given to enable the rural people to effectively participate in the overall process of rural development and also enable them to chalk out their own village development plans according to their determined set of priorities. Accordingly, various government departments provide technical guidance at the time of formulation as well as implementation of the developmental programmes.

The idea of grassroot level planning and development took shape in Nagaland during the Seventh Plan period and the concept of the VDBs came into effect during 1980-81. VDBs were constituted all over the State following the first VDB conclave of 1982. All VDBs in the State are legislated and empowered bodies through the enactment of the Village and Area Council Act 1978 and exercise the powers and functions as per the VDB Model Rules 1980.

VDB in Peren District

The very concept of VDB in Nagaland, is basically based on rich social capital of the Nagas, especially the heritage of a strong community life. Therefore, in Nagaland, VDB structure was initiated mainly to facilitate the institutionalization of a participative process for the implementation of developmental programmes and to benefit from the strengths of the traditional institutions in the village. In Peren district, the VDB programme started as early as 1980-81 under the Lone Jalukie Block with 65 VDBs. The first BDO Office was established by the State Government at Peren Town as early as 1963.[1]

Currently, the district has three (3) RD Blocks viz. (1) Jalukie Block with 31 VDBs; (2) Peren Block with 22 VDBs; and (3) Tening Block with 23 VDBs, with a total of 548 VDB members—433 male and 115 female members each headed by a Block Development Officer. Total rural tax-paying households are 13,475 and total village population stands at 79,391 in persons.

The Village Development Boards (VDBs) in the district carry out various State Governments developmental schemes while the three RD Blocks undertake the following works such as Grant-in-Aid (GIA) for such activities as Piggery, Dairy Farming, Transplantation, Rural Housing, Fishery Ponds, Procurement of paddy etc.Women Programme such as horticulture farming, cash crop farming and poultry framing. Youth Programme like tree plantation, sports goods, for the purpose of construction of link road, approach road, ring well and betel nut plantation. Under SGSY schemes are piggery, dairy, poultry etc.

Socio-economic Profile of Peren District

The Peren District with a total geographical area of 1,647 sq. km (10 per cent of State's geographical area) and a population of 92,339 (4.6 per cent of State's population) as per 2001 Census is the eleventh newest district of Nagaland which was bifurcated from Kohima district on 22nd March, 2004. The district shares common borders with Assam and Dimapur district in the west and north-western part respectively, Kohima district in the east and Manipur in the south.

Peren the district is the home of the Zeliang tribes and serves as an important link between Haflong in Assam and Nagaland. It is situated at about 1,445.36 metres above sea level and is 84 kilometres from the State's only commercial hub of Dimapur. The district receives average rainfall of 2000 mm approximately. The district embraces 6 circles, 3 RD blocks, 76 VDBs and 105 villages with 86 inhabited and 19 uninhabited villages.

The District lies between 93°E—94°E longitude and 25°N—26°N latitudes of the equator. It is strategically bounded by 2 (two) States and 2 (two) districts. On the east and south it shares Nagaland's Inter-State boundary with Manipur, on the

PROFILE OF PEREN DISTRICT

1.	Total No. of RD Block	3
2.	Total Village Population (persons)	79,391
3.	Total No. of Govt. recognised village	86
4.	Total No. of GB	311
5.	Total No. of VC Members	846
6.	Total No. of Farming Household	16,987
7.	Total No. of Tax Paying Households	2,17,194
8.	Total No. of VCM	846
9.	Total No. of VDBs	76
10.	Total No. of VDB Members	548
	(a) Male	433
	(b) Female	115

West also it shares Nagaland's Inter-State boundary with Assam and on the North and North-East it is bounded by 2 (two) Districts of Nagaland—Dimapur and Kohima respectively. The mountain area is rich in forest wealth while the plains contain rich agricultural fields, which receive good rainfall and is called the 'rice bowl' of Nagaland.

Table 4.1 : Profile of the Village

No. of villages	*No. of farming H/hold*	*Village Popu-lation*	*No. of G.Bs*	*No. of VC members*	*No. of VDB Management Board*		
					Male	Female	Total
102	16,987	79,391	311	846	433	115	548

	PEREN	*%*	*NAGALAND*
RD BLOCK	3	5.76	52
VDBs	76	6.97	1089
ADMINISTRATIVE CIRCLES	6	6.45	93
RECOGNISED VILLAGES	86	6.72	1278
RURAL HOUSEHOLDS	13,475	6.20	2,17,194

Source: DAO I/c, Peren.

Composition of VDB in Peren District

The general practice to form VDBs has been one of the uncomplicated procedures wherein the villagers follow a very simple non-technical method of choosing the members from amongst the common villagers to represent VDB. The board members are elected by the villagers in the open public meeting. The term of the VDB members is three (3) years only. As a result, after every three years, new members are nominated by the villagers themselves. The composition or the strength of VDB members depend considerably on the total number of villagers as well as on the number of Clan (*khel*) or Block, existing in the village. A dedicated and relatively educated person is generally elected as the VDB secretary. In some villages, the board inducts one or more women member in line with the State Government standing instruction. The composition VDBs in each of the sampled villages in each block are presented in Table 4.2 (a, b, c). Peren district has a total of

79 VDBs (Tening-23, Jalukie-31, Peren-22) with 548 VDB members (Male-433, Female-115), 79,391 total village population with 13,475 tax-paying households in the district as shown in Table 4.3 (a, b, c).

Table 4.2 (a) : VDBs in Jalukie Block

Sl. No.	*Name of Villages*	*No. of Clan/ Khel/Block in the Village*	*VDB Members*		*Total*
			Male	*Female*	
1.	Samjiuram	3	11	1	12
2.	New Jalukie	2	8	2	10
3.	Nsenlwa	4	8	1	9
4.	Jalukie Old	6	10	2	12
5.	Jalukie 'B'	4	6	1	8

Source: Primary Data collected through Field Survey.

Table 4.2 (b) : VDBs in Peren Block

Sl. No.	*Name of Villages*	*No. of Clan/ Khel/Block in the Village*	*VDB Members*		*Total*
			Male	*Female*	
1.	Kejanglwa	2	6	1	7
2.	Gaili	4	8	2	10
3.	Heningkunglwa	4	6	1	7
4.	Mhainamtsi	3	6	1	7
5.	Dungki	4	8	2	10

Source: Primary Data collected through Field Survey.

Table 4.2 (c) : VDBs in Tening Block

Sl. No.	*Name of Villages*	*No. of Clan/ Khel/Block in the Village*	*VDB Members*		*Total*
			Male	*Female*	
1.	Tening Village	5	10	2	12
2.	New Tesen	4	8	2	10
3.	Nbaulwa	4	4	1	5
4.	Ntu	6	6	1	7
5.	Azailong	4	8	1	9

Source: Primary Data collected through Field Survey.

Table 4.3 (a) : Jalukie Block—Total No. of VDBs = 31

Sl. No.	*Name of Village/VDB*	*Total No. of Tax Paying Household*	*Total Village Population*
1.	Phaikholum	25	225
2.	Lilen	135	576
3.	Jalukie Old	440	2244
4.	Nsenlwa	65	389
5.	Pelhang	190	1257
6.	Phanjang	46	254
7.	New Beisumpui	135	703
8.	Songlhu	82	838
9.	New Soget	45	315
10.	Old Chalkot	80	382
11.	New Ngaulng	99	465
12.	Ikesingram	120	777
13.	Inbung	100	697
14.	Lower Singjol	25	225
15.	Old Beisumpui	121	384
16.	Nkio 'B'	87	455
17.	New Nkio	105	650
18.	Nkwareu	103	447
19.	New Jalukie	282	1951
20.	Saijang	100	1951
21.	Samjiuram	603	3168
22.	Khelma	102	600
23.	Chalkot New	70	382
24.	Sailhem	30	210
25.	Bonkolong	180	836
26.	Songngau	30	270
27.	Phaijol	30	350
28.	Old Soget	70	560
29.	Vongkithem	130	311
30.	Beisumpuikam	336	1965
31.	Jalukie 'B'	309	1774
	Total:	**4275**	**24381**

The major sources of funds for VDBs as the village level rural development institution are the Grant-in-Aid (GiA) from the State Government. This funding is given to all the Village Development Boards having a recognized Village Council every year for carrying out viable developmental activities in the villages. Besides, the Government also contributes a matching grant to the VDB in accordance with the fund created and maintained as fixed deposit with banks by the concerned VDBs.

The VDB has the authority to withdraw an advance payment subsequent to 30 days from the date of approval issued from the BDO for execution of the works. These advances are generally utilized for procuring raw materials.[2] During 2007-08, DRDA Peren made a payment totalling of Rs.138.56 lakh in the ratio of Rs. 45.7 lakh (Jalukie), Rs. 45.49 lakh (Tening) and Rs. 47.37 lakh (Peren Block). While under MCG so far in Peren district it was only during 2007-08 that an amount of Rs. 14 lakh were provided as State share to 9 VDBs. Nevertheless, micro-credit to women particularly the SHGs are proving to be a success in the district. Accordingly, during 2006-07, 4 villages were selected, and in 2008-09, 24 more villages were selected, Tening-7, Jalukie-9 and Peren-8.

Table 4.3(b) : Peren Block—Total No. of VDBs = 22

Sl. No.	*Name of Village/VDB*	*Total No. of Tax Paying Household*	*Total Village Population*
1.	Deukoram	124	351
2.	Kejanglwa	147	698
3.	Peletkie	76	311
4.	Old Puilwa	40	150
5.	Heningkunglwa	397	1825
6.	Gaili	161	1008
7.	New Puilwa	67	354
8.	Kendung	35	110
9.	New Peren	162	408
10.	Ndunglwa	115	633
11.	Old Peren	410	1431
12.	Mhainamtsi	318	1700
13.	Mhaikam	142	587
14.	Dungki	263	918
15.	Mhai Old	125	387
16.	Ngwalwa	343	1038
17.	Poilwa Old	450	3086
18.	Punglwa	282	981
19.	Benreu	223	547
20.	Jaluiekam	117	423
21.	Jalukiezangdi	394	1720
22.	Mpai Old and New	289	980
	Total:	**4680**	**19637**

Table 4.4 : Tening Block—Total No. of VDBs = 23

Sl. No.	*Name of Village/VDB*	*Total No. of Tax Paying Household*	*Total Village Population*
1.	Heiranglwa	60	713
2.	Mbaulwa	119	1502
3.	New Tesen	184	1948
4.	Nkialwa	252	2155
5.	Nzau	310	1565
6.	Nchangram	308	2427
7.	Nzau Namsan	189	1345
8.	Old Nkio	210	1599
9.	Tenning Village	422	4034
10.	Old Tesen	205	1832
11.	Mbaupungwa	182	2799
12.	Azailong	300	2173
13.	Tepun	250	1939
14.	Ngam	60	433
15.	Bamsiakilwa	55	376
16.	Old Ngaulong	75	391
17.	Lalong	240	1802
18.	Nzauna	162	1011
19.	Mechangbung	71	404
20.	Nsong Village	301	1741
21.	Ntu	304	1468
22.	Upper Singjol	60	342
23.	Mbaupungchi	210	1374
	Total:	**4520**	**35373**

Source: Directorate of Rural Development; BDO, (Peren, Jalukie, Tening); DC's Office, Peren; DAO, i/c Peren; PD, RDA Peren.

Table 4.5 : Circle-wise Population Distribution (2001 Census)

Sl. No.	*Name of the Circle*	*Male*	*Female*	*Total*
1.	Ngwalwa	4,373	4,191	8,564
2.	Jalukie	11,048	10,961	22,009
3.	Athibung	7,105	7,045	14,150
4.	Nsong	4,197	4,121	8,318
5.	Tening	15,297	14,889	30,186
6.	Peren	4,684	4,428	9,112
	Total	**46,704**	**45,635**	**92,339**

Source: Statistical Profile of Nagaland 2007, Directorate of Economics and Statistics, GON, page 17.

Achievement and Performance of VDB

VDB in Peren district have uncovered many fruitful plans into the wide-ranging village plans with high prospect to yield sustainable earnings. A number of VDBs have constructed community buildings in towns to sustain their income generating capacity by leasing out the space as well as the building. The developmental activities of VDBs in the district vary from an effortless household assistance to individuals to tide over temporary financial problems as well as providing better rural housing facilities to community, bus services connecting major towns and villages, etc. and all of this are for income generating purposes. It is a recognized fact that poverty alleviation are not easy to achieve without the active participation of people in the village.

In view of the enormous task involved to reach out to large population in rural areas and for their geographical spread and diversities in the State, it was felt that the objective of a well formed target groups could only be achieved through concerted efforts at different levels, with maximum involvement of people at the grassroots.

People in rural areas are inclined to rely mostly on interpersonal contact and customary means as a basis of information. Besides, geographical spread and diversity make it impracticable to attract awareness for income generation activities from the mainland, the District Rural Development Agencies (DRDAs) are, therefore, ideally placed in each district to assess the developmental needs through different programmes and take suitable measures to fulfil the same through locally accessible resources.

However, to reach out to people in remote and interior areas of a backward district like Peren, the major actions lies in putting the different services into prompt delivery and proper distribution of support and assistance. Rural Housing under (IAY) more than 80 per cent coverage of rural household below poverty line are reported to be provided with good quality CGI sheet in Peren District alone which by itself is a huge success. Market Building and Shed under SGSY (Infra) Women Society Market at Dungki Village at the cost of

Rs. 2,66,000 provides benefit of 250 members belonging to BPL families with 5 rooms and employing 5 BPL families for a rent. Piggery Farming (SGSY) KEKU SHG of Mhainamtsi successfully started with subsidy amount of Rs. 30,000 and a loan component of Rs.54,000 from SBI Jalukie during 2006-07. Minor Irrigation Project (SGSY) Kekotei SHG formed in 2002 with 10 members of BPL family started irrigation project with total cost of Rs. 5,65,780 out of which subsidy is Rs. 80,000 and loan was Rs. 4,85,780 during 2006-07. VDB Community Bus (GIA), Punglwa Community Bus was purchased during 2007-08 enabling local people to sell their local products in Dimapur besides normal transportation. Orange Farming (GIA) at Tepun Village under Tening Block with yearly income of Rs. 10,000 for each household through sale proceeds.

From the data collected, it shows that there is a limited impact on poverty removal and reduction through the concept of VDB on the lifestyle and economic condition of people. There has been no marked improvement in their socio-economic status as well as in their standard of living as is evidenced from the data made available through field survey. In fact, the whole life of the villagers revolve round the GIA and IAY schemes for which there is no proper records maintained by any of the VDB in the district.

Implementation of Developmental Programmes through VDBs

The moderately successful implementation of various rural development schemes in the district was because of people's participation to a certain extent. Such participation has the advantage of making local information available to the decision-makers as well as to the agency in implementing policies.

A survey of the villagers' opinion about the workings of VDBs indicates that in general some physical as well as financial achievement has been made in the district. During 2006-07, under SGSY 304 SHGs and 15 individuals were assisted physically involving a financial achievement of Rs.18.77 lakh out of the available Rs. 24 lakh funds in Peren district, while it was 2807 SHGs and 273 individuals involving a total expenditure of Rs. 288.33 lakh out of the available fund of Rs. 311.51 lakh in the whole state during the same year. So far in Peren district, during (2006-07) 9 market sheds constructed (2007-08), Rs. 60 lakh spent for 6 markets shed and 1 VDB Godown for storing agricultural produces at Dungki Village under Peren Block were constructed under SGSY.

Issues and Challenges

There are huge challenges to the performance of VDB as a grassroot level planning machinery in the district. Given the BPL percentage in the State stands at 62.24 per cent, while there are still 4,228 BPL families in the live register of waiting list prepared for availing various schemes of the Government in the district. Poverty eradication programme can be addressed more effectively only when grassroots level organizations are made functioning, more especially in the rural-based communities.

Yet, lack of accountability of the implementing agencies either to the Government or to the people has been the single major cause for misappropriation of funds in the development programmes. In the process, delivery of goods and services to the people in a fair, just and responsive way gets distorted. For successful implementation of any developmental village plans, adequate funds, appropriate policy framework and effective delivery machinery is necessary. But availability of fund alone cannot be sufficient condition for tackling the problems of poverty and backwardness. Optimum utilization of fund is required to achieve sustainable growth.

Key activities were identified by the BDOs based on the local talent and resources in many cases, line departments and banks were not involved in identification of key activities as required under the scheme. Due to non-involvement of banks and right departments, the beneficiaries were deprived of necessary training/skill and infrastructure created by the line departments.

Despite the fact that many attractive and well decorated marketing shed has been constructed in almost all the accessible and marketing strategic points in the district, no appreciable local products or commodities are either being sold or traded so far. There has been no evaluation on the performance of the key activities to determine its success and viability. It seems to be executing projects in the rural areas for project sake only.

The general practice is that beneficiaries of both individual and SHGs categories are selected from the list of BPL households by the BDOs, while VDBs simply agreed and DRDA authorized without actually involving the bankers. This poor participation of banks will be detrimental to the overall financial operation, and failure of the project. No evaluation to ascertain the approved utilization of the assistance received by them had been done at the block or at the district level.

In the absence of good governance and proper implementation, huge resources spent for development stands wasted. Therefore, the system should be so designed to bring better transparency, accountability and streamlining of the structure. Some of the major challenges that faced by VDBs in functioning effectively, are whether—any standard record maintenance system is introduced and followed, proper official records and documents are maintained by the VDB Secretary including bank accounts, loan taken and repayment made from the village account, etc. For selection of beneficiaries in different villages in availing assistance, there has been any marked improvement in the overall living condition of the people after the introduction of VDB programmes, the village plan has been prepared on need-based, any schemes or programme has been forced in the village against their will, members in the village are aware of the village plan, etc. All these issues need to be addressed very meticulously.

Suggestions

Therefore, in the light of the diverse issues and challenges, the following propositions are put forth as a policy measure to contain some of the sluggish problems.

1. Application of technology for value addition giving a new dimension to traditional activities while arranging for regular training programme to build technical and managerial capacity for the rural people particularly the youth and womenfolk, so as to help them in making income generating activities in a more productive and scientific manner. For this to take effective, the implementing agencies have to facilitate the transfer of required technology and facilities.
2. Identify the well managed VDBs in the district and encouraged them to invest in income generating schemes which are not in the VDB Model scheme in order to create more job opportunities particularly for the rural youths.
3. The rate of people's participation in VDB is not encouraging. Village people are not at all aware of the activities. It has been found that more than 70 per cent of the rural population does not know anything about fund distribution, schemes or the programmes being implemented in their own villages including some VDB members. Hence, it is suggested that the schemes/ programmes being implemented and fund allotted against each schemes/programmes be translated into a local language to grow people's consciousness and to become effective in trimming down the probable misuse of fund.
4. To make these 76 VDBs in the district implement the schemes stringently within the guidelines while encouraging them to mobilize their own internal resources for investment in various income generating and economically productive activities.
5. Key activities identified for attaining self-reliance by the self-help groups and individuals should be based on local skills and resources available while the major thrust may be given to livestock-based activities that have local demand for consumption such as piggery and fishery.

6. Imparting professional training of the selected borrowers particularly in the area of income generating activity before sanctioning of the loan/assistance through government or non-governmental agencies would prove to be highly beneficial and worthwhile.

Conclusion

Therefore, given the State Government unyielding efforts to promote and sustain the development of villages through the villagers themselves, it is now for the VDB to rise to the occasion to meet the challenges effectively. The VDBs has to play a catalytic role in raising local resources by unleashing collective initiative, rendering physical labour as well as material for village development purpose.

VDBs can be strengthened by increasing quantum of funds with the full autonomy to use them, have control over personnel deployed in their area with the powers to raise house tax and make the transfer of funds proportional to the revenues raised by them.

The transformed rural set-up, resulting physically from the changed appearance of the village with the richly built infrastructure over four decades of development as an outcome of execution of grant-in-aid and through mobilization of funds for effective implementation of matching grant for confidence building to make the village economy self-sufficient and reliant is worth mentioning. These are apparent in terms of improved housing (CGI roofing), better facilities/services like education, drinking water, health care, sanitation, credit information, electricity, roads and communication in a difficult terrain and topography.

It is the grassroot level organization like VDB, which can ensure precision and answerability in public life through active participation. Determined efforts are, therefore, needed to equip them through proper delegation of powers, functions and funding alongwith necessary training and capacity-building. However, bottlenecks such as lack of adequate infrastructural facilities, poor resource base and shortage of technical know-how continue to handicap the workings of VDBs in the developmental front. As a result, dependency on government agencies is on the rise and the trend is mounting at a much faster pace.

NOTES

1. ADC Office Records, Peren District—Profile in Commemoration of Peren District Inauguration, 11th February, 2004, p. 15.
2. DRDA, Peren.

REFERENCES

Audit Report (Civil) 2002, AG, Nagaland.

Duggal, Ravi *et al.* (1999), Nagaland: Issues in Governance, *Economic and Political Weekly* XXXIV (50)

Karmakar, K.G. and Banerjee, G.D. NABARD, HQ: Mumbai, Village Development Boards (VDBs) in Nagaland.

Nagaland State HDR-2004.

Rural Development News Letter, Volume: 1, Issue—2 Quarterly Issues, October 2008. Directorate of Rural Development, Government of Nagaland.

Saponti Borthakur (2008), People's Participation in Decentralized Planning: A Case Study of Nagaland, Dialogue Vol. 9, No. 3.

5

Hedonic Demand for Rented House in Kohima, Nagaland

S.K. MISHRA and M.L. NGULLIE

Introduction

Unlike his predecessor economists who in promulgating their own theories of consumer's behaviour considered the demand for (or supply of) a commodity merely as an expressed willingness to participate in exchange activity of a quantum of any particular commodity for a quantum of some other commodity (or money), Lancaster (1966) considered a commodity as a bundle of characteristics or a bunch of vectors, $x = [x_1, x_2, ..., x_m]$. A particular commodity, $x^{(0)} = [x_1^{(0)}, x_2^{(0)}, ..., x_m^{(0)}]$ is different from another commodity $x^{(1)} = [x_1^{(1)}, x_2^{(1)}, ..., x_m^{(1)}]$ if and only if $x_j^{(0)} \neq x_j^{(1)}$ for at least one $j; j = 1, 2, ..., m$. The demand for (or supply of) a commodity is, therefore, a demand for (or supply of) characteristics. These characteristics may include time (whether a commodity is old or new), place (its location), positional value (whether it is owned or used by many or only a few), brand name (whether produced by this or that manufacturer), and so on. This view of considering a commodity as a bundle of characteristics opens an immensely wide scope for properly dealing with the demand for (or supply of) a commodity not only as a substitute of but also as a complement to other commodity or commodities.

Rentable house, for example, is a commodity which has a demand (on rent) and often this demand is dependent on the house rent (per month, say), disposable income of the person (family) and the number of members in the family. Had all houses been exactly identical (in matters of location, number of rooms, number of floors, carpet area, available facilities, neighbourhood characteristics, and so on) rent, income and family size (and such variables) would certainly have been sufficient to determine the demand for houses. But on the contrary, each house differs from another house in at least one characteristic. Even if a house, $H^{(1)}$ is exactly the same as another house, $H^{(2)}$ in all characteristics, $j = 1, 2, ..., m$-1, the mth characteristic of it (namely location in the 3-*d* space) must always differ since it is impossible for two houses to occupy exactly the same location. Consumers may have (and often do have) strong preferences for location. This is an awkward situation for the traditional theory of consumer's demand although the characteristic theory can comfortably handle it.

The Objective and Data Base

The objective of this study is to show how the demand for a rentable house can be quantitatively expressed. The data set is obtained by a primary (sample) survey of 209 households randomly selected from the households inhabiting 19 wards of the township of Kohima, the capital city of Nagaland (India) during the first half of the year 2008. Eleven households were chosen from each ward. Besides many other information, the survey collected data on the residential house of the respondent, his/her family size, family income and rent (per month) paid if the house was acquired on rent. Of 209 households, 109 were found living in a rented house. In this study we use the data for those 109 households.

Among the house characteristics, information on the following were collected: (1) House type—(a) *kutcha, pucca* or (b) *pucca*, (2) plot size in sq. ft, (3) floor area in sq. ft, (4) no. of rooms, (5) no. of occupants (persons), (6) nature of ownership—rented, govt. quarter, own, (7) distance from the nearest building in ft, (8) receiving enough sunshine—no, yes, (9) parking space—no, yes, (10) waste disposal facilities—no, yes-near, yes-far, (11) drainage—no, ordinary, very good,

(12) public garden/park nearby—no, yes, (13) having water supply—no, yes, (14) regularity of water supply—not satisfactory, satisfactory, very good, (15) source of water supply—outside common, outside private, inside, (16) nature of toilet—outside common, outside private, inside attached, (17) power connection—no, yes, (18) load-shedding or power failure—frequent, occasionally, rarely, (19) noise pollution—no, yes, (20) air pollution—no, yes, (21) water pollution—no, yes, (22) nature of water pollution—physical, chemical, both, (23) respondent's feeling of satisfaction with the house—no, yes, and (24) safety—unsatisfactory, satisfactory. Most of these characteristics are qualitative in nature and we have used binary variables or an ordinal/nominal scale to measure them such that higher value on the scale refers to a preferred state and *vice-versa*. Further, of these characteristics, we have dropped number 6 since in the subsequent analysis we are concerned with rented house only. In our analysis, rent is used as a price (in Rs.) per sq. ft. of floor area.

Methodological Aspects

We hold that three variables, namely, household (disposable) income *(Y)*, family size *(F)*, and the monthly rental *(R)* should explain the demand for housing. We also hold *a priori* that the coefficient/exponent associated with rent should be negative while the coefficients associated with income, and family size, should be positive—the first measuring the ability to pay and the second measuring a need for larger house which may require higher rent to be paid.

The crudest of the possibilities is to regress each of the characteristics of houses *Y*, *F* and *R*. In that case we will have 22 regression equations to be estimated which will involve 88 parameters (including 22 intercepts). It will be difficult to cogently explain those parameters. Further, this approach may not be suitable in view of interdependencies (substitution as well complementation) among various characteristics since we must consider each equation independently. Simultaneous equation models (such as seemingly unrelated regression equations method of estimation) may not be applicable in want of identifiability and unknown nature of residuals.

Another way to establish the relationship between the demand for house and its determinants is to use factor analysis/ principal components analysis to identify the leading factors in the complex of all house characteristics, regress the factor scores on the determinants (*Y*, *F* and *R*) and back-calculate the coefficients from the factor weights matrix and the regression coefficients. Alternatively, it is also possible that canonical correlations between housing characteristics *(X)* and the determinants, $Z = (Y, F, R)$, of house demand are obtained and canonical factor scores are used to back-calculate the coefficients of the demand equation(s). These methods heavily rely on the correlation matrix, $\Re(X)$, $\Re(Z)$ or both. The degree of success in obtaining the demand equation(s) will depend on the eigen-structure these matrices.

Yet another method was suggested by Stackelberg (1932), although in a different context (Baumgärtner, 2001; Barrett and Hogset, 2003). In the Stackelberg schema, estimation of the demand function for a multi-characteristics commodity is rather simple. Let $X_i = (x_{i1}, x_{i2}, ..., x_{im})$; $i = 1, 2, ..., n$ be observations on *m* joint housing characteristics. Then, a point r_i in m-dimensional (real) space is defined as $r_i = (x_{i1}^2 + x_{i2}^2 + ... + x_{im}^2)^{0.5}$. Only the positive value is taken (since r_i signifies length). One of the characteristics (say, x_1) is considered as a standard measure or reference. The direction vectors for other characteristics are obtained as $\theta_{ij} = \cos^{-1}(x_{ij}/r_i)$; $j = 2, 3, ..., m$. These direction vectors together with the determinants of housing demand $[Z = (Y, F, R)]$ are used as regressors and is used as the regress and variable. Thus, $r_i = f(\theta_{i2}, \theta_{i3}, ..., \theta_{im}; Y_i, F_i, R_i)$; $i = 1, 2, ..., n$ are used to estimate the parameters of demand function of a multi-characteristics commodity such as house. Note that one of the characteristics, here the first one, is used as a standard, and hence θ_1 is not included among the regressors. Implicitly it is assumed that all the characteristics are identically related to the determinants, $Z = [Y, F, R]$. It is also assumed that all the products are measured in the same (Euclidean) space. Since different characteristics are measured in different scales/units, it is appropriate to normalize each of them to have unit norm.

We define $norm_j = \left[\sum_{i=1}^{n} x_{ij}^2\right]^{0.5}$ and $x_{ij} = x^*_{ij}/norm_j$; $i = 1, n$; $j = 1, m$, where x^* is measured in variant units and x is measured with the unit norm. We use this method in our study.

Results and Discussion

In our analysis, we have used the floor area of house as the reference characteristics. We have used the direction vectors of all characteristics (sans number of occupants and nature of ownership, since both of these characteristics are implicitly taken into consideration as we are analyzing the case of rented houses only and the family size of the household is used as an non-characteristic explanatory variable). All variables (dependent, r, as well as independent, θ and Z) are transformed into their (natural) logarithmic values. The results are presented in Table 5.1. Among the house-characteristics variables (direction vectors) only 'house type' is statistically significant at 10 per cent (one-tail) level of significance; others are significant all lower levels. Among the non-characteristics variables, family size is statistically significant at 10 per cent (one-tailed) level. It may be noted that the source of water supply and power connection are complementing floor area and have positive coefficients; other characteristics are substitutes of the floor area as they bear negative coefficients. The negative coefficient associated with rent is not (statistically) distinguishable from zero.

A significant but negative rent-elasticity of demand for rented house may suggest that it is a sticky commodity. This is substantiated by the negative income elasticity of demand (consumption expenditure) for rented houses (Ngullie and Mishra, 2008) although insignificantly different from zero (see Table 5.2).

Table 5.1 : Log-Linear Regression Coefficients of Demand Function for House in Kohima, Nagaland

Sl. No.	*Variable*	*Coefficient*	*t-value*	*Sl. No.*	*Variable*	*Coefficient*	*t-value*
1.	**House type**	-0.1866	-1.42	14.	**Nature of toilet**	-0.6106	-4.74
2.	**Plot size**	-0.6201	-6.63	15.	**Power connection**	1.9809	6.90
3.	**Floor area (Ref. Characteristics)**	-	-	16.	**Load-shedding**	-0.3849	-2.55
4.	**No. of Rooms**	-0.6653	-4.10	17.	**Noise pollution**	-0.2934	-4.42
5.	**Distance from nearest building**	-0.6482	-7.29	18.	**Air pollution**	-0.4547	-5.78
6.	**Availability of sunlight**	-0.3846	-5.80	19.	**Water pollution**	-0.4232	-2.33
7.	**Parking space**	-0.5431	-7.64	20.	**Nature of water pollution**	-0.6117	-3.28
8.	**Waste disposal facilities**	-0.2366	-2.96	21.	**Resident's satisfaction**	-0.3635	-4.60
9.	**Drainage**	-0.4945	-5.01	22.	**Safety feeling**	-0.2544	-3.04
10.	**Adjacency of Park/public garden**	-0.5580	-8.85	23.	**Income**	0.0270	2.29
11.	**Water supply status**	-0.4963	-3.18	24.	**Family size**	0.0174	1.39
12.	**Regularity of water supply**	-0.7605	-6.98	25.	**Rent per sq. ft. floor area**	-0.0009	-0.07
13.	**Source of water supply**	0.4528	1.70	26.	**Regression constant**	1.6642	3.81

R square=0.936787; Table values of 2-tailed t = 0.68 (50%), 1.29 (20%), 1.66 (10%), 1.99 (5%), 2.37 (2.5%), 2.64 (1%).
Regression coefficients are indeed elasticities since regressors and regress and variable are all in natural logarithms.

Concluding Remarks

This chapter draws on the theory of consumer's demand from Kelvin Lancaster who suggested that a commodity may be considered as a bundle of numerous characteristics and consumers are willing to pay for those characteristics. In this chapter we have shown how the demand for a multi-characteristics commodity such as house can be estimated by a method suggested (long back) by Stackelberg that transforms the measures of various characteristics into polar coordinates,

Table 5.2 : Income and Family Size Elasticity of Consumption Expenditure in Kohima

Item of Expenditure	Elasticity: Income	Elasticity: Family Size	Elasticity: Total	Constant	Item of Expenditure	Elasticity: Income	Elasticity: Family Size	Elasticity: Total	Constant
Cereals	3.01E-01	4.54E-01	7.55E-01	4.35E+01	Travel	2.31E+00	-7.15E-01	1.59E+00	1.93E-06
	6.73E+00	8.79E+00	1.55E+01	1.08E+01		9.07E+00	2.43E+00	1.15E+01	6.62E+00
Vegetables	5.50E-01	2.59E-02	5.76E-01	6.34E+00	Education fees	9.04E-01	3.00E+00	3.91E+00	2.15E-03
	1.00E+01	4.07E-01	1.04E+01	4.30E+00		3.79E+00	1.09E+01	1.47E+01	3.29E+00
Non-veg items	6.26E-01	-5.63E-03	6.20E-01	3.09E+00	Cable TV fees	2.01E+00	-6.72E-01	1.34E+00	9.61E-06
	6.54E+00	5.09E-02	6.59E+00	1.51E+00		8.13E+00	2.35E+00	1.05E+01	5.98E+00
Sugar	2.99E-01	4.00E-01	6.99E-01	2.89E+00	Telephone bills	1.99E+00	-6.97E-01	1.29E+00	2.32E-05
	4.57E+00	5.28E+00	9.85E+00	2.08E+00		7.91E+00	2.40E+00	1.03E+01	5.43E+00
Tea leaf	6.15E-01	1.45E-01	7.60E-01	4.32E-01	Guest entertainment	2.30E+00	-2.04E-01	2.10E+00	3.35E-07
	8.16E+00	1.66E+00	9.83E+00	1.43E+00		7.85E+00	6.02E-01	8.45E+00	6.50E+00
Milk	7.14E-01	1.26E-01	8.40E-01	6.66E-01	Hobbies	1.95E+00	-3.74E-01	1.58E+00	1.03E-06
	1.04E+01	1.58E+00	1.20E+01	7.59E-01		6.02E+00	9.97E-01	7.01E+00	5.45E+00
Edible oil	5.33E-01	8.78E-02	6.21E-01	1.11E+00	House rent	-3.69E-01	-3.71E-01	-7.40E-01	1.46E+03
	7.44E+00	1.06E+00	8.50E+00	1.93E-01		8.61E-01	7.47E-01	1.61E+00	2.18E+00
Fruits	1.47E+00	-1.89E-01	1.28E+00	6.28E-04	Toiletries	8.34E-01	-1.00E-01	7.33E-01	2.02E-01
	7.26E+00	8.09E-01	8.07E+00	4.67E+00		7.74E+00	8.05E-01	8.54E+00	1.90E+00
Water supply	1.23E+00	-4.54E-01	7.80E-01	9.72E-04	Addictive items	1.29E+00	-7.49E-01	5.39E-01	1.32E-03
	4.12E+00	1.31E+00	5.43E+00	2.96E+00		3.44E+00	1.73E+00	5.16E+00	2.26E+00
Fuel	4.55E-01	-3.91E-02	4.16E-01	9.47E+00	Clothes/shoes	9.53E-01	4.95E-02	1.00E+00	2.13E-01
	9.16E+00	6.81E-01	9.84E+00	5.79E+00		1.39E+01	6.23E-01	1.45E+01	2.88E+00
Electricity	4.44E-01	4.70E-02	4.91E-01	3.55E+00	Medical bills	1.36E+00	1.94E-01	1.55E+00	3.44E-04
	4.26E+00	3.89E-01	4.64E+00	1.55E+00		4.32E+00	5.32E-01	4.85E+00	3.24E+00
Newspaper	1.47E+00	-6.58E-02	1.40E+00	1.95E-04	Social obligations	2.35E+00	-3.14E-01	2.04E+00	4.29E-07
	5.92E+00	2.30E-01	6.15E+00	4.42E+00		7.99E+00	9.24E-01	8.91E+00	6.38E+00

Note: The first row under each item is the measure of elasticity while the second row under each item gives computed *t* values of the estimated elasticity of expenditure. The results are based on data obtained from 209 sample households.

Source: Ngullie and Mishra, 2008.

and how this method may be useful in identifying the complementary and substitutive characteristics of the commodity concerned. We have not gone in for identification of the demand equation. As for Kohima, an analysis of primary data collected from the households inhabiting 19 wards of the town suggests that consumers of rented house consider floor area, water supply and power supply complementary to each other and other characteristics of house as substitutes of the floor area. It has also been found that in Kohima a rented house is possibly an inferior or sticky commodity and its income elasticity for the overall sample is negative, although statistically insignificant.

REFERENCES

Barrett, C. and Hogset, H. (2003), "Estimating Multiple-Output Production Functions for the CLASSES Model" see at *http://aem.cornell.edu/special_programs/AFSNRM/Basis/Documents/Memos/Multi-output Production Function Estimation for CLASSES. PDF.*

Baumgärtner, S. (2001), "Heinrich Von Stackelberg on Joint Production", *European Journal of History of Economic Thought*, 8 (4): 509-525.

Lancaster, K.J. (1966), "A new approach to consumer theory", *Journal of Political Economy*, 74(2): 132-157.

Ngullie, M.L. and Mishra, S.K. (2008), "Structural Relations among the Components of Household Income and Expenditure in Kohima, Nagaland", Working Paper Series, *SSRN*: *http://ssrn.com/abstract=1215322.*

Stackelberg, H.V. (1932), '*Grundlagen einer reinen Kostentheorie* (Foundations of a Pure Theory of Costs). Verlag von Julius Springer, Wien.

6

Rural Transformation in India
A Study on the Efficacy of DWCRA

J.U. AHMED

Introduction

In India, the Development of Women and Children in Rural Areas (DWCRA) was first introduced in 1978 in 50 districts. It was extended to all the States during 1982-1983. The scheme was promoted by the Central Government with cooperation of UNICEF. Women are the major target group of the scheme. It was observed that the flow of financial assistance through various schemes and programmes was marginal as well as insufficient to enable them to get rid of the poverty line. Therefore, a separate scheme was envisaged which would motivate women to engage themselves in economically viable activities. The Government has taken special efforts to assist these women in marketing their products without any middlemen. The women have been provided an opportunity to expose their products to the urban consumers and also understand customer's choices in a competitive market environment. In this line, DWCRA Bazaars are being set up in several districts to replicate these initiatives at the district level. These bazaars were very successful and response is encouraging. It is also planned to establish marketing outlets exclusively for the sale of DWCRA products to provide an opportunity for the women coming from the rural sector.

With this point in view, the scheme of DWCRA was launched as a sub-scheme of Integrated Rural Development Programme (IRDP). The present chapter is the modest attempt to evaluate the efficacy of the scheme in a backward area, *viz.*, North Karimganj Block of Karimganj District in Assam.

Nature and Scope of DWCRA

The primary thrust of DWCRA scheme has been on the formation of groups of 10-15 women from poor households at the village level, for delivery of services like credit and skill training and infrastructural support for self-employment. The overall aim of the scheme has been to raise income level of women of poor households by making them participate in organized socio-economic activities. As a result of group formation, women's access to basic services of health, education, child care, nutrition, water and sanitation is bound to improve. Wide range of activities related to agriculture and its allied small industries are covered under this programme.

The scheme identifies women in the age group of 18 to 35 years who are living below the poverty line in the rural areas. The identified women are given training for six months and paid Rs. 200 as stipend per month. Also, a group of organizers is selected for each group. The organizers would have to undergo a separate training during which they are paid a stipend of Rs. 250 per month. After the completion of the training, each beneficiary is given a loan ranging from Rs. 4,000 and Rs. 6000 depending upon the nature of activity to start his own business as a self-employed venture.

The DWCRA group generally consists of 15 to 20 women. The group select one of the members as a group organizer, who helps it to select an economic activity in accordance with its skill, aptitude and availability of facilities for procuring raw materials and marketing finished products. 50 such groups can be formed in every block.

The specific objectives of the schemes are :

- To help and promote self-employment among the rural women who are in the BPL by providing training in vocation.
- To organize beneficiaries in some group activities and promote economic and social self-reliance.
- To generate income for the poor by creating avenues for production of good and services.
- To organize production enhancing programmes in rural area. This programme assumes that women in the Below Poverty Line (BPL) can be organized into small groups with a nominated group organizer from amongst themselves to act as a link between the officials of the implementing machinery for delivery of services in one hand and the beneficiary target group on the other.

About the Study Area

Karimganj is the southernmost district of Assam covers an area of 1809 sq. km comprising 933 villages and 4 towns (GoI, 2003). The topography of the district is quadrilateral shape composed of high hills, low lands called *Beel* and *Haor* and level plains dotted with isolated hills called *Tillas* and *Mati-tillas*. The district is densely populated, industrially backward with an agrarian bias. The literacy rate in the district is 57.4 per cent which is higher than the national average (GoI, 2002). Nearly 72 per cent of the workforce and 50 per cent of the geographical area are under agriculture. The soil of the district is highly acidic in nature and is of alluvial origin. High lands within the district are generally planted with tea while plain areas are covered with rice. The rice and tea together occupy more than 90 per cent of gross cropped area of the district. Sugarcane, oil seeds, potatoes, pulses etc. are also produced.

The number of existing industries in the district constituted about 3.5 per cent of the total number of industries of State, Assam during the period 1977-2003. The district Industries Centres (DICs) are imparting training to the rural artisans in trade, leather work, tailoring, bamboo work, carpentry, etc. Only 4.3 per cent of the workers are engaged in manufacturing, processing, etc. as against national average of 10.2 per cent of the workforce in manufacturing sector. A total of 55 per cent of the villages are electrified in the valley while 65 per cent in Assam. The number of registered unemployed in the district increased from 10,125 in 1975 to 1,04,090 in 2001. The adequacy of finance is essential for any developmental activities in rural areas. The rate of growth of flow of institutional finance in the district has not shown significant rise. At present, 9 public sector banks with 32 branches, 1 regional rural bank (Assam Gramin Vikas Bank) with 17 branches and 2 co-operative banks with 3 branches are operating in the district.

The economy of the district is basically agrarian. The economic development of the district is highly dependent on rural development through various development schemes and programmes in the form of the development of agriculture and allied sector, agro-based industries.

DWCRA in the District under Study

DWCRA is being implemented in the block under study from 1992-1993. In order to study the impact of the scheme, we have selected 27 units formed during 1997-2007. The following Table 6.1 exhibits year-wise number of groups formed along with total expenditure incurred for the implementation of the scheme. It has been observed that 210 numbers of group comprising of 3,181 members were formed with an expenditure of total amount of Rs. 41.77 lakh during the period 1997-2007. A provision of an average of Rs. 19,477 was made and supplied to each group as revolving fund. Further, the amount to the tune of around 79 per cent of total receipt of funds has been used for the implementation of the programme.

Table 6.1 : Achievement of DWCRA in the District

Year	*No. of groups formed*	*Membership (No.)*	*Expenditure (Rs. in Lakh)*
1997-98	50	750	5.88 (61.31)
1999-00	25	375	5.89 (93.0)
2000-01	5	75	4.25 (89.5)
2001-02	30	450	7.25 (84.4)
2002-03	25	375	3.15 (68.8)
2003-04	18	270	3.51 (74.6)
2004-05	16	260	3.14 (71.2)
2005-06	20	301	4.51 (81.2)
2006-07	21	325	4.89 (74.5)
Total	210	3181	41 .77 (78.6)

Source: DRDA file record. (Figures in the parentheses indicate percentage to total receipt)

Analysis of Sample

Economic Activities Undertaken by the DWCRA Groups

In the study area a number of income generating activities were undertaken in this scheme includes, cane and bamboo works, weaving, fish-net making, pottery, cane mat (Sital-pati) making and small business which includes chilli-powder making, papad making and betel-nut cutting, *supari* processing, bee keeping, goat rearing, tailoring, poultry, readymade garments. The unit-wise activities undertaken may be presented in Table 6.2.

Table 6.2 : Activities undertaken by the Scheme

Economic Activities	*Number of Units*
Cane and bamboo works	5(22%)
Weaving	11(43%)
Fish-net making	3(13%)
Pottery	2(04%)
Sital-Pati making	3(09%)
Small business	3(09%)
Total	27 (100)

It is observed that the sample groups were formed in six different activities and about 43 per cent of group's pursued weaving activity. Other dominating activities are cane and bamboo works (22 per cent) followed by fish-net making (13 per cent), Sital-pati making (9 per cent) and other small business (9 per cent) and pottery (4 per cent) respectively.

Year-wise Implementation of DWCRA and Present Position

Since the different types of income generating activities were undertaken in the district, it is necessary to study that the present position of the above mentioned units. The following Table 6.3 presents year-wise implementation of DWCRA in the block under study and present position of the units. The Table 6.3 discerns that 27 numbers of unit covering 25 villages were formed during 2000-01 to 2005-06. Out of the 6 units formed during the year 2000-01, 3 were defunct. The reasons are

Table 6.3 : Activities under DWCRA

Year	*Trade*	*No. of Units*	*Villages covered*	*Present Position*
2000-01	Fish-net making	1	2	3 units are defunct, Rare presence of group activities.
	Cane and bamboo	1	2	
	Sital-pati (Cane mat)	2	2	
	Weaving	2	2	
2001-02	Weaving	2	1	No group activities except family-based business activities
	Cane and bamboo	2	1	
	Fish-net making	1	1	
2002-03	Cane and bamboo	2	2	Do
	Weaving	2	2	Do
2003-04	Weaving	1	1	Do
	Small business	1	1	Do
	Pottery	1	1	Do
2004-05	Weaving	3	1	Do
	Net-making	3	1	Do
	Small business	1	1	Do
2005-06	Weaving	2	1	Do
	Small business	2	1	Do
	Total	27	25	

misutilisation of revolving funds, lack of proper initiative for implementing the scheme, absence of group activities, non-formation of group as per the scheme and lack of knowledge regarding the scheme of the members. The units under the scheme are mostly engaged in family based business activities throughout the period 2000-2006.

Overall Appraisal

Since 3 out of 27 sample groups were defunct, an evaluation, therefore, has been made on remaining 24 units. We have conducted an interview in two stages, first the *Gram Sevikas* and then the organizers of the centre. It is revealed that owing to non-availability of common workplace, attempt has been made to improve the economic condition of members individually. In this respect Gram Sevikas are acting a sole authority for improving the scheme. They withdraw a portion of revolving fund and distribute among the members to support their working capital requirements. They maintain both register and accounts of the centre. Thus the group organizers have virtually no role to play.

The members of groups in different villages have acquired knowledge of different activities due to their involvement in family business. It is worth mentioning that selection of members and their inclusion in the group depend on whether she has any knowledge in activity of which the centre is going to be formed. But in most cases it is seen that somehow may be with the political influence, personal motivation, etc., the names of fifteen members are collected and recommended for the scheme. Thus, members in most cases without self-determination and lack of personal zeal even without any earlier knowledge constitute the group. The beneficiaries are aware of hygiene and nutrition aspect needed for their family. They follow certain common rules like use of boil water, washing of hands after work, consumption of green leafy vegetables, use for fresh water for cooking and drinking and also follow the immunization programme for their babies.

The amount of Rs. 15000 has been earmarked for individual unit and the same is released in instalments after reviewing the progress and ability of the group (individual) to repay the amount. In most of the cases it has been observed that a portion of fund ranging from Rs. 500 to Rs. 1,200 distributed among the members as first dose. Out of 24 cases, only 7 units have received first dose, 5 units received second dose and remaining units have received more than two doses. The members of the earlier units have received further instalments due to lack of credit worthiness.

Major Findings

- Economic activities whatever may be the form was mostly undertaken by the individual and as a result the groups as envisaged in the scheme were not formed in the study area and group activities particularly are absent.
- The portion of fund made available to the beneficiaries ultimately goes into the hands of their male partners who take decision of utilization of such funds.
- The revolving fund has not been utilized properly due to beneficiaries' inability to repay and thus help up in the banks.
- The member beneficiaries are already involved in their own traditional family business which is circumscribed by host of problems. Thus loaning her (beneficiaries) name into the centre does not make a significant change in the family income.
- The funds so, received has not been utilized for purchasing materials and thereby the spirit of the scheme of creating assets for the society has been defeated.
- The hand made goods particularly weaving products lost their competitive edge over the machine made goods in terms of price and quality.
- No pragmatic steps either from block or district level were undertaken to implement and monitor the scheme except maintaining related files.
- Inadequate provision of backward and forward linkages needed for the smooth functioning of the

scheme has emerged as another hurdle in the area under study.

- There is a constant time gap between training imparted to the beneficiaries and their commencement of trades, in many cases, it is more than three years. During this period, the trainees usually lost their grip over the skill they have acquired during their training period.
- The assistance has proved to be a liability rather than asset. This happens when the assets fail to generate income and the women groups have to repay loans with high interest rates.
- There is an undue delay in the delivery of development assistance because of lack of functional coordination among the banks, DRDA and the beneficiaries.

Conclusion

The foregoing discussions reveals that DWCRA scheme in the district experienced a number of problems. The appropriate attempt has not been made to address the problems faced by the beneficiaries in the districts. Glamour are only given at both district and block level to the higher percentage of achievement of target size without boosting economic position of the beneficiaries. The potentiality of the programme as a result nipped in the bud due to its non-implementation at the grass-root level. The demanding efforts at all level should be made so that benefits of the scheme may reach to the target groups.

REFERENCES

Ahmed, J.U. and Raul, R.K. 2005. "Implications of PMRY Schemes for Rural Transformation", *Journal of Management Research*, BIT, Mesra, Jharkhand

Ahmed. J.U. 2006. "Bank Financing of Agriculture and Allied Sector in the Reform Era: An Empirical Diagnosis". *Indian Economic Panorama*, New Delhi.

Bhatia D.S. *et al.* (Ed) 1998: *Management of Rural Development*, Deep and Deep Publications, New Delhi.

Dandikar, V.M. and N. Rath, *Poverty in India,* Poona, Indian School of Political Economy

Das, D.K. (ed.) 1994: *Dynamics of Rural Development: Potentials and Constraints,* Deep and Deep Publications, New Delhi.

Desai, V. 1990: *Panchayati Raj* : Himalaya Publishing House, New Delhi.

District Industries Centre, Karimganj, Assam.

Government Manual on *Integrated Rural Development Programme,* January 1980.

Govt. of Assam, 2005. *Statistical Hand Book,* Directorate of Economics and Statistics, Assam.

Lead Bank Office, United Bank of India, Silchar, Assam.

Raul R.K., 2003. *Rural Development in India, Approaches and Applications,* Serial Publication, New Delhi.

Sarma, N.N., 2003. *Consumer Cooperatives and Rural Marketing,* Mittal Publication, New Delhi.

7

Harnessing Agricultural Resources for Socio-Economic Development of North-East India

AMOD SHARMA; K.K. JHA and D.S DHAKRE

Introduction

Food security has been a major area of concern for planners as well as scientists in India especially after the independence. Out of 110 million farm families about 70 per cent belong to the marginal farmers, having operational holding of less than one hectare. The agricultural development efforts need the support of many disciplines, institutions and organizations, so as to accelerate agricultural production and to improve thereby a lot of farming population. Agricultural extension service must be backed by the agencies concerned with various farm inputs, research, training institutions, credit, and marketing cooperative and even by the voluntary organization.

The North-Eastern Hill Region of India comprises of the States of Arunachal Pradesh, Assam, Manipur, Meghalaya, Mizoram, Nagaland, Sikkim and Tripura. These hill States lie between 21.50° to 29.50° North latitude and 85.5° to 97.5° East longitudes representing a distinct agro-climatic zone of the country. These hills occupy the total geographical area of 5.6 per cent with the population of 1.13 per cent of the country (total area of 2.5 lakh sq. km.). Assam is located in the centre and hill States (except Sikkim) are situated around it. Among the 8 hill States of the region, Arunachal Pradesh has the maximum geographical area and Sikkim has the least. However, both have the continental climatic zones in this region (Anon, 2000).

Morphologically, north-eastern hill region of the country is marked by the development of a series of ridges and valleys, terraces, scraps, several geomorphologic or planners, surfaces at different elevations (15 m to 5000 m and above), etc. Only permanent snow cover exist around 28 and 7 per cent of the total geographical area of Sikkim and Arunachal Pradesh respectively. Rivers from the adjoining hill States primarily constitute Brahmaputra drainage basin. The Himalayan (Sikkim and Arunachal Pradesh) rivers originate from the snow-clad mountains, while others originate from the alive hills. It is very difficult to generalize the direction of the rivers. However, the rivers of Arunachal Pradesh and Sikkim usually flow from the north to south.

The climate of Arunachal Pradesh and Sikkim varies from sub-tropical to extreme alpine type. In other States, agro-climate varies from sub-tropical to temperate. The normal mean minimum and maximum temperature vary from 18°C to 32°C in summer and 9°C to 22°C in winter. The temperature in the snow clad mountain remains below—7°C. The NE States as a whole gets mean annual rainfall 2000 mm/annum and heavy precipitation occurs in the form of snow at the top of the mountains. The Brahmaputra and Barak rivers basin drain the water of entire Arunachal Pradesh, Meghalaya, Nagaland, Sikkim and western part of Manipur. The NE region, though having 5.6 per cent of total geographical area of the country, receives 12.1 per cent of the total precipitation. The total surface water potential of the region (data not available for Sikkim) is 928873 mm^3. The soil of this region is broadly classified into 5 orders viz.; *Inceptisols, Entisols, Alfisols, Vertisols* and *Mollisols.*

All the botanical zones from tropical to alpine are found in these States due to its geographical situation, climate and altitude. The forest cover of these hills varies from 44.9 per cent (Sikkim) to as high as 93.8 per cent in Arunachal Pradesh. These States are veritable storehouse of medicinal and economically important plants. Arunachal Pradesh and Sikkim are renowned for its Rhododendrons and orchids and for high altitude Primulas, Meconopsis and Blue poppies. Mithun *(Gravaeus frontalis)* is only confined to Arunachal Pradesh, Manipur and Nagaland in the country. *Yak (Poephagus grunniens* L.) is also in higher elevations of Sikkim and Arunachal Pradesh of the approximately 806 species inhabiting in fresh water of India, 267 species belonging to 112 genera under 38 families and 10 other are found in this region. In that way the region is rich in bio-diversity and endemic species.

Agricultural systems are no longer able to provide adequately for the needs of the increased population pressure on fragile mountain ecosystem. Earlier settlement pattern was dispersed small and people were close to their homesteads, but now there is increasing agglomeration. Semi-permanent cultivation is becoming permanent cultivation with increasing soil erosion and declining soil fertility. There has also been a reduction in the diversity of the crops. A continuous increase in population has further extended cultivation on steeper slopes with much less fertile soil. Soil erosion from agricultural activities on sloping lands has been by and large, the major contributor to the land degradation. In many cases, the loss of top fertile soil from limited cultivated lands has forced many farmers to abandon their traditionally cultivated land and to move on to other marginal lands. During heavy monsoon available human energy is concentrated on repairing damage to the irrigated rice terraces and irrigation system and the rain-fed terraces and other lands have to be left to collapse, because rice is more vital to the survival of the subsistence family in north-eastern hills.

Agriculture in India has made great strides, thanks to the agricultural technology being gradually introduced since the mid-1960s. It encompasses the use of High-Yielding Variety (HYV) seeds, chemicals, fertilizers, irrigation and plant protection measures along with the use of agricultural machinery and implements. The new technology has not been uniform among different States/regions. This has resulted regional imbalances in agricultural development across the States. This may not be entirely due to any policy neglect but could have arisen out of the inherent differences in resource endowments and the extent to which potential resources are being utilized and also, differences in the levels of infrastructure developments.

The deterioration in the productivity of the mountain environment has now been defined as a function of vegetative cover of uncultivated land. The ecology was in association with large variety of other trees, smaller plants and animals from the forest ecosystem. Forests are inter-related with other river and stream ecosystem or neighbouring down or village ecosystems where from visitors like man or his domestic cattle intrude into the forest and remove the forest produce like, timber, leaves, grass, firewood, etc. Thus, forest ecosystems are extremely valuable for the society in the lives of rural poor and tribes. Besides having economic, ecological and scientific values, forests have social, religious and ethnic importance also in our country.

Research Methodology

The present study is mainly based on secondary information, which was collected from several office sources and other publications. The percentages and averages were estimated to meet the objective of the study.

Population: Among the NE States, the lowest density of population/sq. km is Arunachal Pradesh (10) and highest is Tripura (263) and in the rest of States, it is between 33 (Mizoram) and 82 (Manipur). Maximum people live in rural areas (72.5 to 90.9 per cent) except Mizoram (53.9 per cent). The population density in mountain areas has moved from low to very high the decadal rate. The population increase in NE States was almost higher than the national average. In the last three decades (1961-1991) maximum growth was recorded in Nagaland (50 per cent) and it happened to the tune of 78.7 per cent during 1951-1961 in Tripura due to influx of people from Bangladesh. The increased population in subsistence mountain society has led to reduced amount of land per family, deepening poverty and massive deforestation. The NE region is prone to a number of bio-physical, institutional and socio-economical problems resulting into subsistence agriculture with low input and low yield risk technology. The major problems confronting the agricultural growth of the region are enumerated due to: Acidic Soil, high rainfall and humidity, low temperature at higher altitude etc.

Table 7.1 : Percentage Decadal Variation of Population (1951-1991)

Years	*States*								*All*
	A. P.	*Assam*	*Mani-pur*	*Megha-laya*	*Mizo-ram*	*Naga-land*	*Tri-pura*	*Sik-kim*	*India*
1951-1961	+37.23	+34.98	+35.04	+27.03	+35.61	+73.35	+78.71	+17.76	+21.64
1961-1971	+38.91	+33.95	+37.53	+31.50	+24.93	+39.88	+36.28	+29.38	+24.80
1971-1981	+35.15	+23.36	+32.46	+32.04	+48.55	+50.05	+31.92	+50.77	+24.66
1981-1991	+36.83	+24.24	+29.29	+32.86	+39.70	+56.08	+34.30	+27.47	+23.87
1991-2001	+27.00	+18.92	+24.85	+30.65	+28.82	+64.53	+16.03	+33.06	+21.54

Source: Directorate of Economics and Statistics, Government of India, New Delhi.

Table 7.2 : Share of Agriculture (in per cent) in Net Domestic Product and Employment in North-East States

States	*Net Domestic Product*			*Employment*		
	1970-71	*1980-81*	*1990-91*	*1970-71*	*1980-81*	*1990-91*
Arunachal Pradesh	59.1	—	44.5	80.3	69.6	64.0
Manipur	48.0	44.7	29.1	67.0	64.2	62.5
Meghalaya	—	37.8	—	78.9	68.6	64.1
Mizoram	—	—	17.4	—	67.4	55.8
Nagaland	—	28.69	—	79.0	71.9	73.4
Sikkim	—	—	38.7	85.6	61.4	64.3
Tripura	70.0	45.6	31.6	74.3	61.8	57.6
All-India	49.2	36.3	44.5	69.7	60.5	58.9

Source: CMIE Publications (various issues).

Net Domestic Product : In the process of economic development, it is expected that non-agricultural sector would grow faster than agricultural sector in terms of output and labour absorption. However, the share of agriculture in Net Domestic Product (NDP) is higher in NE States except Nagaland as a result of comparatively lower industrial growth in the region. Thc Table 7.2 shows that the decline in the share of agriculture in NDP is higher than the decline in labour force in agriculture. This coupled with population growth has led to an increase in the number of workers per hectare of land in the country as well as for the NE region.

Land Use Pattern: The land use pattern of NE region is strongly influenced by the elevation, climate and mountainous terrain, especially in the field of agriculture and forestry. The NER consists of about 25.539 million hectare of land resources, which comprises of 8 per cent of the total land resource of the country, about 75 per cent area are hilly region. Forest covers accounted 77.9 per cent of the total area and around 60 per cent as a dense forest, which represent 22.5 per cent forest cover of India. The net cultivated land is 6.8 per cent of the total reported geographical area.

Plantation crops like tea, coffee, and rubber were introduced in this region long ago land have been doing very well. This region is the largest producer of tea in the country with an area of 2,36,430 ha. producing 4,32,876 tonnes of tea annually. Meghalaya with an area of 9510 ha. produce about 12,040 tonnes of areca nut. The average productivity of coconut in Assam is about 7000 nuts/ha.

Table 7.3 : Land Use Pattern in Seven States of NE Region (Area in '000 Ha)

States	*Geo. Area*	*Forest*	*Fallow*	*Net Area*	*Total cropped area*	*Irrigated area*	*Intensity*
Arunachal Pradesh	83743	5154	36	164	263	42	170
Assam	78738	1930	82	2701	4065	170	142
Manipur	22327	602	—	140	209	65	134
Meghalaya	22429	938	158	240	277	54	119
Mizoram	21081	1599	170	91	94	9	159
Nagaland	16579	875	77	261	314	72	112
Sikkim	7096	257	9	95	126	17	148
Tripura	10486	606	1	277	428	37	168
Total	262479	11961	533	3969	5776	466	144

[Fertilizer Statistics 1995-96; 111—4, 10, 40, 1996 *Cf.* Fertilizer News. 43 (5): 53-57, 1998].

Shifting Cultivation : In the North-eastern hill region of India, shifting cultivation is a common practice on hill slopes. This practice is known as *Jhum*. As per the Forest Survey of India, 1999 estimated the cumulative area of 1.73 million ha affected by shifting cultivation during 1987-1997 and maximum affected area by this practice of agriculture was Mizoram (603 sq. km.) followed by Nagaland (573 sq. km.). While, in the year 1995-97 the affected area lost because of shifting cultivation was 1875 sq. km. of forest areas. However, an area of 1700 sq. km. of abandoned shifting cultivation came under forest cover as a result of regeneration. Thus, shifting cultivation remains the single largest factor for the loss of forest cover.

Degraded Land : Degraded lands can aptly be described as land whose conditions has deteriorated to such an extent that it can not be put to any productive use, except current fallow due to various constraints. In north-eastern hills the lands affected by different derogative processes accounting 36.57 per cent of the total geographical area of the States. Although conservation measures are being adopted by the State Governments, but yet not keeping pace with time due to agro-climatic conditions of the region. Land degradation occurs mainly due to human interference of the eco-system. Degraded lands and stress sites can be categorized *viz.;* ecologically degraded lands and land degraded as a result of developmental activities.

Table 7.4 : Segment showing the Area involved and No. of Families engaged in Shifting Cultivation (1995-97)

State	*Loss due to Shifting Cultivation (Sq. Km.)*	*Total Districts*	*Families (No's)*	*Net Change in Area*
Arunachal Pradesh	75	10	54000	-19
Assam	257	3	58000	-237
Manipur	603	5	70000	-140
Meghalaya	75	5	52290	-57
Mizoram	292	3	50000	+ 199
Nagaland	573	7	116046	-70
Tripura	—	3	43000	+ 8
Total of NER	1875	36	443336	-316

Source: Forest Survey of India, 1999.

Table 7.5 : Soil Degradation Status in North-Eastern Hill States (lakh ha)

States	*Degraded land due to*		*Total*	*Area trea-*
	Erosion	*Special Problems*	*Problem Area*	*ted till 1996-97*
Arunachal Pradesh	24.44	2.10	26.54	15.80
Manipur	3.74	3.60	7.34	1.40
Meghalaya	8.37	2.65	11.02	1.35
Mizoram	4.21	1.89	6.10	0.40
Nagaland	4.05	6.33	10.38	1.43
Sikkim	3.03	—	3.03	2.72
Tripura	1.67	1.12	2.79	2.32
Arunachal Pradesh	24.44	2.10	26.54	1.40
Total of NER	49.51	17.69	67.20	—
% of Geog. Area	26.94	9.63	36.57	—

Source: Ministry of Agriculture, Directorate of Economics and Statistics, New Delhi.

Infrastructural Development and Inputs Used : Infrastructural developments and inputs used are analyzed in relation to output gains. The development of irrigation has been quite uneven across NE States since organized efforts to harness the water resources started in the country. In the States of Manipur and Tripura where percentage of net irrigated area to net cultivated area was high, which resulted to higher food-grains productivity. Fertilizer consumption per hectare was also higher in Manipur and Tripura, *i.e.,* 84.5 kg. and 31.3 kg. respectively, while in other States it was comparatively very low. It was almost related with the irrigation facilities.

In the States of Mizoram, Manipur, Sikkim and Tripura, the percentage area under HYVs varied from 31.19 to 75.19 per cent. In other States, it ranges from 17.84 per cent in Arunachal Pradesh to 29.13 per cent in Meghalaya. It showed high negative relationship between farm size and area under HYV. The number of pump-sets per unit area was negligible in NE States except Tripura (5.26 per '000 ha). There was significant growth in rural electrification in NE States, which varied from 46.3 per cent in Arunachal Pradesh to 98 per cent in Nagaland.

Understanding the processes, factors and causes of land degradation is a basic prerequisite towards successful

Table 7.6 : Trends in Fertilizer Consumption in NE States (Consumption in '000 tonnes)

States	*Fertilizer*	*1975-76*	*1980-81*	*1985-90*	*1990-95*	*1996-97*	*2000-01*	*2003-04(P)*	*c. g. r.*
A. P.	N_2	0.06	0.06	0.10	0.15	0.32	0.36	0.42	10.9
	P_2O_5	0.01	0.01	0.05	0.09	0.13	0.14	0.05	17.8
	Total	0.08	0.09	0.18	0.27	0.55	0.75	0.73	12.25
Assam	N_2	—	—	—	—	—	73.58	90.37	16.14
	P_2O_5	—	—	—	—	—	28.43	26.46	7.45
	Total	—	—	—	—	—	174.90	189.44	7.68
Manipur	N_2	1.00	2.28	3.90	8.66	11.39	18.41	22.70	10.41
	P_2O_5	0.30	0.56	0.80	4.37	1.25	2.51	2.30	9.14
	Total	1.34	3.00	4.89	13.52	13.18	26.90	27.28	9.90
Meghalaya	N_2	1.20	1.22	1.60	1.79	2.20	2.40	2.73	2.59
	P_2O_5	0.40	0.55	1.30	0.64	1.05	1.19	1.10	4.20
	Total	1.69	2.50	3.07	2.61	3.43	4.46	4.72	3.06
Mizoram	N_2	0.03	0.02	0.05	2.61	0.23	0.55	—	16.04
	P_2O_5	0.06	0.03	0.03	0.36	0.10	0.56	—	12.95
	Total	0.10	0.07	0.08	0.90	0.39	1.87	—	14.74
Nagaland	N_2	0.07	0.06	0.18	0.42	0.41	0.23	0.33	8.33
	P_2O_5	0.03	0.01	0.06	0.28	0.35	0.36	0.17	15.77
	Total	0.11	0.08	0.25	0.87	0.85	0.55	0.68	10.89
Sikkim	N_2	0.06	0.33	0.62	0.58	0.55	—	0.29	10.92
	P_2O_5	0.09	0.23	0.51	0.35	0.18	—	0.07	9.66
	Total	1.00	0.73	1.17	0.35	0.75	1.25	0.44	9.85
Tripura	N_2	0.20	1.39	3.50	6.00	5.41	6.89	7.49	14.74
	P_2O_5	0.04	10.35	1.00	1.58	1.88	1.75	0.76	20.38
	Total	0.29	2.13	4.22	8.43	8.72	9.25	12.57	15.71
All India	N_2	2148.6	3678.1	5660.8	7997.2	10301.8	10920.16	11076.34	7.33
	P_2O_5	466.8	1213.6	2005.2	3221.0	2976.8	4797.93	1696.44	8.26
	Total	2893.7	5515.6	8474.1	12546.2	14308.1	16094.09	16797.65	7.36

Source: Fertilizer Statistics, FAI (various Issues) and C.G.R. (Compound Growth Rate).

restoration of the productivity of degraded lands. Knowing the category of soil degradation is an important stage to restore the soil quality and its productivity by preventing soil erosion, promoting high biological activity, increasing soil organic matter content and increasing rooting depth of plants. There are two approaches that have been used to reclaim degraded land, *viz.*, engineering approaches and ecological approaches.

Agricultural Financial Position : The soil and climatic conditions are favourable for cultivation of variety of field crops and horticultural crops. Rich natural resources including rare species of flora and fauna, numerous seasonal vegetables, tropical and sub-tropical fruits and flowers are available in abundance in the region, which generate vast export potential for valuable foreign exchange and the source of capital formation. Commercial Banks, Regional Rural Banks and Co-operative Banks are the three prominent institutional agencies providing financial assistance for agriculture and rural development in the NER. Over the years, although there is massive expansion of financial infrastructure including agricultural financing in the country, the pace of development in the North-eastern India is however, not up to the mark.

The growth of Scheduled Commercial Bank branches in the N. E. States during 1975-1991 was satisfactory with annual Compound Growth Rate (CGR) of more than 11 per cent. Mizoram appeared to have the highest growth rate (44.34 per cent) and the lowest being 10.97 per cent in Assam during this period. The main reason for high growth rates in the N. E. States is due to low-base arising from a very poor growth of banking institutions in the pre-nationalized period. This expansion is confined mostly to the rural and semi-urban areas. Limited expansion of branches was also seen in urban areas in Assam, Manipur, Meghalaya and Tripura. The population per bank branch is 15000 as compared to 14000 or less in the country during 1990-91. The Credit Deposit Ratio (CDR) for the N.E. India is only 28.03 per cent, which is the lowest in the country (being about 55.49 per cent). The lower CDR in the N. E. India (about half the national average) implies draining, out of the financial resources from this region. Among the north-eastern

States, the CDR is the highest in Manipur (47.60 per cent) and the lowest in Meghalaya (19.11 per cent) during this period. Bank-wise analysis of the CDR shows that in respect of RRB, it was the highest in Arunachal Pradesh (97.93 per cent) and lowest in Mizoram (28.48 per cent). In case of Commercial Banks, it was the highest in Manipur at 45.25 per cent and the lowest being 11.54 per cent in Arunachal Pradesh. Co-operative Banks showed the highest CD ratio in Tripura (82.73 per cent) and the lowest in Mizoram (35.40 per cent).

Livestock Growth : The livestock population has also put tremendous pressure on forest and pasture resources. Unrestricted grazing of livestock, in a situation where both animal and human population is growing rapidly has led to a progressive decline in the density of the vegetative cover and the severe damage of the forest. The species composition changes towards a predominance of useless species while the rate of precipitation, runoff and soil erosion increase. The productivity of livestock itself falls as the animals obtain less available and less green fodder. In over grazed forest, seedlings of broad-leaved trees are grazed or lopped frequently and die due to overgrazing and trampling. In this way overgrazing prevents the replacement of trees cut for timber and fuel wood.

Livestock rearing is an important enterprise, comprises 3.2 million cattle, 0.21 million buffalo, 0.9 million sheep, 1.07 million goat and 1.43 million pig. The compound growth rate of production of milk, egg and fish were in large variation (1.49 to 21.6 per cent). The cattle population in all N.E. States increased significantly which range from 18.99 per cent in Sikkim to 256.99 per cent in Nagaland. The buffalo population increased significantly excepting Arunachal Pradesh, Meghalaya and Sikkim. The significant increase in milk production in Tripura was mostly attributed to improvement in milk breed. There was significant gain in egg production in N.E. States. Out of 7 States, 4 States *i.e.* Nagaland, Mizoram, Manipur and Meghalaya increased at a growth rate of more than all India average of 6.16 per cent per annum.

Table 7.7 : Trend of Milk, Fish and Eggs in N.E. States (Milk and fish in '000 tonns, eggs in lakh, No. of Cattle, buffalo and poultry in '000 numbers. All India egg in million No's. and milk in lakh tonnes)

States	*Year*	*Milk*	*Cattle*	*Buffalo*	*Fish*	*Eggs*	*Poultry*
Arunachal	1975	25.0	168	12	0.2	170.0	764
Pradesh	1997	44.0	324	5	2.1	340.0	1187
	2001	42.0	458.0	11.0	2.70	35.0	1743.0
	c. g. r.	1.49	94.86*	–58.33*	10.8	2.7	55.37*
Assam	1975						
	1997						
	2001	682.0	8440.0	678.0	186.31	507.0	21664.0
	c. g. r.						
Manipur	1975	51.5	294	52	1.8	200.0	938
	1997	62.0	719	114	13.7	612.0	3259
	2001	68.0	418.0	77.0	17.80	72.0	2941.0
	c. g. r.	1.45	144.56*	119.23*	10.1	6.58	247.44*
Meghalaya	1975	46.0	477	40	1.0	220.0	1073
	1997	59.0	635	33	4.1	810.0	1824
	2001	66.0	767.0	18.0	5.64	75.0	2821.0
	c. g. r.	3.12	33.12*	-17.5*	7.6	6.24	169.99*
Mizoram	1975	0.4	49	2	0.2	30.0	1128
	1997	20.0	59	7	2.7	35.0	1086
	2001	14.0	36.0	6.0	3.68	29.0	1125.0
	c. g. r.	21.6	20.41*	250.0*	9.9	6.71	-3.72*
Nagaland	1975	2.4	93	8	1.2	106.0	715
	1997	46.0	332	32	2.9	460.0	2164
	2001	57.0	451.0	34.0	4.90	54.0	2789.0
	c. g. r.	19.40	256.99*	300.0*	-4.3	7.83	202.66*
Sikkim	1975	17.0	158	5	0.1	100.0	221
	1997	35.0	188	2	0.1	170.0	302
	2001	35.0	159.0	2.0	0.14	10.0	332.0
	c. g. r.	3.88	18.99*	-60.0*	-2.41	2.67	36.65*
Tripura	1975	14.0	592	14	-2.41	19.0	665
	1997	470	949	20	25.8	580.0	2597
	2001	88.0	759.0	14.0	19.84	85.0	3057.0
	c. g. r.	5.83	60.33*	42.86*	10.14	5.15	290.53*
All-India	1975	25.09	180140	62029	2265.9	8631.5	160870
	1997	71.0	204516	84239	5360.0	30150.0	307071
	2001		185181.0	97922.0	6304.75	-	489012.0
	c. g. r.	4.4	3.53*	35.81 *	4.6	6.16	90.88*

Basic Animal Husbandry Statistics, Department of Animal Husbandry and Dairy, New Delhi

* Relates to percentage change and CGR (Compound Growth Rate).

Table 7.8 : Area under HYV in North-Eastern States and India during 1997-98

States	*Rice*			*Wheat*			*Maize*		
	Total area	*Area under HYV*	*% of HYV area to total area*	*Total area*	*Area under HYV*	*% of HYV area to total area*	*Total area*	*Area under HYV*	*% of HYV area to total area*
A. P.	120	35	29.17	3.80	3.50	92.11	34.50	—	—
Assam	2489.8	1422	57.11	84.70	84.30	99.53	19.20	12.00	62.50
Manipur	157.9	72	45.60	—	—	—	3.60	—	—
Meghalaya	157.9	42	26.60	4.30	4.00	93.02	17.20	15.00	87.21
Mizoram	68.1	5	7.34	—	—	—	8.20	—	—
Nagaland	145	2	1.38	1.80	0.30	16.67	30.00	3.00	10.00
Tripura	257.8	223	86.50	2.00	2.00	100.00	2.00	2.00	100.00
All-India	43420.2	33399	76.92	26685.60	23726.00	88.91	6305.30	3764.00	59.69

Source: Directorate of Economics and Statistics, Ministry of Agriculture, Government of India.

Table 7.9: Foodgrain Requirement, Production, Productivity and Deficiency in N.E. Region of India

States	*Requirement (000' tonnes)*	*Production (000' tonnes)*	*Deficiency (000' tonnes)*	*Av. Productivity (Kg/ha)*
Arunachal Pradesh	190.0	187.9	-2.1	1040
Assam	4,661.6	3,434.0	-1,227.6	1,288
Manipur	417.9	392.3	-25.6	2,309
Meghalaya	403.6	186.2	-217.4	1,408
Mizoram	155.9	139.6	-16.3	1,686
Nagaland	347.9	280.9	-67.0	1,336
Sikkim	94.5	90.7	-3.8	1,139
Tripura	558.4	503.6	-54.8	1,890
NE Hills	6,829.8	5,215.2	-1,614.6	1,512

Source: Fertilizer Statistics 1999-2000. (Requirement cal. for the pop. of 2001 Census @ 175 kg per Capita per year).

Present Scenario : The N.E. Region produce 5.215 million tonnes of foodgrains against subsistence requirement of 6.83 million tonnes and thus, it faces a deficit of 1.615 miliion tonnes of foodgrains annually. The food productivity is much lower 1512 Kg./ha. as compared to 1620 Kg./ha. during the year 1998-99. Whereas, the major cereals-rice, maize, wheat and millets are much lower in productivity, but the pulse production was higher than the national productivity average. Around 60-70 per cent of the area under foodgrains in the hill region is under upland condition whereas 30-40 per cent area is under irrigated/ low land condition.

Constraints, Issues and Strategies

The N.E. Region is prone to a number of bio-physical, institutional and socio-economical problems resulting into subsistence agriculture with low input and yield risk. The major problems confronting the agricultural growth of the region is of two types : (a) A biotic factors—acidic soil, high rainfall and humidity, land tenure system/operational holding size, low temperature at higher altitude, sunshine and solar-radiation, soil erosion and land degradation and shifting cultivation, (b) Biotic factor—diseases, insect-pests, weeds, etc.

Infrastructural development is the most important step, important in strengthening agricultural production, marketing and research. Marketing of the produces depend on the availability of roads and storage, improving efficiency of animate sources of energy, increased use of high yielding varieties, increasing use of fertilizers and other chemicals (organic-based farming), increasing efficiency of energy sources, increased use of precision and high capacity agricultural implements, development of equipments for mechanization of hill agriculture for improving its productivity, promoting green house technology, watershed management and promotion of appropriate post-harvest technology.

Conclusion

The soils of North-Eastern Region are acidic in reaction resulting poor plant growth as a result of aluminium toxicity and associated nutrient problems. Most of the soils of this region are highly deficient in phosphorus without which it is not possible to get full benefits of other fertilizers response to crops. Establishment of organized networks of market for livestock and livestock diseases is necessary, so that the livestock farmers get due share for their products. Intensive epidemiological studies of the livestock diseases particularly the infectious diseases should be undertaken to plan programme for control and eradication.

Though, modern biotechnology tools for improved livestock production are available in India, applicability of biotechnology tools in rural areas is yet to be assessed and standardized. Cross breeding of indigenous animals with superior germ-plasm, through Artificial Insemination (AI) in extensive manner will surely improve the livestock scenario of this region. Access to information and motivation of farmers towards AI of cattle and other species are the need of the hour.

Technology development is a continuous process requiring dynamic Research and Development (R&D) back-up support. The systematic approach to analyze the impact of recommended technologies for economic upliftment of the farming community is also most essential. Impact analysis will help the policy-makers and researchers to take up future course of action. Demonstrations involving a large group of farmers are expected to have instant impact on adoption and spread of farmer, friendly technologies. Mobilization of available resources towards extensive demonstration of a sound technology identified in forums like Package of Practices (PoP) workshop will go a long way in achieving the desired impact. Inputs required for adoption of technology should be readily available. Privatization of agro-input supply may be encouraged.

The rich resource base in the region such as mega bio-diversity, fertile soil, varied agro-ecological situations of plains as well as valleys, hills, tilla land, immense water resources, human resources of ethnic diversity and cultural groups, could be potential sources of agricultural as well as economic development of the North-East India. However, due to lack of appropriate strategies for development of natural resources, absence of coordination in programme implementation, weak geographical links and poor infrastructural facilities, the region is handicapped in catching up with the agricultural developmental pathways in tune with the national ethos. Slow agricultural development widens the disparities across the States. In this circumstance, agricultural sector needs prioritization of development perspectives for enhancing the adoption of recommended technologies through extension programmes, input supply, support of financial institutions and marketing functionaries. More crucially, the research and developmental programmes must address the problem of generation of need-based location-specific technologies for the specific agro-ecological situations.

REFERENCES

Anonymous (2000) : *Basic Statistics of North-Eastern Region,* North Eastern Council, Shillong (Various issues).

Anonymous (2001) : *Basic Animal Husbandry Statistics,* Department of Animal Husbandry and Dairy, New Delhi.

Anonymous (2003) : *Statistical Handbook of Nagaland,* Government of Nagaland, Kohima.

Anonymous (2006) : *Directorate of Economics and Statistics,* Government of India, New Delhi.

CMIE Publications. Various issues.

Fertilizer News (1998) : '1995-96 Fertilizer Statistics', New Delhi. 43 (5): 53-57.

Forest Survey of India (1999) : *Statistics of Forest,* Directorate of Forest, Dehradun (Uttrakhand).

SECTION II

Population, Migration and Sectoral Development

8

Mining along Indo-Bangla Border

A Study of State Politics, Migrant Labour and Land Relations in Meghalaya

DEBOJYOTI DAS

Introduction

Meghalaya is a land locked State and presents a unique case study of mining where small scale informal coal mining forms the major stay of all mining activity. Because of its limited occurrence, the protected land transfer regime (Land Tenure Act) and its location as a frontier territory of the Indian sub-continent, mineral exploration has not been a very prospective activity. However, in the past couple of decades mineral exploration has gained unique momentum with competition among local entrepreneurs to extract more and more coal through pit-hole technique. Coal mining has today become a lucrative business with oligopolistic control-generating supernormal profits. With the proliferation of mining the ecological consequences have also alarmed local communities and population surrounding mining sites. Thus there is a growing awareness created by civil society groups on the ongoing ecological implication of mining activities on their environment. NGO activism has led to the filing of a Public Interest Litigation in 2006, following which the Supreme Court of India asked a status report on all mining activities carried out in the State from the State Government. These ecological concerns are coupled with other kinds of activism at local level that are linked to questions of ethnic identity and indignity raised by pressure groups. These pressure groups, mostly students union the largest being Khasi Students Union (KSU), who claim to be the custodian of Khasi culture and tribal identity try to link ethnicity and indignity of the Khasis as the central theme in their resistance to mining activity. The immigration of outsiders in the local domain is seen as a major problem that triggers ethnic tension in coal mines. However, there are a series of other issues that remain neglected in the analysis of coal mining in Meghalaya.

These issues relate to the perceptions and interest of local stakeholders who actively participate in coal mining activity in the Khasi-Jaintiya and Garo Hills. The coal mines are operated by local people who have oligopolistic control over production. In the past ecological concerns on unscientific rat-hole mining have hedged broader question of political economy of coal mining in Meghalaya. This needs to be looked at through a historical reflection on how patron-client relations that existed were legitimised by the colonial and later the post-colonial State. The colonial government recognised and legitimised local power hierarchies by formalising the post of *Syiems* and *Dolois* in the Khasi and Garo Hills. In the post-colonial period the establishment of Sixth Schedule status of Meghalaya has marginalised the role of traditional chiefs however their social status within the community is maintained. As my ethnographic field study revealed the village chiefs still enjoys the primacy among his kinsman although his political role in village decision-making was cribbed. These powerful actors at the village level command over mining activity and many a time their blood relations hold high positions in the State bureaucracy. Thus the network, patron-client relations are reproduced. The local power relations within the community still operate and work through kinship relations. As Khan observed in the highlands patronage plays a very important role in exercising State control over local resources. The State patronage is established through these historically evolved structures of *kulaks* who had sustained through State patronage. The village chiefs and democratically elected District Council

(Village Council) members act in connivance with the State bureaucracy to implement their class interest in having control over production and ownership over mines. The State earns revenue from coal export and its role is restricted to revenue sharing. However, in the production of capital the State officials have restrained any action against indiscriminate mining in the pretext of breaching indigenous communities' customary rights over land and forest. However, occasionally this arrangement has been bypassed by the State Government to serve corporate interest by granting them lease to extract minerals to feed large scale cement plants across the international border. This phenomenon will be explored in the following paragraphs.

An intensive fieldwork based study by McDura (2007) reveals that human insecurity in Meghalaya is the outcome of privatization of land holding and its concentration in few hands rather than the constructed notion of insecurity caused by immigrant settling down in coal mining areas across the border. These immigrants mostly Bangladeshis, Nepalis and people migrating from the Hindi speaking belt of central India are most migrant wage earners. They have been termed by Baruah as Denizens in his seminar contribution on the politics of North East, titled *Durable Disorder*. Denizens are people who do not enjoy political or entitlement rights and yet in the north-east they are considered by indigenous community leaders as the biggest threat to local culture and tribal identity.

Here, I would like to concentrate on the issue of class formation within local tribes. The emerging class difference within the community is an effective instrument of social change. The people who own mines also represent the people in the State Legislature. Thus coal mining in the State presents a very complex story of how communities are organised and how they represent their interest in a democratic set-up. Civil society groups today claim to play a very important role in delivering social services, organizing resistance and framing public opinion. However, in the case of Meghalaya they also represent certain class interest. It is interesting to note how the discourse on mining led ecological destruction has resulted environmental and livelihood mayhem in the society in the State. The complexity of the problem I will argue is much more structural and embedded in power relations within the local communities represented in land and land relations and the patronage, clientism that local community has developed with the post-colonial State that facilitates the operation of small mines in Meghalaya. While on the ground the State seems to have no control over mining operation as it is purely governed by private oligopolistic control. The State I will argue is embedded in the day to day struggle over mining. One of the classic examples of State's involvement in coal mines lies in the people who represent the State legislature. The complexity can be defined this way. The civil society group terms it the coal lobby in the State Legislature that prevents the Government taking appropriate action against unscientific mining activity. In fact, Meghalaya is one of the very few States that have yet to draft a State mineral policy. However, given this understanding of why State fails to act upon the coal miners, we see an underpinning of patronage or reciprocal understanding between the State bureaucracy and the local mine owners who form the coal lobby.

These notions of patronage have a colonial history linked to colonial administrative arrangement in the highlands and it is not unique to Meghalaya alone but can broadly be seen all over South-East Asia Li (1999). Thus coal mining in Meghalaya has to be seen in the context of a broader social history of colonial and post-colonial State intervention, rather than concentrating on particular discourses of failed developmentalism, indignity, ethnicity, hegemony and ecological discourse that have come up in civil society critique of coal mining activity in the State. These discourses claim to critique State failure and highlight its inability to control what they call hazardous mining but fail to look at the social complex narratives that underlies the political economy of coal mining in Meghalaya.

Here I will like to draw upon the work done on highland communities by anthropologist in South-East Asia. These works do not necessarily look at coal mining but are implicitly engaging with State, community and extractive industry in the highlands. Some of the most significant contribution has come in understanding South-East Asia's highland in Hafner (1990), Tsing (1993), Li (1999), Khan (1999). These scholars have tried to understand highland production process as embedded in discursive politics of the local, the power relations that circulate within community and is constitutive of the State. As Li (1996) argues in the highlands which are often seen as marginal, less productive and backward spaces some of the most lucrative livelihoods has not been agriculture at all, but focussed rather on extractive industry, trade and wage worker. In Meghalaya, the debate on coal mining have looked at the ethnic dimension of coal mining where migration of labourers across the border into coal mines has played a defining role in farming a identity politics that sees influx as the major problem constraining local identity and indigenous tribal culture.

However, my analysis will shift from these narratives that draw the picture of coal mining in Meghalaya and locate it in a broader picture of capitalist mass production, oligopolistic control over mines, exploitation of wage earners, land consolidation triggering landlessness and the growing nexus between politicians and mine owners that presents a clear picture of privatised land holding and oligopolistic control. The more pressing question of people's livelihood, environment surrounding mines, wage rates of miners and their living condition are subsumed within 'culturisation' and 'environmentalization' of the local problem. Local civil society and pressure group draw popular support to challenge State desire to regulate mining activity by claiming indigenous people's customary right over land and forest resources. Here one has to understand who makes such claims and where do they come from. These claims by pressure groups do not necessarily articulate the resistance of masses but often represent people's stakeholder's interest, the interest of mine owners or the interest of cultural patrons, political and indigenous leaders. The local politics surrounds the ethnic identity crisis. It acts as a depoliticized struggle as the basic question of human insecurity is not questioned in their quest for identity, politics and indignity.

Similarly, implicating State control over day to day life of the indigenous communities, proponents of 'green' development models have declared time and again indigenous tribes to be the appropriate keepers of their resources. The example of 'sacred grooves' collectively owned forest resources of the community are often cited as an example validation local prudence to conservation and management of resources. Such communities are also imagined to possess a set of characteristics counter posed to that of State agency and other forest destroyers : they are tribes, are at least backed by centuries-old environmental wisdom; they have long been located in one place, to which they spiritual and pragmatic attachment. They are relatively homogeneous without class division; they are not driven by motives of exploitation and greed; they have limited consumption requirements; and their collective desire focuses upon long term sustainable management of natural resources for the future generation. The use of indignity as a powerful metaphor in defining ethnic identity and tradition are often misplaces and abrupt simplification of the communities in transition. The transitions are brought about by liberal democracy, market interventions, monetised inflow, the privatization of land ownership, commercialization of farming and the changing attitude towards community life with the growth of services and trade activities in the highlands.

These instruments of social change education, free flow of goods, circulation of cash in a predominantly barter economy has led to modernizing traditional communities and consequently their consumption pattern has changed. As an ethnography among the Bemba shifting cultivators in the northern province of Zambia shows that with the inflow of monetised exchange and market products the Bemba consumption patterns had remarkably changed from purchase of daily necessitates towards a shift in disposable income for manufactured products coming out of industries such as cloths, utensils, soaps, transistors etc. (Moore *et al.*, 1994). Similarly, in the case of Meghalaya the capital produced from export of coal to nearby Bangladesh and mainland India produces conspicuous consumption, the growth of real estate business in the State capital Shillong, and renting capitalism among the indigenous community elites who own mines and have control over production process. Production of coal is achieved through pure human labour as the mines are not mechanised. The immigrant labour power is put to good use under minimal wage rates with no social security. As my fieldwork revealed the wage earners work with extreme risk and enjoy no social security benefits. Their settlements are suffocated in labour lines. Each hut houses a dozen souls where there is not enough space for half of the population. In the cities and district headquarters, these mine owners have ultra-modern houses with flashy cars parked in luxurious lawns and rose gardens. While interviewing one coal mine owner I realised how ethno-centralism can become so deep with the growth of capital in indigenous communities. The mine owners brand their workers to be criminals and fugitives who work in the mines in deep jungles and forest to escape State precaution.

The mining activity provides them with gainful employment which these groups could have never managed in mainland India. Such rhetorics and labelling of workers are quite commonly used even by pressure groups as legitimate claims to flush out all immigrants from the State. The mine workers act as potential disrupters to local economy as they claim all jobs which otherwise are not performed by local tribes as they are low paid and hazardous. The local elites by branding immigrant labour force as illegal migrants protect their illegal status in far flung mines and appropriate their labour power as *quit pro que* (security in return for labour)—providing them shelter from State prosecution. Even mine owners responded that these workers are delinquent and dangerous to associate with. The mine labourers as delinquent, illegal and fugitives taking shelter in coal mines act advantageous towards mine owners bargaining power and in setting terms of contracts for exploring coal. This cultural politics pays huge payoff to mine owners march towards production of capital.

The following discussion dwells on these complexities and tries to locate coal mining crisis in Meghalaya from the prospective of different stakeholders interest in mines and how effectively indignity, tribal identity is played out in a 'cultural-political' discourse that blurs State's control over mines and the various interest it serves in the production of capital.

Mining in Meghalaya

This chapter tries to reformulate the notion of tribal spaces often termed as relative isolation and isolated in the geographical literature in the light of the structural changes that have been brought about by monetised economic exchanges through trade and other secondary activity. The process of mining that dates a history of more than hundred years in the Khasi Hills was first explored by the political agent of the British rule. However, commercial exploration of minerals could only begin in the post-independence period as the colonial power was sceptical about the economic viability of coal mining in these frontier tracks of the then Assam.[1] We don't have any written document that reflects that the indigenous Khasi's used coal before the arrival of the British. But, folklores and collective memory of village elders reveal that gold and similar minerals were mined by the Khasis and became an essential part of their ornamental artefacts. In traditional Khasi society ownership of land was very important. The imposition of colonial governance over the Khasi Hills and the political subjugation of *Siems* under the patronage of the *Raj* transformed the customary and cultural practices of the Khasis.[2] The British had introduced *hoe* tax or house tax for every households practicing shifting cultivation in the State. The *Siems* (kings) were made responsible to collect tax and pay annual tribute to the colonial government.[3] They also introduced the lease system on land by which people outside the community can have *de facto* control over tribal land. The promotion of timber trade and the felling of trees to meet colonial demand for timber started during this period. This transformation had serious impact on the traditional rationale of prestige and power within the Khasi community.[4] Monetised principles of economic exchange and the economic value of land came to be realised.

In the post-independence period, the emergence of Meghalaya as a separate State within the Indian Union necessitated the development of resources within the State to sustain its domestic economy. As Meghalaya became as a Sixth Schedule State land was recognised as owned by the local people. This provision gave local inhabitants right to develop their resources. Coal production during this period boomed as infrastructural facilities were enhanced and border trade with Bangladesh established. In less than three decades of unscientific mining; the ecological footprints are fast emerging manifested in land degradation, aquatic pollution and disruption of local ecosystem. The full-fledged outcry of this plunder made headlines in the region's newspapers with violent outburst of public emotion after a Public Interest Litigation filed in the Supreme Court by the Meghalaya Mountaineering Association an environmental NGO. The public debate on the policy and administrative circles now focussed on the legal status of coal mines in Meghalaya that needed to be regularised.[5] The absence of a State mineral policy necessitated the Supreme Court to order the State Government to submit a status report on all mining activities and their status in the State. This pronouncement created pandemonium in the State Legislative Assembly fuelled by a public outburst of sentiments. The local pressure and civil society organised echoed in solidarity that such assessments would lead to loss of livelihood and closure of mines that would affect the local economy surrounding the mines adversely.

The confusion emerged out of the contradictory position of laws governing mineral resources in Sixth Schedule Areas where historically political and administrative powers have been diffused in the hands of the tribal chiefs and village headman. The coal boom that began in the late 1970's changed the cultural landscape of the Khasi Hills where local entrepreneurs who are at one point community stewards and at other point people's representatives in their collective desire to gain wealth privatised communally owned land and engaged in unscientific mining activity. This resulted in a major mining crisis that destroyed the commons and its heritage. The mining regulations that are in place are often ambiguous and contradictory. The Sixth Schedule status of Meghalaya makes local communities custodians of their own resource. However, the Mines and Mineral Development and Regulation Act 1957 runs contrary to this spirit and claim all private mining activity in Meghalaya illegal.[6]

The State has been historically reluctant to develop mineral resources in frontier territories because of its sporadic availability and limited economic value. However, it claims to protect the interest of small miners in scheduled areas. This has also been clearly spelt out in the National Mineral Policy 2003, that States "Small and isolated deposits of minerals are scattered all over the country. These often lend themselves to economic exploitation through small scale mining. With modest demand on capital expenditure and short lead-time, they also provide employment opportunities for the local population. Efforts will be made to promote small scale mining of small deposits in a scientific and efficient manner while safeguarding vital environmental and ecological imperatives. In grant of mineral concessions for small deposits in Scheduled Areas, preference shall be given to the Scheduled Tribes."[7]

In reality the policy on mining and land tenancy regulation is set with a lot of loopholes. As Mukhim writes "Meghalaya has a Land Transfer Act (LTA) which does not allow non-tribal's to purchase land in the State. But the act has a clause, which states that land can be alienated in favour of a non-tribal if it is in the interest of the tribal's. Several companies have circumvented the act by claiming that they would provide jobs to unemployed tribal's".[8] The transfer of scheduled land to Lafarge the German Multinational to explore limestone to feed its cement plant across the international border was done by the State Government as a step towards opening trade and investment in the region. However, all this was happening in nexus, with District Council, local stakeholders who were partner in Lafarge India Limited.[9] This confusion has emerged out of a broader micro-politics of resource use in which local tribal elites becomes co-partners in appropriation of mineral resources at the expense of local community's right to explore mineral wealth. The illegality of coal mines in Meghalaya creates new ideologies of bureaucratic corruption and misappropriation of resources at the expense of artisanal small scale miner's right to use these resources to create sustainable livelihood.[10] As Lahiri-Dutt observes in Meghalaya a Sixth Schedule State, coal has been classified as major mineral. It keeps nearly thirty thousand people who are depending on mining under extra-legal or non-legal space as technically coal can only be legally excavated by big players like State run corporation or multinationals (Lahiri-Dutt, 2007).

These contradictory statutes of low governing mineral recourse prospecting, use and exploration have created finite ground for illegal mining to be governed by tribal elites who have learnt the art of co-option and wiser ways of safeguarding their interest often in the name of customary right while at times claiming the complex and ambiguous legislation as the main shortcoming in protecting tribal people's rights to resource use. The study aims to analyse power relationship within communities organised at the margins of the nation State. The particular idea envisaged in this chapter is based on reinterpreting how the relationship between subjects and the technology of power works to complicate State legibility at the margins. To rephrase the question I try to understand through the analysis of coal mining in Meghalaya the tribal community as represented in colonial literature as undifferentiated and homogeneous having vagabond lifestyles and how winds of change brought about by colonial administration, western education and the inflow of monetised liberal principles and bureaucratic practices have transformed the community value system from within.

The Khasi community is no longer egalitarian but stratified with interest ridden community stewards—money-lenders, coal mine owners, State bureaucrats, rent-seeking landlords and contractors.[11] The new democratic institutions like the District Council which is a substitute to the *Panchayati Raj* system in the non-scheduled areas, the traditional institution heads the *Siems, Dolois* who preside over the *Darbars* (Village Councils) have played critical role in shaping the cultural politics of land use in the tribal State.[12] Here the question of access as discussed in a separate heading in the preceding paragraphs becomes important as access to resource guaranteed under customary practices becomes critical in maintaining equity and equality in the distribution of resources (Ribot and Peluso, 2003). The question of access is important in understanding common pool resources such as communally owned land, community forest or even communally owned mineral tracts that are subsequently privatised through access that allows certain groups to claim permanent rights over the once held commons while disenfranchising others in the process (Bell 1998). In Jaintiya Hills the transformation of community land to private land has happened in quite subtle ways as commons only exist in collective memory of the people. Land is tightly owned in private hands. This has been made possible by the changes in local value system and attitude towards the economic importance of coal in the life and culture of the indigenous community. Social prestige has given way to cash income. The value system has changed. The people who own mines are also representatives of the community and brokers in transnational coal trade with multinational companies.[13] The illegality of mining creates spaces for local actors to define strategies that themselves eliminate access for other members within the community. Customary laws are codified and modified to suit the interest of vested groups who represent the powerful patrons in the tribal community (Baruah *et al.*, 2005, McDura, 2007).

The political economy of coal mines is closely associated with 'access control' and 'access maintenance'. In Jaintiya Hills where coal mining is most rampant access and maintenance are both in the hands of the community, but is held by the community institutions the village councils or *Darbars*. These traditional institutions decide who should own land and who has the right to private ownership based on customary rules of land use. Here maintenance and control are complementary as the community members who maintain communal land also have the largest access to land (Dev *et al.*, 2003). The question of access is central to control over resources that are often termed as common property. Legality or legislation cannot fully define who can use the commons. These are other factors and interests that legitimize the rationality of jurisprudence on what comprised legal *vis-à-vis* illegal. In Meghalaya the narrative of ecological decline has become the discursive term to regulate coal mining in the light of the ongoing ecological ramifications.

Small scale artisanal mines that are located in frontier territories have been historically neglected attention of official improvement as they were governed by the local customary laws of the tribal lot who were represented in the colonial discourse as a savage race needing special protection from the onslaught of civilization. However, in the contemporary context these small and scattered low productivity mines have become the centre stage of contestation between the State and the community. In defining the legal status of such mining activity claims and counter claims over user rights have been complicated by ill defined legislations and unscientific, indiscriminate exploitation of the resource. However, this tension to regulate coal mining by State legislation and the communities' resistance for autonomy is underpinned by a variety of misreading and complex micro politics of daily practices that are linked to bureaucratic puzzles and the interest of different stakeholders.

It is my hypothesis that the extra-legal space created by the national mineral policy in Meghalaya breeds new ideologies of cash inflow and capital formation that surrounds the mushrooming of pit hole mines. The ambiguity in legislation, conflicting institutional regulation and flexible land tenure rights runs the risk of serving the interest of a few while risking livelihood and ecology of the Khasi village communities. The emergence of civil society institution like pressure groups in the post-independence era after the formation of Meghalaya as a separate State in 1971, has had a major impact in local decision-making.[14] The student pressure groups like the Khasi Students Union act as important voice in framing public opinion and often represent the traditional institutions the *Darbar* (Village Councils). They have close nexus with State bureaucrats and political elites and are influential in public policy-making. My hypothesis runs in three parts. First, given the extra-legal nature of Meghalaya's coal mining activity benefits occur to powerful merchants and coal mine owners rather than forest villagers and mine worker (immigrant labourers) who bear the ecological and social cost. Secondly, this skewed distribution of benefit result from manipulated customary practices by the village chiefs and the elected bureaucracy. Thirdly resistance to State control over local resources in light of their degradation are misrepresentation of the sub-altern voices. The resistance are co-opted voices of the poor reflecting the protection of elite interest in extra legal mines.[15]

The technologies of rule and the rationality of governance carried by the post-colonial nation State particularly in the north-east part of India gave tribes a sense of freedom as the rationalities of State rule remained ill defined and were often superseded by local practice. The logic of subjectivity was different; it gave freedom to the local people to manage themselves through local governance. The actors and networks that evolved out of this unique relationship blurred the boundaries between the subject and objects of rule. With the diffusion of modern education and democratic values by the church and later by the welfare, post-colonial State, a critical section of the local population got involved in the bureaucracy and administrative practices of the State. The development of mineral resources in the absence of State regulation allowed these powerful actors to appropriate the resources that yielded easy money. The collective grab to harness resources resulted in widespread ecological decline that has escalated the present crisis represented in widespread damage to the mining environment.

Concerned with the degrading condition of mines a Public Interest Litigation (PIL) was filed in the Supreme Court in May 2006 by the Meghalaya Mountaineers Association raising concerns on the degrading status of limestone caves in the State. However, the subsequent outburst of violence in Meghalaya was unprecedented and had a tremendous churning of public sentiments that represent resistance to States interference in customary rights to land use and exploration of mineral resources. The Supreme Court directed the State Government to evolve a regulatory mechanism and a workable mineral policy that would make State role legible in mineral exploration. The populist outburst and instant resistance that took severe violent form was recognised as a legitimate reaction to State hegemony. However, this popular outburst of public sentiment created by the civil society is in-built with a variety of misreading of the local social and the political processes that articulates such representation. We shall see in the preceding paragraphs how coal mining in Meghalaya has evolved as a vibrant economic activity and how it appropriates migrant labourers in the cultural politics discourse and creates its own politics or resource appropriation through the narratives of identity crisis and indignity. Here the winners and loser do not represent the conventional local people *versus* the State/multinations. Rather the relationship is more complex. Hegemony of the State is not well defined. People's resistance are co-opted voices of vested interest who represent the community as the guardians of cultural identity. The misrepresentation lies in the local politics of resource use who owns it the State or the community (the powerful networks of local elites who also claim to represent the community) and not on how the resources are used and to whose benefit.

Coal Mining and Miners : In the Pit Holes of the Plateau

Coal mining is one of the primary economic activities of Meghalaya besides the practice of *jhum* (Swidden Cultivation). The history of coal mining in Meghalaya dates back to some 200 years when coal was first mined in Cherra area locally known as *Sorha*. Today these mines are abandoned and mining activity has proliferated in other parts of the State. Colonial records suggest that coal mining started in the Khasi Hills in 1840 by Captain Lister, the Political Agent of East India Company,[16] ever since the coal mining has been carried on with traditional ways. The technique of mining is primitive, hazardous and crude. Commonly known as rat hole mining—in this method the land is first cleared by cutting and removing the ground vegetation and then pits ranging from 5 to 100 metres are dug into the ground to reach the coal seam. Thereafter tunnels are made into the seam side-wise to extract coal which is first brought into the pit by using a conical basket or a wheel borrow and then taken out and dumped on nearby location. The Constitution of India recognises coal mining areas in Meghalaya under the Sixth Schedule that guarantees indigenous people's rights over control to land and forest including natural resources found within it. Coal reserves are thus under the direct control of the indigenous communities who explore it and export to the neighbouring country Bangladesh.

In the past three decades the exponential growth in export of coal has led to its rampant and unorganized exploration by private mine-owners resulting in severe ecological constraints in the plateau region that houses more than 600 endemic plant species. The toxic litter from abandoned coal mines pollutes the fresh water bodies—streams and rivulets. Vast landscapes are littered with coal debris. Much of the research conducted over the past decades tries to explore the physical implication of contamination caused by gases and acidic spills both over land and water and its implication for human settlement surrounding the coal mines (Singh, 2005; Rai, 2002).While others have looked into water quality, corrective solutions to land pollution and issues concerning proper Environment Impact Assessment of coal mines (Shankar *et al.*, 1993; Swer and Singh 2004; Nath *et al.*, 2005). However, there is no significant work of scholarship on the mining communities engaged in informal small scale mines of Meghalaya. It is important to understand their socio-economic status and livelihood strategies given the complex land tenure and private ownership of coal mines. Often the mining ridges owned by the community as commonly perceived are occupied by local elites who lease out their land to contractors who are primarily the middleman responsible for extraction of coal and pay a fixed share to the mine-owner. In this contractual agreement the mine workers are at a disadvantageous position. The contractor who acts as the middleman generates maximum profit from coal exploration which he then shares with the owner. The labourers are not paid daily wages. Instead labour is contracted. According to our survey for extraction of 5 tonnes of coal a labourer is paid around INR 1000.This activity may take one month or more depending on the number of hands engaged. Small cottage-type coal mining is widely prevalent in different areas extending from Jaintia Hills, East and West Khasi Hills in the East ending in East Garo Hills in the West. Unlike other regions of the country coal mines in the State are entirely under private ownership. The process of coal extraction is so careless and indiscriminate that instead of giving suitable benefits it is creating serious problems for environment. Nonetheless coal is the most important mineral for export both to other States of the country as well as to the neighbouring country Bangladesh.

Besides the large scale ecological ramification of coal mining it has attracted a large population of migrants from across the border and within. Migrants are primarily denizen who do not have property rights and are often illegal immigrants. These floating populations who desperately seek jobs for survival have come in conflict with the local communities' finding large scale immigration of outsider "plain population" as a threat to their cultural identity. The identity politics in the past has led to ethnic cleansing and communal outburst leading to disruption of civilian life in the coal mining areas and in labour camps.[17]

Contemporary researches has seldom peeped into the life stories of coal miners and their relationship to the mines. The political economy of coal mining in Meghalaya has a close nexus with the bureaucratic and political elites who control the mines and defines the rules of the game. The newly emerging political class has in connivance with the tradition institutional elites (village headmen) gained control over the mining resources of Meghalaya and very tactfully play the game on identity politics to protect their own class interest. In the absence of State's control over private mines, the minimum safeguards and workers rights fall directly under the purview of local institutions, who manipulate the mining regulations to their advantage.

The Inside Story : Mines and Workers

The inside story of coal miners who work within an informal mining set up is harsh and often violates basic human rights. A close ethnographic survey based on field interviews and live testimonial reveal how mining communities comprise of labourers who had migrated from Bihar, Nepal, Assam and Bangladesh work under terror and threats from local pressure groups of mass exodus. While the local mine owners ensure their safety and lure labourers for work at much cheaper rates than the prevailing market wage rate, the local population provoked by public rhetoric of pressure groups agitate against non-tribal presence in their territory. The common perception of demographic transformation, colonization of local territory by immigration and their assertion over scheduled tribal territory leads to frequent tussles and violent outburst. The local elite's cash upon their customary rights over land-use and mobilise this rational to prevent State intervention thus securing their private interest and *status quo* of indigenous people's rights to manage local resources. In turn, no governmental regulation, safety measures for miners, basic minimum protection from hazard, minimum wage rate apply and the emerging gentry class who have privatized land ownership in the name of customary rights appropriate and internalize all expenditure that would otherwise have gone to the mine workers. The mining communities who are mostly migrant labourers slowly become the denizens[18]. They enjoy no political or entitlements rights and are vulnerable to face exodus when the local community sees them as a threat to their cultural identity. The mine owners exploit their vulnerable social status and fix wages much below the prevailing market rate and under conditions at which the local people will never agree to work. Focus group discussion with one such population in the case study area Laitrumbai revealed that most of the people are migrant labourers willing to work at low wage rate. The Bangladeshi migrants find the job lucrative as they can earn more than what they get for similar kinds of work in their own country. The Rabhas and Hajongs who live at the fringe of Meghalaya plateau as minor ethnic groups find no work in their own territory are naturally attracted towards mining during the lean agricultural season. They live in labour lines where there are no civic amenities. Some of the labour lines look like concentration camps with more than a dozen people occupying a single hamlet. The presence of coal mafia threatens the mine workers from leaking information. Interestingly, most of the coal *mafias* are women who control the economy of the mines in Meghalaya. The mine owners who have made great fortunes with increasing exports of coal to the neighbouring States have relocated their residences to the capital city Shillong buying plots in posh localities while others live in Jawai the district headquarters of East Khasi Hills. The people inhabiting the vicinity of the ever expanding mines fell threatened of caving-in as the ground below the surface is robbed of its black gold.

The recent controversy that has rekindled the environment development debate in the hills of Meghalaya is worth quoting. The Meghalaya Adventures Association had filed a Public Interest Litigation in the Supreme Court stating the degrading status of the plateau cave system. In response the Supreme Court issued public notice to the State Government to provide a status report. This action by the judiciary, the highest court of the land has embroiled the local interest groups who have gone on mass agitation calling such action directly impacting the livelihood of the local people depends on coal mining. There was little concern shown on how private mining should be regularized though a proper policy that looks into miner's rights and amenities. The economic bandwagon of loss of livelihood has been more ethnocentric and a selfish demand based on the sharp divide between the indigenous and the non-tribal world (we and the other outsiders locally called *dkharas)*. What is more interesting to note is the shifting claims made by the local civil society and pressure groups. The cultural politics of resource use is inherently politically motivated. While there has been a long tussle for the past few years on the exploration of uranium in the State by the Uranium Corporation of India Limited (UCL), the local people have resisted its exploration sighting radioactive contamination that would annihilate the surrounding settlements. The civil society groups have been active in supporting the local people's concern by sending memorandum and petition to the State Government to halt the proposed excavation. Such enthusiasms is not to be seen in the context of coal and limestone mining areas where if not less equally noxious toxic litter and chemical spills are polluting and acidifying the aquatic resources of the forest ecosystem. The reference community, the miners are mostly migrants who are dependent on the livelihood provided by mine owners. Their social security and well-being is not a concern for the local the emerging tribal elites who have minted money out of coal trade. The interest of the 'gentry' class lies in exploiting the vulnerable social and economic status of migrant labourers who work in their fields at bare minimal wage rates and help in the creation of wealth and profit for the mine owners who form the new elites within the tribal society.

This draws us to the long standing debate on who should own resources in tribal domains where colonial encounter itself was restricted to revenue generation and political administration (Guha 1991, Bryant 1996). This question echoed in the Parliamentary debates of 1988 when a local member of Parliament representing Meghalaya contested State claims over forest wealth and natural resources as primarily the customary rights that cannot be transuded by State authority. The debate ended in favour of the indigenous community. The indigenous people recognition of their customary rights and exploration were restricted to domestic use of coal explored from their fields. The communities were not permitted to trade in mineral resources found with the territorial limits of the Sixth Schedule areas. However, in spite of such regulations, coal mining has intensified over the years due to the profit earned by its trade. Informal transfer of coal to the main land accounts for more coal being siphoned off to the plains than done through Government check gates. The revenue records earned from coal trade with the neighbouring country Bangladesh, experts claim is just the tip of the iceberg. The recognition of the illegality of coal mining by the State Government itself poses the rhetoric of legalising an informal economic activity. The illegal market has attracted mafia syndicate who extort money from traders. Interestingly, the people who are sent demand notes are no longer the non-tribal *mahajans* but the tribes themselves. It has in the past generated tensions in the coal mining areas with several unrest and kidnapping being reported in the popular press. These events relate to the broader picture how the State participate in the establishment of its rationality through the recognition of customary practices of the community who themselves become perpetrators of violence and brokers in the negotiation and translation of State power. The local tribal elites, coal mine owners have multiple identities. They can be at the same time mine owners, community stewards and local politicians who know his community well. The free trade of coal in the post-liberalization period has further entrenched neo liberal politics in the coal mine where production and exploration are determined by market demand and supply variables and voracious. All this is achieved by sacrificing the interest of mine workers who are the denizens, often quoted by the 'emerging gentry'—tribal elites as criminals and anti-social who work in the coal mines to hide their identity and escape from the surveillance of the State.

Ethno Nationalism and Cultural Politics

The countering of development discourse as hegemony as is well represented in people's resistance to development projects in the south often do not represent the will of the entire community but that of the initiators. They may also be diluted in local attitudes of who owns the resources. There may not be genuine concerns attached to ecological ramification or outcomes of a development project. People's resistance are camouflaged with the communities interest that are hijacked by a few self-interested people who construct the subaltern others oppressed by the nation-state to preserve their self interest. McDura (2007) brings out this duplicity of people's resistance to uranium mining in Meghalaya. Through his field work interview he tries to draw upon the construction of an outsider/insider in the Khasi community.[19] The ethnic identity is posed as the most critical variable in championing resistance against the other. It is quite remarkable to note that the Khasi pressure groups did not mind if uranium mining was in the hands of the local people rather than its present control by the national government. The question of ecological decline and the implication, cost and the nature of development entwined in 'who gains and who pays' has been completely missing in the narrative of people's resistance to State owned resource exploration. This exceptionalism to subaltern struggle and contestation of State control over local resources in the form of new social movement keeps many new questions unanswered. Who are the subalterns? Is there a neglected voice within the subalterns? And how these voices can be articulated to gain a meaningful understanding of civil society's construction of people's resistance to power exercised through bureaucratic control and State regulations.

This brings us to revisit coal mining in Meghalaya and draw the corollary link of civil society's nature of resistance to State led developmentalism. The aftermath of the Public Interest Litigation as discussed in the preceding paragraphs shows the normal attitude of any indigenous community's everyday resistance to State proposed regulation over local resources. While this move can be claimed as a positive step in countering hegemony and exploitative State power, but the principle fails to analyse in depth the nature of people's voice and who represents this voice. The same social group that lives in East Khasi Hills resents against the broad implication that uranium mining would bring to the local area, but keeps silent and resists State policy that would establish proper environmental regulation over mining practices to offset the ecological consequences spelled by such unscientific mining activity. The logic of identity crisis is often seen as anti-development by the mainstream actors who govern resource use. However, the local resistance does not see resource exploration as anti-development till they are controlled by the indigenous people. The cultural politics played out by the front runners in the Khasi society lies in patronising cultural identity to protect the vibrant growth of local cash economy and the interest of the 'emerging gentry' class. Their social capital and command over the local people rally the marginalised behind them and the subalterns within the community can only articulate their oppression through the mirror of cultural identity as the 'collective oppressed'. The inequalities within are enmeshed with a single subalterns that is problematic. There are the others within this marginalised identity and here I classify the marginalised among the perceived subalterns, *denizens* the term used by Sanjib Barual—population who do not have any constitutional or entitlement right yet are constructed as a potential threat for the cultural integrity of the indigenous inhabitants. These are the floating migrants from non-tribal territories. They are not part of the identity politics and hence are excluded from this struggle. They are counted hegemonies by the local people. Then the question emerges can the denizen speak?

This brings us to a more critical engagement as to how the response of the pressure group should be assessed as a collective aggregate of all the local voices or a fragmented interest of a small group who promise to be the vanguard of cultural identity and rebellers to State interference. Quite interestingly much of the literature on coal mining in Meghalaya have dealt on environmental regulation without having any assessment of the nature of the communities and the people engaged in this economic pursuit. The problem has remained a historical and depoliticised in the hands of the 'epistemic communities' (scientific and technical experts engaged by State institutions) who try to find technical solution to problems that are embedded in customary practices, legislation and ethnic identity question of the communities involved in mining activity (Mitchell 2002). The need lies in contextualising the micro processes of resource use and the politics of customary practices, legislation and ethnic identity question of the communities involved in mining activity.

The colonial categorization of tribe and non-tribe, highland and lowland are still constructed in stereotypes, as egalitarian, primitive bastions of indignity. On the ground, the ethnographic representations of tribes have undergone remarkable change both in structure and cultural practices. This has been conjectural with the diffusion of modern education and the involvement of non-State actors like the church that had infused modernity and civilised the untouched frontiers. Thus the post-colonial history of North-East does not represent the 'Golden Ageist'. The protectors of forest and sacred groves are now themselves the perpetrators-actors of environmental violence. While modernity has imbibed antiquates and cosmopolitan cultural habits among the tribal the class consciousness has also grown. The egalitarians nature of co-existence is fast fading that is well represented in privatization of land and the emergence of a landed class. The classic example can be cited in the Garo Hills where the invention of commercial farming as the panacea for developing the rural economy has led to *de facto* control of women's land by male landlords changing the gender equation in predominantly matrilineal Garo social structure. These transformations are significant and get easily negated under the grand narratives of hegemonising state apparatus.

The emerging inequalities with the tribal community's hibernates the micro politics that gets attached to resource alienation and elite capture by communities once stewards, the respected king's man who have patronage and power (tribal chiefs and the emerging political elites). Although the traditional tribal chiefs in Khasi society have been politically disenfranchised to administer their territories with the establishment of District Council they have social power that represent the collective will of the kinsman. No developmental initiative can be initiated without the consent of the village chief, even by the State. This natural collateral and social capital that traditional chiefs wields have in many cases translated into practice of landlordism and control over resources where earning easy money through natural resource exploration has become a grand avenue (timber trade, quarrying and mining). The transforming social order no longer hinges on equity as is commonly portrayed in the popular imagination. The lack of imagination to understand communities changing dynamics has led to the failure of many well intended development projects in South and South East Asia's highlands. (Li 1996; 2000; 2007). The major failure has been elite capture in developmental programmes where the communities are presumed to be egalitarians. (Mounsari *et al.*, 1993). This phenomenon sets out new questions. Why do contemporary studies on tribal societies fail to explore the micro-politics of resource use? Can the counter hegemonising forces within the tribal community functioning with the nexus of State apparatus be effectively challenged by the marginalised? Why is the dominant narrative of outsider/insider so strong in shaping tribal identity and current identity politics? These questions can well bring out the tapestry of transformations that are reshaping tribal society in the post-colonial period.

Anthropological and sociological study on tribes has shaped our present understanding of tribal societies. Often they are static or a historical representation, rather I would argue decontextualised. Leach's classic work on Kachin social structure is a path breaking study that contested earlier ethnographic representation of indigenous tribes of Highland Burma. Leach proposed that primitive societies are ever transforming and the conceptual model of equilibrium does if at all exist only in theory (Leach 1964). The sharp demarcation of tribes and non-tribes in the history of north-east has been a construct of the colonial rule and the political power that shaped discoursed on margin and the core. Anthropological knowledge was organised to serve the interest of the empire. Post-colonial anthropological researches have carried on the colonial tradition of demarcating tribal identities on ethnic lines and advocating protectionism (Elwin 1964). In this process a significant transformation that has been taking place within the community has been undermined. The process of this transformation has had the potential of counter hegemonizing the subalterns' within. As Baruah writes with reference to the Khasi community, there has been a capture of what is formally clan controlled land by powerful individuals. This transformation from egalitarian social formation of primitive accumulation to more broad-based capital accumulation and class consciousness in the tribal economy has been sustained by a network of political process and the lure for commercialization and cash income. The most brilliant evidences are timber trade, mining, quarrying of limestone and other minor minerals that have recently attracted transnational corporations like the Lafarge India Limited (a German multinational engaged in mining exploration) as a move towards integrating the regional economy with South and South-East Asia, as part of North-East India's 'Look East Policy'.

Colonial Intervention and Customary Laws

Here we need to reflect back at the impact that have taken place in the Khasi customary law with the intervention of colonial administration and the legislations under the Sixth Schedule in the post-colonial period. Baruah *et al.*, argues that it is the allocation of modern political function and land distribution powers to the *Darbars* (village councils) that has allowed the elites to capture village land. While others like Nathan trace it to the colonial administration that elevated the status of traditional chiefs locally known as the *Siems* among the Khasis to that of landlords by holding them accountable to collect tax. (This can be seen in the collection of hoe tax that was imposed on Shifting Cultivation areas). This was not unique only to the Khasi Hills tribal chiefs of Chittagong Hill Tracts were made responsible to collect revenue from their subjects as early as 1876. This new practice brought in the importance of monetised economy to the hills[20]. Whether land relations in the Khasi society were predominantly feudal remains contested as colonial ethnographic works do not reflect much on the economic relations of the monarchies that existed within the Khasi society. What can presumably be assumed is that relations were shaped by the power inequalities within families. In the post-colonial period, economic interest attached to land became evident with the exploration of minerals, timber and charcoal trade provided the boost to private *Darbar* ownership of land. However, this was achieved through manipulation of the customary laws by the rural as well as the emerging urban elites who represented the educated English speaking white collar job seekers in public services. The vesting of rights to grant land to individuals on the Village Council by the Sixth Schedule allowed district councils or *Panchayats* and the *Darbars* (traditional institutions headed by the tribal headman) to decide the beneficiary. The process of privatising community owned land has reached a spectacular collaboration where powerful rural elites work tactfully to select their beneficiary.[21]

A direct outcome of this changing land relation is rural indebtedness, landlessness within the Khasi community and the prevalence of absentee landlordism. As McDura shows in his research findings and also observed in our ethnographic survey of villages in Laitrumbai , the busiest coal mining region of Meghalaya, land is leased out to contractors as the owners have resettled in the urban centres with the flow of cash from coal money, while a major section of the rural population who could not develop their land were denied right to permanent settlement by the *Darbar*. In this fashion more and more marginal farmers are losing out their right to claim over common land which has practically vanished in the study area (Laitrumbai) giving rise to private land ownership. The chronic underdevelopment of the region and the growing disparity in incomes is directly linked to this phenomenon of landlessness as more and more people are becoming marginal labourers. However, there are no official statistical figures to substantiate such outcomes on the rates of landlessness and the changes that have occurred in the recent past. This is particularly constrained by the resistance of the *Darbars* to any kind of revenue survey that presumably protects their interest to control over land holding. Nongkynri who has extensively focussed on land relations in Meghalaya observes that in the absence of proper State or district level data generalizations are hard to be made. However, some smaller surveys indicate the persistence of the growing crisis in rural Meghalaya and in areas where coal and limestone mining are carried in a rampant pace.[22]

The changes in land ownership from communal land to private landlordism has resulted in rent seeking, share cropping, land mortgage, landlessness and other forms of private control (Karna, 1990).This has also given rise to middlemen among the rural elites who engage in buying and selling of land and in gaining loans at exorbitant high rates. As Baruah quotes the money-lender is no longer the foxy non-tribal taking advantage of the simple tribal as it used to be. Today the *mahajans* (trader-money-lender) are as tribal as the village folk and as cunning as the old non-tribal money-lenders of the old days.[23] This is fairly evident in a fact finding study on the cash economy of coal mines in Laitrumbai and Jawai the busiest coal mines in Meghalaya. The *mafias* control the land surrounding mines and have become the *de facto* rent seekers from people who open up small businesses. They lease out houses at high rent and extort weekly cash (*hafta*). Interestingly most of the extorters are females. This changing phase of tribal identity has remained unexplored in our understanding of developmental processes and questions of marginality in the north-east. The question of marginality, disempowerment and ecological destruction and the agencies that hegemonise control remain deeply contested. However, what remains interesting is to examine how capitalism and the roots to inequitable social order are created and sustained under the rubric of neo-liberal economic order. It is the task of anthropological knowledge to reconstruct the socio-cultural history of the indigenous society, its evolution and structural transformation at its engagement with modernity.

The assimilation remains self critical. While ethno nationalism and identity politics have become the sole channel through which hegemonic popular culture and State claim over natural resource are contested there is an undercurrent that sustained capitalistic control and exploitation of resources that is in no conflict with market-led developmentalism. While the State and lowland communities the non-tribal's are seen as appropriating and hegemonic agencies the local community fails to imagine the counter hegemony from within, by communities' once stewards the local elites, bureaucrats and politicians who represent the gentry and are the new oligarch in the tribal society. They remain uncontested by the counter hegemonies marginalised population surrounding coal mines. The conceptualization of the other in the local ethnoscape gives little space for the resenting voices within the *Khasi* and *Jaintiya* community to articulate their demand beyond the cultural canvass of ethnic identity.

The cultural politics of rural elites lies in brewing this resentment as an ongoing struggle to secure indigenous peoples rights over local resources as counterpoise to State legitimization. The danger lies in who opens the Pandora box. As has been highlighted by McDura (2006; 2007), that local cultural groups are contesting the ownership rights to control over land and its resources. Given a chance for private ownership over lands community stewards acknowledge mining will no longer be a problem McDura (2007). This has exactly been the case in coal mining areas of Khasi and Jaintiya Hills where individual ownership to land both as *de facto* and *de jury* control (lease and sub-contract) have led to the creation of private property and subsequent proliferation of mining activity. The end result has been the creation of private property where the earlier structure of community owned land has been diminished to oblivion. It has necessitated a crisis, the chaos of unorganised mining rapidly damaging the local ecology resulting in ecological vengeance as is reflected in the pollution of freshwater system of the local area.

The lack of regulation over unscientific privately owned mining has transformed the once community endowment into irresponsible mined landscape necessitating institutional intervention. The State sees these mines as illegitimate and illegal as they do not conform to the mandatory regulations of the Government that define mining activity. Hence there also emerges this question of what comprise a legal definition and how local practices if not conforming to the statutes of the sovereign do not fall into the illegitimate appropriators of wealth. However, this differentiation between legal and illegality is further complicated by the legitimization of such practices by the State Government that collects revenue on coal that is exported with and outside the country. The levying of tax makes the illegal coal mines legal and legitimised by the local administration as it falls within the State subject while not by the Central Government. Part of the nebulousness in violating statutes and State Government not compelling the local people lies in the economic gains and revenue generation that takes place through coal mining and the economy it supports. If coal mining is regularised it is not quite worthwhile whether the environment surrounding mines would be better managed. Several studies have shown that State-owned mines have bypassed Environment Impact Assessment (EIA) regulations and have brought about serious consequences leading to ecological decline because of the sheer scale of mining (Lahiri-Dutt 2006).

Mining Legalities in the Pit-hole Mines

The legality of mining has a unique position in Meghalaya where no complementary large scale State mines exist. As Scott writes with reference to shifting cultivators as illegal citizens, the coal miners of the State also form part of the illegal subjects as their territories do not fall under cadastral revenue settlements (Scott 1998). Inspite of this illegality the paying of tax at the border check posts makes an illegal activity under the jurisprudence of State laws legitimate and legal. To understand the complex legality question that has become so central in the debates on social justice and equitable development surrounding coal mines we have to look back at the colonial encounter with the natives and how it appropriated the frontiers through a discourse of protectionism. In the Sixth Schedule States the processes of mineral exploration is primarily concentrated in the hands of the local people with customary rights to land-use. This unique and isolated departure from mainstream large scale Gondwana coal extraction over the tertiary coal exploration in the north-eastern frontier should be seen from a historical perspective of colonial strategies in managing the frontier tracts of the then Assam that were later carried on by the post-colonial State.

The strategies of governance in the hills till toady remain one of greater political control with limited interference on improving the livelihood condition of the local inhabitants. Improvement was strongly linked to revenue generation that could sustain colonial administration. When coal mining first began in Meghalaya in 1840s the colonial government was reluctant to improve the local mines as there were no incentives to do so. In fact the whole excavation was carried out by a British official named Mr. Darley who was also the acting superintendent of the Cherra mines taking land on lease from the Government. He carried it on till 1951.In a report produced in 1856, it was realised that coal mining in Lakadong, Jaintiya hills could only be made profitable if ancillary activity like clay pot making can be developed. Coal mining completely stopped after the initial exploration in late 1840s. This was also the case of tea gardens in Assam in the initial years of experimentation and exploration until Robert Bruce came into the scene and the loss of global monopoly of Chinese tea by the colonial government necessitated its exploration in the Brahmaputra Valley (Sharma 2006). It is important to note how colonial regulations of the 1880 that demarcated the highland territories from the lowland was more than the immediate administrative manipulation of the colonial government that reshaped and fostered the identity politics that embroils the contemporary ethno landscape of north-east.[24] The 'inner time regulation' was a political project to create secured enclaves in the lowlands where colonial capital could safely play its role in transforming virgin tropical forest (jungles) into profitable tea gardens while counterpoised to that highland became the centres of conservation and regulations that balanced the deforestation of lowlands. Thus scientific forestry has dual meaning in the creation of protected forest in thinly populated frontier tracts while establishing plantation groves at the foothills and the plains. This historical background is significant to revisit the legality and illegality question of coal mines in the post-colonial environment. While inflexible mining regulation and State institutions claim the illegality of coal mining in Meghalaya they rarely could intervene into the cultural landscape of the tribal world that had been constructed by a series of regulation that restricts State's intervention in the daily practices of the natives. This distinction is significant as it distanced the State from taking direct control over coal mines. The emergence of informal coal mining as a co-evolutionary outcome of big mines unable to satisfy the basic needs of its labour force in Central Indian tribal belt was nowhere the reason for the proliferation of small scale informal mining in the Meghalaya plateau.

If the rights to ownership of land remains tightly bounded with the local people with a significant manipulation of land tenure, surrounding mines where the notion of communally owned land now remains in theory. McDura (2007) through his field work concluded that there has occurred significant transformation in the land tenure system of Meghalaya that can only be observed in the field. The traditional classification of land into two nomenclatures *Ri-Kinti, Ri-Raid,* is quite a misnomer. The general transformation has taken a shift from *Ri-Raid* land ownership (community owned land) to *Ri-Kinti* land ownership (private land). How private ownership to land has evolved to supersede community land is quite a complex historical process in which colonial administrative intervention acted as a catalyst (Nathan, 2000). Some argue that the present situation is a continuation of the process started by the British who elevated the *Syiems,* or chiefs to a type of landlord and introduced land taxes. While others have attributed this to the lineages and the power dynamics within the clans that have allowed some clans to be more powerful land owners than others.

The land tenure system of Meghalaya is poorly researched and it is difficult to determine when the existing classification systems as already discussed came into effect (Nongkynri 2002). This has been further complicated by difference in land ownership in different parts of the Khasi Hills (Lahiri 2000).

However, the basic distinction is between privately owned and communally owned clan land. Common land is regulated by the *Darbars* or the Village Council for use by members of a village. Users have no property right over this type of land and they cannot transfer to their children's or relatives. Private land is under the direct control of the individual, who has proprietary, heritable and transferable rights (Nongbri 2003). Private land included both inherited and self acquired land.

There are several ways that land can become private land. Usually, if the occupier and/or cultivator of the common land can show that they have improved the land over a period of three years they are entitled to claim ownership at the discretion of the *Darbars*. As *Darbars* provide land to occupiers those who can pursue the *Durbars* to allow them to occupy land for three years can then develop the land and claim ownership. In future they get every right to personal claims and transfer of land by sale or *de facto* deeds (*benami* transactions). It is interesting to observe that much of the communal land in coal belts of Khasi and Jayantia Hills have been privatised through such sagacious acts of customary transactions and claim to land-use. Here it becomes pertinent to highland the paradox with the new institutional Economic framework that advocates property rights and institutional regulation to check the use and abuse of common pool resources held by the community. We can observe in case of coal mining in Meghalaya the privatization of common resources has led to the proliferation of unscientific pit-hole mines that contests the theoretical claim of free-ridership in community owned natural resource management.

The real human insecurity are not embedded in identity crisis or threats of demographic inhalation from immigrant denizens but are located in land alienation, gender inequality, economic disparity emerging at the village level in tribal territories. This has been brilliantly brought out by Duncan McDura (2006) while analysing the role of civil society in Meghalaya. His analysis draws upon the economic and social reasons behind human insecurity rather than the populist ethno national and nationalist discourse on vulnerability or identity loss that civil society tends to engage with in extra legal landscapes, such as informal coal mines of Meghalaya (McDura 2006). The emergence of new elites within presumed egalitarian tribal social system is not unique to Meghalaya alone. A wealth of ethnographic study among the indigenous Indians in Latin America particularly in Peru, Ecuador and Bolivia represents the hybridization of communities response in resource rich areas where oil and gas reserves in forest territories have led to venture capitalism. Rival (2002) and Sawyer (2004) in their study on the Ecuadorian indigenous Indian communities represent the local politics of the communities and how communities understands transnational interest and struggles to get stakes in their resource rich land. Here we have to deconstruct resistance as it is conventionally understood in the Gramsian sense and detach it from subversion. People's resistance may often involve a sense of subversion as Rival argues in the context of her study on the Huaorani Indians. She looks at the carbon trade phenomena where large multi-nations buy rights to protect forest in lieu of payment to the indigenous communities. The Huaoranis have signed such contracts with multiple corporate by breaking their existing contracts. So the whole process gets disputed. The Huaoranis are fully aware of what they are doing. The claim for ignorant tribes marginalised in the frontiers thus becomes deeply contested. In Meghalaya a similar context is reproduced. The Khasi elites are conscious of the ecological constraints that coal mining will bring to the local landscape yet it is the drive towards easy capital than negates sustainable choices.

The idea of ignorance is falsified. It represents the micro politics of community stewards who constantly negotiate and are well informed of the global politics and corporate interest and competition to gain control over indigenous resources. Here we need to critically engage with the classic notion of resistance to State power and coercion as has been brilliantly highlighted in the works of Scott (2000) and his contemporaries. Resistance can also dissolve into subversion. It is the subverted voices of the local people in extra legal spaces that often construct reality. In extra legal spaces at frontier regions the State maintains a diffused weak inter-locus of administrative control. However, geo-political interest represents the binary of State power with strong border patrol—a strong military presence with limited access to control over local resources and desire for improvement. However, this simplistic binary can be contested. The extra legal nature of tribal territory at the frontiers breeds new ideologies of power that are embedded in daily practices of subjects. As Das and Pool (2004) argue that the margins or frontiers are not mere territorial representation of State power "they are also, and perhaps more importantly, sites of practice on which Laws and other State practices are colonized by others form of regulation that emanate from the pressing need of population to secure political and economic survival". The margins are simultaneously sites of contestation between customary and State laws. These territorial spaces represent wildness where the State is constantly re-founding its modes of order and law making. The illegality of State presence in frontier tracts does not constrain power, but is experienced and undone through the illegality of its own practices, documents and words. The illegal trade of coal as it crosses the international border represents how legality through levying of tax is undone in presence of State institutions. However, it does not constrain the exercise of power.

Complex Land Rights : Its Implications for Small Miners

Given the naivity involved land tenureship in Meghalaya's coal mining belt; the State, community leaders, village elders, democratic institutions (both traditional and modern), State bureaucrats and pressure groups play important role in shaping the discourse on rights and access to resource use. While tension exists between these institutions as their rights to control over resources often overlap and confront each other, coal mining in Meghalaya presents and stand alone a unique case study where local political and bureaucratic practices have given a new meaning to extra-legal coal mining. Here marginality is created from within. The resistance to legislation comes from political and community actors who have best appropriated the exhaustible resource.[25] Although, the extra legal nature of coal mining has raised public debates time and again it has sustained the pressures from the Central Government under the patronage of local politicians, bureaucrats and community elders who are themselves self interested in such projects. However, recent legislation in the post-liberalization period has drawn in more complexity to the debate. The amendments that have been brought in the State industrial policy have allowed big capital to venture into mineral exploration on land lease in tribal areas. The issuing of lease and rampant environment clearance to one such multinational firm Lafarg-*Umiam* mining corporation in 2006 has exposed the complex nexus of interrelationship that tribal elites have developed with big capitalists. While the extra legal nature of coal mining are fought over and protected by the coal lobby, the political actors have let lose the bureaucratic process to allow foreign investment to infringe local customary laws in the name of 'Look East' policy and trade promotion.[26] The political process surrounding coal mining in Meghalaya presents a complex web of interaction in which self interested tribal elites are engaged in redrawing the discourses of development bypassing the customary rights of their community members. However, it would not be wrong to infer that the extra legal nature of coal mining in Meghalaya created by the national mineral policy opens the ground for corrupt local bureaucratic practices. The mineral policy is biased to attract the big players marginalising the specific needs of artisanal and small scale miners engaged in this profession for decades.

However, my philosophy is not to justify State intervention as opposed to local control in the hands of the community. The focus of my argument contests tribe as a homogeneous category. I propose that the exposure of the Khasis to the monetised economic interplay have brought about this transformation (class formation and class consciousness) that survives on a network of practices patronizing identity politics and ethno-nationalism as part of their cultural politics to appropriate and legitimise such transformation. In this process new subjects are produced; counter hegemonising peripheral population within the community and beyond the denizens, immigrants who are a problem category seen as the 'others'. The other's cultural identity as non-tribes disenfranchises them to be part of the local struggle against State hegemony nevertheless are skilfully appropriated in the making and sustenance of the local oligarch who own and control production process in mines. This represents a change in relationship between the hills and the plains people, however, the locus of power does not change with the shift in subjects. It is ingrained in the capitalist rules of primitive accumulation through the exploitation of human labour. The political economy of coal mining in Meghalaya represents a complex set of transformed practices that questions the conventional and mainstream understanding of community, polity, culture, practices and identity that are constantly reshaped to serve individual interest at the expense of communities collective well-being.

NOTES

1. See, 'Report on the Coal Mining in Jaintiya Hills', *India Office Record*, IOR/V/23/93.
2. The native title was officially recognised in 1867. It comprised of twenty-five petty States in the Khasi Hills, fifteen of the first class presided over by *Siems* who, though taken from one family are chosen from by popular election; one confederacy under elected official styled *Wahahars;* five under *Sirdars,* and four under *Lyngdohs,* both of which classes of officials are entirely elective. See, Political Proceedings, March 1867, No 14.
3. The collection of Hoe tax from household was considered as a necessary step for improvement in the condition of the native's livelihood. B.C. Allen writing on the Khasi Hills stated that light and judicial taxation would contribute to the preservation of tranquillity and good order in the Jaintiya Hills. While comparing with the Lurka Coolis of the district Singhbhum, Allen observes, moderate taxation had a beneficial effect upon the savagery of the former. Taxation he proposed was found to make the natives less turbulent and aggressive, and more thrifty, diligent and submissive to the authorities. See, A. Makenzies, 1884, *The North-East Frontier of India*, pp. 240-41.

4. As early as 1853 colonial official posted in these frontier territories observed that the simple character of the Khasias (Khasis)had to some extent become corrupt by civilization and increased wealth; civil wars which continually distracted the country in older times had been put down; trade has been augmented; an increasing demand for hill product has set in .... , . See A. Makenzies, 1884, *The North-East Frontier of India*, p. 239.
5. See the newspaper report, Meghalaya to clean up coal mining act, *The Pioneer*, August 10, 2006.
6. According to Mines and Mineral Development and Regulation Act 1957 amended in 2002, "no person shall undertake any reconnaissance, prospecting or mining operation in any area, except under and in accordance with the terms and conditions of the reconnaissance permit or of a prospecting license or, as the case may be, a mining lease, granted under the act and rule made thereunder". Substituted by MM (RD) Amendment Act, 1999, *vide* G.o.I. Ext. Part II, Section 1, No. 51, dated 20.12.99 (No. 38 of 1999). In the State more that 95 per cent of the coal mines are illegal if one goes by the Act of Parliament passed by the legislature. All private mines operate without reconnaissance permit from the State Government.
7. Available from *http://mines.nic.in/nmp.html* accessed on 26 December, 2007.
8. See the newspaper report, 'Industry *Versus* Environment', *The Telegraph*, Feb. 1, 2005.
9. See the report Meghalaya Limestone Quarries Closed Down to Earth, Dec. 25, 2007. Also see the Supreme Court Judgement on 22 of December allowing resumption of Limestone Mining by Lafarge as appeared in *The Hindustan Times*, December 23, 2007.
10. See the recent controversy that emerged out of bureaucratic and political misappropriation of local resource. The case at hand is the mining rights given to Lafarge Umiam Mining Private Limited in the Shela-Ningtrai village in East Khasi Hills. The gross violation of EIA regulation and the access of forest land for mining activity were objected by the regional office of the Ministry of Environment and Forest after its findings in 2006 that brought mining to a halt in July 2007. However, it is interesting to note that Lafarge Umium Limited had earlier got environmental clearance from The District Commissioner of East Khasi Hills in 1996 and the District Forest Officer in 2001. The autonomous district council also confirmed to it. Lafarge next filed a petition in the Supreme Court in July 2007. In a judgement passed on 22 of December, 2007, the Supreme Court has allowed Lafarge to resume mining in the State. See, Lafarge to resume Meghalaya Mining this Week, *The Hindu Business Line*, November 26, 2007.

11. Since the formation of Meghalaya as a full fledged State in 1972, trible elites have consolidated their power in the society through the expansion of public sector, reserve seat in Parliament, and the capture of development fund allocated to the region from the Central Government. See, Sen Gupta, 2005.
12. The *Darbars* are the traditional institution of decision-making in Meghalaya. In the hierarchical ladder the *Darbars* lie at the bottom of decision-making at village level. However, the *Darbar* decision is binding on the community and no political actor tries to violate its judgement. The *Darbars* are themselves quite heterogeneous. In some areas of the Khasi Hills the *Darbars* can have as many as five different tires : clan level, village level, clusters level, thirty village level and executive level.
13. In the Lafarge Umium Limestone Mining project 29 per cent of the stakes are owned by two tribal chiefs from the State. See 'Meghalaya Limestone Quarries Closed,' *Down to Earth*, 25th December 2007.
14. The Khasi pressure groups in Meghalaya can best be described as ethno-nationalist groups. The main pressure groups are Khasi Students Union (KSU), The Federation of Khasi-Jaintiya and Garo People (FKJGP), The Synguk Seng Samla Snong (SSSS) and the Hyinniewtrp Youth Front (HYF). They are very influential political actors and several of its members go on to become mainstream politicians and legislators.
15. See for a similar kind of work in a different context charcoal production in Senegal. J.C Ribot, *Market, State and Environment Policy: The Political Economy of Charcoal in Senegal.*
16. See Phillemon E.P, (1995) *Cherrapunjee the Area of Rain*, Spectrum Publication, New Delhi, p. 23. In this book the author refers to the trade of coal from the Cherra region to the plains by the British. Preliminary assessment of coal by British Geologist revealed that the coal of Sorha was of exceptionally good quality, equal to some of the English coals. The coal reserves of Sorha were estimated at nineteen million tonnes and its production was estimated around sixty thousand tonnes per year. Between 1840 and 1844 it is estimated that the export increased from 39,750 *maunds* to 90,940 *maunds*. One *maund* equals 40 kg.
17. See, *The Statement* report dated 13th of April, 2007. In this news report the Federation of Khasi, Jayantia and Garo People (FKJGP) have pledged to flush out all non-tribal working in coal mines in Meghalaya. They branded mine workers as criminals.
18. Denizens as used by Baruah to quote in his own words, is not a contemporary legal category. The term goes back to the power of denization that British monarchs once had to grant some aliens, some of the privileges of natural born subjects. Denizens for

instance, could buy land but could not inherit it. At a later stage, the Parliament sought to control the royal power of denizanation by passing laws that disallowed denizens from being members of the Privy Council and the House of Parliament and from occupying civil or military offices of trust, or from obtaining grants of land from the Crown. While the restriction of the rights of the non-tribal population have a very different history and rational, the particular limits, *e.g.* on right of property relationship, access to public employment and elected office are not dismissed to those applicable to denizens.

19. See, Duncan McDuie Ra unpublished PhD thesis submitted in the Department of International Studies and Politics, University of New South Wales titled, "Civil Society and Human Security in Meghalaya: Identity, Power and Inequalities". In his PhD he contests the universal identity of Civil Society and claims that it has been misread in the context of Meghalaya.
20. See, territorial and fiscal jurisdiction of the hill chiefs of Chittagong: Correspondence of the revenue administrator of the Chittagong Hill Tracts, Calcutta, Minute by the Lieutenant Governor General of Bengal, dated 5th July 1876.—MF 957 IOR (India Office Records).
21. The process of privatising community owned land is quite interesting. There are several ways that land can become private land. Usually, if the occupier and/or cultivator of the common land can show that they have improved the land over a period of three years they are entitled to claim ownership at the discretion of the *Darbar.* As *Darbar* provide land to occupiers those who can pursue the *Darbars* to allow them to occupy land for three years can then develop the land and claim ownership. In future they get every right to personal claims and transfer of land by sale or *de facto* deeds (*benami* transactions). It is interesting to observe that much of the communal land in coal belts of Khasi and Jayantia Hills have been privatised through such sagacious acts of customary transactions and claim to land-use.
22. The study by KSO-Kharot Snong Social Organization on landlessness and poverty conducted in 1999 in Kharot Snong area of the East Khasi Hills. According to the survey conducted over 2000 sample household spread over 40 villages, it was found that a quarter of the villagers had common land. A further study conducted by the KSO in 2003 in seven villages, each in seven districts of Meghalaya reveals that landlessness was increasing. The price of land was increasing to lease and buy, and the factors were affecting the rates of deforestation.
23. See, as E.A. Gait in his History of Assam writes the colonial regulations of 1880 was created to facilitate better rule of the colonial government. The inhabitants of the hill tracks, were not

suited for the elaborate rules laid down in the procedural codes and in several other enactments of the same class and they had to be governed in a simple and personal manner then those of the more civilised and long settled districts. It was, therefore, provided by the Frontier Track Regulation, II of 1880, that the operation of suitable laws might be barred in all the hill districts, in the North Cachar Sub-division, the Mikir Hill Tracks in Nowgong and the Dibrugarh frontier track in Lakhimpur.

24. The coal lobby in the State has led to political changes in the past. The committee that was constituted to frame a mineral policy (after the Supreme Court gave its directive to the State Government in July 2006) under the assistantship of the Chief Commissioner involving the coal traders and members of Meghalaya Mountaineering Association has not seen the light of the day. Instead the Ministry of Geology and Mines is now headed by a local legislator who is himself a coal trader.
25. The Lafarge Limestone Mining Project that recently came under controversy is a case in hand. The company Lafarge Surma a subsidiary of Lum Mawshun Minerals Pvt Ltd. has secured a 35-year lease agreement with the villages (Shella-Nongtrai) for about 100 hectares (ha) for the mines and the liberty to use another 26.6 ha for mining-related activities. However, land lease were granted under fudged environmental clearance and a misguided Rapid Environment Impact Assessment by a private consultancy firm. Even the Land Transfer Act was relaxed in 2001 by the State Government to allow Lafarge to acquire land. The company has acquired tribal land otherwise not accessible to outsiders and had mortgaged tribal land to International Banks who have given loan to build state cement plant across the border at Chattak. Bangladesh built at a cost of US$ 225 million. Today, Lafarge Surma owns 74 per cent shares of this company and the remaining shares are owned by two Khasi tribesmen. The controversy sees in policy circles a major setback to the region's Look East Policy.

REFERENCES

Anderson, Benedict (1991), *Imagined Communities; Reflection on the Origin and Spread of Nationalism,* Verson Press, London.

Bareh, Hamlet and R. Kyanti, Eds. (2001), *The Economy of Meghalaya: Tribes in Transition,* Osmond Publication. New Delhi.

Baruah, A.K. (2004), 'Ethnic Conflict and Traditional Self-governing Institution: *A Study of Laithumokhra Dorbar,* London School of Economic Crisis State Programme Working Paper No. 39.

Baruah, Sanjeeb (2005), *Durable Disorder: Understanding the Politics of North-East India,* Oxford University Press, New Delhi

Bryant, Raymond. L, (1996), *Political Ecology of Burma.*

Das, Veena and Pool, Deborah (2004) *Anthropology in the Margins of the State, School of American Research Press,* Santa Fe and Oxford.

Das, Veena and Pool, Deborah (Eds) (2004) 'Introduction' in *Anthropology in the Margins of the State,* School of American Research Press, Santa Fe.

Dev Rajesh *et al.,* (2003) 'Local Liberal Democracy, Traditional Institutions and Politics of Representation: Analysing the Nangkynrih Shynong Dorbar', Unpublished paper published at the Johannesburg Crisis State Workshop.

Elwin, Verrier (1964), *The Nagas in the Nineteenth Century,* Oxford University Press, Bombay.

Guha, Ramchandra (1989), *The Unequal Woods: Ecological Change and Peasant Resistance in Himalayas,* Oxford University Press, New Delhi.

Hafner, Robert W. (1990) *The Political Economy of Mountain Java: An Interpretative History,* Bakerly and Los Angeles, University of California Press.

Karna, M.N (1990), 'The Agrarian Scene', *Seminar,* No. 366, pp. 30-38.

Khan, Joel S., (1999),'Centralising the Indonesian Uplands' in Tania Murray Li. (Ed.), *Transforming the Indonesian Upland,* Amsterdam, Harwood Publication, pp. 79-104.

Lahiri-Dutt, Kuntala (2004), 'My God gives us Chaos, so that we can Plunder: A Critique of Resource Curse and Conflict', *Development,* Vol. 49, No. 3, pp. 14-21.

Leach, E.R (1964) *Political System of Highland Burma: A Study of Kachin Social Structure,* The Athlone Press, London and Atlantic Highlands.

Li, Tania Murray, (1996) 'Images of Community: Discourses and Strategies on Property Relations', *Development and Change,* Vol. 27, pp. 501-527.

Li, Tania Murray., (ed.) (1999), *Transforming the Indonesian Uplands,* Amsterdam Harwood Publishers.

Li, Tania Murray (2000), 'Articulating Indigenous Identity in Indonesia: Resource Politics and the Tribal Slot, *Comparative Studies in Society and History,* Vol. 42, No. 1, pp. 149-179.

Li, Tania Murray (2007), *The Will to Improve: Governmentality, Development and the Practice of Politics,* Duke University Press, Durham and London.

London, Bell, D. (1998) 'The Social Relation of Property and Effeciency', pp. 29-45 in *Property in Economic Context,* Edited by Robert C. Hunt and Anthony Gilman, Lenham, University Press of America, Monograph in Economic Anthropology, No. 14.

Mackenzie. A, (1884), *History of the Relation of Government with the Hill Tribes of the North-Eastern Frontier of Bengal,* Mittal Publication.

McDura, Duncan, (2007), 'Anti-Development or Identity Crisis: Misreading Civil Society in Meghalaya', *Asian Ethnicity,* Vol. 8, No. 1, pp. 43-59.

McDura, Duncan (2006), 'Civil Society Organization and Human Security: Transcending Constricted Space in Meghalaya', *Contemporary South Asia,* Volume 15, March 2006, pp. 35-53.

Mitchell, Timothy (2002), *Rule of Expert: Egypt, Techno Politics, Modernity,* Berkeley, University of California Press.

Moore, H and Vaughan, M (1994), *Cutting Down Trees: Gender, Nutrition and Agricultural Changes in Rural Zambia,* 1890-1990, London: James Curry.

Munsari, Ghazala and Rao, Vijender (2004) 'Community Based and Driven Development: A Critical Review', *World Bank Research Observer,* 19, pp. 1-39.

Nathan, D (2000) 'Timber in Meghalaya', *Economic and Political Weekly,* Vol. 35, Issue 4, pp. 182-187.

Nongbri, T. (2003): *Development, Ethnicity and Gender,* Rawat Publications, Jaipur and Delhi.

Nongkynri, A.K. (2002): Khasi Society of Meghalaya: A Sociological Understanding,New Delhi, Indus.

Nongkynri, A,K (2003): *Human Development in Katanga Shnong,* Shillong, Don Bosco Press.

Ribot, J.C and Peluso, N.L (2003): 'The Theory of Access', *Rural Sociology,* Vol. 68, No. 2, pp. 153-181.

Rival, Laura M. (2002) *Trekking Through History: The Huaorani of Amazonian Ecuador,* Columbia University Press, New York.

Scott, James C. (1985): *Weapons of the Weak: Everyday Forms of Peasants Resistance,* New Haven, CT: Yale University Press.

Scott, J.C (1990) Domination and the Art of Resistance: Hidden Transcripts, Yale, NY-New Haven.

Scott, J.C (1998) *Seeing Like a State: How Certain Schemes to Improve the Human Condition have Failed,* Yale University, New Haven and London.

Scott, James C. (1998) *Seeing Like a State: How Certain Schemes to Improve the Human Condition have Failed,* New Haven, CT: Yale University Press.

Shankar *et al.,* (1993) 'Degradation of Land due to Coal Mining and its Recovery', *Current Science,* Vol. 65, No. 9, pp. 680-687.

Sharma, Kiranmoi (2003) 'Impact of Coal Mining on Vegetation: A Case Study of Jaintiya Hills of Meghalaya, India, unpublished Masters Dissertation submitted to Indian Institute of Remote Sensing, Dheradun.

Sharma, Aradhana and Gupta Akhil, (eds.), (2006) 'Introduction' in *The Anthropology of the State*, A Reader, Blackwill Publishers.

Sharma, Jayeta (2006), 'British Science, Chinese Skill and Assam Tea: Making Empires Gardens', *Indian Economic and Social History Review*, Vol. 43, pp. 429-455.

Singh, O.P (2005): *Mining Environment: Problems and Remedies*, Regency Publication, New Delhi.

Suwayer, Suzana (2004) Crude Chronicles: Indigenous Politics, Multinational Oil and Neoliberalism in Ecuador (American Encounters/Global Interactions).NC, Duke University Press, Durham.

Swer, S. and Singh, O.P (1994) 'Status of Water Quality in Coal Mining Areas of Meghalaya', in Inder N., Singh and Manik, K. Ghosh, Proceeding of the National Seminar on Environmental Engineering with Special Emphasis on Mining. Shillong College, Shillong.

Tsing, Anna Lowenhaupt (1993) *In the Realm of the Diamond Queen*, Princeton, Princeton University Press.

9

Levels of Living, Demographic Changes and Consumption Growth Divergence

A Study of North-East India

D.P. PAL and DEBOTTAM CHAKRABORTY

Introduction

India is a federal state. India's overall development is monitored at the central level. Total development funds are allocated among different States according to priorities and needs of the States.

Rural development schemes are undertaken by the States as formulated centrally by the Government of India towards development of infrastructure and generation of employment and income. But implementation of these schemes does not occur equally in the States. States vary in the speed as well as in the extent of implementation of the schemes, particularly infrastructure development and employment generation. Such differences create differences in the per capita income, particularly rural per capita income across the States. Per capita income determines per capita expenditure on consumption which is indicative of levels of living of the people (Varian, 1992). Per capita consumption consists of different food and non-food items. The composition of the consumption basket differs from household to household in a State and from State to State in a country. Changes in per capita income are manifested in changes in the composition of the consumption basket and hence in the living pattern (welfare) of the people.

Per capita income and hence per capita consumption expenditure vary across the States in India, so also the living pattern. The purposes of this chapter are :

(a) To examine the extent and the nature of variation in per capita consumption expenditure and hence level of living across States in India during 1993-2004. More specifically, rural-urban differences in variations in living as reflected in the ratio of food and non-food expenditures are examined in terms of Engel elasticities, expenditure-elasticities and household-size elasticities,
(b) To examine the effects of changes in the household-size on per capita consumption. A decomposition model is formulated in the comparative static framework to analyse the effects of changes in total consumption expenditure and household-size on changes in the per capita consumption expenditure
(c) To examine the nature of inter-State divergence in the growth of consumption expenditure *i.e.*, whether inter-State differences in per capita consumption have been exploding or disappearing over time.

The present study discusses some of the above issues mainly in respect of the major States of India and ignores the issues in respect of minor States (Meenakshi and Ray 1999; Chakraborty, Pal and Sen 2004). Our purpose is to consider the issues in the minor States of India in the North-Eastern Region (NER). The States are Arunachal Pradesh, Assam, Manipur, Meghalaya, Mizoram, Nagaland, Tripura, and Sikkim. These are minor States in terms of State domestic product, population and size .The combined share of these States in country's net domestic product is only 3 per cent in 2004-05. Assam (1.87 per cent) is ranked first among these States followed by Tripura (0.31 per cent). The Table 9.1 containing the Net State Domestic Product data is provided in the Annexure (Table 9.A.1).

The study has been undertaken for the period of 1993-94 to 2004-05. 50th (for 1993-94 data), 55th (for 1999-2000 data) and 62nd (for 2004-05 data) rounds of NSSO data on Monthly Per Capita household Consumption Expenditure (MPCE) have been used. MPCE data are deflated at 1993-94 prices.

Per Capita Consumption

Monthly Per Capita Consumption Expenditure (MPCE) serves as a proxy for income to measure well-being of the people. It differs across the States and across different income groups in a State. At the household level the composition of the consumption basket differs among income groups in a State and also across States (Chakrabarty and Pal 2008). It also changes over time.

Divergence across States

It is observed (Table 9.1) that except in 1993-94 Nagaland occupied the top position in respect of MPCE in rural as well as urban areas. Tripura slipped to the last position in rural areas in 2004-05, and in urban areas the last position is all through occupied by Manipur. In all the States under consideration MPCE and hence level of living have increased during the period irrespective of the regions. Judged by the level of MPCE Nagaland people are in a position to have better level of living while the people of Manipur lag behind among the states under comparison.

The Coefficient of Variation (CV) of MPCE across States has declined from 34.87 per cent in 1993-94 to 26.02 per cent in 1999-2000 and to 23.54 per cent in 2004-05 in case of rural areas. But in case of urban areas, CV has increased from 14.85 per cent in 1993-94 to 18.81 per cent in 1999-2000 and then to 21.34 per cent in 2004-05. *While in case of rural areas disparity in*

MPCE among the north-eastern states has been declining, in case of urban areas it has been increasing as in the major Indian States (Chakraborty, Pal and Sen 2004).

Table 9.1: MPCE of Different North-East States (Rs)

Year/States	*1993-94*		*1999-2000*		*2004-05*	
	Rural	*Urban*	*Rural*	*Urban*	*Rural*	*Urban*
Arunachal Pradesh	316.85 (6)	494.12 (5)	446.90 (3)	525.97 (7)	412.58 (3)	471.18 (7)
Assam	258.11 (8)	458.57 (7)	293.88 (8)	561.46 (6)	290.47 (7)	565.77 (5)
Manipur	391.17 (1)	319.55 (8)	370.90 (5)	488.12 (8)	328.45 (6)	388.44 (8)
Meghalaya	356.98 (4)	530.55 (2)	388.59 (4)	670.47 (3)	350.43 (5)	636.41 (3)
Mizoram	389.55 (3)	549.51 (1)	497.82 (2)	728.71 (2)	416.23 (2)	641.98 (2)
Nagaland	441.46 (2)	510.01 (4)	649.18 (1)	856.82 (1)	540.54 (1)	801.32 (1)
Sikkim	298.72 (7)	518.44 (3)	366.74 (6)	624.61 (4)	368.20 (4)	591.87 (4)
Tripura	343.93 (5)	489.94 (6)	364.42 (7)	604.55 (5)	260.76 (8)	535.05 (6)
Coefficient of Variation (%)	34.87	14.85	26.02	18.81	23.54	21.34

Note: Figures in parentheses indicate rank in descending order.

Divergence across Expenditure Classes

People in a State have different income levels .They have hence different MPCE. MPCE varies across different expenditure classes (Table 9.2). The coefficient of variation of MPCE across expenditure classes is indicative of the size-class variation in the level of living. Its high (low) value reflects the high (low) degree of size-class disparity in the level of living. The CV is all through higher in urban areas than in rural areas. It has increased almost everywhere during the period. It thus emerges that the size-class disparity in the level of living has been more in urban areas than in rural areas and it has risen during the period.

Table 9.2: Coefficient of Variations (%) among different income classes within a state

Year/States	*1993-94*		*1999-2000*		*2004-05*	
	Rural	*Urban*	*Rural*	*Urban*	*Rural*	*Urban*
Arunachal Pradesh	67.65 (2)	73.08 (4)	67.08 (2)	62.80 (8)	70.65 (1)	87.97 (3)
Assam	60.17 (5)	76.23 (1)	59.72 (3)	74.37 (3)	64.18 (5)	100.14 (1)
Manipur	62.00 (4)	68.49 (5)	55.17 (5)	114.17 (1)	65.03 (3)	77.93 (6)
Meghalaya	111.79 (1)	75.06 (2)	52.22 (6)	63.59 (6)	56.51 (7)	81.36 (5)
Mizoram	52.21 (7)	58.90 (8)	51.92 (7)	63.58 (6)	58.99 (6)	71.87 (7)
Nagaland	45.77 (8)	60.97 (7)	49.79 (8)	66.11 (7)	54.17 (8)	65.44 (8)
Sikkim	57.01 (6)	65.59 (6)	59.37 (4)	72.75 (2)	67.69 (2)	82.88 (4)
Tripura	62.50 (3)	74.27 (3)	70.25 (1)	70.25 (4)	64.63 (4)	89.58 (2)

Note: Figures in the parentheses indicate rank in descending order.

Demographic Change

Household consumption depends on, among others, household income and household-size. In Tables 9.3A to 9.3C the household size of different income classes in the States has been enlisted. It is observed that for both rural and urban areas, Sikkim is all through having the smallest household-size. Manipur is having the highest household-size in both rural and urban areas till 1999, and thereafter Mizoram and Nagaland have enjoyed the prime position.

Nagaland has exhibited the highest CV (80.1 per cent) in household-size among different income classes in 1993-94 in rural areas. In case of urban areas Mizoram (64.67 per cent) has the highest CV. In 1999-2000 also Nagaland is having the

Table 9.3A : Family Size of Different MPCE Classes in 1993-94

States/Size Class (Rs.)	Arunachal Pradesh		Assam		Manipur		Meghalaya		Mizoram		Nagaland		Sikkim		Tripura	
	Rural	Urban	Rural	Urban	Rural	Urban	Rural	Urban	Rural	Urban	Rural	Urban	Rural	Urban	Rural	Urban
Overall	4.59	3.64	5.09	4.30	5.33	5.08	4.44	3.97	5.01	4.60	5.29	4.99	4.11	3.58	4.45	4.32
1.	4.85	5.05	6.01	6.39	3.46	8.00	1.60	4.00	0.00	0.00	0.00	0.00	0.00	0.00	5.80	4.84
2.	7.18	4.40	5.59	5.87	4.00	5.95	4.51	3.01	0.00	0.00	0.00	0.00	6.44	0.00	5.13	5.43
3.	6.10	5.84	5.93	5.49	6.20	6.36	5.51	6.33	7.00	0.00	0.00	9.00	6.04	4.98	5.64	5.34
4.	5.07	5.22	5.62	5.57	6.24	5.89	5.49	6.97	6.50	6.03	0.00	7.50	5.13	5.89	4.95	5.09
5.	4.54	5.79	5.70	5.47	5.97	5.59	5.27	5.36	4.62	5.47	9.35	7.18	5.65	5.85	4.69	4.64
6.	5.81	3.60	5.40	4.85	5.85	5.55	5.52	5.10	5.23	5.44	5.84	5.58	4.76	4.94	4.60	4.49
7.	5.01	3.46	4.93	4.96	5.55	4.30	5.01	4.32	5.71	5.27	6.53	6.29	4.73	4.70	5.01	4.57
8.	3.82	4.90	5.16	4.64	5.42	3.87	4.80	4.85	5.66	4.97	7.12	6.48	4.31	4.94	4.80	4.84
9.	4.79	3.20	4.56	3.47	5.44	3.60	4.90	3.64	5.71	4.74	6.11	4.80	4.13	3.21	4.33	4.61
10.	3.71	3.04	4.31	3.27	4.66	2.21	3.96	3.54	5.05	4.04	5.70	3.90	3.63	2.39	4.17	3.70
11.	3.85	2.59	3.94	2.57	4.64	2.23	3.26	2.64	4.78	3.20	4.84	2.65	2.96	2.04	4.09	3.11
12.	3.32	1.98	3.66	2.95	3.43	4.73	2.37	2.07	3.18	3.44	3.98	2.24	1.74	2.08	3.64	2.92
Coefficient of Variation (%)	23.14	31.4	15.6	27.18	20	35.23	29.9	34.06	51.42	64.67	80.1	63.06	44.7	61.68	13.3	18.17

Table 9.3B : Family Size of Different MPCE Classes in 1999-2000

States/Size Class (Rs.)	Arunachal Pradesh		Assam		Manipur		Meghalaya		Mizoram		Nagaland		Sikkim		Tripura	
	Rural	Urban	Rural	Urban	Rural	Urban	Rural	Urban	Rural	Urban	Rural	Urban	Rural	Urban	Rural	Urban
Overall	4.93	4.21	5.41	4.03	5.18	5.40	5.05	4.04	5.21	4.83	5.01	4.17	4.62	3.99	4.63	4.15
1.	8.29	5.71	7.05	6.68	6.95	0.00	6.00	0.00	0.00	0.00	0.00	0.00	6.09	7.64	4.38	5.77
2.	6.19	0.00	6.50	5.43	3.00	8.23	0.00	0.00	0.00	0.00	0.00	0.00	5.92	5.41	5.64	5.13
3.	6.93	6.56	6.12	5.30	6.06	5.91	5.95	7.00	5.32	5.99	0.00	8.00	6.50	7.01	5.43	5.31
4.	5.89	4.94	6.01	5.28	6.39	6.25	6.30	5.41	7.30	6.50	5.00	3.00	5.94	4.77	5.12	5.01
5.	5.96	4.73	5.70	4.74	5.09	5.55	6.09	6.72	5.74	5.14	7.00	5.00	5.40	5.48	4.58	4.70
6.	5.72	3.66	5.54	4.05	5.43	5.47	5.77	5.52	6.29	5.61	6.38	7.74	5.99	6.47	5.19	4.32
7.	6.19	3.88	5.36	4.28	5.68	4.93	5.94	4.28	6.42	5.18	6.67	5.79	5.12	4.94	4.83	4.25
8.	5.76	4.41	4.92	3.59	5.31	5.68	5.59	4.33	6.08	5.42	6.10	5.29	4.76	3.54	5.13	4.36
9.	4.77	2.86	4.89	3.71	5.20	5.12	5.06	3.63	5.80	4.88	5.58	4.97	4.75	3.13	4.56	3.91
10.	4.49	3.37	4.43	2.87	4.59	4.55	4.53	3.80	5.81	4.18	5.78	4.40	3.52	3.59	4.05	3.37
11.	4.71	3.43	3.98	3.21	4.62	4.42	3.53	3.71	4.76	4.06	5.72	3.11	4.09	2.58	3.80	3.27
12.	3.29	3.83	3.32	2.77	4.64	3.75	3.33	1.40	3.68	4.17	4.19	2.28	2.37	2.09	3.83	3.00
Coefficient of Variation (%)	22.46	41.27	20.2	27.51	19.4	38.67	37.6	60.94	50.3	49.8	62.6	62.56	24.2	37.58	13.1	19.84

Table 9.3C : Family Size of Different MPCE Classes in 2004-05

States/Size Class (Rs.)	Arunachal Pradesh		Assam		Manipur		Meghalaya		Mizoram		Nagaland		Sikkim		Tripura	
	Rural	Urban	Rural	Urban	Rural	Urban	Rural	Urban	Rural	Urban	Rural	Urban	Rural	Urban	Rural	Urban
Overall	4.85	3.78	5.13	3.84	5.07	4.80	4.84	4.30	4.32	4.88	5.38	4.88	4.34	3.40	4.38	3.89
1.	7.95	1.41	5.76	6.03	5.00	5.24	0.00	0.00	0.00	0.00	0.00	0.00	2.96	1.00	5.10	4.57
2.	6.59	4.45	5.82	4.57	7.00	5.02	0.00	5.23	0.00	6.00	0.00	0.00	8.00	6.32	5.42	4.36
3.	5.83	4.19	5.59	4.71	4.75	5.80	5.00	5.29	6.12	5.80	0.00	0.00	6.58	1.98	4.66	4.91
4.	6.59	4.40	6.08	4.35	5.30	4.90	7.13	5.99	4.79	5.96	0.00	4.12	6.39	5.54	4.70	4.27
5.	6.23	4.31	5.43	5.26	5.74	5.08	5.37	6.34	5.99	6.22	0.00	5.31	5.70	4.88	4.71	4.49
6.	5.97	4.73	5.02	4.62	5.42	5.01	5.89	5.11	5.73	5.52	6.07	6.37	5.15	3.64	4.44	4.28
7.	5.48	3.70	5.14	4.00	5.72	4.48	5.75	5.81	5.64	5.48	6.83	5.59	4.74	3.97	4.42	4.00
8.	5.71	3.04	5.11	4.13	5.36	4.32	5.49	4.51	5.28	4.98	6.40	4.93	4.56	3.61	4.38	3.42
9.	5.07	3.70	5.00	3.02	4.92	4.14	5.10	3.94	4.51	4.67	5.96	5.21	4.47	4.16	3.98	3.60
10.	4.53	3.27	4.76	3.14	4.54	3.10	4.31	3.87	4.02	4.44	5.75	4.37	3.81	3.37	3.70	3.56
11.	4.17	2.95	4.33	3.17	4.22	3.02	3.61	3.16	3.67	4.08	5.09	4.91	3.91	1.91	3.64	2.92
12.	3.61	2.03	4.13	1.84	3.97	6.79	2.70	1.51	2.96	3.08	4.73	4.01	2.80	1.00	2.89	2.37
Coefficient of Variation (%)	21.03	29.13	11.4	27.77	15.6	22.14	53.9	44.9	52.42	37.14	89.7	62.7	31.2	49.48	16	19.05

Note: It may be noted that the expenditure class varies between rural and urban areas. Expenditure class also changes over the period of time. Expenditure classes are described in Table A2.

highest variation in case of rural areas (62.6 per cent) as well as in urban areas (62.56 per cent). It is also true in 2004-05: in rural and urban Nagaland CV is 89.7 per cent and 62.7 per cent respectively. The lowest variation is observed in case of Assam in rural areas (11.4 per cent) and in Tripura in urban areas (19.05 per cent) in 2004-05. In general, *the household-size is higher in lower income groups in rural areas as well as in urban areas. But in urban areas, the variation among different expenditure classes is higher than in rural areas than in urban areas. In most of the States considered the household-size has declined over time.*

Engel Functions : Engel Elasticities

Engel functions have been estimated with the household-size and MPCE as explanatory variables for food and non-food groups for three years (1993-94, 1999-2000, and 2004-05) in rural and urban areas separately. Here our main objectives are (a) to estimate the expenditure-elasticities of food and non-food consumption so as to examine the changing importance of the items in consumption; and (b) to estimate the effects of household size on consumption so as to examine how the economization effects (size-effects) of household-size on consumption vary depending upon the nature of the goods in consumption.

There are numerous studies, both national and international, on the effects of household-size on consumption. To mention a few Tobin (1950), Houthakker (1957), David (1962), Iyengar, Jain and Srinivasan (1968), Iyengar (1968), Nelson (1988), Figini (1998), Tasciotti (2007) are cited. They have studied how family-size affects consumption of a household. Most of the studies have taken the headcount number of the family as the size of the household. But in Houthakker's and in Nelson's studies the equivalent scale has been used to determine the family size. The importance of relationships among the household members has been studied by David. In the following section, in this chapter, we attempt to demonstrate the model to be used in estimating the effects of MPCE and household-size on consumption.

Model for Estimation

Suppose that X_i^h is the expenditure on item *i* by household *h*, X^h is the total expenditure of household h, and N^h is the total number of family members of household *h*.

Then the specific expenditure function is

$$X_i^h = f(X^h, N^h) \qquad ...(1)$$

In estimation we may take the logarithmic form or any other form depending upon the purpose and theoretical necessity. We take here the logarithmic form:

$$ln\ X_i^h = \beta_0 + \beta_1\ ln\ X^h + \beta_2\ ln\ N^h + u^h \qquad ...(2)$$

By OLS we estimate , $\hat{\beta}_0, \hat{\beta}_1$ *and* $\hat{\beta}_2$

The problem of this estimation is that $ln\ X^h$ and $ln\ N^h$ are directly related. Multicollinearity problem appears in the estimation. Precision of estimates is reduced; it is no doubt a serious problem. However, if one can tolerate such problem, one can get the effects of total expenditure and family size on specific expenditure. It is possible to overcome the problem to some extent if we assume that the specific expenditure function is one degree homogeneous in X^h and N^h.

Using this relation we get,

$$f\left(\frac{X^h}{N^h}, \frac{N^h}{N^h}\right) = \frac{1}{N^h} f(X^h, N^h) \frac{X_i^h}{N^h} = x_i^h$$

$$\text{Hence } x_i^h = \varphi(x^h, 1) = \varphi(x^h) \qquad ...(3)$$

As before we take the logarithmic form:

$$ln\ x_i^h = \alpha_0 + \alpha_1 ln x^h + u^h \qquad ...(4)$$

which is the specific expenditure function in terms of per capita variables, in contrast to the earlier one where total variables are used. This form does not contain *explicitly* the family size variable (N^h). But N^h is implicitly used in per capita terms. OLS estimates are $\hat{\alpha}_0, \hat{\alpha}_1$.

Here multicollinearity is avoided, but the family size effect on specific expenditure is not explicitly determined.

However, we can proceed further. We go back to the original functional form :

$$\ln X_i^h = \beta_0 + \beta_1 \ln X^h + \beta_2 \ln N^h + u^h$$

$$\Rightarrow \ln X_i^h = \beta_0 + \beta_1 \ln X^h + \beta_1 \ln N^h - \beta_1 \ln N^h - \ln N^h + \ln N^h + \beta_2 \ln N^h + u^h$$

$$\Rightarrow \ln X_i^h = \beta_0 + \beta_1 \ln X^h + \beta_1 \ln N^h - \beta_1 \ln N^h - \ln N^h + \ln N^h + \beta_2 \ln N^h + u^h$$

$$\Rightarrow \ln X_i^h - \ln N^h = \beta_0 + \beta_1 \ln X^h - \beta_1 \ln N^h + (\beta_1 + \beta_2 - 1) \ln N^h + u^h$$

$$\Rightarrow \ln\left(\frac{X_i^h}{N^h}\right) = \beta_0 + \beta_1 \ln\left(\frac{X^h}{N^h}\right) + (\beta_1 + \beta_2 - 1) \ln N^h + u^h \qquad ...(5)$$

This contains family size variable explicitly and other variables in per capita terms.

Comparing (5) with (4), we observe that (5) gives more information than (4). Here, effect of family size together with the effect of total per capita expenditure is estimated and multicollinearity problem seems to have been minimised. Furthermore, when $\beta_1 + \beta_2 - 1 = 0$ the form reduces to (4), which is one degree homogeneous. Thus, one can test the hypothesis, $H_0 : \beta_1 + \beta_2 - 1 = 0$ against the alternative hypothesis $H_1 : \beta_1 + \beta_2 - 1 \neq 0$ in the form (5) and calculate whether the original form is one degree homogeneous.

So, to infer whether the household-size affects consumption or not we must test the hypothesis $H_0 : \beta_1 + \beta_2 - 1 = 0$ against the hypothesis $H_1 : \beta_1 + \beta_2 - 1 \neq 0$. If H_0 is true we can infer that the household-size does not have any effect on the consumption of the *i*-th item, otherwise the household-size affects positively or negatively the consumption of the *i*-th item, depending on the sign of $(\beta_1 + \beta_2 - 1)$, whether it is positive or negative.

In Tables 9.4A to 9.4C, the estimate of Engel function has been provided. As the log-log form has been considered, the coefficients are Engel elasticities: expenditure elasticities and household-size elasticities. If the coefficients are significant in

5 per cent level of significance, they are marked by asterisks in the Table.

Taking food and non-food items together in comparison, we can say that the demarcation line between the necessary items and the luxury items shifts over time towards the latter if elasticities (expenditure) of the non-food items decrease and come down below unity. This means that although to start with a low level of income only food items of low value remain necessary items, over time as income increases, many food items of high value and some luxury items become necessary items and still at a later stage many of the non-food items enter into the basket of necessary goods. The living standard improves. This phenomenon is called Engel's Law.

Our estimates reveal that only in few States the expenditure-elasticity of the non-food items has come down below unity, *i.e.*, non-food items have turned out as necessary items during the period. In case of Assam in rural areas, non-food expenditure-elasticity has come down from 1.070 in 1993-94 to 0.115 in 1999-2000, although it has again increased above unity (1.384) in 2004-05. For Manipur, in rural areas, it was 0.998 in 1993-94, but it has then increased to 1.253 in 2004-05. Only in case of Sikkim, it has consistently declined from 1.606 in 1993-94 to 1.251 in 1999-2000 and further to 0.987 in 2004-05 in urban areas. So, it can be inferred that *in case of north-east States, there are few States where the levels of living as judged by declining no-food expenditure-elasticity have improved during 1993-2004.*

Economization in consumption (household-size effect being negative) is significantly observed mostly in non-food items in the rural regions of Assam, Manipur and Meghalaya in 1993-94; in Assam, Sikkim and Tripura in 1999-2000; in Nagaland and Sikkim in 2004-05. Interestingly all the States under consideration have exhibited the negative size-effect indicating the presence of economization in non-food consumption (though not all statistically significant). In some States economization in food consumption has also been observed. These are Sikkim in urban areas in 1993-94, Arunachal Pradesh in rural areas and Meghalaya in urban areas in 1999-2000, Meghalaya and Manipur in urban areas in 2004-05. So, *economization in consumption due to household size is more pronounced in rural areas than in urban areas and for nonfood items than for food items (Tables 9.4A to 9.4C).*

Table 9.4A: Estimates of Engel Functions: 1993-94

States		*Food*			*Non-food*		
		Co-efficient of Total Expen-diture	*Co-effi-cient of House-hold-Size*	R^2	*Coeffi-cient of Total Expen-diture*	*Coeffi-cient of House-hold-Size*	R^2
Arunachal Pradesh	Rural	0.790 (27.181)	-0.071 (-0.940)	0.996	1.470 (17.060)	0.311 (1.382)	0.987
	Urban	0.833 (9.186)	0.159 (0.879)	0.967	1.344 (8.564)	-0.121 (-0.387)	0.970
Assam	Rural	0.973 (8.720)	0.564 (1.517)	0.987	1.070 (6.627)	-1.107* (-2.058)	0.991
	Urban	0.817 (17.347)	0.101 (0.930)	0.997	1.313 (19.450)	-0.125 (-0.804)	0.998
Manipur	Rural	1.308 (8.803)	1.792 (4.065)	0.912	0.998 (8.842)	-1.663* (-4.967)	0.920
	Urban	0.602 (13.078)	-0.117 (-1.519)	0.984	1.522 (19.298)	-0.045 (-0.345)	0.991
Megha-laya	Rural	0.746 (13.973)	0.611 (5.820)	0.960	1.238 (46.617)	-0.819* (-15.685)	0.997
	Urban	0.772 (32.005)	0.114 (2.457)	0.994	1.394 (23.580)	-0.101 (-0.888)	0.991
Mizoram	Rural	0.732 (16.701)	0.021 (0.216)	0.991	1.571 (17.978)	0.170 (0.897)	0.992
	Urban	0.801 (5.234)	0.108 (0.286)	0.983	1.236 (6.733)	-0.083 (-0.183)	0.991
Nagaland	Rural	0.801 (20.696)	0.050 (0.780)	0.997	1.426 (15.351)	-0.116 (-0.753)	0.995
	Urban	0.745 (11.170)	0.004 (0.053)	0.996	1.529 (7.546)	0.138 (0.555)	0.990
Sikkim	Rural	0.883 (15.496)	0.161 (2.059)	0.997	1.491 (10.591)	0.038 (0.195)	0.995
	Urban	0.540 (5.267)	-0.262* (-1.840)	0.981	1.606 (21.755)	0.386 (3.764)	0.997
Tripura	Rural	0.843 (8.991)	0.282 (0.697)	0.986	1.336 (10.276)	-0.548 (-0.975)	0.992
	Urban	0.796 (18.249)	0.170 (1.139)	0.994	1.436 (37.909)	0.189 (1.451)	0.999

Table 9.4B: Estimates of Engel Functions: 1999-2000

States		*Food*			*Nonfood*		
		Co-efficient of Total Expen-diture	*Co-effi-cient of House-hold Size*	R^2	*Coeffi-cient of Total Expen-diture*	*Coeffi-cient of House-hold Size*	R^2
Arunachal Pradesh	Rural	0.580	-0.578*	0.993	1.699	1.072	0.995
		(8.536)	(-3.569)		(18.390)	(4.865)	
	Urban	0.817	-0.006	0.982	1.260	-0.015	0.985
		(13.629)	(-0.037)		(15.149)	(-0.062)	
Assam	Rural	1.649	2.087	0.992	0.115	-2.956*	0.996
		(7.487)	(3.789)		(0.449)	(-4.632)	
	Urban	0.633	-0.260	0.992	1.316	-0.133	0.996
		(7.796)	(-1.282)		(12.577)	(-0.511)	
Manipur	Rural	0.627	0.053	0.986	1.781	-0.190	0.986
		(24.951)	(0.890)		(24.557)	(-1.104)	
	Urban	0.270	-0.962	0.730	1.366	0.166	0.973
		(1.083)	(-1.023)		(7.690)	(0.248)	
Megha-laya	Rural	0.908	0.153	0.993	1.187	-0.168	0.991
		(16.745)	(1.261)		(13.567)	(-0.857)	
	Urban	0.655	-0.192*	0.993	1.352	0.178	0.994
		(11.876)	(-2.696)		(16.539)	(1.690)	
Mizoram	Rural	0.835	0.182	0.993	1.299	-0.325	0.980
		(22.626)	(2.031)		(10.981)	(-1.132)	
	Urban	0.678	-0.298	0.992	1.317	0.182	0.999
		(10.812)	(-1.312)		(32.812)	(1.253)	
Nagaland	Rural	0.827	0.038	0.974	1.331	-0.060	0.950
		(12.012)	(0.197)		(8.429)	(-0.136)	
	Urban	0.882	0.051	0.980	1.126	-0.041	0.989
		(14.325)	(0.563)		(18.431)	(-0.453)	
Sikkim	Rural	0.938	0.217	0.993	1.090	-0.249*	0.995
		(16.681)	(2.114)		(15.718)	(-1.963)	
	Urban	0.772	-0.020	0.997	1.251	0.040	0.998
		(22.571)	(-0.360)		(25.720)	(0.497)	
Tripura	Rural	0.900	0.235	0.997	1.183	-0.456*	0.994
		(39.588)	(2.612)		(26.348)	(-2.569)	
	Urban	0.868	0.363	0.996	1.249	-0.345	0.999
		(9.859)	(1.295)		(15.078)	(-1.310)	

Table 9.4C: Estimates of Engel Functions: 2004-05

States		*Food*			*Nonfood*		
		Co-efficient of Total Expen-diture	*Co-effi-cient of House-hold Size*	R^2	*Coeffi-cient of Total Expen-diture*	*Coeffi-cient of House-hold Size*	R^2
Arunachal Pradesh	Rural	0.716	-0.010	0.992	1.415	0.096	0.994
		(8.401)	(-0.043)		(10.044)	(0.249)	
	Urban	0.670	-0.105	0.980	1.475	0.613	0.994
		(20.605)	(-1.551)		(37.475)	(7.455)	
Assam	Rural	0.803	0.319	0.974	1.384	-0.195	0.993
		(6.668)	(0.544)		(12.120)	(-0.350)	
	Urban	0.788	0.410	0.971	1.345	-0.015	0.999
		(7.680)	(1.588)		(29.857)	(-0.132)	
Manipur	Rural	0.742	0.442	0.871	1.253	-0.437	0.948
		(5.938)	(0.959)		(8.107)	(-0.767)	
	Urban	0.415	-0.268*	0.955	1.415	-0.069	0.998
		(12.132)	(-2.604)		(63.548)	(-1.037)	
Megha-laya	Rural	0.764	0.094	0.997	1.388	0.051	1.000
		(24.662)	(1.664)		(70.832)	(1.435)	
	Urban	0.521	-0.243*	0.994	1.518	0.401	0.999
		(13.871)	(-3.816)		(60.851)	(9.499)	
Mizoram	Rural	0.807	0.261	0.966	1.278	-0.280	0.990
		(6.318)	(0.961)		(9.212)	(-0.949)	
	Urban	0.856	0.597	0.992	1.223	-0.264	0.997
		(12.809)	(2.874)		(15.691)	(-1.090)	
Nagaland	Rural	0.784	0.844	0.989	1.131	-2.152*	0.996
		(9.836)	(2.899)		(7.887)	(-4.110)	
	Urban	0.670	0.247	0.983	1.313	-0.249	0.995
		(17.148)	(1.609)		(29.572)	(-1.425)	
Sikkim	Rural	0.792	0.274	0.987	1.261	-0.500*	0.992
		(23.472)	(4.330)		(24.195)	(-5.115)	
	Urban	1.250	0.641	0.936	0.987	-0.289*	0.979
		(11.168)	(4.593)		(18.851)	(-4.417)	
Tripura	Rural	0.833	0.306	0.993	1.523	0.386	0.995
		(10.769)	(1.176)		(12.721)	(0.960)	
	Urban	0.726	0.471	0.990	1.480	0.292	0.996
		(12.574)	(2.286)		(17.089)	(0.946)	

Decomposition of Change in MPCE into Change in Total Consumption Expenditure and Change in Household Size: Comparative Static Analysis

MPCE (x) is monthly total expenditure (X) divided by the number of household members (household-size, N). The change in MPCE during the period t to t+1 can thus be divided into two parts: change due to family size and change due to total expenditure. This can be estimated using the following decomposition scheme in respect of household h:

$$\Delta X_t = X_{t+1} - X_t = x_{t+1}N_{t+1} - x_tN_t$$

$$= X_{t+1}N_{t+1} - x_{t+1}N_t + x_{t+1}N_t - x_tN_t$$

$$= X_{t+1}\Delta N_t + N_t\Delta x_t \qquad \text{...(6)}$$

where x=X/N

Also,

$$\Delta X_t = X_{t+1} - X_t = x_{t+1}N_{t+1} - x_tN_t$$

$$= X_{t+1}N_{t+1} - x_{t+1}N_t + x_{t+1}N_t - x_tN_t$$

$$= X_{t+1}N_{t+1} - x_tN_{t+1} + x_tN_{t+1} - x_tN_t$$

$$= X_t\Delta N_t + N_{t+1}\Delta x_t \qquad \text{...(7)}$$

Now by adding (6) and (7) and dividing by 2, we get,

$$\Delta X_t = \frac{1}{2}(N_{t+1} + N_t)\Delta x_t + \frac{1}{2}(x_{t+1} + x_t)\Delta N_t$$

$$\Rightarrow \Delta x_t = \frac{2}{N_t + N_{t+1}}\Delta X_t - \frac{x_t + x_{t+1}}{N_t + N_{t+1}}\Delta N_t \qquad \text{...(8)}$$

where Δx is the change in MPCE of household h. x_{t+1} and x_t are the MPCE of household h at time $t+1$ and t respectively. N_t and N_{t+1} total household size of household h at time t and $t+1$ respectively. Again, ΔN_t is the change in household-size of household h and ΔX_t is the change in total consumption of household h. The first term of (8) indicates the change due to total income or income effect (X) and the second term indicates the change due to family size or family-size effect (N). Change in MPCE (x) is the weighted change in total expenditure net of the weighted change in household-size.

In Table 9.5, the decomposition of changes in MPCE has been provided during the period 1993-94 to 2004-05. In Manipur, Meghalaya and Tripura MPCE has declined in rural areas by Rs. 62.72, Rs. 6.55 and Rs. 83.17 respectively. In urban areas, only in case of Arunachal Pradesh MPCE has declined by Rs. 22.94. Otherwise in case of Nagaland it has increased by Rs. 99.08 in rural areas and by Rs. 291.31 in urban areas. This was the maximum increase across all north-east States.

For Manipur, in rural areas, both total expenditure and family-size have declined; but the negative expenditure effect has more than offset the negative family-size effect resulting in the fall in MPCE *and thus the situation is too vulgar in this case. The same thing is true for the case of Tripura in rural areas.* MPCE has declined (by Rs. 83.17) as total expenditure has declined (by Rs. 87.90) more than the family-size (Rs. 4.73).

In urban areas, the decline in MPCE in Arunachal Pradesh has occurred because of decline in total expenditure *i.e.,* negative expenditure effect (by Rs. 5.37) and positive family size effect (by Rs.17.57). For Assam, Manipur, Nagaland, Sikkim, the increase in MPCE in urban areas is due to the negative family-size effect and positive expenditure effect. But for Tripura, the rise in MPCE (by Rs. 45.11) is due to the negative family-size effect (–Rs. 53.44) which has more than offset the negative expenditure effect (–Rs 8.33).

MPCE Growth Divergence

We have earlier said that the States have been divergent in monthly per capita household consumption. The question in which we are now interested is whether such inter-State divergence in consumption has been disappearing or exploding over time. If the previous year's expenditure determines the next year's expenditure, it may have very serious implication for the State-wise expenditure distribution in the economy. This, in effect, means that inequality in expenditure distribution will increase across States and divergence in MPCE growth will explode over time.

Table 9.5: Decomposition Changes in MPCE due to Family Size and Total Expenditure (in Rs.).

States	*Change due to Family Size*		*Change due to Total Income*		*Change in MPCE*	
	Rural	*Urban*	*Rural*	*Urban*	*Rural*	*Urban*
Arunachal Pradesh	19.95	17.57	115.69	-5.37	95.73	-22.94
Assam	2.16	-58.23	37.66	55.08	35.5	113.31
Manipur	-25.89	-20.44	-88.61	48.45	-62.72	68.89
Meghalaya	30.88	45.63	24.33	151.50	-6.55	105.86
Mizoram	-60.01	35.59	-33.33	128.06	26.68	92.47
Nagaland	8.06	-14.51	107.14	276.80	99.08	291.31
Sikkim	18.35	-29.91	87.83	43.52	69.48	73.43
Tripura	-4.73	-53.44	-87.90	-8.33	-83.17	45.11

To examine whether the consumption-expenditure growth divergence among the States has exploded or disappeared over time, we have estimated the following equation, separately for rural and urban areas (taking State as the unit) :

$$\ln\left(\frac{MPCE_t}{MPCE_{t-1}}\right) = a + b\ln MPCE_{t-1} + u \qquad ...(9)$$

where $MPCE_t$ is the monthly per capita consumption expenditure of the *t*-th year, and $MPCE_{t-1}$ is the MPCE of the (*t*-1)th year and *u* is the standard error term spherically distributed. If the coefficient *b* (in Table 9.6) is significant, we can infer that MPCE of year *t*-1 determines its value in the *t*-th year. Again if the value of *b* is positive we can conclude that more consumption-expenditure in the current year induces more growth in the next year; that means growth divergence happens. If *b* is negative, then we can say that consumption in the next year declines and growth divergence disappears.

Here we have considered the years 1993-94, 1999-2000 and 2004-05. MPCE growth rate for each State has been determined using terminal values during 1993-1999, 1999-2004 and 1993-2004. For each period Equation (9) is estimated using the OLS technique.

In Table 9.6 the coefficients of $MPCE_{t-1}$ are presented. It is observed that only when *t*=2004-05 and *t*-1=1993-94, in rural areas the coefficient of $MPCE_{t-1}$ is negative and significant at the 5 per cent level of significance. At 10 per cent level of significance, for *t*=1999-2000 and *t*-1=1993-94, in rural areas the coefficient of $MPCE_{t-1}$, becomes negative and significant. In urban areas the value of the coefficient (*b*) is negative, though not significant. This reveals that there is no statistical evidence of consumption growth divergence among the States to explode particularly in the rural areas of the north-east States.

Table 9.6: Estimation of Equation: $\ln\left(\frac{MPCE_t}{MPCE_{t-1}}\right) = a + b \ln MPCE_{t-1} + u$

Cases	*Rural*			*Urban*		
	Coeffi-cient	*Constant*	R^2	*Coeffi-cient*	*Constant*	R^2
t=2004-05	-0.837	4.932	0.566	-0.039	0.410	0.002
t-1=1993-94	(-2.796)	(2.781)		(-0.116)	(0.199)	
t=2004-05	-0.155	0.807	0.120	0.143	-1.015	0.135
t-1=1999-2000	(-0.906)	(0.783)		(0.968)	(-1.066)	
t=1999-2000	-0.730	4.422	0.484	-0.296	2.089	0.122
t-1=1993-94	(-2.372)	(2.426)		(-0.914)	(1.046)	

Conclusion

In conclusion we can summarize our findings as follows:

Irrespective of the regions in the North-East States of India the level of living has been improving since 1993. In case of rural areas, inter-State disparity in consumption and hence well-being among the region has been declining, and in case of urban areas, it tends to be increasing. In case of urban areas the variation of consumption (well-being) among different expenditure classes has increased over time, but in rural areas it has declined.

The household-size is higher in lower expenditure group than in higher expenditure group in rural areas as well as in urban areas. But variation in household-size among different expenditure classes is higher in urban areas than in rural areas.

The economization effect of household-size on consumption is more pronounced in rural areas than in urban areas and in case of non-food items than in case of food items. There is no evidence of consumption growth divergence among the North-East States in India to explode during the period of on-going reforms particularly in rural areas.

REFERENCES

Atkinson, A.B. (1970): On Measurement of Inequality, *Journal of Economic Theory*, Vol 2.

Chakraborty, D. *et al.* (2004): "Changing Levels of Living in India in the 1990s" in Singh, Ravishankar Kumar, (ed.) *Economic Reforms in India*, Abhijit Publications, Delhi.

Chakraborty, D. and Pal, D.P. (2009): "Changing Consumption Pattern in India" in Pal, P.K. (ed.), *Reforms and Structural Changes in India*, Regal Publications Ltd., New Delhi.

David, M.H. (1962): *Family Composition and Consumption*, North Holland Publishing Company.

Figini, Paolo (1998): *Inequality Measures, Equivalence Scales and Adjustment for Household-Size and Composition*, Working Paper, Department of Economics, Trinity College.

Gupta, S.P. (1996): "Recent Economic Reforms in India and their Impact on the Poor and Vulnerable Sections of Society" in C.H. Hanumanta Rao and Hans Linnemann (eds.), *Economic Reforms and Poverty Alleviation in India*, Sage Publications.

Houthakker, H.S. (1957): "An International Comparison of Household Expenditure Patterns", *Econometrica*, pp. 159-174.

Iyengar, N.S. *et al.* (1968): "Economics of Scale in Household Consumption—A Case Study ", *Indian Economic Journal*, Vol. 15.

Maity, P. (1998): "Studies on Absolute Level of Living and Poverty in India", in Chakravarty, S. (eds.) *Quantitative Economics*, Allied Publishers Ltd.

Meenakshi, J.V. and Ray, Ranjan (1999): "Regional Differences in India's Food Expenditure Pattern: A Complete Demand Systems Approach" *Journal of International Development*, Vol. 11.

Meenakshi, J.V. and Ray, Ranjan (2000): Impact of Household-Size and Family Composition on Poverty in Rural India, *Australian Research Council*.

Nelson, Julie A. (1988): "Household Economies of Scale in Consumption: Theory and Evidence", *Econometrica*, Vol. 56, No. 6. (Nov. 1988), pp. 1301-1314.

NSSO: Level and Pattern of Consumer Expenditure 1993-94, 1999-2000, 2004-05

Pal, D.P and Sen, J (2002): "Social Sector Reforms and Relative Income Deprivation in India: A Note", Conference Volume, *Indian Economic Association*, 2002.

Pal, D.P. and Sen, J (2003): "On Dimensions of Poverty: A Cross-Section Study in India with Rural-Urban Disaggregation", Conference Volume, *IEA*, 2003.

Pal, D.P. and Sen J (2003): "Relative Income Deprivation: An analysis of Sub-Group Decomposition" in Reddy, K. Malla (ed.) *Economic Reforms and Indian Economy: A Development Experience*, Deptt. of Economics, Osmania University, India.

Sandhu, H.S. (1992): *Consumer Demand in India*, Guru Nanak Dev University, Amritsar.

Sen, A.K. (1973): *On Economic Inequality*, Oxford University Press.

Shorrocks, A.F. (1983): "Ranking of Income Distributions", *Econometrica*, Vol 50, No. 197.

Tasciotti, Luca (2007): *Expenditure Pattern in Italy, 1875-1960: A Complete Quadratic Demand System Estimation with Demographic Variables*, Working Paper, University of Tor Vergata.

Tobin, James (1950): "A Statistical Demand Function of Food in the USA", *Journal of the Royal Statistical Society*, 113.

Varian, H. (1992): *Micro Economic Analysis*, 3rd Edition, W.W Norton & Company, New York.

ANNEXURE

Table 9.A.1: Net State Domestic Product (at factor cost at 1999-2000 prices (in Rs. crore), 2004-05

States	*NSDP*	*%age*
Arunachal Pradesh	2241	0.11
Assam	39777	1.87
Manipur	4070	0.19
Meghalaya	4318	0.20
Mizoram	1839	0.09
Nagaland	4304	0.20
Sikkim	1102	0.05
Tripura	6639	0.31
Total of North-East States	64290	3.02
Indian NDP	2126018	100.00

Table 9.A.2: Different Expenditure Classes (MPCE Rs.)

Years	*Areas*	*1*	*2*	*3*	*4*	*5*	*6*	*7*	*8*	*9*	*10*	*11*	*12*
1993-94	Rural	<120	120-140	140-165	165-190	190-210	210-235	235-265	265-300	300-355	355-455	455-560	>560
	Urban	<160	160-190	190-230	230-265	265-310	310-355	355-410	410-490	490-605	605-825	825-1055	>1055
1999-2000	Rural	<225	225-255	255-300	300-340	340-380	380-420	420-470	470-525	525-615	615-775	775-950	>950
	Urban	<300	300-350	350-425	425-500	500-575	575-665	665-775	775-915	915-1120	1120-1500	1500-1925	>1925
2004-05	Rural	<235	235-270	270-320	320-365	365-410	410-455	455-510	510-580	580-690	690-890	890-1155	>1155
	Urban	<335	335-395	395-485	485-580	580-675	675-790	790-930	930-1100	1100-1380	1380-1880	1880-2540	>2540

10

Rural Poverty and Rural Non-Farm Employment in India

An Inter-State Analysis

PRANKRISHNA PAL

Introduction

According to World Development Report (2000/01) poverty implies lack of adequate food and shelter, deprivations that keep them away from a decent standard of living-implying better housing,.sanitation, access to safe drinking water and so on. So it is a multidimensional concept. The main dimensions are: (i) lack of income and assets to attain basic necessities—food, shelter, clothing and acceptable levels of health and education, (ii) sense of voicelessness levels and powerlessness in the institutions and society, and (iii) vulnerability to adverse shocks, linked to an inability to cope with them.

The Planning Commission in India has estimated the incidence of poverty on the basis of the Task Force Method based on monthly PCCE at the national and State level since early 1970's. Later on, the Planning Commission has constituted the Expert Group in 1989. The Expert Group has estimated the poverty lines and poverty ratio both at the national and State level at six points of times: 1973-74, 1977-78, 1983, 1987-88, 1993-94 and 1999-2000. Subsequently, the Planning Commission has estimated poverty in 2004-05 using two consumption distributions known as Uniform Recall Period (URP)

Consumption Distribution and Mixed Recall Period (MRP) Consumption.

Rural economy in India is basically a farm economy. Development of the rural economy occurs when dependence on farm activities decreases and non-farm activities increases. Increasing participation of labour in rural non-farm activities is indicative of such development of the rural economy. Agriculture being almost saturated, off-farm jobs are to be created in the rural area through creation of new production centres like food processing, ancillary industry, repairing based on transport and construction etc. for reducing rural poverty and employment generation.

In this chapter an attempt has been made to examine the different aspects of rural poverty and rural non-farm employment in India during 1973-74 to 2004-05. The changing scenario of inter-Sate differentials of rural poverty line in India is discussed in Section I. Section II contains the changing scenario of inter-State differentials of rural poverty level in India. Section III discusses the changing scenario of rural non-farm employment and occupational distribution of labour in India. The growth rate of rural non-farm employment in India is discussed in section IV. Section V contains the relationship between rural poverty and rural non-farm employment in India. Section VI contains the concluding remarks. The NSSO data and Planning Commission data, Government of India, are used in the analysis.

Changing Scenario of Rural Poverty Line

Poverty is defined as the head count ratio, which is expressed as the percentage of people living below the poverty line. The Planning Commission in India has estimated the incidence of poverty on the basis of the Task Force method at National and State level since the early 1970's. The Task Force method has defined the poverty line as monthly per capita consumption expenditure of Rs.49.09 in rural areas and Rs. 56.64 in urban areas in 1973-74. Later on, the Planning Commission has constituted the Expert Group in 1989 on Estimation of

Proportion and Number of Poors and the method is known as Expert Group Method. The Expert Group has estimated the poverty lines in rural and urban areas of 18 States and UTs. Poverty line and poverty ratio at both rural and urban areas have been estimated at six points of time: 1973-74, 1977-78, 1983-84, 1987-88, 1993-94 and 1999-2000. Subsequently, in 2004-05 the Planning Commission has estimated the poverty line by using original state specific poverty lines identified by the Expert Group and updating them to 2004-05 prices using the Consumer Price Index of Agricultural Labourers (CPIAL) for rural poverty line and Consumer Price Index for Industrial Workers (CPIIW) for urban poverty line.

Let us now discuss State-wise poverty line in rural India for the years of 1973-74, 1983-84, 1993-94 and 2004-05. Rural poverty line has increased in India and its constituent States over time (Table 10.1). At the all India level rural poverty line in terms of monthly per capita consumption expenditure has increased from Rs. 49.63 in 1973-74 to Rs. 89.50 in 1983-84, to 205.84 in 1993-94 and to Rs. 356.30 in 2004-05. During this period it has increased by more than seven times. It has varied across the States over time. It is lowest in Andhra Pradesh at all points of time. It is highest in Bihar in 1973-74, Orissa in 1983-84, Kerala in 1993-94 and Uttarakhand in 2004-05. Thus there exists an Inter-State variation of rural poverty.

Changing Scenario of Poverty Level in Rural India

Let us now turn to aspect of the incidence of rural poverty in Indian States. Based on the rural poverty line, poverty level (percentage of people below the poverty line) is estimated in rural area at different points of time: 1973-74, 1977-78, 1983-84, 1993-94 and 2004-05. Here we use the poverty level for the years of 1973-74, 1983-84, 1993-94 and 2004-05. At the all-India level, poverty level was as high as 54.88 per cent in 1973-74 which come down to 44.48 per cent in 1983-84, to 35.97 per cent in 1993-94 and to 27.5 per cent in 2004-05. Thus the extent of poverty has been reduced by more than 50 per cent.

Table 10.1 : State-wise Poverty Line in Rural India during 1973/74-2004/05 (Rs. Monthly Per Capita)

Sl. No.	States	1973-74	1983-84	1993-94	2004-05*
1.	Andhra Pradesh	41.71	72.66	163.02	292.95
2.	Assam	49.82	98.32	232.05	387.64
3.	Bihar	57.68	97.48	212.16	354.36
4.	Chhattishgarh	—	—	—	322.41
5.	Dadra & Nagar Haveli	—	—	—	362.25
6.	Goa	—	—	—	362.25
7.	Gujarat	47.10	83.29	202.11	353.93
8.	Haryana	49.95	88.57	233.79	414.76
9.	Himachal Pradesh	49.95	88.57	233.79	394.28
10.	Jammu & Kashmir	46.59	91.75	0.00	391.26
11.	Jharkhand	—	—	—	366.56
12.	Karnataka	47.24	83.31	186.63	324.17
13.	Kerala	51.68	99.35	243.84	430.12
14.	Madhya Pradesh	50.20	83.59	193.10	327.78
15.	Maharashtra	50.47	88.24	194.94	362.25
16.	Orissa	46.87	106.28	194.03	325.79
17.	Punjab	49.95	88.57	233.79	410.38
18.	Rajasthan	50.96	80.24	215.89	374.57
19.	Tamil Nadu	45.09	96.15	196.53	351.86
20.	Uttarakhand	—	—	—	478.02
21.	Uttar Pradesh	48.92	83.85	213.01	365.84
22.	West Bengal	54.49	105.55	220.74	382.82
23.	Delhi	49.95	88.57	233.79	410.38
24.	All-India (Implicit)	49.63	89.50	205.84	356.30
	Disparity Index (DI) (%)	7.07	9.81	10.08	11.05

Source: Planning Commission, Govt. of India.
* Based on URP-Consumption.

Like total poverty, rural poverty has also reduced in India and in its constituent States over time. Estimates (Table 10.2) reveal that at the all-India level it has reduced from 56.44 per cent in 1973-74 to 45.65 per cent in 1983-84, to 37.27 per cent in 1993-94 and to 28.3 per cent in 2004-05. Thus poverty has been reduced by 50 per cent during the period under study. Declining annual growth rate of poverty has rising from 1.5 per cent in 1973-77 to 5.3 per cent in 1993-2000. So during the reform periods the declining rate of rural poverty is very high due to implementation of rural poverty alleviation programmes for employment generation through non-farm activities.

Table 10.2 : Percentage of People below Poverty Line in Rural India during 1973/74-2004/05

Sl. No.	States	1973-74	1983-84	1993-94	2004-05*
1.	Andhra Pradesh	48.41	26.53	15.92	11.2
2.	Arunachal Pradesh	52.67	42.60	45.01	22.3
3.	Assam	52.67	42.60	45.01	22.3
4.	Bihar	62.99	64.37	58.21	41.1
5.	Chhattisgarh	—	—	—	40.8
6.	Goa	46.85	14.81	5.34	5.4
7.	Gujarat	46.35	29.80	22.18	19.1
8.	Haryana	34.23	20.56	28.02	13.6
9.	Himachal Pradesh	27.42	17.00	30.34	10.7
10.	Jammu & Kashmir	45.51	26.04	30.34	4.6
11.	Jharkhand	—	—	—	46.3
12.	Karnataka	55.14	36.33	29.88	20.8
13.	Kerala	59.19	39.03	25.76	13.2
14.	Madhya Pradesh	62.66	48.90	40.64	36.9
15.	Maharashtra	57.71	45.23	37.93	29.6
16.	Manipur	52.67	42.60	45.01	22.3
17.	Meghalaya	52.67	42.60	45.01	22.3
18.	Mizoram	52.67	42.60	45.01	22.3
19.	Nagaland	52.67	42.60	45.01	22.3
20.	Orissa	67.28	67.53	49.72	46.8
21.	Punjab	28.21	13.20	11.95	9.1
22.	Rajasthan	44.76	33.50	26.46	18.7
23.	Sikkim	52.67	42.60	45.01	22.3
24.	Tamil Nadu	57.43	53.99	32.48	22.8
25.	Tripura	52.67	42.60	45.01	22.3
26.	Uttarakhand	—	—	—	40.8
27.	Uttar Pradesh	56.53	46.45	42.28	33.4
28.	West Bengal	73.16	63.05	40.80	28.6
29.	Andaman & Nicoar	57.43	53.99	32.48	22.9
30.	Chandigarh	27.96	23.79	11.35	7.1
31.	Dadra & Nagar Haveli	46.85	14.81	51.95	39.8
32	Daman & Diu	0.00	0.00	5.34	5.4
33	Delhi	24.44	7.66	1.90	6.9
34	Lakshadweep	59.19	39.03	25.76	13.3
35	Podicherry	57.43	53.99	32.48	22.9
	All-India (Implicit)	56.44	45.65	37.27	28.3
	Poverty Disparity Index (PDI) (%)	23.19	40.96	44.73	53.70

Source: Planning Commission, Govt. of India.

* Based on URP Consumption.

Wide variations in the poverty level are observed among the States in India over time. That is, at different time periods the relative ranking of the States have changed. Poverty is low in the States of Delhi (24.44 per cent in 1973-74, 7.66 per cent in 1983-84, and 1.90 per cent in 1993-94) and J & K (4.6 per cent in 2004-05) while it is high in the States of W.B (73.16 per cent in 1973-74), Orissa (67.53 per cent in 1983-84), Bihar (58.2 per cent in 1993-94) and Orissa (46.8 per cent in 2004-05). Thus Bihar and Orissa are the poorer States in India during the reform periods under study.

It thus follows from the above discussion that Indian States have exhibited a divergent poverty line and hence poverty level in rural India during 1973/74-2004/05. Poverty level (line) is low in some States while it is relatively high in some other States. All this clearly indicates the existence of inter-State disparity in poverty level (line). Such inter-State disparity in poverty level is clearly revealed by the Poverty Disparity Index (PDI) as :

Where,

$$PDI= 100\ [\Sigma\ (p_i-p)^2/(n-1)]^{1/2}/p$$

p_i : poverty level (or line) in the State i, i=1, 2,................, n

p : poverty level (or line) in India as a whole

n : Number of States and UTs in India

Estimates (Tables 10.1 and 10.2) reveal that PDI has risen over time in rural India at both line and level. The index for poverty line has increased from 7.07 per cent in 1973-74 to 9.81 per cent in 1983-84, to 10.08 per cent in 1993-94 and to 11.05 per cent in 2004-05 while the index for poverty level has also increased from 23.19 per cent in 1973-74 to 40.96 per cent in 1983-84, 44.73 per cent in 1993-94 and to 53.70 per cent in 2004-05. This indicates that inter-State disparity has widened more in poverty level rather than in poverty line during the period under study. This is to say, although the percentage of people below the poverty line has shown a steadily declining trend, yet the rising values of the index shows that instead of convergence, the Indian States have experienced rather a divergence in respect of the incidence of poverty in rural India. As a result, the richer States have shown a tendency to become relatively richer while the poorer one becomes relatively poorer.

Deprivation in India : Human Poverty Index

As per UNDP's Human Development Report (1997) human well-being has three dimensions :

- (i) Longevity—the ability to live long and healthy life.
- (ii) Education—the ability to read, write and acquire knowledge.
- (iii) Command over resource—the ability to enjoy a decent standard of living and have a socially meaningful life.

So deprivation is of three types: (a) Longevity deprivation. (b) Education deprivation; and (c) Economic deprivation. Based on all these deprivation, Human Poverty Index (HPI) has been constructed by taking equal weights:

$HPIj = [(P_1^3 + P_2^3 + P_3^3)/3]^{1/3}$,
where j: state
Pi : deprivation in *i*-th dimension, $i = 1, 2, 3$.

The HPI lies between 0 and 100. Closer the HPI to 100 higher will be the deprivation of a state and *vice versa*. It implies that the entire population of the State is deprived of the minimum attainments on each of the three dimensions. Here,

P_1: Longevity deprivation captured by the indicator persons not expected to survive beyond the age of 40 years,

P_2: Composite indicator on educational deprivation (taking illiteracy rate in the age group 7 years and above, and proportion of children in the age group 6-18 years not enrolled in the schools),

P_3: Composite indicator on economic deprivation:

- (i) proportion of population below the poverty line,
- (ii) proportion of population not receiving medical attention at birth,

(iii) proportion of population living in *kutcha* houses,

(iv) proportion of population without access to basic amenities like safe drinking water, sanitation and electricity.

As per the estimates of the National Human Development Report (2002) the HPI in India has declined from 47.33 in 1981 to 39.36 in 1991. This is also true both in rural (53.28 to 44.81) and urban (27.21 to 22) areas. Thus the HPI in rural areas is significantly higher than that in urban areas in India and its constituent States. But the decline in the HPI in rural areas is slightly higher than that in urban areas in India and its constituent States. In both rural and urban areas the relative ranking of the States have changed during the period under study. In rural areas the HPI was low in Delhi (27.36 in 1981) and Lakshadweep (19.04 in 1991) and high in Orissa (62.50 in 1981) and Bihar (55.85 in 1991). The respective figures in urban areas were: low in H.P. (14.10 in 1981 and 10.14 in 1991) and high in Orissa (37.90 in 1981) and U.P. (31.52 in 1991).Thus inter-State disparity arises in respect of HPI during the period under study (Pal, 2004).

Rural Non-Farm Employment

Rural labour is employed in alternative sectoral activities like (a) Primary Sector (PS) consisting of cultivation, agricultural activities, forestry, fishing, mining and quarrying; (b) Secondary Sector(SS) including manufacturing, servicing and repairing in both household and non-household industries and construction; (c) Tertiary Sector (TS) consisting of transport, trade and commerce, storage and communication and services. The last two sectors jointly we called it Non-Farm Sector (NFS) while the first one is the Farm Sector (FS). The FS and NFS are to a great extent interdependent. With the transportation of the rural India, inter-sector or inter-farm sector shifting of rural labour occurs. Villages are linked with the cities and towns through a wide net of transport, markets are developed and expanded, farm output are transported, agricultural machinery and repairing shops are opened, small electrical units are set up etc. All these necessitate increasing absorption of rural labour in NFS.

Estimates (Table 10.3) reveal that employment in NFS has increased all through in India at the cost of farm employment both for male and female. For male it has increased from 16.2 per cent in 1972-73 to 21.8 per cent in 1983, to 25.2 per cent in 1993-94 and to 33.2 per cent in 2004-05. While for female it has increased from 10.1 per cent in 1972-73 to 12.1 per cent in 1983, to 13.6 per cent in 1993-94 and to 18.2 per cent in 2004-05. Thus male non-farm employment is more than female ones in rural India due to expansion of the non-farm activities more for male relative to female.

Table 10.3 : Rural Non-Farm Employment in India during 1972/73-2004/05

Year	*Male*		*Female*	
	FE	*NFE*	*FE*	*NFE*
1972-73	83.6	16.4	89.9	10.1
1977-78	81.1	18.9	88.3	11.7
1983	78.2	21.8	87.9	12.1
1987-88	75.2	24.8	85.1	14.9
1993-94	74.8	25.2	86.4	13.6
1997	76.3	23.7	87.8	12.2
1999-00	71.9	28.1	94.4	15.6
2004-05	66.8	33.2	81.8	18.2

Source: NSSO data.
Notes: FE: Farm Employment, NFE: Non-Farm Employment.

Rural NFE (RNFE) has varied across the States in India over time. It is expected that more and more a State is economically and educationally developed, more and more is the supply of labour in the NFS. So, irrespective of sex, Indian States have exhibited wide variations in NFE during the reform period. Estimates (Table 10.4) reveal that rural NFE for male has increased in all the constituent States in India during 1983-2004 at the cost of farm employment while for female it has also increased in almost all the States excepting Karnataka and West Bengal during the reform periods of 1993/94-2004/05. The

Table 10.4 : Rural Non-Farm Employment in Indian States during 1983-2004/05

States	*1983*				*1993-94*				*2004-05*			
	Male		*Female*		*Male*		*Female*		*Male*		*Female*	
	FE	*NFE*	*FE*	*NFE*	*FE*	*NFE*	*FE*	*NFE*	*FE*	*NFE*	*FE*	*NFE*
A.P.	77.4	22.6	83.7	16.3	76.6	23.4	83.9	16.1	68.0	32.0	79.5	20.5
Assam	79.3	20.7	82.1	17.9	78.0	22.0	84.6	15.4	69.3	30.5	82.7	17.3
Bihar	81.3	18.7	88.3	11.7	82.3	17.7	91.2	8.8	75.6	24.4	82.8	17.2
Gujarat	79.7	20.3	92.9	7.1	71.9	28.1	88.4	11.6	69.7	30.3	87.5	12.5
Haryana	71.5	28.5	90.0	10.0	60.8	39.2	84.7	15.3	50.9	49.1	80.9	19.1
H.P.	70.0	30.0	96.9	3.1	61.4	38.6	94.7	5.3	46.6	53.4	89.5	10.5
Karnataka	81.7	18.3	88.3	11.7	79.8	20.2	83.5	16.5	78.3	21.7	87.3	12.7
Kerala	57.8	42.2	70.9	29.1	54.3	45.7	51.4	48.6	38.2	31.8	43.8	56.2
M.P.	87.3	12.7	95.6	4.4	86.6	13.4	94.2	5.8	79.7	20.3	88.5	11.5
Maharashtra	79.7	20.3	93.0	7.0	75.5	24.5	91.6	8.4	71.7	28.3	91.0	9.0
Orissa	78.2	21.8	81.1	18.9	79.6	20.4	85.2	14.8	66.4	33.6	72.5	27.5
Punjab	77.2	22.6	92.8	7.2	67.9	32.1	65.5	34.5	54.4	45.6	48.4	51.6
Rajasthan	80.8	19.2	93.9	6.1	71.6	28.4	92.6	7.4	61.8	38.2	87.6	12.4
T.N.	68.7	31.3	81.8	18.2	64.2	35.8	77.7	22.3	59.3	40.7	73.2	26.8
U.P.	79.0	21.0	89.8	10.2	75.9	24.1	89.0	11.0	65.6	34.4	81.4	18.6
W.B.	73.2	26.8	75.2	24.8	64.4	35.6	45.3	54.7	64.3	35.7	54.1	45.9
India	78.2	21.8	87.9	12.1	74.4	25.6	85.2	16.8	66.8	33.2	81.8	18.2

Source: NSSO data.

Notes: FE: Farm Employment, NFE: Non-Farm Employment.

NFE for male is lowest in M.P. (12.7 per cent in 1983, 13.4 per cent in 1993-94 and 20.3 per cent in 2004-05) and highest in Kerala (42.2 per cent in 1983, 45.7 per cent in 1993-94 and 61.8 per cent in 2004-05). Thus these two States have maintained their respective position during the pre-reform and post-reform periods. On the other hand, the NFE for female is lowest in H.P. (3.1 per cent in 1983 and 5.3 per cent in 1993-94) and Maharashtra (9.0 per cent in 2004-05); and highest in Kerala (29.1 per cent in 1983), West Bengal (54.7 per cent in 1993-94) and Kerala (56.2 per cent in 2004-05). Thus among the States only Kerala has significantly enjoyed more the absorption of the rural NFE for both male and female due to the generation of the non-farm activities particularly rural industrialization during the reform period of 1993/94-2004/05.

Sex-wise analysis also reveals that male NFE is more than female one in India and its constituent States during the pre-reform period. But during the post-reform period this is also true excepting Kerala, Punjab and West Bengal. Thus these three States have enjoyed more female NFE than male one during 1993/94-2004/05. This is presumably due to the fact that during the reform periods various types of non-farm activities have been generated in these States compared to other States in favour to rural female so that these States can utilize more female relative to male at a low wage rate.

As to the structure of labour utilization we note the following :

(a) Among the 3 (three) constituent sectors, the share of PS has all through been the highest both for male and female in India and its constituent States. At the national level, its share has decreased marginally from 74.4 per cent in 1993-94 to 71.8 per cent in 1999-2000 and to 66.8 per cent in 2004-05 for male; from 85.2 per cent in 1993-94 to 84.5 per cent in 1999-2000 and to 81.8 per cent for female. The share has also decreased in all the States for male; excepting Karnataka and West Bengal for female during the period of 1993-2005. Also we note that the female employment is more than the male ones in India and its almost all the constituent States excepting Punjab and West Bengal in this sector during the globalization period.

(b) TS has the second largest share in India and its almost all the constituent States both for male and female followed by SS. At the national level, its share has risen from 14.7 per cent in 1993-94 to 16.2 per cent in 1999-2000 and to 18.1 per cent in 2004-05 for male; from 6.2 per cent in 1993-94 to 6.6 per cent in 1999-2000 and to 7.8 per cent in 2004-05 for female. The share has also risen in almost all the States excepting Tamil Nadu for male; excepting Assam, Haryana and Orissa for female during the period of 1993-2005. Interestingly we note that among the States we considered Punjab is the only State where TS has utilized more rural female labour than male ones due to the expansion of the service sector activities for female during the globalization period.

(c) Employment in SS has also risen in India and its almost all the constituent States. Its share has risen from 10.6 per cent in 1993-94 to 12 per cent in 1999-2000 and to 15.1 per cent in 2004-05 at the national level for male. The respective figures for female are 8.6 per cent, 8.9 per cent and 10.4 per cent. Sex-wise analysis reveals that SS has absorbed more rural female than male ones (i) in 1993-94 in the States of Assam, Karnataka, Kerala, Maharashtra, and West Bengal, (ii) in 1999-2000 in the States of Andhra Pradesh, Bihar, Haryana, Karnataka, Kerala, Madhya Pradesh, Orissa, Punjab, Rajasthan, Tamil Nadu, U.P and West Bengal and in 2004-05 in the States of Bihar, Orissa and West Bengal. Thus the job opportunities for rural female relative to rural male have been expanded in these States due to rural industrialization during the globalization period.

Measures of Occupational Diversification

We have so far discussed the occupational distribution of rural employment for sex. The occupational distribution of employment has changed during the period under study. Employment has risen in some occupations while it has declined in some others. We shall now measure the extent of variations in the occupational distribution of employment. For this we have estimated the Occupational Diversification Index (DI) based on Theil (1967) entropy measure which is defined as:

$DI = E/\log n$,
where $E = \Sigma\, e_i \log (1/e_i)$,
e_i : share of the i=th occupation in the total
n = number of occupations.

Here (a) $DI = 0$ for $E = 0$. It means that a particular occupation captures all workers: employment is not diversified occupationally. (b) $DI=1$, when $E=\log n$=maximum value. This happens when all workers are employed equally by different occupations: employment is completely diversified occupationally. So, $0 \leq DI \leq 1$, the higher (lower) the value of *DI*, the higher (lower) the degree of diversification of rural employment occupationally.

Estimates (Table 10.5) reveal that in rural India *DI* for male has increased from 0.481 in 1993-94 to 0.518 in 1999-2000 and 0.557 in 2004-05. The rising trend is also observed in case of female: 0.284, 0.333 and 0.351. *DI* for male exceeds that for female. Thus the occupational distribution of rural employment for male has been more and more diversified than that for female during the reform period.

Across the States we also observe that *DI* for male has increased in all the constituent States in India during 1993/94-2004/05. The rising tendency is also observed in case of female excepting Haryana, Karnataka and West Bengal. *DI* for male is lowest in M.P. (0.279 and 4.00) and highest in Kerala (0.709 and 0.822) during 1993/94-2004/05. Also, *DI* for female is lowest in H.P. (0.157 in 1993-94) and Maharashtra (0.209 in 2004-05) and highest in Kerala (0.609 and 0.622) during the period under study. Thus among the States Kerala has occupied more and more occupational diversification in both rural male and female employment. But the diversification for male is more than that for female during 1993/94-2004/05. This is also true in all the States excepting Punjab and West Bengal during 1993/94-1999/2000, and only Bihar in 2004/05.

Table 10.5 : Indices of Occupational Diversification in Rural India during 1993/94-2004/05

States	*1993-1994*		*1999-2000*		*2004-2005*	
	Male	*Female*	*Male*	*Female*	*Male*	*Female*
A.P	0.439	0.345	0.511	0.362	0.564	0.448
Assam	0.386	0.180	0.531	0.443	0.497	0.345
Bihar	0.352	0.233	0.398	0.294	0.433	0.453
Gujarat	0.482	0.267	0.489	0.244	0.519	0.318
Haryana	0.618	0.372	0.608	0.594	0.716	0.357
H.P.	0.594	0.157	0.724	0.184	0.734	0.243
Karnataka	0.397	0.335	0.408	0.296	0.416	0.273
Kerala	0.709	0.609	0.782	0.685	0.822	0.662
M.P.	0.279	0.184	0.263	0.217	0.400	0.307
Maharashtra	0.453	0.195	0.468	0.172	0.498	0.209
Orissa	0.402	0.375	0.418	0.397	0.561	0.481
Punjab	0.570	0.594	0.618	0.683	0.668	0.614
Rajasthan	0.522	0.238	0.543	0.260	0.617	0.286
T.N.	0.577	0.379	0.591	0.414	0.625	0.467
U.P.	0.504	0.264	0.490	0.349	0.551	0.368
W.B.	0.533	0.608	0.534	0.581	0.572	0.548
India	0.481	0.284	0.518	0.333	0.557	0.351

Source: NSSO, Different Round.

Growth Rate of Rural Non-Farm Employment

We have already discussed the changing structure of rural NFE in India and its constituent States during 1983-2004/05. Let us now examine the growth rate rural NFE in India and its constituent States during the pre-reform periods of 1983-1993/94 and the post-reform periods of 1993/94-2004/05.

Estimates (Table 10.6) reveal that the annual compound growth rate of rural NFE has varied in India and its constituent States during the pre-reform and the post-reform period. At the all-India level the growth rate of employment has increased from 1.46 per cent during the pre-reform period to 2 per cent during the post-reform periods for male. But for female the growth rate has decreased from 2 per cent to 0.62 per cent. Sex-wise analysis reveals that the growth rate of female employment is higher than that of male one during the pre-reform period while the reverse has happened during the post-reform period in India and its constituent States.

Table 10.6 : Annual Compound Growth Rate (%) of Rural Non-Farm Employment in India

States	1983-1993/94		1993/94-2004/05	
	Male	Female	Male	Female
A.P	0.32	-0.11	2.40	1.86
Assam	0.55	1.37	2.51	0.89
Bihar	-0.50	-2.59	2.47	5.16
Gujarat	2.95	4.46	0.58	0.57
Haryana	2.90	3.87	1.73	1.71
H.P.	2.29	4.87	2.50	5.26
Karnataka	0.89	3.12	0.55	-2.01
Kerala	0.72	4.66	2.32	1.12
M.P	0.49	2.51	3.19	5.26
Maharashtra	1.71	1.66	1.11	0.53
Orissa	-0.60	2.22	3.84	4.76
Punjab	1.39	14.24	2.70	3.10
Rajasthan	3.56	1.76	2.28	3.97
Tamil Nadu	1.22	1.85	0.99	1.41
U.P	1.25	0.68	2.74	4.04
W.B	2.58	7.19	0.02	-1.35
India	1.46	2.98	2.00	0.62

Source: NSSO Data.

Indian States have exhibited wide variations in the growth rate of NFE during the pre-reform and post-reform periods. The growth rate of male NFE has increased in almost all the States in India excepting Gujarat, Haryana, Karnataka, Maharashtra, Rajasthan, Tamil Nadu and West Bengal from pre-reform period to post-reform periods. While for female NFE the growth rate has also increased in almost all the States excepting Assam, Gujarat, Haryana, Karnataka, Kerala, Maharashtra, Punjab, Tamil Nadu and W.B. during the period under study. The growth rate is negative (i) in Bihar and Orissa for male during the pre-reform period, (ii) in A.P. and Bihar for female during the pre-reform period, and (iii) in Karnataka and West Bengal for female during the post-reform periods. However, the growth rate has varied from (a) -0.60 per cent in Orissa to 3.56 per cent in Rajasthan during the pre-reform periods and 0.02 per cent in West Bengal to 3.84 per cent in Orissa during the post-reform periods for male; (b) -2.59 per cent in Bihar to 14.24 per cent in Punjab during the pre-reform periods and -2.01 per cent in Karnataka during the post-reform periods for female. Also, compared to male employment growth rate, female employment growth rate is higher in the States of Assam, Gujarat, Haryana, Himachal Pradesh, Karnataka, Kerala, Madhya Pradesh, Orissa, Punjab, Tamil Nadu and West Bengal during the pre-reform periods, and (b) Bihar, H.P., M.P., Orissa, Rajasthan, T.N. and U.P during the post-reform periods. Thus we observe that the growth rate of female employment is higher than male one in most of the States during the reform periods.

Relationship between Rural Poverty and Rural Non-Farm Employment

In our earlier sections we have discussed the changing structure of rural poverty and rural NFE in India and its constituent States during the pre-reform and post-reform periods. Let us now examine the relationship between rural poverty and rural NFE during the period of study. Our hypothesis is that more the NFE of a State, less the poverty of that State. So there is an inverse relationship between them.

For this purpose we have taken 16 large States in India: Andhra Pradesh, Assam, Bihar, Gujarat, Haryana, H.P., Karnataka, Kerala, Maharashtra,, Orissa, Punjab, Rajasthan, T.N., Uttar Pradesh and West Bengal. States are ranked according to rural poverty and rural NFE (both male and female) in the years of 1983, 1993-94 and 2004-05. Rank correlation coefficient between these variables is estimated for these years. The coefficients are, in turn, statistically tested. Estimates (Table10.7) reveal that for male the coefficient is negative in all the years but statistically significant in the years of 1993-94 and 2004-05. But for female the coefficient is positive in 1983 and negative in the years of 1993-94 and 2004-05, not statistically significant. Thus during the globalization periods there has been a gradual fall in the percentage of the rural people below the poverty line and a gradual increase in the percentage of the people engaged in rural non-farm activities in the rural areas. This suggests that employment generation in the non-farm sector plays a significant role in the reduction of rural poverty in India.

Table 10.7 : Rank Correlation Coefficient between Rural Poverty and Rural Non-Farm Employment : (1983, 1993-94 and 2004-05)

Variables	*Rank Correlation Coefficient*		
	1983	*1993-94*	*2004-05*
Male Non-Farm	-0.271	-0.482*	-0.609*
Employment	(-1.049)	(-1.868)	(2.358)
Female Non-Farm	0.482	(-0.376)	-0.126
Employment	(1.867)	(-1.456)	(0.490)

Source: NSSO Data, Planning Commission Data.
Notes: *: significant at 10% level of significance. Figures in parentheses indicate z-values.

Concluding Remarks

Rural poverty line has increased in India and its constituent States during 1973-74 to 2004-05. At the all-India level rural poverty line in terms of monthly per capita consumption expenditure has increased from Rs. 49.63 in 1973-74 to Rs. 89.50 in 1983-84, to Rs. 205.84 in 1993-94 and to Rs. 356.30 in 2004-05. Poverty level has declined in India and its constituent States during the period under study. But the rate of declining has varied among the States over time during the pre-reform and the post reform periods. But the declining rate of poverty level is very high during the post-reform periods as compared to the pre-reform periods in rural India. Also, inter-State disparity arises in respect of Human Poverty Index during the period under study.

Irrespective of sex, the rural employment in Non-Farm Sector has increased all through in India at the cost of Farm Sector during 1983 to 2004-05. But male non-farm employment is more than female ones. Among the States only Kerala has enjoyed significantly the absorption of the rural non-farm employment for both male and female due to the generation of the non-farm activities during the reform periods of 1993-94 to 2004-05.

In rural India the occupational distribution of rural employment for male has been more and more diversified than that for female during 1993-94 to 2004-05. Among the States we also observe that Kerala has occupied more and more occupational diversification for male and female employment. But the diversification for male is more than that for female during the period under study. This is also true in all the States except Punjab and West Bengal during 1993-94 to 1999-00, and only Bihar in 2004-05.

The annual compound growth rate of rural NFE has varied in India and its constituent States during the pre-reform and the post-reform periods. At the all-India level the growth rate of employment has increased from 1.46 per cent during the pre-reform periods to 2 per cent during the post-reform periods for male. But for female the growth rate has decreased from 2 per cent to 0.62 per cent. Sex-wise analysis reveals that the growth rate of female employment is higher than that of male during the pre-reform periods while the reverse has happened during the post-reform periods in India and its constituent States.

Thus during the globalization periods there has been a gradual fall in the percentage of the rural people below the poverty line and a gradual increase in the percentage of the people engaged in rural non-farm activities in the rural areas. This suggests that employment generation in the non-farm sector plays a significant role in the reduction of rural poverty in India.

REFERENCES

Ahluwalia, M.S. (1978): "Rural Poverty and Agricultural Performance in India", *Journal of Development Studies.*

Datt, G. (1999): "Has Poverty Decline since Economic Reform?" *EPW,* Vol. 34, No. 50.

Datta, K.L. (2002): "On Measurement of Poverty", Occasional Papers, *State Institute of Panchayats and Rural Development,* Government of West Bengal, 2002.

Datt, R. (2001), "Economic Liberalization and its Implications for Employment in India", *The Indian Economic Association,* Conference Volume, Vellore.

Dutta, R. (1995), "New Economic Reform—Need for Some Rethinking", *The Indian Economic Journal,* Vol. 42, No. 3.

Economic Survey, Government of India, Various issues.

Koutsoyiannis, A. (1979): *Theory of Econometrics,* 2nd Edition.

Mohendra Dev, S. (1988): "Economic Reforms, Poverty, Income Distribution and Employment", *EPW,* Vol. XXXV, No. 10.

National Accounts Statistics of India: 1950-51 to 1995-96, *EPW,* Research Foundation.

NSSO (1997): *Employment and Unemployment in India 1993-94,* Government of India.

NSSO (2000): *Employment and Unemployment Situation in India 1999-2000,* Government of India.

NSSO (2003): *Household Consumer Expenditure and Employment-Unemployment Situation in India,* Government of India.

National Human Development Report (2002), Planning Commission, Government of India.

Nayyar, Rohini (1991): "Rural Poverty in India: An Inter-State Difference", *OUP,* Mumbai.

Pal, P.K. and Pal, D.P. (2000), "Structural Reforms, Development and Employment Projection in India" in P.D. Hajela and M.P. Goswami (eds.) *Economic Reforms and Employment,* Deep & Deep Publication Pvt. Ltd., New Delhi.

Pal, P.K. (2001), *Development Pattern in India: An Inter-State Analysis,* Occasional Papers, Department of Economics, Rabindra Bharati University, Vol. IX, 2001.

Pal, P.K. (2002), *Globalisation and Labour Utilization in Rural India: An Inter-State Analysis,* The Indian Economic Association Conference Volume, Trivandrum

Pal, P.K. (2004): *Poverty and Deprivation in India: An Inter-State Analysis,* Occasional Papers, Deptt. of Economics, Rabindra Bharati University, Vol. XII, 2004.

Pal, P.K. (2005), "Workforce in India: An Inter-State Analysis", *Artha Beekshan,* Vol. 13, No. 4, March, 2005

Pal, P.K. (2006), *Pattern and Growth of India's Economy since 1980s,* Occasional Papers, Department of Economics, Rabindra Bharati University, Vol. XIV, 2006.

Pal, P.K. *et al.* (1997), *The Indian Economy: A Structural Analysis: 1950-95* (Summary). The Indian Economic Association Conference Vol. 1997.

Panda, Manoj (2004-05): "Macro-economic Science: Growth and Equity Perspective" in Kirit. S. Parikh and R. Radhakrishna (eds.): *Indian Development Report, 2004-05,* Indira Gandhi Institute of Development Research, Oxford.

Rao, C.H.H (1996):"Economic Reforms, Agricultural Growth and Rural Poverty" *The Indian Economic Journal,* No. 4.

Shetty, S.L. (1978), "Structural Retrogression in the Indian Economy since the Mid-Sixties", *EPW,* Special No.

Sundaram, K. (2001), "Employment-Unemployment Situation in the Nineties: Some Results from NSS 55th Round Survey, *EPW,* Vol. 36, No. 11.

Theil, H. (1967): *Theory of Econometrics.*

Vaidyanathan, A. (1994), "Employment Situation: Some Emerging Perspective", *EPW,* Vol. 29, No. 50.

Vaidyanathan, A. (2001):"Poverty and Development Policy", *EPW,* Vol. XXXVI, No. 21.

Visaria, P. (1995), "Rural Non-Farm Employment in India: Trends and Issues for Research," *Indian Journal of Agricultural Economics,* Vol. L, No. 3 (Conf. Number).

www.indiabudget.com

11

Sericulture for Rural Development in Assam
Problems and Prospects

P.C. DUTTA and A. KHERKATARY

Introduction

Assam is a State of multi-cultural, multi-cultural mix bag. Majority of the population in the State live in rural areas and agriculture is the main source of their livelihood. But the very sector agriculture has not been able to alleviate poverty and solve the problem of unemployment. Under such circumstances agriculture needs to be diversified to other avenues, such as Sericulture.

Sericulture, the technique of silk production is an agro-based labour intensive cottage industry, providing gainful employment and generation of income to weaker sections in the rural and semi-urban areas. Since its discovery, the sericulture has been playing an important role in the socio-economic life of the people. Sericulture as a whole involves a series of economic activities, like cultivation of silk worm food plants, seed production, rearing of silk worm for production of cocoons from which the filament is derived. The post-cocoon activities involved reeling, spinning, twisting, dyeing, weaving, printing, finishing and processing of silk fabrics.

Assam has the distinction of producing all kinds of commercial silk namely, *eri, muga, mulberry* and *tassar*. Silk occupies a very important place in the life and culture of the people of Assam, regardless of community and caste. The climatic condition and natural environment in Assam is favourable for cultivation of host plants and rearing of silk worms. All types of silk yarn have to undergo through certain pre-processing operations before weaving. The availability of agricultural and semi-agricultural labours has widened the scope to develop this industry in the State. Sericulture is an enterprise, offers a tremendous opportunities for sustainable employment and economic growth of the State. Being a production and employment oriented industry; it can reshape the rural economy to a great extent.

The eri silkworm is the easiest of the four silk varieties to produce, as the worms are grown indoors and not very sensitive to temperature or humidity, unlike the muga worms. Humidity is especially a problem, and the monsoon limits muga production to two or three commercial harvests a year, whereas eri can be harvested up to six times. Eri is also genetically more diverse, and resistant to outbreaks of disease, whereas muga is not. Moreover, food plants for eri are abundantly available in the State, unlike muga which needs continuous nourishment to be provided by the growers. Although silk constitutes a negligible amount of the tune of 0.2 per cent of the total textile fabric production of the world (1995), it has been a luxury fabric through the ages.[1] Mukherjee, in the year 1919 (as quoted by Watt, 1893) advocated that "sericulture in India depends upon perfecting it as a peasant enterprise."

The industrialisation of urban areas created more employment opportunities and labour forces from rural areas started migration to urban areas for their better employment. It necessitated development of cottage and village industries for creating employment opportunities in the village itself. The performance of any economic policy should not be judged by looking merely at its national level performance. Its impact should also be evaluated by looking its performance at the sub-national or State-levels and in a backward State like Assam where more than 88 per cent of the population live in rural areas; an analysis of the impact of the policy on the rural development assumes an additional significance. In this context, a study meant to analyse the performance of income generating institutions in the rural areas of Assam will be an important issue to deal with (Dutta, 2008). Under these circumstances, sericulture plays a vital role in generating gainful employment opportunities to the villagers.

Sericulture industry offers many advantages like :

(i) helping to keep rural and semi-urban population employed and to prevent migration to the town;
(ii) securing gainful employment;
(iii) increasing income and reducing income inequality;
(iv) increasing the socio-economic status of women;
(v) requires little investment and infrastructure to start with;
(vi) providing raw materials for cottage and even large scale textile industries;
(vii) earning much needed foreign exchange; and
(viii) helps in maintaining ecological balance.

Literature Survey

Narasimhanna (1988) emphasised the need of quality silk worm seed cocoons and standards to be followed in production of silk worm egg on which stability and success of sericulture depends. He is of the opinion that sound seed is sound sericulture. Jolly (1987) dealt with important aspects such as sericulture and its economies, mulberry cultivation under rain-fed and irrigated conditions, silk worm seed production technology, silk worm diseases, pest and their control and silk reeling techniques. Thangavelu (1988) along with others dealt extensively with government activities. According to them one tree (food plant) can be utilized for two rearing in a year yielding 1000 number of cocoons and thus 1 kilogram of muga silk can be produced from 5000 cocoons which can be obtained from 5 trees only. Tendulkar (1999) discussed about the advantages of indoor rearing. He opines that through indoor rearing one can increase the production of cocoons by 40-50 per cent in comparison to outdoor rearing and hence one can earn more money practicing muga culture by applying the indoor rearing technique. Sarkar (1988) dealt with the problems of marketing and the various promotional steps undertaken by the Government. He showed that an eri rearer can earn a net income of Rs. 4100 from one hectare of castor plantation by way of sale of eri cocoons, castor seeds and eri pupae. Choudhury (1992) has dealt extensively with the origin of sericulture, its economies and sericultural technology. As the most labour intensive agro-industry covering host plant plantation and rearing and even the reeling stages, sericulture provides job to a large section of the agricultural population as a secondary occupation and generate income to supplement the income from agriculture (Baishya, 2005).

Sericulture has traditionally been carried out under a regulated trade regime with restrictions on imports, exports, movement of goods between States, and highly controlled markets. Since 2001, globalization has exposed the industry to several risk factors and has necessitated changed responses. However, infrastructure, rapid industrialization, loans for promoters of industries and encouragement to agro/food industries may be considered as some of the driving forces of the development of sericulture. The development is a complex process and has multi-dimensional structure depending upon its resources in general and infrastructural facilities in particular (Dutta 1996). The industry with its rural character fits well with modern concept of village organisation, where economics, technology and specialization based on small working units, community ownership and regional work places can be utilized with local labour and resources (Schumacher, 1977).

Objectives

Keeping in view the importance of the subject discussed above, the broad objectives of the present study aims at examining the problems and prospects of sericulture industry in the State of Assam. However, the main objectives of the present study may be classified under the following heads :

(i) To investigate the overall production and families engaged in sericulture industry in Assam.
(ii) To identify the problems and constraints associated with the industry.
(iii) To find out the prospects of sericulture in Assam.
(iv) To suggest some remedial measures for the development of this industry.

Methodology

The study is mainly based on the secondary sources of materials collected from different published and unpublished Government reports, journals, magazines, etc. The study is being concluded with some viable suggestions for future planning in regard for improvement of sericulture industry in the State.

Analysis and Discussion

Assam is well known for its sericulture and weaving practices. Since the time immemorial, sericulture activity is being practiced by the people in the State. According to Assam Government records, about 2,625 hectares of land are utilised for production of Muga Silk in the State. About 30,000 Assamese households are related with Muga Silk production. There are 15 Muga Silk Reeling units in Assam now.

The total area under the cultivation of food plants of Eri Silk Worm in the State counts for about 2,993 hectares. At present, the State has 21 Eri Silk Spinning training centres. There is also a sub-Silk Mill in Assam, located at Jagiroad. About 1.28 lakh families of Assam are engaged in rearing and production of Muga Silk.

Paat or mulberry silk also occupies an important place in Assam's Sericulture. About, 40,000 families of the State are engaged in the production of mulberry silk. The total area under the cultivation of food plants for the mulberry silk worms is about 2,300 hectares. In Assam, the mulberry silk worm culture is practiced on a large scale in the districts of Upper

Assam. Lakhimpur, Sibsagar, Dibrugarh and Jorhat districts are the important producers of mulberry silk. In order to produce more and more mulberry silk worm seeds, the State Sericulture Department has also organised a systematic "Seed Organisation Programme". A cold storage plant has also been set up in the Kamrup District of Assam for the preservation of mulberry silk worm seeds.

The Table 11.1 gives a comparative picture in production among some countries of the world. China occupies the first position with the production of 1,02,560 tonnes, followed by India (16500 tonnes) and Brazil (1512 tonnes). A minute look at the Table 11.1, it can be noted that India produces only 13 per cent in comparison to China. Sericulture has also been attempted in the United States, but these endeavours have been sporadic and largely unsuccessful.

Table 11.1 : Production from Sericulture Industry

Country	*Production (in Tonnes)*
China	102560
India	16500
Japan	287
Brazil	1512
Korea Republic	150
Uzbekistan	950
Thailand	1420
Vietnam	750
Others	1500

Table 11.2 shows the production of Mulberry and Vanya Raw Silk in different states of India. A close look at the Table 11.2, it is observed that Karnataka (48.37 per cent) occupies the first position in the production of mulberry raw silk, followed by Andhra Pradesh (34.80 per cent) and West Bengal (10.05 per cent). However, Assam contributes only 0.05 per cent.

In case of Tasar Raw Silk, Jharkhand is on the top sharing 31.17 per cent of the total production in India, followed by Chhattisgarh (29.22 per cent) and West Bengal (11.04 per cent).

In case of Eri production, Assam occupies first position sharing 51.66 per cent followed by Meghalaya (29.42 per cent) and Manipur (16.3 per cent).

Table 11.2 : State-wise Mulberry and Vanya Raw Silk Production in 2005-06 (Unit: Metric tonnes)

		Vanya Silk			*Total*
States	*Mulberry*	*Tasar*	*Eri*	*Muga*	
Andhra Pradesh	5375	20	27	—	5422
Assam	8		745	104	857
Arunachal Pradesh	1	neg.	10	0.24	11
Bihar	3	14	2.8	—	18
Chhattisgarh	3	90	2	—	96
Himachal Pradesh	16	—	—	—	16
Haryana	—	—	—	—	—
Jammu & Kashmir	95	—	—	—	95
Jharkhand	1	96	neg.	—	97
Karnataka	7471	—	—	—	7471
Kerala	12	—	—	—	12
Madhya Pradesh	23	16	—	—	39
Maharashtra	44	6	—	—	50
Manipur	48	3	235	0.06	286
Mizoram	6	neg.	3.2	0.07	9
Meghalaya	3	—	280	5.4	288
Nagaland	1	neg.	130	0.18	131
Orissa	2	21	2	—	25
Punjab	4	—	—	—	4
Rajasthan	0	—	—	—	—
Sikkim	—	—	—	—	—
Tamil Nadu	739	—	neg.	—	739
Tripura	4	—	—	—	4
Uttar Pradesh	19	3	0.5	—	24
Uttranchal	14	5	neg.	neg.	19
West Bengal	1552	34	4	0.2	1591
Total	15445	308	1442	110	17305

It is remarkable to note that in the production of muga silk, the State of Assam contributes 94.55 per cent followed by Meghalaya (4.91 per cent)

The Indian Silk Export Promotion Council (ISEPC) has asked the Union Government to include sericulture industry under Visesh Krishi and Gram Udyog Yojana (VKGUY) scheme that promotes export of agricultural products and forest-based products. China is looking at collaborations with India in certain areas of sericulture industry. However, India already has collaborations with Japan and has developed certain bivoltine races from Japanese silk races. As a majority of sericulture industry in India is covered in tropical States, original races from temperate climate of Japan are trivialized before being released into field for bivoltine silk production in India.

Some of the north-eastern States like Assam, Manipur, Meghalaya, Tripura and Mizoram have accorded a fairly high priority to sericulture. In Tripura, around 4,500 beneficiaries are directly involved in the subsidiary occupation further improving their socio-economic status.

Assam has virtual monopoly in the production of muga silk and in the production of eri silk it has a major share in the total production of the country. Tassar silk is a newly introduced variety in Assam and was undertaken by the Government of Assam in Karbi Anglong and North Cachar Hills district. In the North Cachar district, one experimental centre was set up in 1972 and subsequently 4 and 1 in North Cachar and the Karbi Anglong district or simply 5 seed centres under different nomenclatures were set up.

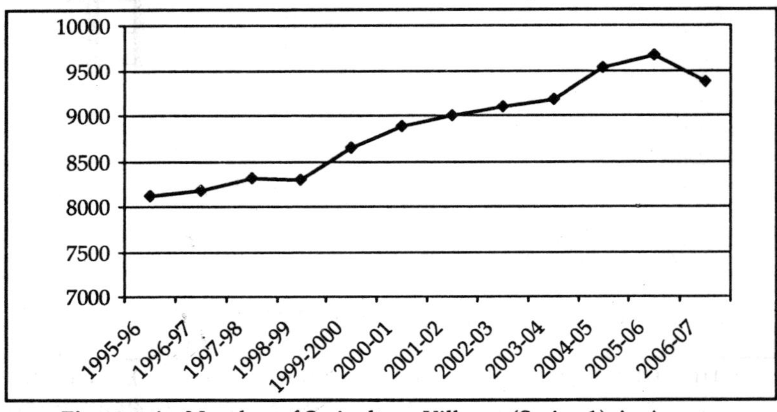

Fig 11.1-A : Number of Sericulture Villages (Series-1), in Assam, 1995-96 to 2006-07

Source: Statistical Hand Book, Assam, Various Issues.

In 1995-96, the State had 8,127 sericulture villages under the supervision of the State Directorate of Sericulture and in 2006-07, the number increased to 9,373 showing an increase of 13 per cent during the period considered (Fig. 11.1-A)

Fig 11.1-A shows number of sericulture villages in Assam over the period 1995-96 to 2006-07. It is observed that the number of sericulture villages shows an increasing trend excluding the years 1998-99 and 2006-07. It is further observed that over the period under consideration, the number of villages increased by 13 per cent.

Fig 11.1-B shows that the total number of families engaged in sericulture were 1,28,186 in Eri, 29,409 in Muga and 38,822 in Mulberry in 1995-96. The respective numbers in the year 2006-07 were 1,34,597, 27,063 and 29,775 showing 4.8 per cent increase in eri, 8 per cent decrease in muga and 23 per cent decrease in Mulberry.

A close look at the figures (11.1-A and 11.1-B) , it is interesting to note that though the number of sericulture villages shows an increasing trend, the number of families engaged in eri, muga and mulberry culture shows a fluctuating trend over the period considered. It is observed that the percentage of the number of families engaged in Eri culture

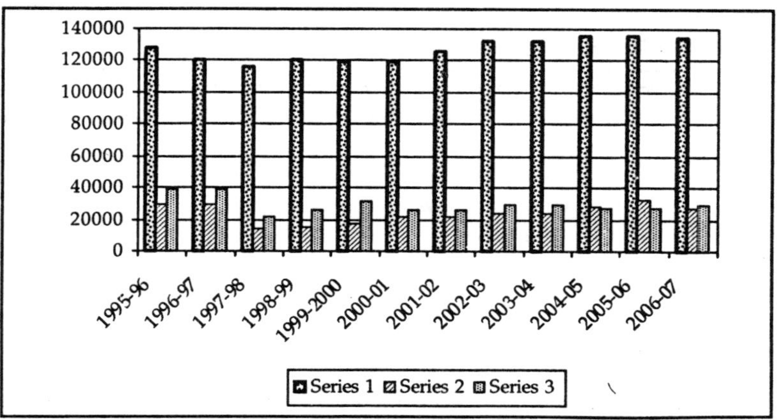

Fig: 11.1-B: Number of Families engaged in Eri (Series-1), Muga (Series-2) and Mulberry (Series-3) in Assam, 1995-96 to 2006-07

Source: Statistical Hand Book, Assam, Various Issues.

has decreased in the years 1999-2000, 2000-01, 2006-07, the percentage of families in case of muga has decreased in the years 1997-98 and 2006-07 and in case of mulberry the respective years are 1997-98, 2000-01, 2001-02, 2004-05.

The figure 11.2-A shows the total number of employment in sericulture (eri, muga and mulberry) over the period 1995-96 to 2006-07. It is clear from the table that the total number of families decreased with the tune of 2.54 per cent over the period considered. It is to be pointed that during the year 1997-98, the total employment decreased to 152978 which is 18.78 per cent over the previous year. However, after 1997-98, the total employment shows an increasing trend.

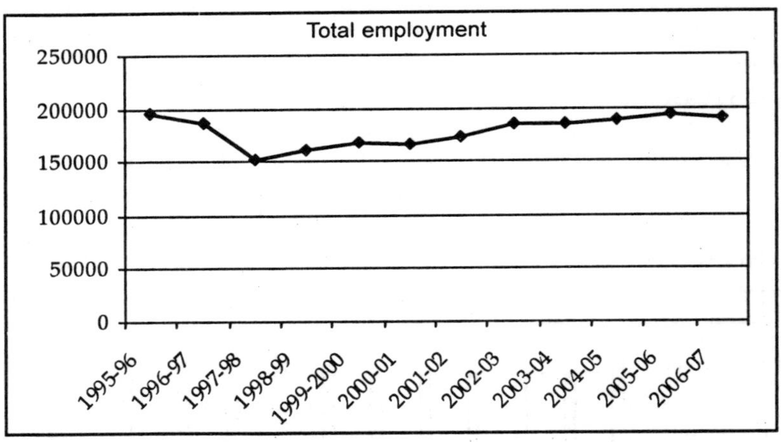

Fig. 11.2-A: Total Employment in Sericulture (Eri, Muga and Mulberry)

Source: Statistical Hand Book, Assam, Various Issues.

Fig.11.2-B shows the share of employment (in percentages) in eri, muga and mulberry culture in respect to the total employment in sericulture. It is evident from the above diagram that the employment generation in case of eri culture varies between 63.77 per cent to 76.19 per cent of the total employment in this industry showing the highest percentage in the year 1997-98 and the lowest in the year 1996-97. For muga, it varies between 9.22 per cent to 16.81 per cent and that of mulberry culture, the variation ranges from 13.89 to 20.61 per cent.

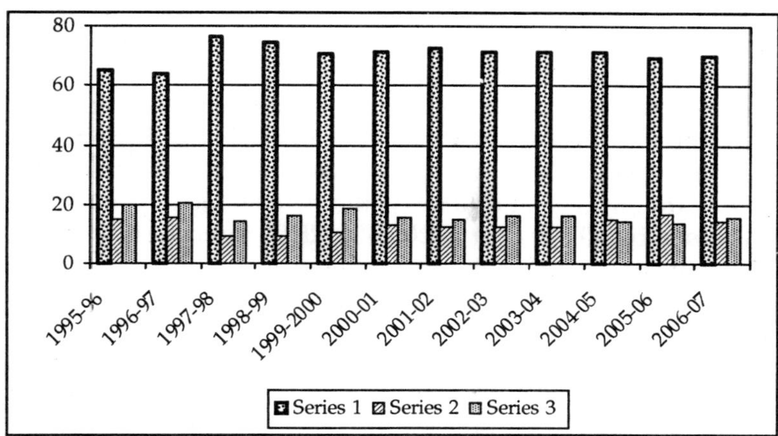

Fig. 11.2-B: Percentage of Employment in Eri (Series 1), Muga (Series2) and Mulberry (Series 3) over the period 1995-96 to 2007-08

Source: Statistical Hand Book, Assam, Various Issues.

A minute look at the Figure 11.3, it is observed that the share of eri, muga and mulberry silk yarn to the total silk yarn

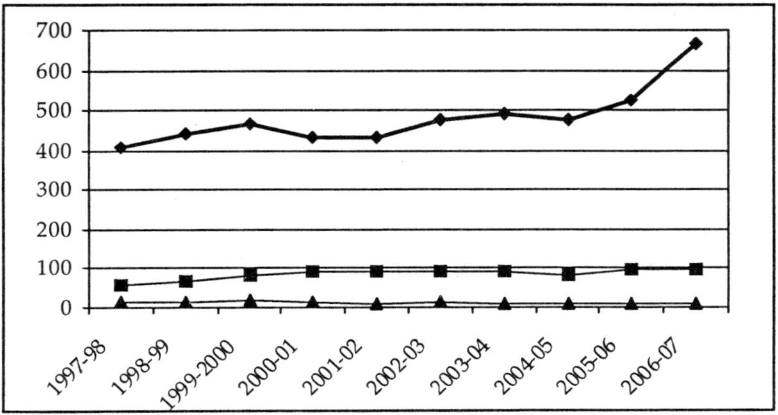

Fig 11.3: Production of Eri (Series 1), Muga (Series 2) and Mulberry (Series 3) Silk Yarn (in Million tonnes) in Assam, 1997-98 to 2006-07

Source: Statistical Hand Book, Assam, Various Issues.

varies 79.52 per cent to 86.08 per cent, 12.28 per cent to 17.38 per cent and 1.18 per cent to 3.21 per cent respectively over the period 1997-98 to 2006-07. It is to be noted here that the percentage of production in case of eri-silk yarn decreased by 7.48 per cent in 2000-01 and 3.07 per cent in 2004-05 over the previous years. It is also to be noted that in case of muga silk yarn, the production decreased by 2.8 per cent in 2001-02 and 14.1 per cent in 2004-05 over the previous years. It is remarkable to note that in case of mulberry, the percentage of production decreased by 40 per cent in 2003-04, 28.95 per cent in 2001-02, 23.59 per cent in 2006-07 and 14.33 per cent in 2004-05 over the previous years.

Thus it is to be noted here that the contribution of eri is the highest amongst the total silk yarn production in the State.

Figure 11.4-A shows the picture drawn on the basis of production statistics (Target and Achievement) of eri cut cocoon of Assam for a period of 21 years data starting from 1985 to 2006. It is observed from the Figure 11.4-A that the achievement in eri cut cocoon production in Assam during 1985-1995 was more or less satisfactory according to the targeted amount with only exception in the year 1992-93. But the production could not achieve the targeted amount during the period 1995-2006. However, the production of Eri increased from 2.95 lakh Kg., in 1985 to 9.31 lakh Kg. in 2006 showing an upward trend during the period under consideration.

Ericulture *i.e.*, rearing of eri cocoon and spinning as well as weaving of endi clothes has been an integral part of the rural economic activities especially of the rural women in Assam. Ericulture plays an important role in reducing the hardship by improving economic condition and standard of living of the rearing and weaving families.

Production (in lakh Kg.) statistics (Target and Achievement) of muga for the period of 1985-2006 is being shown in Fig. 11.4-B. A close look at the figure, it is observed that the production achieved the targeted level during the period of 1985-88 and 1990-92 only. It is important to note that only in the period 1990-91, the achievement level was much above the targeted level but after 1992 it shows a declining trend till 2006. However, during the period under consideration, the production of muga increased from 0.521 lakh Kg. to 0.985 lakh Kg. showing an increase of 89.06 per cent.

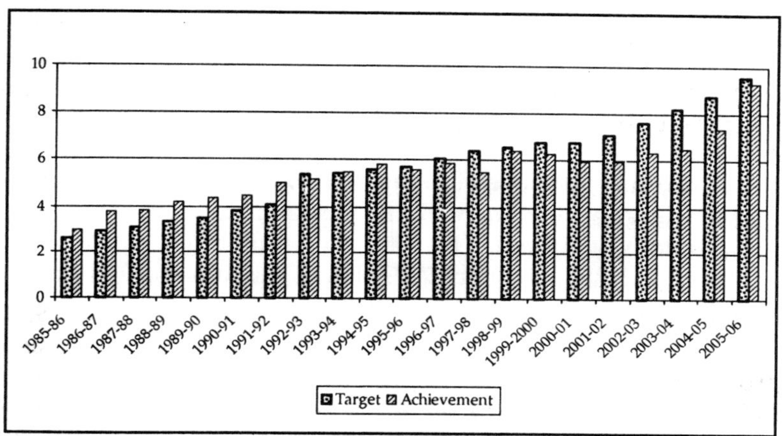

Fig. 11.4-A : Production of Eri Cut Cocoon (in lakh Kg,)

Source: Directorate of Sericulture, Govt. of Assam.

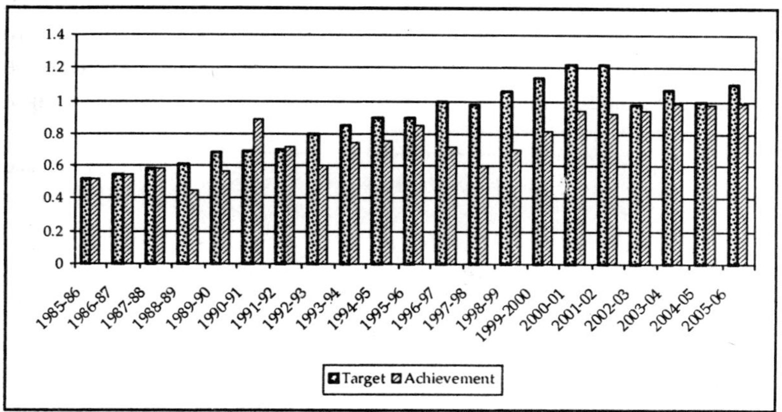

Fig. 11.4-B : Production of Muga (in lakh Kg.)

Source: Directorate of Sericulture, Govt. of Assam.

The Fig. 11.4-C shows the graph of production of Mulberry (In lakh Kg,) in the State of Assam for a period of 21 years (1985-2006). It is important to note that over the period of 21 years, the production decreased from 0.152 lakh Kgs. to 0.0645 lakh Kg. with highest production occurred in the year 1993-94 (0.277 lakh Kg.). The graph shows the fact that production could not touch the targeted amount during the period under consideration. Thus in case of mulberry, achievement in raw silk production is totally failed to reach the target and this failure was more stringent from 1996-97 onwards.

In 2006-07 the State of Assam had 9,373 sericulture villages under the supervision of State Directorate of Sericulture, Government of Assam. The total area under silk worm food plants were 7,382 ha. of eri, 7,299 ha. of muga and 3,711 ha. of mulberry. The number of families engaged in sericulture were 1,34,597 in eri, 27,063 in muga and 29,775 in mulberry and the production of silk yarn from the sericulture villages were 664.97 MT of eri, 98.59 MT of muga and 9.10 MT of mulberry.

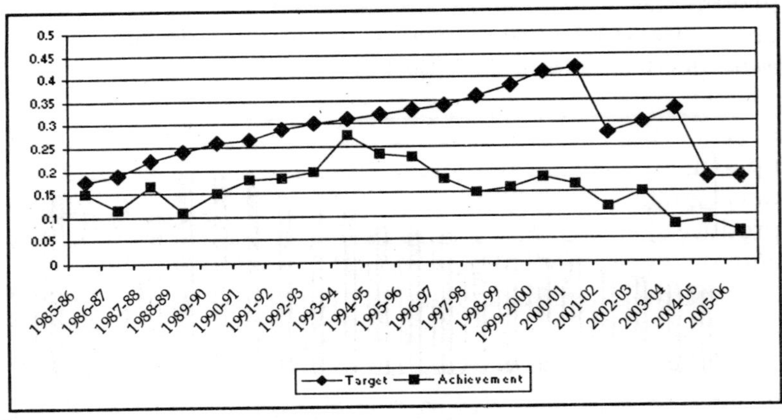

Fig. 11.4-C: Production of Mulberry (in lakh Kg.)

Source: Statistical Hand Book, Assam, Various Issues.

Research findings have shown that significant involvement of women is observed in silk rearing and farming activities—in tending mulberry plants, feeding silk worms and removing waste. Poverty programmes based on data that do not adequately capture the extent of women's work in sericulture.

Problems and Constraints

The main weakness of mulberry is related to a poor database, diverse range of practices leading to a divergence in productivity and quality. Generally, there is weak accent on quality consistency in production, poor transfer of technology to the decentralized sector both due to poor technology absorption and poor/inadequate follow-up on laboratory findings; poor market linkages. Unlike mulberry silk production, non-mulberry silk production is unsteady and fluctuates from year to year. The central silk board has not given enough attention to their R&D and extension activities in the area of non-mulberry sericulture inspite of its potential to directly help the poor. Presently, muga and eri silks are produced mostly for self-consumption. But with their uniqueness to India, they have great potential for value-added exports.

Due to several problems and constraints faced by the sericulturists in the State, this industry has not been developed up to the satisfaction although there is huge potentiality for its development. As a result, this industry has not been able to produce the required silk yarn. The eri sector has not been endowed with viability under the present level of technology. Despite the potential, this industry has lost its pre-eminent position as silk producer and sericulture is now stagnant. Both sericulture and silk weaving are age-old avocations. Natural disasters and a number of factors stand on the way for a harmonious growth of both. Oak *tassar* culture has not yet been properly adopted, as people are new to this culture and economies are yet to be established. Also lack of disease monitoring and of control measures is noticed.

Many institutional, non-institutional problems and technological problems which stand as barriers in the development of this industry may be outlined as follows :

1. There is absence of systematic cultivation of silk worm food plants for speedy supply of leaves.
2. Lack of sufficient grainages for production of silk worm seeds as required by the rearers in each district of the

State resulting to depend on other districts and sometimes they find it difficult to get seeds in sufficient quantity and in time.

3. Frequent occurrence of flood in the State always lead to huge losses to the sericulturists.
4. Non-availability of Disease Free Laying (DFL) leads to production of low quality cocoons.
5. There is unorganized silk yarn market and lack of assured market facilities for the end product *i.e.* 'Silk'.
6. The use of insecticide and pesticide in the tea gardens severely effect during the rearing of silk worms.
7. Lack of exposure to the farmers to modern rearing technologies.
8. Majority of technical buildings, rearing houses and staff quarters are found collapsed due to their non-renovation. The fencing around the sericultural farm are being damaged resulting hardship in the maintenance and protection of these farms.
9. Due to transport and communication bottlenecks, the rearers and reelers are unable to supply their production to the marketing centres and outside the region.
10. The Government does not publish the price list of cocoons regularly.
11. Non-availability and insufficient credit facilities compelled the sericulturists to depend on village money-lenders and middlemen who exploit them.
12. Lack of awareness about its commercial exploitation.
13. Age-old method of reeling and spinning.
14. Lack of research and development in the State.
15. Difficulties in absorption of funds is a greater impediment than the availability of resources, funds are not being utilized due to a number of reasons, which include delay in submission of proposals, non-release of the State Government's share in case of Centrally Sponsored Scheme and non-submission of utilization certificates etc.

Prospects

India is the second largest producer of silk, contributing to about 13 per cent to the world production. USA, Britain, and Germany are the major consumers of India's silk. Owing to heavy internal consumption, Japan has become an importer of silk, thus widening the gap between production and demand. What is, however, more noteworthy is the fact that India's requirement of raw silk is much higher than its current production at present. Thus, there is considerable scope for stepping up production of raw silk in the country, overcome the persistent conflict of interest between exporters of silk products and producers of raw silk.

It is needless to mention that there is tremendous scope of prospects for all-round development and improvement of sericulture industry in the State of Assam due to the following reasons :

- Conducive and suitable climate for sericulture.
- Scope for extension for the growth of host plants.
- Availability of agricultural and semi-agricultural labours.

However, adequate and strategic measures may be adopted to overcome the existing problems and constraints in this industry.

1. Imparting training and skill upgradation for rural farmers, particularly in the pre- and post-cocoon technologies.
2. Providing infrastructural facilities like modern reeling/ spinning machines and supply of DFLs.
3. Development of organized and co-operative market facilities for marketing their products.
4. Provision for cheap and available credit facilities to the sericulturists.
5. Renovation of the existing technical buildings, rearing houses and provision of research and development.

6. Need for full fledged silk worm seed production farms.
7. Diversification of sericultural products.

Action taken up by the Government

In the backdrop of growing unemployment and slow industrialisation, developmental strategies are increasingly focusing on this traditional, income earning cottage activity in the State. Efforts are now under way to transform sericulture from a household occupation into a vibrant commercial activity.

The Central Silk Board (CSB) is supplementing the efforts of the State Government by implementing a number of schemes which include distribution of high yielding varieties of mulberry at subsidized rates, supply of quality silkworm seeds to sericulturists, through a network of seed production centres and providing development and extension support through research and extension units. Besides post-cocoon harvest technology, namely silk reeling, twisting, weaving, dyeing, printing, processing and finishing of silk fabrics are receiving attention.

The Central Silk Board (CSB) has evolved a standardized package of practices for increasing productivity by upgrading technology. However, this intermediate technology is yet to reach all farmers and reelers.

Fortunately, the Department of Sericulture, Assam is having an adequate infrastructural network for providing extension services to the farmers. During the last few years it could be possible to percolate some of the packages of practices developed by the CSB through extension machineries under Catalytic Development Programme (CDP), United Nations Development Programme (UNDP), Sonali Suta Prakalpa etc. The overall outcome of these schemes although have been encouraging but they have to go a long way for achieving their goals.

During the Ninth Plan the Directorate of Sericulture, Assam, has implemented various schemes under the State plan for development and expansion of sericulture in the State. Some of the major schemes were :

- Development and expansion of Eri silk, Muga silk, Mulberry silk and Tassar silk.
- Schemes for training in sericulture.
- Schemes for cocoon marketing and silk growers cooperative.

Moreover, during the Ninth Five Year Plan and Tenth Five Year Plan, thrust has been given on the following points :

1. To increase systematic plantation of silkworm food plants in both government and private sector.
2. To produce and supply disease free and healthy silk worm seeds to the rearers.
3. Organization of entrepreneurs for establishment for reeling/spinning units and to create employment avenues in private sector.

North-Eastern Action Plan was launched in the year 1996 by the Central Silk Board through the State Department with an aim to familiarise the traditional and non-traditional pockets with the new technique of silkworm rearing in Bivoltine races and cultivation of improved variety mulberry and soil management.

According to the final report of a Marketing Study of muga and eri silk industry in Assam, conducted by Central Silk Board (CSB) under the Ministry of Textiles, the State has about 3000 commercial looms engaged in muga fabric production, which is about 12 per cent of the total silk looms. The report prepared in February 2008 states that despite the shortage of yarn, the muga weaving ventures is increasing due to entrepreneurship development programme and income generation. It also reveals that considering the present production of yarn and its utilization, there is shortage of about 40-50 MT (metric tonnes) of yarns.

The Golden Muga silk, despite being the pride of Assam is adulterated to a large extent due to high demand and shortage of sufficient silk yarn. The adulteration is done by mixing muga yarn with local and Chinese tassar silk or tassar-like silk polyester during weaving, thereby camouflaging the products as that of original muga. Similar adulteration also takes place with eri silk products.

To check such illicit practices and to protect the purity of the silk, the Central Silk Board under the Ministry of Textiles has introduced the Silk Mark for pure silk products, since 2005 separately for eri and muga weaving products. Mamata Sharma, a senior official of the CSB says that there are around 80 authorised users of the Silk Mark in the north-eastern States. Central Silk Board (CSB), the apex body of the Indian Silk Industry, has decided to give a facelift to eri silk, the only silk that does not require killing of the silkworms to get the fibre. Muga silk has also received official 'Geographical Indication' status during the year 2007 under the Geographical Indications of Goods (Registration and Protection) Act, 1999; it is first commodity from Assam to get this protection against fake substitutes. This will definitely provide better legal protection to this golden yarn, its fabrics and the people connected with their production.

Recently Government of Assam has also introduced the Oak Tassar in Assam. Hill areas of Assam are suitable for cultivation of Oak Tassar, as Oak trees grows in abundance there. In the two hill districts of Assam—Karbi Anglong and North Cachar, five Tassar Centres have been set up for the production of seeds and rearing of Oak Tassar.

UNDP Programme

For the development of non-mulberry silk in the State project under the UNDP has been implemented for a period of 4 years starting from 1999 to 2003 with an approved outlay of Rs. 1107.96 lakh of which UNDP's share is Rs. 298.31 lakh and beneficiaries share is Rs. 809.65 lakh. The project has been implemented through non-government organisation/societies in 9 districts for production of 11.27 MT of Muga raw silk, 8.9 MT of muga spun yarn and 152.86 MT of Eri spun yarn.

Conclusion and Suggestions

To conclude, it can be considered that there is high potential and suitable environment for the development of this industry. It is the time on the part of the Governments both Central and State and the concerned departments to prepare comprehensive schemes and programmes so that it can attain the commercial viability at its earliest and become a source of socio-economic development in the rural areas of the State. The necessary budget allotment for the sericulture industry has to be increased. There is an urgent need to make concerted effort to enhance the utilization of Plan funds for the rapid development of this industry. The various schemes sponsored and financed by the Central Silk Board (CSB) need also be implemented properly.

Today the Indian Silk Industry is already a major player in the global scenario and the growth prospects for the industry seem to be bullish. The North-Eastern Council should take necessary steps for its all-round development.

To improve the quality of muga and eri silk yarn, the existing reeling and spinning machines are to be improved or replaced by modern efficient machines available in other advanced states and countries. The introduction of such improved modern machines will help in producing quality, standardized twisted silk yarns for production of superior quality silk clothes. This improved reeling and spinning machineries may be popularized by proper demonstration in the fields and among silk rearers of the State.

The Directorate of Sericulture should motivate more and more farmers by imparting necessary training to them for taking up all sericultural activities from silkworm rearing to silk yarn production. Sericulture is one of such industries where majority of workers are women. Women in rural areas consider it as one of their important source of livelihood. Thus special care and facilities should be extended to the women by the concerned departments so that they would encourage and come forward for the actual development of this industry.

Over and above people's active participation and co-operation in implementing all the projects and schemes is the pre requisite in this regard, and by which the vision of the State Sericulture Department "Transforming of rural economy of Assam through leadership in the International Silk Market" will come up into a reality.

NOTE

1. CSB, *Compendium of Statistics of Silk Industry*, 1999, Table-1.

REFERENCES

Baishya, P (2005): *The Silk Industry of Assam*, Spectrum Publications, Delhi.

Choudhury, S.N. (1992): *Silk and Sericulture*, Directorate of Sericulture, Government of Assam.

Dutta P.C. (1996): "Quality Variation of Some Food Items of Consumption in North-Eastern Region (NER) India", *IJRS*, Vol. 28, No. (1).

Dutta, P.C. (2008): *Society, Culture and Development in NE India: Essays in Memory of Dr. Basudev Datta Ray*, in A. Ray and S.B. Chakrabarty (eds.), Concept Publishing House, New Delhi.

Government of Assam; *Economic Survey Assam : 2002-03, 2003-04, 2006-07 and 2007-08.*

Government of Assam: *Statistical Hand Book, Assam : 2005, 2006 and 2007.*

Jolly, Manjeet, S. (1987): "Sericulture and its Economics" in Jolly, Manjeet, S. (ed.) *Appropriate Sericulture Techniques*, International Centre for Training and Research in Tropical Sericulture, Central Sericulture Research Institute, Mysore.

Mukherjee, N.G. (1919): *Hand Book of Sericulture*, Government Book Depot, Calcutta.

Nagendran, R. and K. Joseph (2007): *Networking of Sericulture Industries in Urban-Semi-Rural Area Near Hosur/Bangalore, India*, Project Report, Centre for Environmental Studies, Anna University, Chennai.

Narasimhanna, M.N. (1988): *Manual on Silk Worm Egg Production*, CSB, Bangalore.

Sarkar, D.C. (1988): *Eri Culture in India*, Central Silk Board, Bangalore.

Schumachaer, E.F (1977): *Small is Beautiful*, Radhakrishnan, New Delhi.

Thangavelu, K., *et al.* (1988): *Hand Book of Muga Culture*, CSB, Bangalore.

12

Agriculture and Forestry
A Road Map to Rural Development

K.C. KABRA and R.K.P.G. SINGHA

Introduction

The still increasing order of rural-urban migration at the face of visibly minimal diffusion of non-agricultural activities in rural areas *prima facie* indicates a high order of regional imbalance if not underdevelopment in absolute sense. Suggestion as emerged in economic literature urges upon entrepreneurship development process so as to generate able entrepreneurs who, by acting as agents of change, can bring about economic enterprises to create employment opportunities, enhance income, fill the market gaps, and ultimately foster the process of development in rural areas. While giving a pragmatic approach to the above process, there is a need to visualize the opportunities available in the rural environment and develop the required entrepreneurial knowledge, skills, attitude in order to actualize those opportunities in the interest of the rural masses. This chapter in the aforesaid background makes an attempt to identify the opportunities of self-employment available to educated youths (graduates and post-graduates of rural development) in and around rural areas where instead of seeking jobs, they can start and operate small scale business enterprise in agriculture and forestry. For better and clearer understanding, this chapter is concentrated mainly to Mizoram, the easternmost State of the country.

Entrepreneurship

Collectively, entrepreneurship is governed by four dominant forces such as: (1) The Socio-Sphere System, (2) The Support System, (3) The Resource System, and (4) Self-Sphere System. These four systems are inter-linked, constantly interacting and adjusting with each other. Any attempt to effect change in one system neglecting the other is bound to fail and distorts the very objective of promoting entrepreneurship. Entrepreneurship is a phenomenon performed by an entrepreneur that is a person who starts, operates, organizes and manages a business venture (undertaking) assuming the risk in anticipation of profit. In this process, an entrepreneur need to possess: ability to recognise avenues and opportunities, technical ability, motivation, creativity and originality in generating new business ideas in the form of new products or services, new markets, new methods, new organizations, and new mix of inputs, critical thinking, knowledge about products and markets, analytical ability from new perspectives, communication skills, high dedication for long hours working with less stress, marshalling and commitment towards resources and aptitude for human relations.

Agricultural entrepreneur is an agri-skilled person who implements, operates and assumes financial risks in farming activities with modern business outlook like Agro-processing, Raising Livestock, Dairy, Piggery, Poultry, etc.

Agri-Business Centre

Any venture or business can be made successful if the operator or entrepreneur is perfect. Agriculture Graduates can undertake business ventures like (a) Rural Marketing Dealership of farm Inputs and Outputs, (b) Retail Marketing Outlets for Processed Agro-products, (c) Custom Hiring, Repairs and Maintenance of Agricultural Implements and Machinery including Micro-irrigation Systems (sprinkler and drip), (d) Seed Processing Services, (e) Facilitation of Agricultural Insurance through Agency Service, (f) Livestock

Health Cover Services through Veterinary Dispensaries, Frozen Semen Banks and Liquid Nitrogen Supply, (g) Access to various agriculture related portals through setting up of Information Technology Kiosks, (h) Feed Processing and Testing Units, (i) Post-harvest Management Services of Value Addition like Processing, Standardization, Grading, and Packaging, (j) Metallic/Non-Metallic Storage Godowns including Cold Chain, (k) Production of Bio-fertilizers, Bio-pesticides, Bio-control agents by setting up of Vermi-culture Units, etc.

Agri-Plant Clinics

A correct diagnosis about plant health can save money, time and avoid the use of toxic chemicals. A plant clinic provides analysis of plant materials and soil for insect and nematode pests, bacterial, fungal and viral pathogens and recommends appropriate control measures. It facilitates nutrient analysis of soils, fertilizers, manure and growing media as also on-site inspection and diagnosis of plant health problems at ground location. Agriculture Graduates can offer their professional extension services to farmers in the form of providing: (a) extension consultancy services, (b) consultancy services on soil fertility, chemical and physical soil properties essentially needed for plant growth, (c) consultation and training on plant protection service (pest surveillance, diagnostic and control service including Integrated Pest Management and Pesticide Applications), (d) laboratory and field evaluations on pest control efficacy for phyto-chemicals and pesticides, (e) input testing laboratory services for testing and improvement of soil and water quality, (f) Micro-propagation through Plant Tissue Culture Labs. and Hardening Units, etc.

To make clinic more attractive, some special features can be added like the centre serves as a valuable resource for many different groups such as: (a) Home Gardeners, (b) Plant Lovers, (c) Golf Courses, (d) Garden Societies and Clubs, (e) Property Management Corporations, (f) Hydroponics, Orchid Vegetable and Ornamental Plant Farms, (g) Agri-chemical Companies,

(h) Landscape Companies and Maintenance Contractors,
(i) Plant and Plant Product Traders, Importers and Exporters.

Local Resource-based Industries

Industrialization is based on either availability of raw materials or market for finished goods. Mizoram has a market for many things but non-availability of raw materials puts barriers in the production. A better option in industrialization is, therefore, to concentrate on the development of locally available raw materials-based industries. Among these, bamboo-based industries, timber-based industries, medicinal plant-based industries, agro-horticulture and agro-based industries such as food and fruit processing, animal feed, tea, coffee, rubber and tung plantations, orchid cultivation, floriculture based industries, etc. are prominent. According to Forest Survey of India (State of Forest Report, 2001), Mizoram with forest cover of 82.98 per cent State's geographical area ranked third[1], after Lakshadweep (89.91 per cent) and Andaman & Nicobar (84.01 per cent) in India. In terms of economic value of goods (*i.e.* timber, fuelwood, etc.) and service (income and employment) annual contribution of forest is estimated at Rs.100 crore.[2] Considering the local resource base the branch SISI, Aizawl through Industrial Potential Survey, 1996 had identified industries having scope in Mizoram. This included[3] wooden furnitures, wooden handicrafts, wooden doors and windows, wooden rulers, graduated scale, handmade pencils, cane furniture, bamboo craft, baskets, wooden packing boxes, etc., tent poles, bamboo ladders, agarbatti sticks, artistic photo frames, trays etc., umbrella handles, walking sticks, canes for police, handles for sports goods, ginger processing, and de-hydration, potato chips, mushroom processing, fruit juice, jams, jellies, banana chips and processing, corn flakes, papaya processing, starch from tapioca, oils extraction, meat, fishes, vegetables and fruits, animal, cattle and poultry feed, handmade paper from wooden waste, agro waste, plastic recycling, waste particle board from wooden shavings, fuel briquettes from charcoal dust, wooden waste country type bricks and clay tiles. A brief description of some of these industries is given here.

(1) **Coffee Plantation :** In Mizoram, coffee is cultivated without any core and maintenance, with practically no technical inputs being applied. The Coffee Board has identified 4,000 hectares of land as potential for coffee cultivation, while presently 300 hectares of land only is being used. According to MS Swaminathan Report about 10,000 hectares may be used for coffee plantation in seven blocks. Black pepper and orange may be sown as companion crops. This source may earn an income of Rs. 15,000 per hectare from fourth year that may be raised to Rs. 88,000 from eighth year. It may promote allied services of pulping machines and drying yards. It is important to note that the Coffee Board is presently meeting 50 per cent of the cost of coffee cultivation. Further, several incentives are given by the Coffee Board. It is suggested that necessary inputs, supply and requisite technology may be extended to coffee growers by introducing "coffee grower card". This in turn is expected to discourage *jhoom* cultivation.

(2) **Tea Industry :** In Mizoram, land measuring 10,000 hectares has been identified as ideal for tea growing and it is estimated that this can earn a net income of Rs. 13,000 per hectare from fourth year, which may rise to Rs. 82,000 in eighth year and onwards. It may promote allied services needed for processing the green tea leaves such as pruning knives, trailer basket, tea sample containers, wire fencing nails, nuts, bolts, aprons, rain coats, umbrella, pesticides, fertilizers, weedicides, polythene bags, soaps, detergents, phenyl, dettol, bandage, cotton, drugs, pharmaceuticals, tea chests with polythene lining and aluminium lining etc. Further, the Tea Board also offers benefits and incentives that may be availed by the entrepreneurs.

(3) **Rubber Plantation :** In Mizoram, Rubber Plantation need to be resumed as this source has a potential for

raising Rs.13,000 per hectare from seventh year onwards. The literature on Mizoram shows that rubber plants existed in plenty during pre-British time. This indicated that the land is fit for rubber plantations. It was estimated that about 5,000 hectares of land is presently suitable for rubber plantations near the Western Border, which may produce/extract rubber 1,000 kg per annum from seventh year to 1,500 kg per annum in the tenth year and onwards. At the same time banana and pineapple may be grown during gestation period.

(4) **Tung Plantation :** Mizoram's land is suitable for Tung Plantation. Tung is an important input for paint and wax industries. Mizoram is the only State/place in India where tung trees are grown on large scale. Technical estimates revealed that about 275 trees per hectare may be raised and tung seeds after shelling and drying may be sold to the oil extraction companies at Rs. 10 per kg ex-factory price. This source may earn a net income from one hectare of Tung Plantation in the fifth year at Rs. 1,000, which may rise to Rs. 13,000 from the tenth year and onwards. Mushroom cultivation may be also promoted, as the land and climate is congenial to its production. Commercial orange farming on large scale may be encouraged.

(5) **Orchid Cultivation :** Mizoram has rich diversity of natural orchids, which have domestic and international potential in cut flowers and medicinal market. More than 200 varieties of orchids are found in Mizoram. Mizoram is the only natural home of Vanda Coerules (Blue Vanda), Renanthera Imschootiana (Red Vanda)) among the North-Eastern States. Cymbidium variety may be cultivated for sale as cut flowers in Delhi/ Kolkata markets with the assistance of forest department. Cultivation of 1000 plants of cymbidium hybrid may earn an income of Rs. 67,000 from third year that may go upto Rs. 1,21,000 from fifth year onwards. However, these natural orchids are not

properly conserved and developed to a sustainable level of utilization due to lack of eco-scientific management in Mizoram. In order to conserve and attain sustainable utilization of natural orchids certain measures such as 'survey and demarcation of orchid rich areas' within the State, framing of proper rules and regulation to stop illegal collection and export of wild orchids, establishment of proper orchid research and development centre, to adopt latest technology of breeding, multiplication, cultivation and management etc., establishment of an orchid farming society, etc. are necessary. This is expected to generate employment of local youth, and commercialization of orchids may be adopted[4].

(6) **Rural Nurseries :** There exists scope for establishment of nurseries in Kolasib district to produce quality-planting material for cash crops. This source may earn an annual income of Rs. 2.37 lakh from each nursery. There is a scope for growing new crops *viz.* mango, cashew, banana, cinnamon, clove, arecanut, geranium, mint, etc.

(7) **Bamboo-based Industries :** Mizoram has abundant natural bamboo resource, while bamboo resource is depleting in other parts of the country. Around 57 per cent of the geographical area of Mizoram is under bamboo cover, ranging from 400-1500 metres above the mean sea level. There are twenty species of bamboo in Mizoram of which *Melocanna baccifera* is dominating variety of the State, which fetches Government a revenue of Rs. 80 lakh annually[5]. The Government receives a sum upto Rs. 66 lakh per year as royalty on bamboo. Annual availability from the total growing in the State is 5.83 million MT, but aggregate annual consumption of bamboo including paper mills supply stands at 28,315 MT only. Bamboo-based products such as fibre-board, mat-ply, bamboo pens, umbrella handles, wall hangers, traditional hats, water piping, broomsticks, ceiling cleaners, decorative and household

items, etc., can be manufactured without much investment. Bamboos grow upto 8-10 metres height and are widely used for construction of *Kutcha* houses, furnitures, weaving, pulping, and fencing. The shoots are eaten in large scale during rainy season and constitute a dominant food item. There is no proper management of the bamboo resources of the State. The Government has recently framed a bamboo policy for ensuring optimum utilization of this resource. A Bamboo Institute may be opened in the State to train young entrepreneurs in producing different products and caring for its varieties.

In view of the vast potential of bamboo resource, a paper mill was set up at Panchagram in Cachar district, under the ownership of M/S. Hindustan Paper Mills Ltd, a public sector undertaking. Bulk of the raw material to this mill is sent from Mizoram. During 1976-77, the Government had initiated for another paper mill within Mizoram. The feasibility study suggested for a plant at Bairabi with capacity of 200 MT per day of printing and writing paper. But it could not materialize. There might have been some flaws in the project, which should be removed by redesigning the same and it may be taken up again to turn the vast untapped bamboo resource known as 'green gold' of the State into 'cash gold'. Paper and pulp projects may encourage ancillarisation of alum, salt cake, starch, lime, sulphuric acid, resin, paper cones, telcum powder, gum taps, wooden plugs and sodium chloride.

(8) Timber-based Industries : Mizoram receives 778 cm rainfall annually. It is home of a great variety of ever-green as well as deciduous timber species. Among these *Michelia Champaca* is a big evergreen tree with high quality timber. Its timber is graded as A-II class, which is the highest grade among the indigenous species in Mizoram. It is a fast growing variety with a long, clean and cylindrical bole. Artificial regeneration of the variety is found to be quite successful and widely tried in the State. *Terminalia Myriocarpa* is the second highest graded timber in the State, next to Michelia variety. It is a big tree found in almost all parts of Mizoram. Its timber is widely used and is moderately hard and moderately refractory and durable. *Artocarpus Chaplasha* is one of the best timbers for manufacturing motor bodies and country boats. It is indigenous to the State and graded as A-II class. Artificial regeneration has been largely tried with good success. *Tectona Grandis* teak is exotic to Mizoram but due to its high quality in furniture making it is widely planted both by private and Government agencies. Majority of the Government plantations are teak plantations in pure form as well as mixed with *Gmelina Arborea*. Plantations of economic tree species on abandoned *jhum* land and degraded forest area is the best alternative.

Timber-based industries have good scope in the State. Mizo carpenters manufacture good quality furniture. To make it commercially viable and export oriented, industrial units may be set up with efficient managerial skill. However, deforestation due to timber-based industry should be accompanied by afforestation to prevent environmental hazards. In view of Supreme Court order dated 15th January 1998, which banned fresh felling of forest trees except in accordance with the working plan of State Government, there is a need to frame such a plan at an early date.

(9) Medicines : Mizoram is rich in bio-diversity. Work on botanical collection and botanical research was started since 1990 and by now more than 400 medicinal plants have been identified in Mizoram, of which 62 are recorded as new medicinal plants. Further, it was reported that existence of estimated 90 per cent of India's medicinal plant diversity in forests and 10 per cent in non-forests habitat suits Mizoram conditions[6]. Entrepreneurs with exposure and training in forestry should be encouraged to undertake medicine extraction.

Agro-based Small-Scale Processing Industries

These small-scale industries simply process the agricultural produce. They do not manufacture any new product. The important feasible processing industries are:

(a) *Rice Mill* for hulling paddy into rice, rice bran oil,
(b) *Dal Mill* for grinding pulses like Arhar, Moong, Pea, Gram and lentil into Dal,
(c) *Maize Hulling* unit for separating maize grains from cobs,
(d) *Oil Mill* for extracting oil from Mustard, Groundnut, Soybean, Til, Sunflower, Linseed etc.

The agro-climatic conditions of the north-eastern region favour the growth and development of ginger, turmeric, black pepper, large cardamom and cinnamon. Except cardamom, all the spices need processing for marketing and human consumption. Unemployed educated mass can switchover to this sector for remunerative enterprise.

Agro-based Small-Scale Manufacturing Industries

Small-scale industries manufacture entirely new products based on agricultural produce as the main raw materials. The finished product will be entirely different compared to its raw material. Some of the important units which have potential in NER are as follows.

(1) Gur and Khandsari Unit: In north-eastern India sugarcane cultivation is in practice at small scale. It grows extremely well due to favourable climatic conditions. Setting up of Gur/Khandsari units availing KVIC subsidy and loan facility by power-driven crushers for making gur/khandsari from sugarcane gives scope of employment generation in rural area. The National Sugar Research Institute, Kanpur had conducted a study on feasibility of establishing a Mini-Sugar Plant during Fifth Five Year Plan period and had recommended that a plant with an installed capacity to crush 50 MT of cane should be set up. During the year 1978-79, it was contemplated to make it operative. However it remained on paper. It may be taken up again in the light of annual sugarcane production of 9360 MT.[7]

(2) **Fruits and Vegetable Preservation Units :** Some of the agricultural products that are perishable in nature and need processing for value addition in the form of condensing, slicing, powdering, canning, preserving, dehydrating, drying, pickling to make them available throughout the year which can be attained by setting up small preservation industries in the region. This will give permanent engagement to the entrepreneurs and may earn a comparatively large and stable income. The most common and widely cultivated fruits in the region are mandarin, pineapple, banana, apple pear, stone fruit, passion fruits, lemon, coconut, and guava.

In view of high quality of banana of Mizoram, scope exists for its processing into banana slices (chips). Similarly, concentrated fruits squash may be converted into powdered form and after packing on the lines of Kissan/Maggi Tomato Soup pouch or milk powder may be sold in the country and outside. There is a need for making these products value added, at competitive cost, which can be achieved by applying management techniques, improving production technology, etc.

Despite the well established and distinctive quality character of khasi mandarin, the annual production of fruits is progressively declining due to lack of marketing facilities. If orange squash industry comes up near the feeder area, it will lessen the burden of quick disposal and at the same time fetch a high value. Pineapple occupies the second largest hectare in the region and the climate of the region favours its luxurious growth. The pineapple juice extraction units and other allied preservation activities will give a further boost to the pineapple cultivation. Among the temperate fruits apple and pear has shown great sign of development in the region. But difficulties in transportation remains a great bottleneck and this problem could be solved to some extent by opening up of the preservation units.

(3) **Food Processing Industries :** Ginger, banana, orange, pineapple, sugarcane, chilly, bamboo shoots, passion fruits etc. are produced in large quantity and are in excess of domestic consumption in the State. Ginger is available between Rs. 5 to Rs. 10 per kilogram. When pickle is made, it becomes worth Rs. 175 per kg. Similarly, passion fruit a rare product in the country is available in Mizoram in plenty, it may be exploited profitably and may become a monopoly item if squash or juice or powder is made. Recently, the MIFCO's has installed an Integrated Fruit Juice Concentrate Plant at Chhingchhip, which needs regular supply of various types of fruits for further processing. This may lead to ancillarisation for packing material from plastic, polythene and glass, spices (*masala*), label printing, etc.

Allied Agro-based Industries

These small-scale industries are basically genetic in nature and produce very important basic items of daily dietary requirement irrespective of consumers' food taste, *e.g.*, milk, eggs, etc. and make use of mainly agricultural by-products as feed. The products are in great demand in every corner across the globe. Some of them again constitute an important raw material in the course of further processing say milk products. Some of such important industries having potential in North-East Region are discussed as follows :

(1) **Dairying :** Dairy Farming is mostly practiced as a means of creating employment opportunities for small/ marginal farmers including educated unemployment youth all over the country. According to World Bank estimates about 75 per cent of India's population (940

million) lives in 5.87 million villages and cultivates over 145 million hectares of cropland. The average size of the farm is about 1.66 hectares. Of the 70 million rural households, 42 per cent operate on 2 hectares of land and 37 per cent are landless. These landless small farmers rear 53 per cent of domesticated animals and consequently occupy 51 per cent market share in total milk production in the country which was 84.6 million MT for the year 2001-02 when the per capita milk availability was 226 ml. per day only as against the minimum of 250 ml. per day as recommended by ICMR. Thus, small/marginal farmers and landless agricultural labourers play a prominent role in the field of milk production in the country.

Though, dairy farming has become an important business and is being carried out at all levels ranging from small-scale to large-scale using all types of business organisations say proprietorship, partnership, company, cooperatives, etc., small/marginal farmers and landless labourers normally keep 1-2 milk yielding animals as a subsidiary occupation to supplement their income. A viable economic dairy farming unit as full time occupation requires minimum 8-10 high milk yielding animals and preferably 1 hectare cultivable land that demands capital investment of about Rs. 1 to 1.50 lakh. According on one estimate, a farmer can earn a net surplus of about Rs. 24,000 p.a. from a pair of 2 milking cows. Thus, there lies potential for increase of milk production.

Besides, the manure from animals provides a good source of organic matter for improving soil fertility and crop yields. The *gobar* gas from animal dung is used as fuel for domestic purposes as also for mechanical pulling of water from well. The surplus fodder and agricultural by-products are gainfully utilized as animal feed. Most of the draft power for farm operations and transportation is provided by bullocks. Though the agriculture is seasonal, dairy farming is for throughout the year renders stable employment to people. This paves way for dairy farming to be taken up at different scales as one of the main occupation in and around big urban centres where obviously the demand for milk is high. Hence, dairy development programme in India is not only aimed at increasing milk production, but also to provide stable employment to rural population as it is the most appropriate policy instrument for ensuring equitable distribution of income.

(2) **Poultry :** The poultry farming renders it possible of converting grains and other agricultural products into eggs and poultry meat for nutritional benefit of mankind. Poultry farming offers opportunities for full time as well as part-time employment particularly for women and children on the farm. Liquid egg, egg powder, dried yolk, etc. are value added products of poultry farming not only furthers employment opportunities but also help raising income. The term poultry refers to wide variety of birds of several species including dressed one or alive and it applies to chickens, turkeys, ducks, swans, etc. Chickens start laying eggs since 6 months of age. Broilers can be marketed for poultry meat at the age of 8-10 weeks. As compared to the other livestock rearing occupation, poultry farming requires not only less space but less investment to start with and pays return early. Thus, people from low income group find it easy to start the same on a small-scale. Of the entire country, the NER constitute 3.70 per cent of livestock and 8.13% of poultry population (Verma1998). After piggery, poultry farming comes as a next preferred occupation of people in the entire NE region. But, various surveys conducted so far in the different parts of the region at different points of time revealed the major constraints that are being faced by the poultry entrepreneurs in the region are the high cost of feed, high cost of marketing poultry products, non-availability of

improved variety of breed and adverse climatic conditions that lead to high mortality.

(3) **Piggery :** Pig farming in the region is as common as the practice of cattle rearing in Gujarat (buffaloes), Haryana and Punjab (cows). It is a profitable occupation of converting waste food and low value feed into valuable animal protein. Pigs do not compete with other animals for feed. The kitchen waste like food (rice), waste parts of vegetables and other waste like wheat bran, fish bran, fish meal, rice bran, maize, molasses, oil cakes, etc. are also used as pig feed in the same manner as the other people makes use of the same in rest parts of the country as cattle feed. Pig with its special characteristics of high feed efficiency conversion, gains a body weight of 100 kgs in just 300 kgs of animal feed and stores more fat than any other animal. Pigs also excel in dressing percentage of around 80 per cent over any other animal. Because of prolificacy, shorter generation period, rapid rate of growth and economic feed conversion ability, pigs, thus, play an important as well as dominant role in meat production.

Forestry-based Enterprises

Timber in NER attained its prime importance only after establishment of forest-based industries and development of roads and rail network during last 6 decades. Earlier, non-wood forest products were the main sources for mankind. Though, over the years, area under forests shrinks owing to their depletion; dependence of people on forests remained by and large very high. Many of the non-wood forest products from NER like fibres, flosses, tanning, dyes, gums, resins, essential oils, raw drugs from medicinal plants, edible wild fruits, lac, honey, wax, silk, lac larvae, horn, hides and ivory have high demand in rest of the country. Many people living in and around forests are unaware of the potentials of these forest resources and because of this, sustainable exploitation of these resources did not receive adequate attention. Some of the important forest-based employment generation enterprises of the region are as follows :

(1) Mushroom Cultivation : Mushroom is a healthy and nutritious vegetable. Since early times, mushroom has been treated as special kind of food. Mushrooms are a good source of proteins, minerals, vitamins etc.; low in sugar content and as such used as selective food for diabetics. Thus, mushrooms provide a high protein and low calorie diet. Due to its nutritional and medicinal value, mushroom is in high demand these days and has become a profitable enterprise for earning handsome livelihood. Mushrooms are used as food either in fresh, dried or canned form. A variety of products like mushroom ketchup, soup, powder, dehydrated mushroom etc. can also be prepared. It forms a valuable fodder for pigs, poultry and fishes. Fresh mushrooms are sold as vegetable in the market as also preserved in the form of pickle, drying and canning which have got internal market in metro cities. Canned mushrooms have got a good export market also. Mushroom cultivation is one of the self-employment programmes where low paid employees and landless labourers may take it up as their additional source of income. Thus, one can think of small-scale mushroom cultivation on purely commercial basis under contract farming if he has little cultivable land. Government also gives loans to mushroom growers besides 35 per cent subsidy.

The climatic conditions of the north-east is most suitable for cultivation of paddy straw mushroom and White oyster mushroom that can be grown throughout the year except in winter on hills. Mushroom entrepreneurs do not require huge investment in the form of seed, land, soil, machinery, fertilizer, etc. Just with the help of agricultural waste, plastic bags and seeds mushroom can be grown in a shed of room size or balcony for 365 days. Mushroom farming can be practiced both indoors and outdoors. It can also be grown in basements, verandah, garage, abandoned farm house, mud huts, wooden/bamboo framed thatch houses etc. Though commercial cultivation demands maintenance of controlled conditions particularly temperature and humidity, experiments have shown that it can be practiced successfully in variable natural conditions of north-east on small-scale. White button mushroom gives 2-3 crops in a season on hills, but, it requires two different temperature ranges for growth and production. While spawn run (vegetative growth) it needs temperature of 22°-28°C and while fruit body formation the need is of 15°-18°C. Besides, it demands presence of humidity at 85-95 per cent and enough ventilation during fructification.

Since paddy cultivation is the main occupation of the people of North-East, large quantity of paddy straw is easily available for making compost (8-28 days) for mushroom cultivation which can be used as manure after mushroom cultivation. Light spray of water on cased trays brings mushroom in about 3 weeks time. Individual tray of size 3'x 2' produces 5-6 kg of fresh mushroom per cropping cycle of 8-12 weeks. Thus, there is a vast scope of commercial mushroom cultivation in this region as an income generating venture and creating employment opportunity specially unemployed/underemployed youths.

Oyster mushroom (Dhingri) requires cold weather of 20°-28°C and relative humidity of 75-85 per cent. In its case neither compost preparation nor a precise temperature control is required. It grows on a variety of crop refuses; saw dust, paddy straw, sugarcane molasses, etc. It can also be grown in polythene bags where individual bag of 25 x 40 cm size produces 1-2 Kg. of fresh mushroom per cropping cycle of 25-30 days and gives 3-4 flushes (crop) in one season.

(2) Agar Oil : Agar oil, one of the perfumes, is obtained from the infected wood of *Aquilaria agalocha* Roxb, which has a high demand in international market particularly in the Middle-East countries for mixing with their best grade of scents and is a good source of handsome revenue. Agar bearing trees are found growing naturally in some parts of forest area of Assam, Manipur, Meghalaya and Nagaland. Some inner fungus infected parts of mature agar tree contains the precious oil which is highly priced by the European perfumeries. It is reported that the infected agar wood itself fetch a price of Rs. 20,000-40,000 a Kg. and the oil sells at any price ranging between Rs. 2-4 lakh a litre. Proper and planned cultivation of this wild plant may help generate good revenue

(3) **Sericulture :** Silk is secretion of insects belonging to *Lepidoptera* family. There are many kinds of silk producing insects. Some are reared artificially while others are found wild feeding on a variety of host plants in the forest. The most important are *Antheraea paphia* which produces *Tassar* silk and *Antheraea assamensis* which produces *Muga* silk. Assam in particular, boasts of its silk weaving. The golden *Muga* having unique properties has placed Assam with such potentials for development that cannot be challenged by any other in the world. The NER has all the potentials for production of Mulberry, Eric and *Tassar* silk production and this can become an effective tool in employment generation.

(4) **Honey and Wax :** Honey is considered as one of the most prized free gifts of nature and is commonly used as natural sweet. It is known by different names in different parts of the country such as *madhu, shahad,* etc. It needs to be stored in cool and dry place and is used as sweetening eatables. Medicinal properties have also been attributed to it. In fact, honey is collected by honey-bees. The colour and flavour of honey depends on the nature of nectar and the fragrance of flowers which these bees visit. They built their combs on the branches of big trees or on the buildings. They store

the honey in the upper part of the comb particularly bigger cells. When these are full are sealed with wax. Unsealed cells contain the honey that is not fully ripe. Honey is collected in containers, which is slipped down with the help of a rope. To skim off wax, honey is separated sometimes after it is given heat over a bath of water. Too much of heating decomposes honey.

Bee-keeping is most profitable venture for the reasons that it does neither require any land nor demand continuous physical work, nor need heavy investment. Therefore, even landless unemployed youths, women and children can also maintain beehives. Other valuable products like wax, jelly, bee-venom, pollen and propolis are also obtained from honey-bees. Wax is used for making artificial hives, polishes and water-proofing of leather goods.

(5) **Rope Making :** Long lengths of rope are obtained by twisting moist fibres of grasses and sedges together. Though a certain degree of twist is essential, but excess twisting weakens the rope and in this process, certain amount of compactness is essential for preventing infiltration of water so that rope is preserved from decomposition. These days, rope making machines are also available. Where ropes are made for commercial purposes the fibre is fed to machines.

(6) **Broom Grass :** The inflorescences of broom grass from which brooms are prepared are found naturally grown in the forest belt of entire NE region. Every year many truck loads of broom sticks are being transported to other parts of the country. Surprisingly, no commercial cultivation has yet taken place in the region. Moreover, it can easily be propagated by vegetative part at one metre distance in the month of May/June and has equally good chance of being remunerative on commercial basis.

(7) **Gums and Resins :** Gums and resins are important forest products which are used for mixing in manufacture of water colours, paint and polish

industry as binding agent, and also used in food and confectionery industry.

The nature and flow of gum differs considerably depending on different species of trees varying in size and shapes. Often, unhealthy plant produces more gum than healthy plant. Usually gum and resin plant requires a large number of cuts with an axe on its bark. The gum exudes from blazes all over the year but its flow is more in hot weather. Collection of gum and resin is done by hand picking on daily basis in summer and on alternate days in winter except rainy season. After collection, the gum may be sun-bleached before it is sent to market. Cleaning to remove particles of bark, sand or soil dirt may be carried out as a preliminary step to grading. The better grades of gum show uniformity in size of fragment and are pale in colour with an absence of dust or powder.

(8) **Basket and Wicker work including Canes :** Roots, stems, dry leaves, splints of bamboo and some of the reeds and rushes from the forest species are used for making baskets, chairs, stools, tables, fishing rods, hand fans, trays, musical pipes, bags, screens and inner ceiling. For different types of mats like plain, and striped, the culms of mat grass are used after splitting them into 2, 4, 8, or 12 strands. The thinner strands are used for exceptionally superfine mats. For sleeping mats, floors mats, hats, fine bags, the stems of *fimbristylis* herbs are cut, bleached by exposure to the sun and used either whole or after splitting.

The cane sticks are used for making furniture frames, walking sticks, ski-sticks, polo sticks, alpenstocks, umbrella, handles, etc. Thinner ones are used for making multipurpose, useful, durable, and portable baskets. They are also used for making articles. Splits of thin canes are used for retuning chairs. The bottom portion of the *culm* which is strong and rigid and is used for various purposes where strength and rigidity is required while making furniture frames. The middle portion of the *culm* is used for general purpose where pliable cane is required. The top portion of the *culm* which is weak and unsuitable for generation purpose is separated. The demand for canes in the country has been much more than the supplies available from the indigenous sources.

(9) **Katha and Cutch :** Katha and cutch are produced from the heart wood of *Acacia catechu* (*Khair* tree) and *Acacia chundra* (*Sundra* tree) and is mainly used for flavouring betel leaf as masticator and valued for its catechuic content. Cutch, the bye-product of *katha* industry largely used in paper and pulp industry for dyeing, colouring purposes.

Conclusion

In a positive note, it is always better not to rationalize the failures, if one wants to bring about any change; it has to set an example. There is no force more powerful than leading by example. To quote what Mahatma Gandhi said "Bring the change you want to see in the world." Moreover it is important always to seek the "truth" and Samuel Johnson has rightly said, "If you don't have courage, you may not have an opportunity to use any of your other virtues". Further, to become the best, one has to benchmark with the best in the world. Anything below this does not work in reaching the top. This requires discipline and hard work and refrains from cynicism. Cynics know the price of everything but the value of nothing. They do nothing but criticize those who are doing something worthwhile which takes away the enthusiasm and builds a negative mindset. In order to overcome this, one has to be in action. In Gandhi's words, "A man is the sum of his actions". Bringing about change requires a mindset and a mindset makes one determined to change for better. In the words of Dr. Mashelkar, "today, the struggle is between the mind and the mindset". Societies those win this struggle succeed. Certainly, everything is not under one's control. However, it does provide no excuse for not doing what is under one's control.

People aspiring high when not matched with opportunities to fulfil certainly realize discontentment and look for easy alternative ways. But, this cannot lead to sustained development in the society. We cannot ignore the higher values developed in our society, solutions which can improve the conditions of our society, have to be found, while responding to the globalization, so that we do not lose our bearings. People are the key resources to any society. Therefore, transformation and development of a society can never take place without the willingness and harmonious efforts of its people.

Opening of Agri. Clinics/Agri-Business centre in remote areas at the grassroot level is the road to destination for both to the unemployed graduate youths and to the nation as it offers exciting future opportunities with a variety of challenges, provided one works hard with full determination. The following small poem that reflects this sentiment beautifully: "Life's battles do not always go to the strongest or the fastest man. Sooner or later the man who wins is the man who thinks he can".

NOTES

1. Department of Environment and Forests, *Mizoram Forest*, 2003, Government of Mizoram, Aizawl, p. 4.
2. *Ibid.*
3. Assistant Director-in-charge, *Small Industries Service Institute*, Aizawl, July 1996.
4. *Ibid.*, p. 46.
5. *Ibid.*, p. 15.
6. *Ibid.*, p. 22.
7. Department of Environment and Forests, *Mizoram Forest*, 2003, *op cit.*, p. 3.

REFERENCES

Gupta, R. C. (2006): Entrepreneurship in Agriculture, Emerging Dimensions: Soil Plant Health Clinics, A paper presented at the Seminar on "Promotion of Entrepreneurship in North-Eastern Region —Issues and Challenges" organised by the Department of

RDAP, North-Eastern Hill University, Tura Campus, Tura on 24th-25th March, 2006.

Kabra, K.C.: Business and Industry in Mizoram, unpublished Ph.D. thesis of J.R. Nagar Rajasthan Vidyapeeth University, Udaipur, 2005.

Mani Sunil (1995): 'Economic Liberalisation and the Industrial Sector,' *Economic and Political Weekly*, May 27, pp. M-38-50.

Sandeseva, J.C. (1991): New Small Industrial Policy: Implications and Prospects, *Economic and Political Weekly*, October 19, pp. 2423-2426.

13

Employment, Well-being and Growth in Rural India

An Inter-State Comparison

GUNENDRA PRASAD PAL

Introduction

India's rural economy is a part of its overall economy. Any change in the structure of the overall economy can affect directly its rural economy. Since the inception of the reforms in India in 1991, a lot of changes have occurred in the structures of income, employment, levels of living, assets and debts in both rural and urban areas of India. All such changes have obviously created divergent effects on people's well-being. Structural changes have expectedly been different in the States.

Let us now look into the rural socio-economic scenario. Majority of population in the country live in the rural areas and depend primarily on agriculture and its allied activities (farm activities). Though rural population has tended to decline, its share in total population is around 72.2 per cent in 2001. Rural poor has recorded 77.7 per cent of total poor in 1983 and it has marginally declined to 76 per cent in 1993-94 and then to 73.4 per cent in 2004-05. Since Independence, overall incidence of poverty has declined over the years. But disparity has continued to prevail in the poverty ratio among the States and also between rural and urban areas. Rural poverty ratio has declined from 45.7 per cent in 1983 to 37.2 per cent in 1993-94 and then to 29.2 per cent in 2004-05. It is still higher as compared to its counter part (NSSO Reports).

Adequate infrastructure creates employment and hence generates income and in turn increases people's level of living. Rural Infrastructure Development Fund (RIDF) has increased to Rs. 42,000 crore in 2004-05 with an initial sum of Rs. 2,000 crore in 1995-96 for different rural infrastructure projects such as irrigation, soil conservation, flood protection and watershed management for increasing production of crops, rural roads and bridges, rural market godowns, construction of schools and health centres. Out of the sanctioned loan amounting to Rs. 34,678 crore under RIDF, only 60.7 per cent have been disbursed on March 31, 2004 (Annual Report, NABARD, 2003-04) and the remaining amount was not at all disbursed, signalling a dim picture of the implementation of the programme.

India's economic structure consisting of thirteen economic activities is separated into three major sectors such as Farm Sector (FS), Industry Sector (IS) and Service Sector (SS). Here we have studied only five broad activities because of their prime places in their respective sectors: agriculture including fishing, forestry and logging as farm activities (FS); manufacturing (MF) of IS; construction (CST), trade, hotel etc. (TC) of SS and Non-Farm Sector (NFS) of IS and SS taken together.

The area of our study is threefold: (1) Structure of Rural Employment, (2) Rural Poor and Incidence of Poverty, and (3) Structure of Rural Monthly Per Capita Expenditure (MPCE). Based on NSSO data of 38th, 50th, 55th and 61st Rounds on Employment and Unemployed; and of 43rd, 50th and 61st Rounds on Consumer Expenditure Surveys we have examined the nature and the extent of the structural growth of rural employment by sex and MPCE in respect of the rural areas in 17 major rural States during 1983-2005. The period is sub-divided into (1) 1983-1994; and (2) 1994-2005.

The following aspects are hence of interest to us :

1. Changes in the distribution of rural employment among the activities for the sector(s) and the inter-State differentials in the employment structure.

2. Changes in the distribution of employment among the sectors and the inter-State differentials in the distribution.
3. Changes in the distribution of mode of employment and the inter-State differences in the distribution.
4. Nature and extent of growth rate of rural employment in different sectors and the consequent inter-State disparities in employment growth.
5. Nature and extent of rural poor and poverty and the inter-State disparities.
6. Nature and extent of inequality in MPCE distribution and its growth rate.
7. Classification of States on the basis of poverty ratio and inequality index of MPCE.

For easy understanding, this chapter is divided into five sections. The *Section 1* deals with the nature and the extent of growth patterns of rural employment occupationally, sectorally and categorically in 17 major States of India during 1983-05. In *Section 2,* the incidence of rural poor and poverty as the level of well-being of rural people is examined across the States. *The Section 3* analyses the nature and the extent of inequality in MPCE distribution as people's levels of living are analyzed. In *Section 4,* the changing socio-economic scenario of the rural States on the basis of poverty ratio and inequality index of MPCE is discussed. The concluding remarks are given in Section 5.

Pattern of Employment

It is well known that the level of well-being of individuals in any country like India depends on their absorption in economic activities and hence income. Labour is employed in alternative activities (sectors) in both rural and urban locations. Since the process of liberalization has been going on and the economy has also been growing, it is essential to examine the growth pattern of rural employment in different States of India occupationally, sectorally and categorically during the period under study.

Inter-Sector Pattern

Variations in the activity structures of rural employment have resulted in changes in their growth pattern in the States and India as a whole. The inter-sector (intra-sector) heterogeneities in the distribution of employment (Tables 13.1-13.2) are prominent everywhere in India.

In rural areas agriculture and its allied activities (farm activities) are predominant while non-farm activities are not very significant. Estimates reveal that rural workers fall back upon the non-firm activities for their survival from farm activities everywhere in India. *The steady decline in the share of farm sector in rural employment has been accompanied by non-farm employment irrespective of sex. The monotonous decline in employment share of farm sector is relatively less for female than that for male in all the States during the period.*

Among the States the decline in farm employment ranges between a minimum of 0.8 per cent in West Bengal and a maximum of 16.4 per cent points in Himachal Pradesh for male while for female it is 0.1 per cent in West Bengal and 11.3 per cent points in Kerala. The low value of decline in employment share is observed on Karnataka, Gujarat and Maharashtra for male (less than 2 per cent points) while Kerala, Punjab, Orissa and Haryana have exhibited its high values (more than 10 per cent points). *Karnataka has only exhibited the steady increase in the share of farm employment for female.* The overall steady declining in the share of farm employment is 7.6 per cent and 2.9 per cent points respectively for male and female.

Intra-Sector Pattern

The share of rural employment under manufacturing has declined over the 12-year period (1993-2005) in Gujarat, Karnataka and West Bengal (highest) for male; and in Assam (highest), Karnataka and West Bengal for female. *Increase in the share of female employment is relatively high as compared to its male counterpart.* Rural male employment in construction seems to have increased very substantially over the 12-year period in

Table 13.1 : Sectoral Distribution (%) of Rural Employment (UPSS) by Sex in India

States	*1993-94*						*2004-05*						*Annual Growth Rate (%)*			
	Male		*Female*		*All*		*Male*		*Female*		*All*		*1983-94*		*1994-05*	
	FS	*NFS*	*FS*	*NFS*	*FS*	*NFS*	*FS*	*NFS*	*FS*	*NFS*	*FS*	*NFS*	*FS*	*NFS*	*FS*	*NFS*
AP	75.6	24.4	83.7	16.3	79.3	20.7	66.4	33.6	78.5	21.5	71.8	28.2	2.13	2.68	-0.16	3.65
Assam	78.2	21.8	83.3	16.7	79.2	20.8	69.6	30.4	88.3	11.7	74.3	25.7	2.54	2.85	2.05	4.54
Bihar	82.0	18.0	91.9	8.1	84.3	15.7	75.8	24.2	86.4	13.6	77.9	22.1	1.37	0.79	1.14	6.24
Gujarat	71.1	28.9	90.6	9.4	78.7	21.3	69.3	30.7	89.1	11.9	77.3	22.7	0.83	5.10	1.87	2.72
Haryana	60.9	39.1	93.2	6.8	71.9	28.1	49.4	50.6	90.6	9.4	64.1	35.9	1.82	4.58	2.00	5.54
HP	65.8	38.2	95.5	4.5	80.3	19.7	49.4	50.6	91.0	9.0	69.6	30.4	-	-	-	-
J & K	61.3	38.7	95.4	4.6	75.8	24.2	53.8	46.2	86.6	13.4	63.9	36.1	-	-	-	-
Karnataka	78.8	19.2	84.6	15.4	81.2	18.8	77.7	22.3	85.5	14.5	81.0	19.0	1.74	3.83	1.53	1.67
Kerala	53.2	46.8	63.0	37.0	56.4	43.6	37.1	62.9	51.7	48.3	42.0	58.0	-0.92	1.80	-1.29	4.04
MP	87.2	12.8	93.9	6.1	89.8	10.2	79.1	20.9	88.1	11.9	82.5	17.5	1.76	2.76	0.74	6.02
Maharashtra	75.3	24.7	91.2	8.8	82.6	17.4	71.4	28.6	90.7	9.3	80.0	20.0	1.22	3.56	1.24	2.84
Orissa	78.7	21.3	85.0	15.0	80.9	19.1	65.9	34.1	74.6	25.4	69.0	31.0	1.95	0.86	0.08	6.20
Punjab	68.1	31.6	92.7	7.3	74.7	25.3	54.7	45.3	89.7	10.3	66.9	33.1	-0.91	3.63	1.23	4.80
Rajasthan	69.6	30.4	93.0	7.0	79.9	20.1	60.2	39.8	89.5	10.5	72.9	27.1	1.37	6.19	0.83	4.51
TN	64.0	36.0	78.5	21.5	70.5	29.5	58.7	41.3	73.8	26.2	65.4	34.6	0.51	2.46	-1.41	0.73
UP	76.3	23.7	90.0	10.0	80.0	20.0	66.3	33.7	86.5	13.5	72.8	27.2	1.81	3.34	1.25	5.02
WB	64.7	35.3	58.9	41.1	63.3	36.7	63.9	36.1	58.8	41.2	62.7	37.1	0.93	5.70	1.58	1.85
India	74.1	25.9	86.2	13.8	78.4	21.6	66.5	33.5	83.3	16.7	72.7	27.3	1.24	3.05	0.86	3.81
Range	34.0	34.0	35.0	35.0	33.4	33.4	42.0	42.0	39.3	39.3	40.5	40.5	81.4*	53.1*	126.8*	46.0*

Source: *NSSO Report Nos. 409 and 515, 1993-94 and 2004-05.*
Note: UPSS = Usually Principal plus subsidiary Status. * Growth Divergence Index (CV %).
FS = Farm Sector; NFS = Non-Farm Sector.

Table 13.2 : Percentage Point Change between 1993-94 and 2004-05 in the Share of Activity-Employment (UPSS) in Rural India

States	*Farm sector*			*Manufacturing*			*Construction*			*Trade and Commerce*			*Non-farm Sector*		
	M	*F*	*All*	*M*	*F*	*All*	*M*	*F*	*All*	*M*	*F*	*All*	*M*	*F*	*All*
AP	-9.2^{m}	-5.2^{n}	-7.5^{m}	1.3^{n}	2.3^{n}	1.7^{n}	2.5^{m}	0.5^{m}	1.6^{m}	2.6^{m}	1.5^{n}	2.1^{m}	9.2^{m}	5.2^{n}	7.5^{m}
Assam	-8.6^{m}	5.1^{n}	-4.9^{m}	0.8^{m}	-5.0^{m}	-0.4^{m}	2.2^{m}	0.7^{m}	1.8^{m}	3.4^{m}	-0.8^{m}	2.1^{m}	8.6^{n}	-5.0^{n}	4.9^{n}
Bihar	-6.2^{m}	-5.5^{m}	-6.4^{m}	1.6^{m}	4.2^{m}	2.8^{m}	1.6^{m}	-	1.2^{m}	3.4*	-7.6^{m}	3.2^{m}	6.2^{m}	5.5^{m}	6.4^{m}
Gujarat	-1.8^{n}	-1.5^{n}	-1.4^{n}	-2.2^{m}	40.3^{n}	-1.4^{m}	0.7^{m}	0.5^{m}	0.6^{m}	2.7^{m}	0.2^{m}	1.8^{m}	1.8^{n}	1.5^{n}	1.4^{n}
Haryana	-11.5^{m}	-2.6^{m}	-7.8^{m}	6.5^{m}	2.2^{m}	4.9^{m}	6.3^{m}	0.1^{m}	4.0^{m}	3.7^{n}	-0.2^{m}	2.2^{m}	11.5^{m}	2.6^{m}	7.8^{m}
HP	-16.4^{m}	-4.5^{m}	-10.7^{m}	2.4^{m}	0.8^{n}	1.6^{m}	6.4^{m}	0.2	3.5^{m}	2.5^{m}	0.5*	1.3^{m}	16.4^{m}	4.5^{m}	10.7^{m}
J and K	-7.5^{n}	-8.8^{n}	-11.9^{n}	4.2^{n}	8.8^{m}	6.2^{m}	0.3^{m}	-0.6^{m}	1.1^{m}	2.8^{m}	0.1^{m}	2.5^{m}	7.5^{n}	8.8^{m}	11.9^{n}
Karnataka	-1.1^{m}	0.9^{m}	-0.2^{n}	-0.1^{m}	-0.8^{m}	-0.5^{m}	1.1^{m}	-0.1^{m}	-0.6*	1.1^{m}	0.3^{m}	0.8^{m}	3.1^{m}	-0.9^{n}	0.2^{m}
Kerala	-16.1^{m}	-11.3^{m}	-14.4^{m}	0.4^{n}	1.7^{m}	0.9^{n}	7.6^{m}	1.3^{m}	4.9^{m}	4.0^{m}	1.6^{m}	3.2^{m}	16.1^{m}	11.3^{m}	-14.4^{m}
MP	-8.1^{m}	-5.8^{m}	-7.3^{m}	1.3^{m}	2.6^{m}	1.8^{m}	3.4^{m}	0.8^{m}	27^{m}	73.1^{m}	0	2.4^{m}	8.1^{m}	5.8^{m}	7.3^{m}
Maharashtra	-3.9^{m}	-0.5^{n}	-2.6*	1.0^{m}	0.1^{n}	0.6^{n}	0.8*	0.7^{n}	0.5^{m}	2.1^{m}	-3.3^{m}	1.4^{m}	3.9^{m}	0.5^{n}	2.6^{m}
Orissa	-12.8^{m}	-10.4^{m}	-11.9^{m}	2.8^{m}	8.2^{m}	4.7^{m}	4.5^{m}	2.3^{m}	3.8^{m}	3.9^{m}	0.3^{m}	2.3^{m}	12.8^{m}	10.4^{m}	11.9^{m}
Punjab	-13.4^{m}	-3.0^{m}	-7.8^{m}	3.2^{m}	2.4^{m}	2.5^{m}	8.8^{m}	0.1^{m}	5.3^{m}	3.0^{m}	0	1.5^{m}	13.4^{m}	3.0^{m}	7.8^{m}
Rajasthan	-9.4^{m}	-3.5^{m}	-7.0^{m}	2.2^{m}	2.2^{m}	2.2^{m}	3.6^{m}	1.3^{n}	2.6^{m}	2.8^{m}	0.1^{n}	1.7^{m}	9.4^{m}	3.5^{m}	7.0^{m}
TN	-5.3^{m}	-4.7^{m}	-5.1^{m}	0.7^{m}	17^{m}	1.1^{m}	5.0^{m}	1.3^{m}	3.8^{m}	1.6^{m}	1.6^{m}	1.6^{m}	5.3^{m}	4.7^{m}	5.1^{m}
UP	-10.0^{m}	-3.5^{m}	-7.2^{m}	2.6^{m}	2.7^{m}	2.5^{m}	4.8^{m}	0.4^{m}	3.3^{m}	3.1^{m}	-0.4^{m}	1.9^{m}	10.0^{m}	3.5^{m}	7.2^{m}
WB	-0.8^{n}	-0.1^{m}	-0.6^{n}	-2.8^{m}	-1.1^{n}	-2.5^{n}	2.3*	-1.1^{m}	1.5^{n}	2.4^{m}	0.7^{m}	2.0^{m}	0.8^{n}	0.1^{n}	0.4^{n}
India	-7.6^{m}	-2.9^{m}	-5.7^{m}	0.9^{m}	1.4^{m}	1.1^{m}	3.6^{m}	0.6^{m}	2.5^{m}	2.8^{m}	0.4^{n}	1.8^{m}	7.6^{m}	2.9^{m}	5.7^{m}

Source: As in Table 13.1.

Notes: M = Male, F = Female, All = Male + Female.

m = Monotonous change, n=Non-monotonous tendency.

* = Ref.

Table 13.3 : Percentage Shares of Self-Employment (SE) and Casual Employment (CE) in Total Employment (UPSS) in Rural India

States	*Male*						*Female*					
	1993-94		*1999-2000*		*2004-05*		*1993-94*		*1999-2000*		*2004-05*	
	SE	CE	SE	CE	SE	CE	SE	CE	SE	CE	SE	CE
AP	49.1	42.8	48.4	44.0	48.4	41.9	45.3	52.8	42.6	53.8	47.2	48.7
Assam	60.0	26.6	59.0	25.3	41.3	19.4	49.1	32.7	54.8	25.4	70.3	21.3
Bihar	55.4	39.9	53.9	41.9	62.4	34.7	41.9	56.4	47.7	50.8	51.7	46.5
Gujarat	46.9	43.2	50.9	39.5	49.6	40.2	55.4	43.1	59.1	39.3	59.5	37.9
Haryana	63.3	23.2	59.0	24.4	58.0	22.0	77.4	21.5	86.0	12.5	84.9	12.8
HP	75.1	12.7	62.9	20.4	61.4	20.4	96.7	1.6	95.9	1.2	92.9	2.0
J & K	72.0	11.8	73.3	14.5	69.9	13.5	96.2	1.8	97.4	0.5	94.5	2.4
Karnataka	57.9	35.6	51.8	40.6	49.6	44.1	53.4	44.3	47.6	50.5	48.9	48.1
Kerala	40.8	46.9	38.1	48.9	41.5	43.5	55.0	35.3	53.0	32.0	53.1	27.6
MP	62.4	31.7	58.0	37.1	61.4	32.1	61.2	37.6	54.4	44.1	59.1	37.7
Maharashtra	49.3	38.8	44.1	44.1	50.6	37.1	48.1	49.4	44.5	54.0	51.7	45.8
Orissa	56.6	37.2	48.4	45.8	56.4	36.1	56.2	42.5	49.2	49.5	61.9	35.9
Punjab	54.7	32.1	54.0	28.5	47.1	33.5	85.0	11.8	88.9	7.4	88.9	6.5
Rajasthan	71.8	20.8	73.3	18.9	70.0	21.5	88.4	10.7	89.0	10.0	87.0	11.6
TN	41.4	46.1	35.8	48.9	39.9	46.7	41.9	52.9	38.0	55.1	46.1	47.3
UP	72.4	21.9	70.8	22.1	72.4	20.5	79.5	19.6	77.5	20.9	85.2	13.1
WB	54.7	35.0	49.2	43.3	53.4	39.3	59.0	33.7	62.4	32.5	61.0	30.7
India	57.7	33.8	55.0	36.2	58.1	23.9	58.6	38.7	57.3	39.6	63.7	32.6

Source: As in Table 13.1.

Punjab (highest), Kerala, Himachal Pradesh and Haryana. The very small increase in male employment share is only observed in Gujarat, Maharashtra and J & K (Less than 1 per cent point). The percentage of female employment in construction is smaller than that of male employment in all the States.

The increase in the proportion of rural male workers undertaking trade and commerce activities has been rather modest everywhere. Female engagement in these activities is relatively less as compared to its counterpart. It is clear from the study that transformation of labour utilization has taken place in two ways: (1) from farm activities to non-farm activities; and (2) from rural activities to urban activities. It is due to modernization of farming system, extension of rural-urban linkages, and expansion of rural market, rural electrification, and quality of labour and reasonable labour wage.

Overall Pattern

In India as a whole the activity pattern of employment reveals that the steady increase in employment share of the non-farm sector is exhibited at the cost of the farm sector irrespective of sex over the 22-year period. The non-farm employment growth is due to trade and commerce, construction, transport and communication and manufacturing. Though manufacturing dominates the pattern of the industry sector, trade and commerce of the service sector has accounted relatively high share in non-farm employment compared to other activities over time. It is clear from estimates that manufacturing has shared relatively more female employment over time as compared to male employment. It is explained by the fact that female workers enjoy easy access to their works at the houses.

Mode of Employment

Labour is employed not only in alternative activities but also under different managements. Some workers have managed their own works and they are called self-employed. Some others have worked against regular salary and they belong to the category of regular employed. A section of workers are also absorbed by others casually or occasionally. They are called casual labour and they have no permanent jobs.

Among three categories of employment *self-employment is the main feature of rural employment irrespective of sex: it dominates the employment pattern of over time. The pattern has now moved towards casualization and feminization. Female workforce has been employed relatively more as compared to male workforce in the category of self-employment during 1983-2005. Share of self-employment for male has declined during the period in most of the States at the cost of casual employment. On the contrary, the reverse has happened in case of female.*

Growth Pattern of Employment

The annual compound' growth rate of rural employment has varied across sectors among the States. Employment prospects are not bright in farm sector. Growth rate of employment in this sector becomes slow-moving and thus rural workers fall back upon the non-farm sector for their survival. *The States that have exhibited low growth rate of farm employment have registered high growth in the non-farm sector in the post-reform period as compared to the pre-reform period.*

The overall non-farm growth of employment has increased in the post-reform period while the reverse has happened in case of farm employment. The growth rates are 1.24 per cent during 1983-1994 and 0.86 per cent during 1994-2005 for farm employment and those for non-farm employment are 3.05 per cent and 3.81 per cent in the respective periods. Turning to the growth of the activity employment in India as a whole it is noted that the rate ranges from 0.06 per cent in farm activities to 8.6 per cent in transport and communication. Retrogression in employment is observed only is mining and quarry, electricity-gas-water supply in the post-reform period. Employment growth in construction is 7.4 per cent. It is next to that of transport and communication. Employment in manufacturing has grown at the rate of less than 2 per cent.

Across the States, retrogression in farm employment is observed in Tamil Nadu, Kerala and Andhra Pradesh in the reforms period. The growth rate is highest in Assam followed by Haryana, Gujarat and West Bengal during 1994-2005, while for its counterpart Bihar has exhibited the highest growth followed by Orissa, Madhya Pradesh, Haryana and Uttar Pradesh. However, Bihar and Orissa have marked initially a very low growth in the pre-reform period. The growth of non-farm employment has declined in Gujarat, Karnataka, Maharashtra, Rajasthan, Tamil Nadu and West Bengal. *As to the diversification of rural employment among the States, it is noted that employment growth divergence is relatively more in the post-reform period in case of farm sector (12.7 per cent) than in the pre-reform period (81 per cent) while it is relatively less in case of non-farm sector (46 per cent and 53 per cent).*

Sector-Diversification in the Employment Structure

To examine the overall aspects of rural employment pattern a macro index is needed. Based on Thiel's equality index (Thiel, 1967) Diversification Index (DI) of rural employment is defined as:

$$DI = \sum_{i=1}^{n} x_i \log\left(\frac{1}{x_i}\right) / \log n$$

Where x_1= share of the i=th sector in rural employment,
n= number of sectors.

The value of *DI* lies between 0 and 1. When *DI* = *0*, total rural employment is completely shared by one sector and for *DI=1* all sectors share total rural employment equally. It follows that

$$0 \leq DI \leq 1$$

Estimates reveal that the values of *DI* are less than 0.400 everywhere in India during 1993/94-2004/05 indicating that a few sectors have assumed higher importance in rural employment. Thus the sectors have not been diversified in employment. In India indices are 0.194 in 1999-2000 and 0.218 in 2004-05. Among the States the value of index is highest in

Kerala (more than 0.300) over time while it is lowest in MP (less than 0.150). The rural employment is highly concentrated in farm sector everywhere in India while the other sectors are lagged behind.

Incidence of Poor and Poverty

Well-being of rural people in the State (country) can be judged from different angles. Among them here we have taken two: (1) extent of rural poor and poverty, and (2) that of rural monthly per capita expenditure. Higher (lower) the number of poor and poverty in the rural States, lower (higher) the level of people's well-being and hence they are not able to afford their required expenses for livelihood. On the other hand, higher (lower) the level of rural MPCE, greater (smaller) the spending power rural people have and they hold high standard of living.

Poor

The extent of the poor has varied across the States. Across the States, a group of 3 States comprising Bihar, MP and UP has shared jointly 43 per cent of the rural poor of the country in 1983. Their share has increased to 48 per cent in 1993-94 and then to 52.4 per cent in 2004-05: it indicates high concentration of rural poor in these States. But other States such as Punjab, Haryana and J & K have accounted jointly for 2.4 per cent, 3.3 per cent and 2.1 per cent of the poor of the country in the respective years. The share is highest in UP (more than 18 per cent) over time followed by Bihar, MP, Maharashtra and West Bengal. It is lowest in HP followed by J & K and Punjab (less than 1 per cent each). *The number of the poor have decreased everywhere excepting Bihar, M.P. and UP during the period under study.*

India, as a whole, the rural poor as a percentage of the total number of poor has declined marginally from 78 per cent in 1983 to 76 per cent in 1993-94 and then to 74 per cent in 2004-05. Across the States the share of rural poor in the State's total number of the poor ranges from 61 per cent in Punjab to 94 per cent in Assam in 1983. The corresponding figures are 58 per cent in Gujarat and 97 in Assam; 42 per cent in TN and 97 per cent in Assam in the respective years *Assam's share is the highest over time. The States such as UP, Orissa and West Bengal belong to the limit of 80-90 per cent over time. Punjab, Gujarat and AP belong to the limit of less than 70 per cent.*

Poverty

Poverty (Headcount Ratio) is measured by the number of rural people below the poverty line as percentage of total population. *Rural poverty is reduced in most of the States. It is very high in the States of Orissa and Bihar (more than 40 per cent).* It ranges from 30 per cent to 40 per cent in MP, UP and from 20 per cent to 30 per cent in Maharashtra, TN, Karnataka and West Bengal in 2004-05. *Orissa's poverty is almost 5 times that of Punjab (9.5 per cent) and 10 times that of J & K.* Poverty is lowest in J & K (4.8 per cent) followed by Punjab, AP, Kerala, HP and Haryana. In 1983 it is as low as 14 per cent in Punjab being preceded by HP, Haryana, AP and J & K (less than 30 per cent each) while it is as high as 68 per cent in Orissa followed by Bihar, West Bengal and TN (more than 56 per cent each).

Levels of Living

Extent of MPCE

The nature and the extent of the levels of living are manifest in MPCE. The level of living in rural areas is compared with that in urban areas in terms of rural MPCE as percentage of urban MPCE. It has declined over time almost everywhere in India. It is lowest (45 per cent) in MP preceded by Gujarat, West Bengal, Karnataka and Assam (less than 55 per cent each) in 2004-05 while the level of living is highest (91 per cent) in Kerala followed by Haryana, J & K (more than 80 per cent each). *Maharashtra is the State where the level of living is almost stable (51 per cent).*

Inequality of MPCE

In some States a section of rural people are wealthy and hence they have more purchasing power and higher standard of living while other people are economically backward and their capacity of purchasing is very low. The pattern of rural MPCE is not uniform among rural people in the States. So to find out the degree of variation in the distribution of MPCE we have used the Gini measure as a system (macro) index of inequality. The value of index (Gini coefficient) ranges between 0 and 1. For 0, the MPCE pattern is completely egalitarian. Rural people have equal MPCE and there is no disparity in the MPCE distribution. For 1, only one person among the people shares total MPCE and there is a complete concentration in the MPCE distribution. Higher (lower) the value of the index, greater (smaller) the concentration of rural MPCE the rural State has. The States that have exhibited increasing concentration of MPCE are Haryana, Maharashtra, Kerala and TN (More than 0.3). Out of 17 States, 13 States have registered increase in inequality index of the MPCE distribution in 2004-05 as compared to that in 1993-94. *However, the distribution of MPCE has tended to be diversified in Assam and Bihar.*

Inequality Growth of MPCE

Let us now turn to the trend of inequality. Across the States inequality growth rates are heterogeneous in both pre- and-post-reform periods. It is highest in Haryana (0.9 per cent) and lowest in HP (0.1 per cent) in the pre-reform period. The corresponding figures are 2.2 per cent in Kerala and 0.14 per cent in Maharashtra in the post-reform period. It is also noted that *the retrogression in MPCE inequality is observed in almost everywhere in the pre-reform period while the reverse has happened in the post-reform period. Inequality growth rate has declined in the States of Maharashtra and J & K in the reform period. Inequality growth divergence among the States is very high (more than 118 per cent) during the periods, though it has marginally declined in the reform period.*

Growth Rate of MPCE

A depressed performance is observed in the States of Karnataka, MP, Orissa and Rajasthan (less than 0.8 per cent each) in the reform period. Four States such as Assam, Haryana, HP and J & K have displayed MPCE growth in the range of 2 to 3 per cent. The States that have registered relatively higher growth in the post-reform period compared to the pre-reform period (less than 0.5 per cent each) are Bihar, Gujarat, Haryana and Uttar Pradesh. *Two States such as Assam, HP have achieved spectacularly higher MPCE growth (more than 2 per cent) leaving the path of retrogression in MPCE in the pre-reform period. The growth has declined in West Bengal, Tamil Nadu, Madhya Pradesh, Orissa. Kerala is the exception from other States. Its performance is worth mentioning. It has achieved a very high growth: 0.8 per cent in 1983-94 and 3-8 per cent in 1994-2005. MPCE growth divergence among the major 17 States is very high, though it has declined from 123 per cent to 81 per cent.*

Poverty and Inequality

We have classified the States of India so as to find out changing the socio-economic scenario of the rural States on the basis of rural poverty ratio and inequality index (Gini) of rural MPCE during the period under study. The Table 13.6 exhibits the mode of classification in terms of disparity.

We have got 4 cells : (L, L), (H, L), (L, H) and (H, H). The cell (L, L) implies the State has a low poverty and low inequality while the cell (H, H) signifies that the State displays a high poverty with high inequality. The cell (L, H) indicates that the state records a low poverty with a high inequality while the cell (H, L) depicts that the state exhibits high poverty with low inequality. Among the cells the cell (L, L) is preferable. It is expected that lower the level of poverty, higher the degree of equality in the distribution of MPCE. The other cells are not preferable.

From estimates (Tables 13.4-13.5) we have got four types of the classification of the States in relation to India : some States

Table 13.4 : Incidence of Poor and Poverty in Rural India

States	*Poor across States (%)*			*P/TP (%)*			*Poverty Ratio (%)*			*Growth Rate of Poor (%)*	
	1983	1993-94	2004-05	1983	1993-94	2004-05	1983	1993-94	2004-05	1983-94	1994-05
AP	4.66	3.41	2.72	69.85	54.49	53.42	27.31	16.64	10.85	-2.56	-2.29
Assam	2.86	3.76	2.46	94.25	97.08	97.44	41.92	44.43	23.05	2.65	-3.50
Bihar	16.66	18.77	19.51	90.53	91.16	89.74	64.89	57.24	43.06	0.95	-0.21
Gujarat	2.70	2.58	2.88	61.33	58.14	72.43	27.92	22.44	19.76	-0.57	0.44
Haryana	0.92	1.42	0.93	74.92	81.25	66.36	21.77	26.62	13.41	4.60	-0.35
HP	0.29	0.58	0.31	93.67	97.31	96.05	17.77	29.27	12.50	8.72	-4.51
J & K	0.50	0.51	0.17	90.07	89.36	74.07	25.23	19.73	4.81	-0.07	-6.20
Karnataka	4.11	3.94	3.73	65.94	61.94	56.52	37.51	30.24	23.73	0.53	-0.01
Kerala	3.18	2.36	1.29	76.99	74.42	62.84	38.46	26.49	12.27	-2.47	-4.41
MP	8.41	8.82	10.77	77.62	72.88	76.15	48.21	40.43	38.17	0.26	1.37
Maharashtra	7.64	7.72	7.74	67.22	61.77	56.78	45.04	37.66	30.36	-0.08	-0.53
Orissa	6.52	5.79	6.78	90.92	88.35	84.18	67.52	50.11	47.76	-1.16	0.90
Punjab	0.72	0.82	0.69	61.28	72.34	75.23	14.30	13.72	9.55	1.10	-1.91
Rajasthan	4.31	3.99	3.91	78.24	74.06	67.23	37.72	26.89	18.91	-0.82	-0.74
TN	7.49	4.82	3.37	70.35	58.88	42.05	56.22	32.99	22.96	-3.35	-3.12
UP	17.70	20.46	22.13	80.80	82.21	80.39	46.38	42.33	34.06	1.21	0.15
WB	10.37	7.85	7.57	84.41	80.76	79.62	61.56	37.35	28.49	-2.35	-0.85
India	100.00	100.00	100.00	77.71	76.16	73.53	45.76	37.26	29.18	-0.17	-0.55
CV (%)				14.33	18.13	20.72	29.0	34.4	47.4		

Source: Sarvekshana, Vol. 13, No 2 (1989); NSSO Report Nos. 402 (1996) and 508 (2006).
Note: P/TP = Rural poor as percentage of total poor in the State.

Table 13.5 : Rural-Urban MPCE Ratio (R/U), Gini Coefficient of MPCE (G) and Growth Rate of MPCE (g) in Rural India

States	*R/U (%)*			*g(%)*		*Gini Coefficient (G)*			*Growth Rate of G (%)*	
	1983	*1993-94*	*2004-05*	*1983-94*	*1994-05*	*1983*	*1993-94*	*2004-05*	*1983-94*	*1994-2005*
AP	63.61	70.66	60.74	1.02	1.09	0.296	0.289	0.294	-0.24	0.15
Assam	78.71	56.29	54.56	-0.26	2.00	0.201	0.179	0.199	-1.11	0.98
Bihar	69.10	61.84	59.61	0.62	1.23	0.2630	0.225	0.212	-1.47	-0.51
Gujarat	74.07	66.78	52.93	0.39	1.02	0.269	0.240	0.271	-1.08	1.11
Haryana	82.25	81.24	82.60	0.01	2.18	0.285	0.313	0.339	0.90	0.73
HP	64.85	46.94	62.13	-1.02	2.51	0.281	0.284	0.310	0.09	0.79
J & K	83.73	67.08	82.34	0.91	2.36	0.228	0.243	0.248	0.58	0.18
Karnataka	02.96	63.66	54.29	0.21	0.43	0.311	0.269	0.265	-1.34	-0.15
Kerala	87.05	79.06	91.34	0.86	0.80	0.320	0.301	0.382	-0.57	2.18
MP	62.92	61.76	45.10	0.72	0.26	0.298	0.279	0.277	-0.62	-0.09
Maharashtra	50.66	51.46	50.51	1.09	1.00	0.291	0.306	0.311	0.50	0.14
Orissa	50.16	54.60	56.51	2.02	0.72	0.271	0.246	0.285	-0.92	1.32
Punjab	96.44	84.78	66.94	-0.31	1.07	0.293	0.283	0.295	-0.33	0.39
Rajasthan	84.26	75.90	67.86	-0.54	0.49	0.382	0.265	0.250	-3.41	-0.51
TN	58.90	66.99	68.27	2.34	1.21	0.392	0.312	0.321	-2.16	0.26
UP	82.63	70.40	66.15	0.36	1.03	0.291	0.281	0.290	-0.34	0.28
WB	53.36	58.79	53.58	2.70	1.09	0.301	0.254	0.273	-1.61	0.65
India	65.82	61.44	56.47	0.83	1.16	0.308	0.285	0.304	-0.72	0.59
CV (%)	22.48	18.68	24.86	122.7	80.7	15.78	13.58	16.07	147.66	118.23

Source: As in Table 13.4.
Mahendra and Ravi, EPW Feb 10, 2007.

have displayed low poverty and low MPCE inequality while some others have exhibited high poverty with high inequality. Again some States have recorded low poverty with high inequality and some others have depicted high poverty with low inequality. *Out of 17 States, only three States such as Gujarat, J & K and Punjab have registered low poverty with low inequality in MPCE. On the contrary, Maharashtra and Tamil Nadu has high poverty with high inequality in the reforms period (1994-2005).*

Table 13.6 : 2×2 Classification of the States

Inequality/Poverty	*Low (less than national level) (L)*	*High (greater than or equal to national level) (H)*
Low (less than national level) (L)	(L, L)	(L, H)
High (greater than or equal to national level) (H)	(H, L)	(H, H)

Concluding Remarks

The level of rural poverty will be reduced if rural labour force is engaged intensively in rural alternative activities as scheduled in the rural developmental programmes of the Government. The quality of rural workforce should also be improved through rural training programmes. Rural employment programmes and poverty eradication schemes should be implemented on priority basis with active involvement of rural representatives (Gram Panchayats) who have more accountability to ensure employment in rural areas so as to reduce the extent of poverty and to increase the level of MPCE. Simultaneous, the programme for the removal of poverty from the States (country) should be time bound.

REFERENCES

Annual Report, NABARD, 2003-04.

Bhaumik, S.K. (2007), "Growth and Composition of Rural Non-farm Employment in India in the Era of Economic Reforms", *Indian Economic Journal*, Vol. 55, No. 3.

Chakraborty, D. *et al.* (2004). "Changing Levels of Living in India in the 1990s" in Singh, Ravishankar Kumar (ed.) *Economic Reforms in India*, Abhijit Publication, Delhi.

Dev, S.M. and Ravi, C. (2007), "Poverty and Inequality: All India and States, 1983-2005", *Economic and Political Weekly*, February 10.

Dutta, R. (2007). "Poverty, Employment and Growth: Pre- and post-Reform Experience". *Indian Economic Journal*, Vol. 54, No. 4.

NSSO Reports—38th, 50th, 55th and 61st rounds of Employment and Unemployment in India.

NSSO Reports—43rd, 50th and 61st rounds of Consumer Expenditure Surveys in India.

Pal, D.P. and Sen, J. (2002). "Social Sector Reforms and Relative Income Deprivation in India: A Note", Conference Volume, *Indian Economic Association*.

Pal, D.P. and Sen, J. (2003). "On Dimensions of Poverty: A Cross-Section Study in India with Rural-Urban Desegregation, Conference Volume, *Indian Economic Association.*

Pal, P.K. *et al.* (1995), "Non-Farm Employment and Rural Economic Transformation in India", *Journal of Agricultural Economics*, Conference Volume, Indian Economic Association.

Pal, G.P. (2007), "Impacts of the Economic Reforms on Indian Rural Economy: Growth, Employment and Capital Formation", *National Seminar Volume*, Nov. 3-4, Kakatiya University, Warangal.

Sundaran, K. (2001), "Employment-Unemployment Situation in the Nineties Some Results from NSS 55th Round Survey", *Economic and Political Weekly*, Vol. 36, No. 11.

Sen, Abhijit and Himansu (2004), "Poverty and Inequality in India', *Economic and Political Weekly*, Vol. 39, No. 38.

Sarvekshana, (1989), Vol. 13

14

Agricultural Functions in Purnia

A Study of North Bihar

MAHMOOD ANSARI

Conceptual Foundation

Peasantries are actually economically differentiated groups in the countryside. Such groups differ with each other not only in the matter of ownership, control and operation of land but also the use and exploitation of outside labour hired on the farms. The degree of use of hired-in labour *vis-à-vis* family labour differentiates the peasantries into at least five economic classes: petty/poor peasant, small peasant, middle peasant, rich peasant, and landlord/capitalist. Agricultural production is organized by combining a number of non-land inputs with the land on the farms of peasantry. The output obtained and the inputs applied bear a definite relation of association. Such relation is usually captured by the conventional input-output analysis with the help of a theoretical concept called an agricultural production function. It shows the technical relationship between the physical quantities of inputs used and output obtained on the agricultural farms. A production function in agriculture describes the maximum output for each specified combination of agricultural inputs. It refers to the physical relation between inputs and output. It represents the purely technical relations between inputs and output on the peasant farm. It describes the laws of proportions of inputs at any particular point of time. A production function can be represented mathematically in the form of algebraic equations, and diagrammatically by a series of isoquants (the negatively sloped curve in an input-output space). A production function describes not only a single isoquant but the whole array of the isoquants on the map, whereby each isoquant represents a method of economizing on the use of agricultural resources by a peasant-producer. The method commonly used for statistical fitting of an agricultural production function in the literature is the least square method of the regression analysis. In the perspective of the present work, the conceptual doubt towards such a technique of production analysis is premised on the fact that it simplifies the complex realities of the production process in agriculture. The concept of production function abstracts from the concrete economic differentiation among the peasantry, which is the core of Marxist perspective on peasantries. Since all operators are not theoretically the profit maximizers (Bhardawaj 1974:61-62), a hierarchy of production functions specific to each class of farms is possible and must be estimated in a realistic analysis.

It is worth arguing that there are no motivational forces, which are definable, *a priori* for any peasant household independently of the entire gamut of production and market relations in which it is involved. The objective behind peasant production may not be unequivocally the profit-seeking. There may be a situation for classes of peasantry whereby a peasant-cultivator of a specific class location may not even make both ends meet. A peasant may be in debt. It may not be the net returns for a peasant of this class but the gross yield, which he/she may be seeking to maximize with the burden of debt allowed to be accumulating. In such circumstances, it is clearly futile to reduce all operators to the status of the profit maximizers. The assumption of a given qualitatively identical materials, equipment and machinery and, therefore, almost uniform technology used by each cross-section of farms is then far from reality. It is worth arguing that there cannot logically and realistically be a uniform technology adopted by the peasantry, who are in reality differentiated on the basis of inequality in the resource endowments and land ownership base. In such a circumstance, the minimization of deviations from the average relation between inputs and output characterizing the least-square method of regression analysis so as to derive a unique aggregate production function is antithesis of the phenomenon of differentiation of peasantry.

In the alternative standard model, it is invariably assumed that a peasant owns and controls a profit-seeking production enterprise in agriculture. Peasants are rational, and the objective of agricultural production is profit maximization. It is assured by running the production unit on the basis of utilization of the inputs in technically efficient manner. The State of knowledge about the various methods that might be used to transform the inputs into agricultural outputs, that is, production technology in agriculture used by a peasant is assumed to be given for a given period of time. It is further assumed that the agricultural inputs are perfectly divisible. These assumptions are at the core of neo-classical thinking in the mainstream economics. Under such postulates of theorists of the neo-classical persuasions, a vital tool and technique of input-output relations have been devised in the literature. This is called the agricultural production function. The basic theory of production is built on the basis of such a function, and concentrates only on the efficient methods or processes or activity. A rational entrepreneur in agriculture is not assumed to be using any inefficient method of production. In the neo-classical literature, agricultural growth is then measured by statistical fitting of an aggregate production function for agriculture, and there are sophisticated tools available for the statistical fitting of the function, for example, the multiple regression analysis. The marketable and marketed output functions of individual crop as well as aggregate basket of crops are fitted and statistically estimated with the help of simple and multiple regression analysis. There are, however, debates surrounding the statistical estimates, and the associated measurement methods. It is affirmed that there may be a possibility of 'specification bias' in fitting a production and marketed output function. The specification bias arise when the specification of the list of relevant factors in a relation is either wrong or a particular factor is omitted. While fitting a production function in agriculture, the omission of variables like human labour, draft power, etc. are very much likely because of disregard of importance to measurement of the variable itself (Minhas 1966:176). In a statistical fitting of a production function of Cobb Douglas type, there are further serious problems of isolating the marginal productivity of human labour from that of other inputs like livestock (Bardhan, 1973). On methodological grounds, the statistical procedures employed to fit a function have been found to be unsatisfactory (Rudra 1982; Bhardawaj 1979; Jodha and Anderson 1973; Sen 1975). It is, therefore, asserted that such functions are usually too simple to capture adequately the complexities of the agricultural production processes (Booth and Sundaram 1984:248). It is not to say that the function is not at all an improved and rigorous tool of analysis of the production activity of the peasantry on uniformly controlled experimental farms. But when it comes to applying it to the actually existing uncontrolled non-experimental farms, the case is different. The statistical fitting of an agricultural production function moreover involves a departure from the theoretical concept. The departure consists in the fact that the measurement of variables (*i.e.* input and/or output) in the value terms is possible on the assumption of a uniform "price regime". It is also the case that the statistical fitting affords only average or "expected" estimate of the functional relation. Its deviation from the "maximum" or maximal estimate (the theoretical concept of neo-classical vintage point) needs to be measured (Rudra 1982: 273-75). With such caveats, we attempt below the build-up of models of agricultural functions and estimates of regression analysis.

Peasant Strata and Multiple Models of Agricultural Functions

In order to classify the peasantry, Utsa Patnaik (1976 : A-83-89) has put forward a labour-exploitation index. Symbolically, it is defined for a given rural household as follows :

$$E = X/Y = [(H_i\text{-}H_o) + (L_o\text{-}L_i)]/F$$

In the above formulation, E is the labour-exploitation index, and H_i refers to labour days hired on the operational holdings of the household, H_o to family labour days hired-out to others, L_i labour days worked on leased-in land (whether by family or hired labour), L_o labour days similarly worked on land leased-out by household, and F labour days worked by family labour on the operational holding. The extreme values of E are infinity for the big landlord and minus infinity for the landless labourer *i.e.* $\propto \geq E \geq -\propto$. It is possible to approximately identify a capitalist, a landlord, a petty tenant and an agricultural labourer on the basis of the estimated value of labour-exploitation index of a rural household.

In the present study in Purnia district of north Bihar, we have primary data on randomly sampled 268 rural producing households and their farms. The farms are sampled from three villages of the district. We have the labour use data in sufficient detail for the major crops paddy and jute but not in sufficient detail for the minor ones. The definition of exploitation index, E, is thereby modified as follows (we expect that this modification will not seriously affect the validity of the economic class divisions obtained).

E=(Plhi+Alhi) - (Plho+Alho) + (Renttakn-Rentgivn)/ (Padfl+Jutfl)

The notations *'Plhi'* and *'Plho'* refer to the annual total number of mandays of plough labour hired-in and hired-out respectively, *'Alhi'* and *'Alho'* to the annual total number of mandays of daily casual, contract and other labour hired-in and hired-out respectively, *'Renttakn'* and *'Rentgivn'* to the estimated annual number of mandays (of all labour used on the piece of land leased-out) appropriated through rent and (of all labour used on the piece of land leased-in) parted away as rent respectively, and *'Padfl'* and *'Jutfl'* to the annual total number of mandays of family labour used in the production of paddy and jute crop respectively by a peasant household on the farm during 1991-92 kharif season.

The value of E is estimated for each one of 268 cultivating households of the three sampled villages. The households are then grouped into economic classes as per the limits specified in Patnaik (1976, 1986). In our present sample, the value of E ranges from minus 2.96 to plus infinity. In other words, the poor/petty peasants work for others to almost three times the extent of self-employment on their operated holdings while at the other pole the landlord/capitalists do not work at all. Excluding landlord/capitalists, the lowest and highest average values of E for peasant classes range from -2.96 for poor peasants to +588.33 for rich peasants. This means the rich peasants use others' labour to the extent of nearly six times the work the family puts in on its operational holding. This observed range is of course specific to our particular sample and will be different for another sample.

$E \leq -1$	the petty and poor peasant class
$0 \geq E > -1$	the small peasant class
$1 > E > 0$	the middle peasant class
$E \geq 1$	the rich peasant class
$E \rightarrow \alpha$	the landlord and capitalist class

We do not have any landless labour households in our sample.

The classification of households by the labour-exploitation index gives us 12 households of petty/poor peasants, 42 households of small peasants, 51 households of middle peasants, 108 households of rich peasants and 55 households of the landlord/capitalists in the sample pooled for the three villages. While landlords are theoretically distinguished from capitalists on the basis of whether their main source of income is through net leasing out land rent, as opposed to net hiring in and profit, we have not applied the distinction, as exact demarcation is difficult on the basis of our data. In Table 14.1, the distribution of sampled households into economic classes is furnished, and Chart 14.1 presents the visuals.

Table 14.1 : Distribution of Sample Households by Economic Class : Purnia, 1991-92

Economic Classes	*Number of Households/Farms*	*Percentage of Households/Farms*
Petty/Poor Peasant	12	4.5
Small Peasant	42	15.5
Middle Peasant	51	19.0
Rich Peasant	108	40.0
Capitalist/Landlord	55	21.0
All Economic Classes	268	100.0

Source: Field Sample Survey, 1991-92.

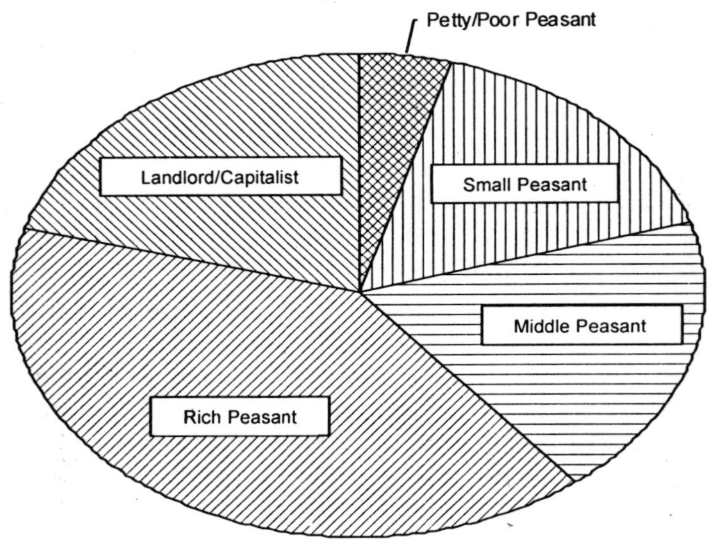

Chart 14.1: Distribution of Sample Households into Economic Classes : Purnia, 1991-92

Source: Derived from Table 14.1.
Note: The number of households and their percentage is given in the Table 14.1.

We have applied the Fisher's Discriminant Function Analysis, which makes it also possible to obtain the classification statistics. Such statistics gives the predicted class membership of the sample rural households under investigation (Burns and Bush, 2000). In the present work, it shows that the prior probabilities for the sample households to belong to the respective five economic classes are 0.045, 0.157, 0.190, 0.403, and 0.205 respectively. There is almost 48.1 per cent of original class membership based on the labour-exploitation criterion, which is correctly classified according to Discriminant Function Analysis. The classification function coefficients are, however, full of error and, therefore, the predicted class membership cannot be relied upon. One must read this classification with caution.

The most widely used and popular agricultural function is the Cobb-Douglas production function. It was a pioneering piece of economic work, which came up towards the close of the third decade of the present century (Cobb and Douglas 1928 : 139-65; Douglas 1948 : 1-41). It was a power production function. The function made it possible to use the statistical data on the volume of labour and stock of fixed capital employed to plot the shape of the production map. The original function was later modified by Douglas (1948) to account for the increasing and diminishing returns (Mitra 1980 : 18). There later emerged also the possibility of incorporating the input of land in the function (Mellor 1986 : 24). It was later argued further that there was a vital input called the raw material, which had not been taken care of in this function (Mitra 1980 : 19-21). There have thus been attempts to broaden the functional form in later years. There exists today a general mathematical form, which can be represented as:

$$Y = f(L, K, R, S, \upsilon, \gamma),$$

where L refers to the amount of labour, K to capital, R to the raw materials, S to land amount, υ to the returns to scale, and γ to the efficiency parameter. All the variables are flows, and measured per unit of time. The raw materials bear a constant relation to output for all levels of production and land can be assumed to be fixed for the economy, and thus may be lumped together with capital for individual firm. The abbreviated form of the function is then of the following form :

$$Y = f(L, K, \upsilon, \gamma).$$

The variable υ is relevant only in the long run. If land and capital are constant, then the output is simply a function of the efficiency parameter only. The parameter refers to the entrepreneurial organizational aspects of the production (Koutsoyiannis 1985 : 67-70). According to Yujiro Hayami (1975), there may be residuals, which may remain unexplained by the growth in inputs. This residual may be explained by the changes in the rate of growth in total factor productivity. The changes in the rate of growth in total factor productivity may be explained by including non-conventional factors such as education of farmers, public expenditure on agricultural research and extension, and improvement in land infrastructures in a production function. The growth rate of agricultural output on the peasant farms across the historical junctures shows distinct growth phases—distinct regions of total factor productivity growth. It is influenced by the technology.

In the present analysis of cross-section of agricultural farms, the general linear production function is conceived as follows:

$$X_c = f(A, e, L, B, M, C, P_L)\, g + D + F$$

The linear equation form is :

$$X_c = \alpha_0 + \alpha_1 A + \alpha_2 e' + \alpha_3 L + \alpha_4 B + \alpha_5 M + \alpha_6 C + \alpha_7 P_L + D + F,$$

where the notations X_c refers to the volume of output of a crop per acre, A to the amount of cultivated land area in acres, e to the percentage of cultivated area under artificial irrigation, L to the number of mandays of human labour input per acre, B to the number of mandays of bullock labour (or plough labour) per acre, M to the aggregate monetary value of material inputs of the seeds, manure, fertilizers, irrigation water, and pesticides per acre, C to the monetary value of expenses on the machinery like pump-sets, tractors, threshers, etc. running on farms per acre, P_L to the annual money cost of hiring-in the permanent labour per acre, g to the random multiplicative error term, D to the dummy representing village effect, and F to the dummy capturing the land fertility effect. The letter '*f*' refers to the functional notation. The notations α_0 refer to the intercept value, and notations α_1 to α_7 to the respective regression coefficients with respect to relevant inputs. It is to be noted that the letter '*g*' stands for an error term that arises from two sources: a stochastic-error-component, resulting from the effects on X_c of many omitted variables operating in different directions and each with a relatively small effect, and a measurement-error-component. All the variables are expressed in 'per-acre' terms to ensure homoskedasticity. The general linear model entails the restriction that the structure of the relationships is linear in α_is. Furthermore, it is assumed that the independent variables are measured without error.

In the case of **paddy crop**, the regression analysis is run over the aggregate sample of farms, and the statistical estimate of coefficients obtained. The linear **production function** fitted is found to be of the following reduced form:

$$Pp = \alpha_0 - \alpha 2e^r + \alpha_5 M + V$$

The least-square criterion of linear regression analysis gives statistically non-significant values of slope coefficients for other input variables of the original regression model; these independent input variables are thus eliminated, and a trimmed model is run. The input variables are, therefore, reconstituted to consider only those explanatory variables, whose *t*-value was respectively statistically significant. It is revealed that even the slope coefficient value for dummy variable of land fertility index show insignificant *t*-value. Putting the estimated values of intercept and slopes or the regression coefficients of the considered inputs, we get

$$P_p = 8.75 + 0.001\ M - 0.02e^r + 3.64V$$

The linear regression analysis has a 'goodness of fit'. The estimated *F*-value of the analysis of variance stands at 33.828, which is higher than the table value and, therefore, meaningful at 1 per cent level of significance. What is more significant is the reading that the test of Durbin-Watson gives the value of 1.796, which is of course closer to two—a desirable trait. The collinearity statistics referred to as Variance Inflation Factor (VIF) for all independent variables in the multiple regression equation is much less than 10, establishing that there is no concern for the multicollinearity in the backward step-wise regression. In other words, there is no need of reconstituting the set of determining variables under consideration.

Table 14.2 : Linear Regression Analysis of the Determinants of Annual Volume of Paddy Output per Acre on a Farm : Purnia, 1991-92
Mean Value : 10.37 quintals per acre
Standard Deviation : 3.65 quintals per acre

Regressors/Explanatory Variables	*Regression coefficient statistics*	*Standard error*	*t-value*	*Significance*
Constant	8.748	0.380	23.007	0.000
Total cost incurred on seeds, manure, fertilizers and irrigation per acre of operational land (rupees)	0.0007	0.000	5.082	0.000
Net area under irrigation as percentage of operated area	(-)0.018	0.006	(-)3.312	0.001
Paddy village dummy variable	3.641	0.399	9.131	0.000

In this regression analysis, the number of observations is 268 paddy farms of the sample peasantry in Purnia. The estimated *R*-value is 0.527. The R^2 value is the square of the correlation coefficient. The value of R^2 stands at 0.278. This R^2 value is important because it reveals how well the straight-line model fits the scatter of points in the regression plain. It is evident that it fits rather less well in the exercise under consideration. The statistical fitting of the cross-sectional paddy-crop production function is rather a poor one because it explains only 27.80 per cent of the variation in the annual volume of the paddy output per acre. The intercept value is positive one; which is a high numerical figure closer to the mean value of output variable. In statistical theory, the adjusted R^2 reduces the R^2 by taking into account the sample size and the number of parameters estimated. In the present exercise, the adjusted R^2 is at the numerical figure of 0.269. Be that as it may. The *F*-value of the analysis of variance signals, however, that null hypothesis of no linear relationship is to be rejected. The contribution of the total cost incurred on seeds, manure, fertilizers and irrigation per acre of operational land to the paddy output per acre is positive. The contribution of the irrigation input in explaining the change in the paddy output is, however, negative one. This is expected in a rainfed farming area. The most important part is nonetheless played by the area and village specificity clubbed under the dummy of so-called 'paddy-producing village'. Theoretically, the standard error of the estimate is a measure of the accuracy of the estimates of the regression equation. It is analogous to the standard error of the mean but based on residuals *i.e.* the difference between the predicted and actual value of paddy output per acreage under the crop. It is of course found to be low presently. The standard error of the estimate is found to be equivalent to 3.117.

In the case of **jute crop**, a trimmed linear model of the regression analysis is statistically fitted on the aggregate sample of 268 farms under consideration. This is again obtained by reconstituting the explanatory variables of the original regression model under consideration. The linear **production function**, which is statistically fitted, is found to be of the following reduced form :

$$P_J = \alpha_0 + \alpha_3 L + \alpha_6 C + \alpha_7 P_I + V$$

The other input variables of the original model were dropped from the analysis to improve the "goodness of fit". The regression coefficients of the dropped variables have *t*-value, which was significant not even on 10 per cent level of statistical significance. The estimated fit of the linear jute production function, obtained by least square method of multiple regression analysis with the statistical estimate of coefficients obtained, is as follows :

$$P_j = 2.50 + 0.01L - 0.0003M + 0.002P_I + 2.03V$$

The goodness of fit of the regression analysis of the annual volume of jute output per acre is established by the high numerical estimated and statistically significant *F*-value of analysis of variance. The estimated *F*-value, which stands at 45.098, is significant at 1 per cent level of significance. The Durbin-Watson value is also closer to two; the estimated value is 1.772. The collinearity statistics referred to as Variance Inflation Factor (VIF) for all independent variables in the multiple regression equation is much less than 10, which does unfailingly establish that there is no need of any concern about the multi-collinearity in the backward step-wise regression. In other words, there is no need of further reconstituting the set of determining variables under consideration.

Table 14.3 : Linear Regression Analysis of Determinants of Annual Volume of Jute Output per Acre on a Farm : Rural Purnia, 1991-92
Mean value = 4.85 quintals per acre
Standard deviation = 3.30 quintals per acre

Explanatory variables (Regressors)	*Regression coefficient*	*Standard error*	*t-value*	*Significance*
Constant	2.498	0.248	10.080	0.000
Total mandays of family, casual and contract labour employed per acre of jute production	0.009	0.001	9.294	0.000
Total cost incurred on seeds, manure, fertilizers and irrigation per acre of operational land (Rupees)	(-)0.0003	0.000	(-)1.995	0.047
Cost incurred in employing the permanent labour per acre of operated land (Rupees per acre)	0.0017	0.000	1.024	0.000
Jute village dummy variable	2.034	0.361	5.638	0.000

The number of observation is 268 farms of jute crop. The estimated *R* coefficient is high at the figure of 0.638. The significant coefficient is however the R^2 which is 0.407. It means that 40.70 per cent of the variation in the jute output per acre on the sample farms is explained by the input variables considered in the model. This is still high in a situation of a highly heterogeneous cross-section of farms of the sample. The adjusted R^2 value of course reduces to stand at 0.398. In other words, it is justifiable to use a straight-line relationship to model the selected variables. The contribution of the mandays of family, casual and contract labour per acre, and the monetary cost incurred on employing the permanent labour per acre on the jute farms are positive, along with the positive intercept value in the model. The role played by the annual cost incurred on seeds, manure, fertilizers and irrigation per acre of operational land in the change in the output of jute per acre is however negative. The village specific dummy variable is having a positive contribution in the changes in jute output on the farms. Be that as it may. The standard error of estimate is low at 2.561. It is worth to note that the regression equation of jute output cannot be strictly compared with the regression equation of paddy output in terms of the goodness of fit, because the R^2 value in each case pertains to two different trimmed model altogether. Despite this it is the linearity characteristics of the models are common. Nonetheless, it is understood that the variation in the jute yield is robustly explained by the inputs under consideration.

A simple linear cross-section marketed output function is likewise statistically fitted based on least-square method of multiple regression analysis in case of a crop in the following form :

$$Si = f(\chi_p, \chi_j, P_{mi}, I) + M,$$

where S_i refers to the proportion of net marketed output to net output of a crop over a year, χ_p to the annual volume of output of food crop per adult in quintals, χ_j to the current market price-based value of output of a commercial crop per adult in rupees, and P_{mi} to the weighted average market price of a crop per quintal received by a household across season in the year, I to the average income of a peasant householding from non-crop production, and M to the dummy variable called the market-type chosen by a household in disposing the surplus of a food crop. The goodness of fit is estimated based on the significance of R^2 value of estimates, t-value of a pair of determinant variable and the value of standard error of estimate. The diagnosis of multi-collinearity is particularly taken care of.

In the case of **paddy crop** marketed by the cross-sections of aggregate sample farms, a rather trimmed model is run, because the variables relating to the income and dummy are dropped due to these being found statistically not significant. The **marketed output function** of paddy crop on the basis of reconstituted independent variables is of the following linear equation form :

$$S_p = A + \alpha_1 \cdot \chi_p + \alpha_2 \cdot \chi_j + \alpha_3 P_{mp},$$

where A refers to the intercept value, the subscript p for the paddy crop, and α_1 to α_3 to the respective regression coefficients with respect to relevant independent variables. In the multiple regression analysis, the estimated values of intercept and regression coefficients give the following marketed output function for paddy crop:

$$S_p = -16.60 + 1.28\chi_p - 0.001\chi_j + 0.17\, P_{mp}$$

Table 14.4 : Linear Regression Analysis of the Determinants of the Proportion of Net Marketed Output to Net Output of Paddy Crop on a Farm : Purnia, 1991-92

Mean Value = 33.36

Standard Deviation=37.04

Explanatory Variables (Regressors)	*Regression coefficient*	*Standard error*	*t-value*	*Significance*
Constant	(-)16.603	2.700	(-)6.149	0.000
Annual volume of paddy output per adult (quintals)	1.284	0.160	8.038	0.000
Annual market value of jute output per adult (Rupees)	(-)0.0013	0.000	(-)3.472	0.001
Average market price of paddy per quintal (Rupees)	0.165	0.011	15.033	0.000

The linearity assumption and the set of explanatory variables chosen gives a statistical 'goodness of fit' with a high and significant value of R^2 and F-value of analysis of variance. The standard error of the estimate is nonetheless high. The model has goodness of fit on the cross-section of farms under consideration. The number of observation is 268 paddy farms. The F-value of analysis of variance is pretty high at 170.064, which is significant at 1 per cent level of significance. The Durbin-Watson value is 1.645. The estimated R-value is 0.812. The R^2 value is 0.659. In other words, the present linear model and the determining variables considered therein do explain 65.90 per cent of the variation in the proportion of the net-marketed output of paddy. The adjusted R^2 value is of course a reduced value, that is, 0.655. The standard error of the estimate is high at 21.666. The intercept value is negative, which is of course expected. We get the negative intercept, which captures the fact that there is phenomenon of positive sales of marketed output alongwith negative phenomenon of repurchases. In case of a few peasant farms, the net-marketed output of paddy is a negative figure due to high repurchases and zero marketed output. The contributions of the paddy output on the farm and paddy price in the market are positive to the variation in the proportion of the net-marketed output of paddy. It is but the role played by the market value earned by selling a commercial crop is negative. The annual jute output value per adult has otherwise weak significance in explaining the proportion of net marketed output to net output of the food crop of the sample farm. The three determining variables considered in the model, given the t-values estimated, are statistically significant. There is no need to reconstitute the set of variables considered, because the collinearity statistics referred to as Variance Inflation Factor (VIF) for all independent variables in the multiple regression equation is much less than 10, establishing that there is no concern for the multi-collinearity in the backward step-wise regression.

In case of **commercial crop of jute**, there is again the need to reconstitute the explanatory variables in the marketed output function. The income and dummy variables are statistically not significant. The trimmed model was, therefore, run. The statistically fitted **marketed output function** over the cross section of farms is of the following linear form :

$$S_j = A + \alpha_1 X_j + \alpha_2 P_{mj},$$

where S_j refers to the proportion of net marketed output to net output of jute in the year, X_j to annual volume of jute output per adult in quintals in the year and P_{mj} to the average current market price of jute per quintal in rupees received by a household. The least square method of the multiple regression analysis on the cross section of all sample farms gives the following marketed output function for jute crop estimate :

$$S_j = 1.85 + 0.181\ P_{mj}$$

Table 14.5 : Linear Regression Analysis of the Determinants of the Proportion of Net Marketed Output to Net Output of Jute Crop on a Farm : Purnia, 1991-92
Mean Value = 60.95
Standard Deviation = 38.83

Explanatory Variables (Regressors)	*Regression coefficient*	*Standard error*	*t-value*	*Significance*
Constant	1.850	1.236	1.496	0.136
Average jute market price per quintal (Rupees)	0.181	0.003	56.499	0.000

The number of observation is 268 jute-producing farms. The model has a highly satisfactory goodness of fit. The Durbin-Watson value is highly close to the desirable value, it stands at 1.927. It is almost close to 2.0. The *F*-value is pretty high numerical figure; it is 3192.160. This estimated value is of course significant at 1 per cent level of significance. The estimated *R*-value is 0.961. The value of the R^2 is 0.923. In other words, almost 92 per cent of the variation in the proportion of the jute-marketed surplus is explained by the trimmed linear model. The adjusted R^2 is 0.923. The standard error of the estimate is quite low at 10.791. There is no concern for the multi-collinearity phenomenon. The market price of the jute crop received by the farmers is the sole explanatory variable worth consideration. This is highly expected in case of a commercial crop. The intercept value is quite low but positive. The jute marketed output function is a comparatively better statistical fit with linearity assumptions of regression analysis than the paddy marketed output function of the overall sample farms.

Agricultural Functions : "Class Differentiated" Results

The present production function of cross-section of agricultural farms captures the input-output relation as one moves from farm to farm. This is irrespective of the size and qualitative features of the farms. The peasant farms are, however, operationally quite different and diverse rather qualitatively due to the differing economic class-locations of the owner-peasantry. The linear paddy regression equations are estimated, therefore, for each cross sub-section of the paddy and jute farms pertaining to the diverse agrarian locations of peasant classes. The linear production functions of paddy and jute crops for the cross-sections of each class farms, which are fitted and estimated, are all different in terms of coefficients and independent variables.

Petty/Poor Peasant

In the case of petty/poor peasant class farms, the statistical fitting gives the following linear form of paddy output regression equation :

$$P_p^{mg} = 7.50 + 0.014\,M - 0.04e^r + 1.21V$$

The number of observations is only 12 paddy farms. The estimated R-value of the regression analysis is 0.703. The R^2 coefficient is standing at 0.495. The adjusted R^2 is 0.305. The standard error of estimate is 2.699. The value of the Durbin-Watson value is 2.095. The F-value is 2.611, which is significant at 12.4 per cent level of significance. The intercept value is positive. The monetary expenditures on the seeds, manures, fertilizers, and irrigation do contribute positively to the variation in paddy yield. The village dummy is also contributing to the variation in the paddy output per acre rather positively. The area under irrigation contributes rather negatively in the variation of paddy yield on the marginal farms of the peasantry.

The statistical fitting gives the following linear form of jute output regression equation :

$$P_j^{mg} = 0.11 + 0.01L - 0.91V$$

The number of observations are 12 jute farms. The estimated R is 0.986. The estimated R^2 is 0.972. In other words, almost 97 per cent variation in the jute yield on the petty/poor peasant farms is explained by the inputs under consideration in the model. The adjusted R^2 value reduces to stand numerically at 0.966. The standard error of estimate is 0.515. The Durbin-Watson value is found to be 2.118. It is of course closer to the desirable value of two. The F-value of the estimate is 156.580. This is significant at 1 per cent level of significance. The intercept value is positive. The contribution of the jute specific village dummy is however negative. It is the mandays of human labour, which has a positive contribution to the jute yield on such farms.

The statistical fitting gives the following linear form of paddy marketed output regression equation:

$$S_p^{pp} = -22.70 + 0.16\ P_{mp}$$

The number of observations are only 12 paddy farms. The estimated R-value of the regression analysis of marketed output proportion of paddy is 0.722. The crucial R^2 value is 0.522. The adjusted R^2 value is 0.474. The standard error of estimate is 25.817. The Durbin-Watson value is highly close to the desirable value and stands at 2.152. The F-value of variance is 10.918. It is significant at 1 per cent level. The intercept value is negative, which is of course expected. There is positive contribution of the paddy price received by the farmers in explaining the variation in the proportion of the paddy-marketed output.

The statistical fitting gives the following linear form of jute marketed output regression equation :

$$S_j^{PP} = 0.009 + 0.21\ P_{mj}$$

The number of observations in this cross sub-section of paddy farms are 12 jute farms. The estimated *R*-value is 1.000. The coefficient of determination, represented by the R^2 stands at 0.999. This is certainly a high numerical figure. The adjusted R^2 reduces to the value of 0.999. The standard error of estimate is 0.846. The crucial test of the goodness of fit of the regression analysis is nonetheless performed by checking the value of the Durbin-Watson. It stands at the value of 1.471. The *F*-value is higher than the table value for the degree of freedom under consideration. It is 17961.795, which is significant at 1 per cent level of significance. There is no concern for the multi-collinearity phenomenon. The market price of the jute crop received by the farmers is the sole explanatory variable worth consideration. The intercept value is quite low but positive.

Small Peasant

In the case of small peasant class farms, the statistical fitting gives the following linear form of paddy output regression equation:

$$P_p^{sp} = 7.71 + 0.02\ P_{LM} + 2.48V$$

The number of observation is 42 paddy farms. The estimated *R*-value is 0.631. The R^2 is 0.398. In other words, close to 40 per cent of the variation in the yield of paddy on small class farms are explained by the inputs considered in the trimmed linear model. The adjusted R^2 is 0.368. The standard error of estimate is found to be at 2.335. The Durbin-Watson value is closer to two at 2.250. It is found that the null hypothesis of no relation is to be rejected because the *F*-value is 12.911, and it is significant at 1 per cent level. The intercept value is positive. The cost incurred in employing the permanent labour per acre of operated land contributes positively to the variation in the paddy yield on the small farms. The village dummy is also contributing to the variation in the paddy output per acre rather positively.

The statistical fitting gives the following linear form of jute output regression equation :

$$P_j^{sp} = 0.64 + 0.02L + 2.97V$$

The number of observations in the present regression exercise are a cross sub-section of 42 jute producing farms. The estimated R-value is found to be 0.846. The estimated R^2 value is standing at 0.715. In other words, almost 71.5 per cent variation in the jute yield on the small peasant class farms is explained by the inputs under consideration in the model. The adjusted R^2 value is a reduced one at 0.700. The standard error of estimate is pretty low at 1.759. The Durbin-Watson value is 1.823, which is close to two. The F-value of the analysis of variance is certainly positive. It is considerably high value at 48.938, which is significant at 1 per cent level of significance. The intercept value is positive. The contribution of the jute specific village dummy is also positive. It is otherwise the mandays of human labour alone which has a positive contribution to the jute yield on the farms of the small class peasantry.

The statistical fitting gives the following linear form of paddy marketed output regression equation :

$$S_p^{sp} = -20.22 + 0.18P_{mp}$$

The number of observations in this cross sub-section of paddy farms are in total 42 farms. The estimated R-value is 0.792. The coefficient of determination, represented by the R^2 stands at 0.627. This is certainly a high numerical figure. The adjusted R^2 reduces to the value of 0.618. The standard error of estimate is 20.778. The crucial test of the goodness of fit of the regression analysis is nonetheless performed by checking the value of the Durbin-Watson. It stands at the value of 2.021. The F-value of the analysis of variance is higher than the table value for the degree of freedom under consideration. It is 67.238, which is significant at 1 per cent level of significance. The intercept value is negative, which is of course expected. There is positive contribution of the paddy price received by the farmers in explaining the variation in the proportion of the paddy-marketed output. It is evident that the farms, which do belong to the petty/poor and small farmers, are influenced principally by the market price of the crop while taking a decision to market the food crop.

The statistical fitting gives the following linear form of jute marketed output regression equation:

$$S_j^{SP} = 1.18 + 0.18\,P_{mj}$$

The number of observations in this cross sub-section of farms are in total 42. The estimated *R*-value is 0.957. The coefficient of determination, represented by the R^2 stands at 0.915. This is certainly a high numerical figure. The adjusted R^2 reduces to the value of 0.913. The standard error of estimate is 12.288. The crucial test of the goodness of fit of the regression analysis is nonetheless performed by checking the value of the Durbin-Watson. It stands at the value of 2.079. The *F*-value of the analysis of variance is higher than the table value for the degree of freedom under consideration. It is 430.501, which is significant at 0.1 per cent level of significance. There is no concern for the multi-collinearity phenomenon. The market price of the jute crop received by the farmers is the sole explanatory variable worth consideration. The intercept value is quite low but positive.

Middle Peasant

In the case of middle-peasant class farms, the statistical fitting gives the following linear form of paddy output regression equation :

$$P_p^{mp} = 9.26 - 0.03e^r + 3.44V$$

The number of observations are 51 paddy farms. The estimated *R*-value stands at 0.558. The estimated R^2 value is 0.311. Accordingly, the adjusted R^2 value is 0.282. The standard error of estimate is 2.460. The Durbin-Watson value is little far off from the desirable value of two at 1.341. The *F*-value is 10.830, which is significant at 1 per cent level of significance. The intercept value is positive. The village dummy is also contributing to the variation in the paddy output per acre rather positively. The contribution of the net area under irrigation as percentage of operated area to the paddy yield on the middle class farms is negative.

The statistical fitting gives the following linear form of jute output regression equation :

$$P_j^{mp} = 1.24 + 1.29A + 1.57V$$

The number of observations are 51 sample jute farms. The estimated R-value of the present regression analysis is 0.795. The estimated R^2 value is 0.633. It is clear that the form of the trimmed models is changing across the divergent peasant class jute-farms, and the coefficient of determination value is subsequently decreasing. The adjusted R^2 value is 0.617. The standard error of estimate is found to be at 2.244. The Durbin-Watson value is a little far off from the desirable value; it is at the numerical figure of 1.629. The F-value of the analysis of variance is high enough at 41.341. It is significant at 1 per cent level of significance. The intercept value is positive. The contribution of the jute specific village dummy is also positive. In the case of the middle peasant farms, there is a positive contribution of the acreage under jute to the jute yield.

The statistical fitting gives the following linear form of paddy marketed output regression equation :

$$S_p^{MP} = -11.14 + 1.05\ Xp + 0.15\ P^{mp}$$

The number of observations in this cross sub-section of paddy farms are in total 51 farms. The estimated R-value is 0.860. The coefficient of determination, represented by the R^2 stands at 0.739. This is certainly a high numerical figure. In other words, almost 74 per cent of the variation in the proportion of marketed output of paddy on the middle class farms is explained by the paddy output and its price being considered in the trimmed linear model. There is positive contribution of both the paddy volume produced on the farms as well as the price received by the farmers in explaining the variation in the proportion of the paddy-marketed output. The adjusted R^2 reduces to the value of 0.728. The standard error of estimate is 13.600. The crucial test of the goodness of fit of the regression analysis is nonetheless performed by checking the value of the Durbin-Watson. It stands at the value of 1.795. The *F*-value of analysis of variance is higher than the table value for the degree of freedom under consideration. It is 67.992, which is significant at 1 per cent level of significance. The intercept value is negative, which is of course expected.

The statistical fitting gives the following linear form of jute marketed output regression equation:

$$S_j^{MP} = 1.61 + 0.19\, P_{mj}$$

The number of observations in this cross sub-section of paddy farms are in total 51. The estimated *R*-value is 0.972. The coefficient of determination, represented by the R^2 stands at 0.945. In other words, almost 94 per cent of the variation in the proportion of marketed output of jute on the middle class farms is explained by its price being considered in the trimmed linear model. This is certainly a high numerical figure. The adjusted R^2 reduces to the value of 0.944. The standard error of estimate is 9.999. The crucial test of the goodness of fit of the regression analysis is nonetheless performed by checking the value of the Durbin-Watson. It stands at the value of 1.468. The *F*-value is higher than the table value for the degree of freedom under consideration. It is 848.712, which is significant at 1 per cent level of significance. There is no concern for the multi-collinearity phenomenon. The market price of the jute crop received by the farmers is the sole explanatory variable worth consideration. The intercept value is quite low but positive.

Rich Peasant

In the case of rich peasant class farms, the statistical fitting gives the following linear form of paddy output regression equation :

$$P_p^{rp} = 9.64 - 0.02e^r + 0.04P_L + 4.03V$$

The number of observations in this cross sub-sectional regression analysis are 108 farms. It is estimated that the *R*-value is 0.585. The estimated R^2 is 0.343. In other words, almost

34 per cent of the variation in the yield of paddy on rich class farms are explained by the inputs considered in the trimmed linear model. The adjusted R^2 value is 0.324. The standard error of estimate is pretty low at 2.872. The Durbin-Watson value is 2.042. Of course, it is closer to the desirable figure of two. The F-value stands at 18.066. This establishes that the regression estimate is meaningful at 0.1 per cent level of significance. The intercept value is positive. The mandays of plough labour hired-in contributes positively but the area under irrigation rather negatively to the variation in the paddy yield on the rich class farms. The village dummy is also contributing to the variation in the paddy output per acre rather positively.

The statistical fitting gives the following linear form of jute output regression equation :

$$P_j^{rp} = 4.53 + 0.003L + 0.03\, P_L + 1.81V$$

The number of observations in this regression analysis are 108 jute farms belonging to the rich class peasantry. The estimated R-value is 0.501. The estimated R^2 value is 0.251. In other words, merely 25 per cent of the variation in the yield of jute on the rich class farms is explained by the inputs considered in the trimmed linear model. A non-linear model would be probably a better fit. The adjusted R^2 value is 0.229. The standard error of estimate is 2.001. The Durbin-Watson value is 1.998, which is very close to the value of two. The F-value of the analysis of variance is comparatively low at 11.605. This is, however, significant even at 1 per cent level of significance. The intercept value is positive. The contribution of the jute specific village dummy is also positive. There is definite contribution of the mandays of human and plough labour to the yield of jute on the farms of the rich peasant. The t-values of the regression coefficients of these agricultural inputs are of course are statistically significant at 5 per cent level of significance.

The statistical fitting gives the following linear form of paddy marketed output regression equation:

$$S_p^{RP} = -10.71 + 1.14\, Xp - 0.002\, X^v_j + 0.16\, P_{mp}$$

The number of observations are 108 paddy farms. The value of estimated R is 0.770. The value of the coefficient of determination, R^2 is 0.592. The adjusted R^2 is 0.580. The standard error of estimate is 23.429. The Durbin-Watson value is 1.677. The ANOVA F-value is 50.355. It is significant at 0.1 per cent level of significance. The intercept value is negative, which is of course expected. There is positive contribution of the paddy price received by the farmers in explaining the variation in the proportion of the paddy-marketed output. The contribution of the market value realized by selling the commercial crop is of course negative.

The statistical fitting gives the following linear form of jute marketed output regression equation :

$$S_j^{RP} = 6.30 + 0.17\, P_{mj}$$

The number of observations are in total 108 paddy farms. The estimated R-value is 0.862. The coefficient of determination, represented by the R^2 stands at 0.742. This is certainly a high numerical figure. The adjusted R^2 reduces to the value of 0.740. The standard error of estimate is 12.302. The crucial test of the goodness of fit of the regression analysis is nonetheless performed by checking the value of the Durbin-Watson. It stands at the value of 2.138. The F-value of analysis of variance is higher than the table value for the degree of freedom under consideration. It is 305.498, which is significant at 1 per cent level of significance. There is no concern for the multi-collinearity phenomenon. The market price of the jute crop received by the farmers is the sole explanatory variable worth consideration. The intercept value is quite low but positive.

Landlord/Capitalist Class

In the case of landlord/capitalist class farms, the statistical fitting gives the following linear form of paddy output regression equation :

$$P_p^{cp} = 10.68 - 0.02B + 2.90V$$

The number of observations are 55 paddy farms. The estimated R-value is 0.437. The estimated R^2 value is 0.191. In other words, merely 19 per cent of the variation in the yield of paddy on landlord class farms is explained by the inputs considered in the trimmed linear model. A non-linear model would be a better fit. Be that as it may. In the present linear model, the adjusted R^2 value is 0.160. The standard error of estimate is found to be at the numerical figure of 4.346. The value of the Durbin-Watson value is 1.917. Undoubtedly, it is closer to two. The F-value is at 6.126, this is lower than the table value. This is significant only at 5.0 per cent level. The intercept value is positive. The contribution of annual number of mandays of plough labour hired-in per acre of operated land to the yield of paddy on the landlord farms is negative. The village dummy is, however, contributing to the variation in the paddy output per acre rather positively.

The statistical fitting gives the following linear form of jute output regression equation :

$$P_j^{cp} = 2.96 + 0.01L - 0.0004C + 0.003P_l$$

The number of observations are 55 jute farms. The estimated R-value is 0.555. The estimated R^2 value is 0.308. The adjusted R^2 value is 0.268. The standard error of estimate is 2.909. The Durbin-Watson value is 1.620. The F-value of the analysis of variance is 7.580, which is significant at 1 per cent level of significance. The intercept value is positive. The contribution of the jute specific village dummy is nil, that is, statistically not significant at all. The human labour mandays used per acre and the cost incurred on hiring-in the permanent labour do have statistically significant contributions to the jute yield on the landlord farms. It is surprising to note that the expenditures incurred on the tools and machinery do contribute to the jute yield on the farms of this class only, and that too rather negatively.

The statistical fitting gives the following linear form of paddy marketed output regression equation:

$$S_p^{LP} = -1.26 + 1.15\ Xp - 0.002\ X^v_j + 0.15\ P_{mp}$$

The number of observations are 55 farms. The estimated R value is 0.758. The value of R^2 is 0.575. The adjusted R^2 value is 0.550. The standard error of the estimate is 22.062. The

Durbin-Watson value stands at 1.165. The *F*-value of analysis of variance is 23.017, which is of course significant at 1 per cent level. The intercept value is negative, which is of course expected. There is positive contribution of the paddy price received by the farmers in explaining the variation in the proportion of the paddy-marketed output. The contribution of the market value realized by selling the commercial crop is of course negative.

The statistical fitting gives the following linear form of jute marketed output regression equation :

$$S_j^{LP} = 1.43 + 0.18\ P_{mj}$$

There are 52 farms in this cross sub-section of observations. The estimated *R*-value of the regression analysis is 0.981. The coefficient of determination, represented by the R^2 stands at 0.961. This is certainly a high numerical figure. The adjusted R^2 reduces to the value of 0.961. The standard error of estimate is 7.425. The crucial test of the goodness of fit of the regression analysis is nonetheless performed by checking the value of the Durbin-Watson. It stands at the value of 1.536. The ANOVA *F*-value is higher than the table value for the degree of freedom under consideration. It is 1321.642, which is significant at 0.1 per cent level of significance. There is no concern for the multi-collinearity phenomenon. The market price of the jute crop received by the farms is the sole explanatory variable worth consideration. The intercept value is quite low but positive.

Concluding Remarks

This chapter has been built upon gathering two facts about agricultural farms: one, that peasantries who run the farms are economically differentiated mass of rural actors in the countryside; second, such farms run by divergent peasantries are characterized by heterogeneity of agricultural production and marketed output functions fitted to these, at least in north Bihar. The farms are quite different in matter of both the production technology adopted as well as the behaviour with regard to the crop sales on the market. A single linear production function for all 268 sample farms in Purnia district is not at all warranted. The only commonality is the linearity characteristics of the production function, and the positive role played the village-specific dummy variable in explaining the variation in the paddy output per acre in all exercises, except the farms belonging to the landlord/capitalist class. It is otherwise human labour alone which has a positive contribution to the jute yield on the farms of the petty/poor as well as small class peasantry. In the case of the middle peasant farms, there is a positive contribution of the acreage under operated land to the jute yield. There is definite contribution of the mandays of human and plough labour to the yield of jute on the farms of the rich peasantry. In the case of jute farms operated by the landlord/capitalist, the intercept value is positive. The contribution of the jute specific village dummy is nil, that is, statistically not significant at all. The human labour mandays used per acre and the cost incurred on hiring-in the permanent labour do have statistically significant contributions to the jute yield on the landlord farms. It is surprising to note that the expenditures incurred on the tools and machinery do contribute to the jute yield on the jute farms of this peasant class only and that too rather negatively. In other words, the conclusion of analysis on statistical fitting of production functions of subsistence and commercial crops on a sample of farms in Purnia is sharp: the two functions do differ. In case of both paddy as well as jute farms, the statistical fitting of production functions on farms belonging to different economic class of peasantry are different. A homogeneous peasantry in terms of input-output relations of crop farms is then a misnomer.

The economic behaviour of divergent classes of peasantries with regard to the marketing a proportion of the net output is equally interesting in Purnia. In case of petty/poor as well as small class farms, the proportion of paddy output marketed is explained by merely the paddy price factor. In case of middle class farms, the marketed output volume is, however, explained by both price as well as paddy output variables. In case of rich peasant and landlord class farms, almost three variables explain the sales: price of paddy; output of paddy; and jute output value. The current value of jute output per adult does contribute of course rather in the negative way. On the farms of commercial crop of jute, price is the most significant explanatory variable of marketed output for all classes of peasantry; the output volume of food and commercial crops is, however, explanatory variable on the farms of the rich peasant and landlord/capitalist class in case of marketed output of the paddy. The intercept and the coefficient value of the jute price variable are quite different to further establish that the degree of commercialization is quite diverse among the farms across the dissimilar class positions in the agrarian countryside of Purnia. In short, there exists a hierarchy of marketed output functions of both food as well as commercial crop across the farms of different peasant sectional clusters, and the best fit for the rich peasant class is probably a non-linear marketed output function. In such a situation, it is highly plausible to argue that the commercial and distress sales coexist and affect upon the diverse factions of peasantry rather differently.

The policy implication is then simple: a rural development programme must recognize the existence of differentiated peasantry, multiplicity of technical-organizational complex on heterogeneous farms and coexistence of commercial and distress sales of crops by peasantries on the market. A uniform rural development policy would fail to reach all sections of peasantry in successful way; and would be self-defeatist as far as the stakeholders of petty/poor and small peasantries are concerned.

REFERENCES

Anderson, J.R. and N.S. Jodha (1973), 'On Cobb-Douglas Production Function and Related Myths', *Economic and Political Weekly* (Reviews of Agriculture), June.

Bardhan, Pranab (1973), 'Size, Productivity and Returns to Scale: An Analysis of Farm-level Data in Indian Agriculture', *Journal of Political Economy*, Vol. 81.

Bharadwaj, Krishna (1974), *Production Conditions in Indian Agriculture*, Cambridge: Cambridge University Press.

Bharadwaj, Krishna (1979), 'Technical Relations in Agriculture' in C.H. Shah (Ed.), *Agricultural Development in India: Policy and Problems*, New Delhi: Orient Longman.

Booth, Anne and R.M. Sundaram (1984), *Labour Absorption in Agriculture: Theoretical Analysis and Empirical Investigations*, Delhi: Oxford University Press.

Burns, A.C. and R.F. Bush (2000), *Marketing Research*, New Jersey: Prentice Hall International, Inc.

Cobb, C.W. and P.H. Douglas (1928), 'A Theory of Production', *American Economic Review*, Vol. 18.

Douglas, P.H. (1976), 'Cobb-Douglas Production Function Once Again: Its History, its Testing and Some New Empirical Values', *Journal of Political Economy*, Vol. 84, No. 5.

Field Sample Survey, 1991-92, Purnia, North Bihar

Koutsoyiannis, A. (1985), *Modern Microeconomics*, Hong Kong: Macmillan.

Mellor, John (1986), 'Determinants of Rural Poverty: The Dynamics of Production, Technology and Price' in John Mellor and G. M. Desai (Eds.), *Agricultural Strategy and Rural Poverty*, Delhi: Oxford University Press.

Minhas, B. S. (1966), "Rapporteur's Reports", *Indian Journal of Agricultural Economics*, Vol. 2.

Mitra, Ashok (1980), *The Share of Wages in National Income*, Delhi: Oxford University Press.

Patnaik, Utsa (1976), *Identifying the Peasant Classes in themselves in Rural India: A Methodological and Empirical Exercise*, New Delhi: Centre for Economic Studies and Planning, Jawaharlal Nehru University (Mimeo.)

Patnaik, Utsa (1987), *Peasant Class Differentiation: A Study in Method with Reference to Haryana*, Delhi: Oxford University Press.

Patnaik, Utsa (1988), 'Ascertaining the Economic Characteristics of Peasant Classes in themselves in Rural India: A Methodological and Empirical Exercise', *Journal of Peasant Studies*, Vol. 15, No. 3.

Rudra, Ashok (1982), *Indian Agricultural Economics: Myths and Realities*, Delhi: Allied Publishers.

Sen, A.K. (1975), *Employment, Technology and Development*, Oxford: Clarendon Press.

SECTION III

Infrastructure, Education and Participation

15

Infrastructure Development in Coastal Karnataka

Major Challenges and Key Policy Issues

V. SHAM BHAT and MUSTHAF

Introduction

Access to adequate and feasible infrastructure brings progress and prosperity to both individual as well as the economy. The low level of human development is both a cause and consequence of inadequate and insufficient infrastructure. Thus infrastructure support is the pre-requisite for economic development. Further it is universally accepted that if the goals of development are to reach full employment along with high standard of living, an adequate and efficient infrastructure is called for.

This chapter is an attempt to give a brief profile of Coastal Karnataka and high light major challenges and key policy issues with respect to infrastructure and a few possible suggestions are given at the end.

This study is an exploratory one and secondary information is used for strengthening arguments. Documents published by various Government departments and the local bodies have also been used.

Profile of Coastal Karnataka

Coastal Karnataka comprises of three districts, Dkshina Kannada (DK), Udupi, and Uttra Kannada. In (Uttra Kannada) was a part of greater district called Canara, which was under a single administration in the Madras Presidency before 1860, the British split then area into South Canara and North Canara.

The entire Coastal Karnataka has rich interlard. Its demographic features are unique; it has population of 43.64 lakh; has high literacy rate; the percentage of people living below poverty line is lower than the State average. In terms of Human Development Index (HDI), DK ranks second, Udupi ranks third and Uttara Kannada ranks seventh in the State. Industrialization has made much progress with few mega projects operating in the region. The service sector has been growing at a galloping rate.

Table 15.1: Brief Statistical Profile of Coastal Karnataka

Particulars	*Dakshina Kannada*	*Udupi*	*Uttara Kannada*
Area	4,771 Sq. Km.	3,575 Sq. Km.	10,291 Sq. Km.
Population	18,97,730	11,12,243	13,53,644
Males	9,38,434 (49.45 per cent)	5,22,231 (46.95 per cent)	6,86,876 (50.74 per cent)
Females	9,59,296 (50.55 per cent)	5,90,012 (53.05 per cent)	6,66,768 (49.26 per cent)
Literacy	83.4 per cent	79.90 per cent	76.6 per cent
Density of Population	416	286	132
Sex Ratio	1022	1130	971
Urban Population	38.43 per cent	18.55 per cent	28.65 per cent
Rural Population	61.57 per cent	81.45 per cent	71.35 per cent
HDI Rank	2	3	7
Health Rank	3	1	22
Education Rank	4	2	5
Gender Related Index	2	3	7
GDP Rank	2	5	11
Per capita GDP at 1993-94 prices (Rs.)	20,682	15,471	12,043

Note: Data is for the year 2001.

The entire coast of Karnataka stretches for 300 kilometres. Of these, Uttara Kannada has 160-kilometer long coastline while 98 kilometres in Udupi district and the rest in the Dakshina Kannada. It (Karnataka) lies between the Arabian Sea and the Western Ghats, which is one of the recognized 'biodiversity hot spots' in the world, and comprises estuaries, beaches, monsoon wetlands, agricultural and forestlands, and mountains upto a height of 2000 metres. It has three distinct agro-climatic zones, which ranges from coastal flatlands in the west with undulating hills and valleys in the middle and high hill ranges in the east that separates it from the peninsula. 22 rivers flowing down from the Western Ghats traverse the costal stretch. Traditionally, agriculture was the main occupation of the entire Coastal Karnataka and majority of the land holdings are either marginal or small in nature. The Table 15.1 provides brief profile of Coastal Karnataka.

However, the coastal areas of Karnataka present quite a contrast. Dakshina Kannada and Udupi are the affluent regions bustling with entrepreneurial energy. Uttara Kannada on the other hand is not as developed as the other two districts. However, this is changing at the fast rate. The coastal districts are undergoing a major transformation. Significant improvements in infrastructure are underway. Many mega projects are on their way and some are already in the stage of implementation.

Components Infrastructure

Broadly speaking, infrastructure encompasses three vital components. Economic or physical infrastructure which includes engineered structures, equipment, and facilities, and the services they provide in economic production and by households. Public Utilities such as power, telecommunications, water supply, sanitation and sewerage, solid waste collection and disposal, public works such as major dam and canal works for irrigation and roads, and other transport sectors like railways, urban transport, sea ports and waterways and airports fall within the ambit of economic infrastructure.

Social infrastructure encompassing education, health care, labour and labour welfare, rural development and poverty alleviation programmes, represents equally or perhaps even more important set of issues.

Financial infrastructure which consists of institutions such as Commercial Banks, Rural Banks, Co-operative Banks and a host of other organizations associated with financial services is an important as the other two sectors.

Infrastructure Development : Achievements and Constraints

Infrastructure development scenario in coastal region presents an interesting mixture of positive achievements and negative fallouts. Positive achievements are clearly visible in the developments that have taken place in information and communication technology. The result is one can have access to information easily and in a cost-effective manner. Similar are the benefits made available by the innovations in communications technology. Telephones, cellular phones, telex, fax and other facilities have given an impetus to economic activities. The entry of private providers of some of the infrastructure services has also led to improved efficiency and lowering of prices.

Nonetheless, in certain other areas of infrastructure investment and maintenance, there is need for improvement. For example, despite the increase in the creation of installed capacity and generation of electric power, one would notice grave inefficiency and irregularities in its supply. Because of poor quality equipment and lack of proper maintenance, transmission and distribution losses have been put at 40 per cent of the output. Further, added to this, unscheduled load shedding, brownouts and blackouts have been very common. The Electricity Supply Companies have not been able to ensure quality power supply even during the limited hours. This visible fact is more pronounced in rural areas where the farmers are made to wait anxiously to run the irrigation pump sets.

Since quality power supply is not assured, they resort to the use of condensers, which would quite often cause damage to the vital electrical installations and equipment.

Again, consider the provision of road transport. Despite phenomenal increase in road construction and the fleet of transport vehicles, travel by road is tiresome and hazardous. A well constructed, paved road surface should last for 10 to 15 years before needing resurfacing. But poor quality of construction coupled with inadequate maintenance would lead to serve deterioration in half of normal life time. There are instances where bridges have collapsed even before they were thrown open to vehicular traffic. Quite recently, a major chunk of bus stand under construction had collapsed in Udupi City. Driving or travelling even on the so-called National Highways has been found to be a tortuous experience. The condition of other roads is even more pathetic. Cities locations having a high level of accumulation and concentration of economic activities and are complex spatial structures that are supported by transport systems. The most important transport problems are often related to urban areas, when transport systems, for a variety of reasons, cannot satisfy the numerous requirements of urban mobility. Urban productivity is highly dependent on the efficiency of its transport system to move labour, consumers and freight between multiple origins and destinations. Additionally, important transport terminals such as ports, airports, and rail yards are located within urban areas, contributing to a specific array of problems. Some problems are ancient, like congestion, while others are new like urban freight distribution or environmental impacts.

The provision of irrigation facilities presents a similar picture. Evidently, detailed technical and other feasibility studies will have been undertaken before an irrigation project is actually sanctioned and its execution taken up. But consequently it would be realized that the site selected for the construction of the dam is not so well suited either on geo-seismic considerations or on the type of soil which it is supposed to irrigate. Further to these, there are cost and time overruns which lead to enormous cost escalation and inexplicable delay in completion. Again, the construction and maintenance of irrigation canals leaves much to be desired. Faulty planning with respect to alignment, poor maintenance, substandard revetment etc, would prevent the flow of water upto the targeted destination. The tail-enders of the command area would experience non-flow of water to their fields. Also, there are frequent instances of breach of canal bunds leading to the surge of water into the fields destroying standing crops and rendering crop fields unsuited for cultivation until the silt is removed and the land is restored. Eventually, the society has to bear the burden of such omissions and wrong decisions. Similar is the experience with respect to the provision of safe, potable drinking water. Owing to indiscriminate drilling of tubewells, almost everywhere sources of surface water have dried up necessitating recourse to tubewells even for drinking water purposes. Added to this, the water yielded by the bore-wells may not be safe for consumption. Presence of excessive chloride content in water makes it a health hazard. The travails associated with urban water supply are equally worrisome. Use of sub-standard, poor quality equipment for supply of water, frequent breakdown of water pumping equipment, lack of standard water storage and treatment plant, result in the spread of many water-borne diseases.

The Education Sector is considered as an important component of Human Development and Social Infrastructure. No doubt, the financial outlay on education—primary, secondary, higher and technical—has increased enormously during the last few decades.

A number of programmes are being implemented for the realization of the objectives. The private managements in this sector, starting from pre-primary upto pre-university, strive to create a hype that education imparted in their institutions is excellent and world-class, thereby impelling the parents to opt for such schools even though they are made to bear a heavy financial burden. A corollary of this scenario is that the Government educational institutions are being presented in a poor light, giving an impression that they are meant only for the underprivileged children who cannot afford to go to private schools. What are the implications of such a provision for the national economy? The main defect in the education sector is that lack of academic industry collaboration. While these programmes are laudable conceptually, there are serious shortcomings noticed in their implementation. This is another glaring example for the failure of public providers of vital components of social infrastructure to ensure high quality primary and secondary education.

It is true that the performance of private healthcare providers has been quite spectacular in recent decades. A number of world class private hospitals have come into being and medical facilities offered—in terms of equipment, diagnosis and treatment—are on par with the best medical practices available even in the West. But then, the question is whether such services are available to majority of the people in the country. Only rich and affluent sections of society can afford the cost of such healthcare delivery system.

What Ails Infrastructure Development ?

Infrastructure development scenario in the coastal area is not so enthusing. In terms of quality of stock or in terms of efficiency of the delivery system of infrastructure services, it could be endorsed to lack of commitment, non-accountability and politics of self-interest. Most of the infrastructure projects are formulated and undertaken for execution not based on their technical and economic superiority but on extraneous considerations. In many cases, premature investments are made in infrastructure capacity creation entailing enormous resources that could otherwise have been devoted to maintenance, modernization or improvements in service quality. Again, infrastructure investments have often been misallocated. Too much to new projects, woefully inadequate for maintenance; too much to low priority projects but not enough to essential services. The delivery of services is also hindered by technical inefficiency and waste. The operation and management of infrastructure services is marked by and attitude of casualness because of the absence of accountability.

In many circumstances, public infrastructure projects are administered and managed by generalists rather than professionals. The argument put forward to justify the preference for generalists is that they have the mindset to take a holistic view in the decision-making process. Added to this, Government's policy of *ad hoc* interventions in the management of infrastructure sectors leads to inefficiency and waste. It is very much clear that, the self seeking attitude of the functionaries responsible for the delivery of infrastructure services is also a major contributing factor. In this context, it would be pertinent to recall the observation made by the Late Rajiv Gandhi, Former Prime Minister of the country. He remarked in great anguish that only 15 per cent of infrastructure project fund reaches to the poor community of the country. Precisely noted that "Indians are better talkers than doers; better planners than executors".

The availability and accessibility of infrastructure has increased significantly over the past several decades. In many cases the full benefits of past investments are not being realized, resulting in a serious waste of resources and economic opportunities that have been lost. This has been mainly caused by inadequate incentives embodied in the institutional arrangements for providing infrastructure services. It is the fact that special technical and economic characteristics of infrastructure give and pervasive intervention by Governments has in many cases failed to promote efficient or responsive delivery of services. Hence, the record of success or failure in infrastructure is largely a story of Governments' performance. In relation to the growth and performance of infrastructure services in the coastal Karnataka, there can be no dispute that it has been quite spectacular in some respects. The growth rate and the coverage achieved by telecommunication and power sectors in this regard are really commendable.

The Causes for Poor Performance of Infrastructure Services

The World Bank Research Team have listed out the problems of inadequate maintenance, misallocated investment, unresponsiveness to users and technical inefficiencies as reasons for the disappointing performance of certain infrastructure services. The same Team has identified three principal reasons for the poor performance of infrastructure services. They are :

(a) The absence of competition,
(b) Lack of managerial and financial autonomy to those charged with the responsibility for delivering efficient and high-quality services. Precisely for the same reason, public sector infrastructure agencies are rarely held accountable for their actions.
(c) The users of infrastructure are not given an opportunity to make their demands felt. Also, the actual and potential users are seldom allowed to participate in planning and implementing new infrastructure investment. Quite often, decisions are based on extrapolations of past consumption rather than on true assessments of effective demand and affordability.

Some of the Research Studies have also highlighted a number of issues that are especially relevant for developing regions, like coastal Karnataka :

- Primarily the various studies indicate that public infrastructure in different parts of State is of poor quality and is used inefficiently.
- Significantly, it has been found that corruption can distort the entire decision-making process associated with Government investment projects. The greater the potential for bribery for this type of Government spending may lead to an increased quantity of public infrastructure, but it may also account for its very poor quality.
- Finally, public infrastructure spending appears to bear a larger burden of the fiscal cuts that developing economies often have to undertake in times of financial crises, raising questions about whether it is the wrong

kind of spending that is cut. In the light of these considerations, it is important to focus on Government's role in investing, regulating and maintaining a country's infrastructure as also the appropriate mix of public and private investment and participation, in order to reap the full benefits of the public capital.

- The question that arises in this context is what factors determine appropriate Government policy regarding infrastructure development. As in the past, Government itself can provide infrastructure facilities. Alternatively, Government can also influence private infrastructure investment maintenance and management by means of direct subsidies, by regulation of prices, or by regulation of the rules of conduct in an industry.

Future Challenges and Key Policy Issues

In the backdrop of the scenario of currently prevailing coastal Karnataka, our next task is to find effective ways of overcoming the problems and ensuring realization of the targeted objectives. The hallmark of success registered in any sector is efficiency which should find manifestation in continuous improvement in the quality of product or service—combined with cost-effectiveness. This calls for improvement in technology through innovation and option of best management practices.

In the recent decades, revolutionary changes have taken place in information and communication technology, which have opened up opportunities for the emergence of knowledge-based society. Similar changes have been taking place in all other branches of human knowledge including management sciences. Industry-University interaction programmes, the process of technical and legal consultancy, public-private partnership schemes have all opened up new vistas in development process. The authors suggest the following measures to the challengers confronting us relating to infrastructure developments.

Emphasizing Stress on Infrastructure Management

First, the Government should shed its colonial mores where the objective was one of administration rather than development. The administrative structure was hierarchical and bureaucratic with emphasis on points of control and command, top down approach. Now there is imperative need to adopt corporate style of administration and management where each one has a specified role to play. There are well defined goals to be achieved and the means of achieving the targeted goals are also suggested. Such governance requires a paradigm shift in the approach to tackle the problems. It requires adoption of a policy of partnership in progress than that of a 'big boss'. Such a fundamental change in the style of governance would give room for adoption of greater consultation and co-ordination in decision-making process with emphasis on transparency. When once this mode of governance comes to be accepted then it would be relatively easy to formulate and implement policies designed to achieve optimum results.

Infrastructure Development—A Continuous Process

Infrastructure development is not a once over affair. On the contrary, it is a continuous process. Further, infrastructure must adapt to support changing patterns of demand because the shares of different components of economic infrastructure such as power, roads, railways and telecommunication in the total stock of infrastructure are likely to increase relative to those of such basic services as water and irrigation.

Along with increase in infrastructure investments, there is need for efficient utilization of available infrastructure services. Further, there is also need for optimization of costs and design of infrastructure projects and minimization of cost and time overruns. Improvements in and efficient delivery of infrastructure services call for wider application of commercial principles, increasing recourse to competition and increased involvement of users where the scope for adoption of commercial principles and competition is limited. In sum, the most important challenge with respect to the radical changes in the psyche of the people. The level of awareness has to be increased; the desirability of each project or programme has to be decided purely on objective considerations. Scientific reasoning and temperament has to be encouraged. Further, certain ethical values have to be inculcated so that each individual would be sensitized to the problems of the poor and the underprivileged.

People's Participation and Community Involvement

Setting up of Committees of well-informed and concerned citizens to oversee and monitor the infrastructure projects taken up for implementation either by public or by private agencies could be one such solution. Care should be taken to ensure that such voluntary organizations comprise of persons with proven technical knowledge, experience and expertise coupled with impeccable character and personal qualities. It may not be difficult to find some people with the attributes outlined above who would act as a watch-dog committee and ensure quality assets and service.

Infrastructure and Environmental Link

The relationship between each of the infrastructure sectors and the environment is complex. Infrastructure has got both the positive and negative effects on the individuals, society, economy and the natural environment. Negative environmental effects often result from a failure to take account of interdependencies among infrastructure sectors. For example, under investment in sewerage relative to water supply in many places has led to harmful contamination of water reserves, exacerbated flooding, and reduced the health benefits from investments on water. Poor management of solid waste and inappropriate disposal further complicates wastewater disposal and urban street drainage leading to health hazards in the big cities.

There are also some positive environmental impacts of infrastructure. For example, reclaimed landfill sites and wetlands used for sewerage treatment can be developed into recreational parks. Duckweed ponds can serve both as wastewater treatment and a source of high-quality protein feedstock for animals. A good infrastructure in the form of improved transport can increase the productivity of worker through better management of time spent by them on non-productive activities. Improvements in water supply and sanitation also can have positive impact on the health of the workers, thereby increasing their productivity. A better infrastructure in various forms helps the poor earning more for their livelihood and thus leading to reduction in poverty and inequality.

Infrastructure Development and Local Government Reforms

In continuation with the infrastructure development of the coastal region there is heavy need of reforms in municipal governance, the Government of India has approved that an strategic Action Plan is needed to keep citizens abreast with the local developments and provide basic municipal services. The cities should generate outcome oriented pro-poor plans through participatory processes. Creation of effective linkages between asset creation and asset management so that the infrastructure services created in the cities are not only maintained efficiently but also become self-sustaining over time. The urban development plans are prepared to promote development of the well planned cities including peri-urban areas, out growths, urban corridors, so that urbanization takes place in a dispersed manner

Reforming Transport Sector Development

There is acute awareness that lack of transport capacity could be the stumbling block in realizing the growth potential. Further development of national highways appears to have slowed down though impetus is being given to ensure that the national highways network continues to expand its capacity. The Government is keen to link the national highways network and the rail network with ports. Indian Railways, however, is largely dependent on budgetary support for capacity expansion. A review of recent investment decisions would indicate that while road and ports have made quite a few positive moves in the recent past, the Railways' action plan is somewhat hazy. The port sector is also expanding and there is competition to develop large container port capacity. A massive national maritime development programme is set to be launched to rejuvenate the port sector and strengthen it in the face of increasing traffic. Existing airport infrastructure is being augmented and new airports are at various stages of development to be able to serve national and international travellers. New developments in the civil aviation sector have included many budget airlines and low-cost, no-frills airlines, which have commenced to offer services in a big way.

The Development of Urban Infrastructure

The development of urban infrastructure has been fairly stop-gap in the last few decades. Barring a few large projects in a handful of cities, paucity of urban infrastructure projects is glaring. Whereas city mass transport systems and airports have found place in developmental plans, essential services such as roads, drinking water, sewage management, drainage, and primary health—the under belly of urban infrastructure have not yet come on the developmental radar. Efforts are being made to develop urban infrastructure in a sustainable fashion.

Carrying Capacity of Coastal Region for Sustainable Development

Planning for sustainable development calls for trade off between the desired production-consumption levels through exploitation supportive capacity, and environmental quality with assimilative capacity of regional ecosystem. In this context, an understanding of carrying capacity provides an operational framework enabling planning for sustainable development.

Any level of development or economic activity that does not exceed the carrying capacity of the planning region is sustainable in ecological terms. Human society depends on many ecologic and economic resources for survival and the carrying capacity study helps to identify the single vital resource that is in least supply. Thus in endeavour, scarce resources must be managed in the face of many competing demands in the natural and human environments, which in turn must withstand perturbations caused by changes in man's social and economic activities. Carrying capacity studies aims to bring out the steps to raise the levels of ecologic compatibility and economic efficiency while ensuring sustainable development in a region. Since there is a limit for the total waste that can be discharged in the area without environment problems, the best combination of the industries, which ensures optimum utilization of the gas and oil produced in the area, generating maximum employment opportunities and wealth in the area, subjected to the environmental constraints

Conclusion

The development of adequate infrastructure is a critical prerequisite for sustaining the growth momentum and to ensure inclusiveness of the growth process. The challenges in implementing projects in this sector are immense. Each segment in the physical infrastructure sector has its own specificities, be it of land acquisition, environment, regulation, financing or of designing of contracts. In case of land acquisition, the problems are well known. There is no option but to squarely address them with foresight, sensitivity, fairness and transparency for all stakeholders. The need to develop appropriate mechanisms for financing infrastructure, especially the development of a domestic debt market, is challenging. It is also important to ensure synergy in the efforts being made to develop different types of infrastructure through effective coordination between different agencies. Only then can the sum total be greater than its parts. These challenges are serious, but they are by no means insurmountable. The critical requirements would be determined and well designed efforts by the Government(s) and the private sector partners to implement the policy initiatives already underway with the requisite amount of detailed technical, managerial, administrative and human skill and, not the least, with the will to implement in a transparent and inclusive manner.

Recommendations

Following are some of the recommendations we would like to propose :

1. There is need for a Master Plan for development of coastal region.
2. Utilize the potentials of harbours and ports by considering the bottlenecks in road transports.
3. There is a need of Metro Rails connecting three district centres.
4. Any development plan should be prepared by taking into account the needs of next 100 years.
5. There is a need to develop indigenous power generation for domestic use.
6. The growth of real estate sector resulted in the use of hilly lands that has depleted ground water resources. Actions are needed in this direction.
7. Small ports can be well developed across the coastal region.

16

Rural Development in India
The Strategic Leadership Model of an Education Enterprise

G.V. CHALAM; C. SURESH BABU; and J. SUCHARITHA

Introduction

Knowledge is a buzzword, which has transformed the management discourse of 1990s in much the same fashion as sustainability colonized the environment and development. With all the positive attention being directed to knowledge and intellectual capital, the causal observer might be puzzled about the gloom and doom in the academy. Ironically, this new bullish attitude towards knowledge is one of the factors that possess the greatest threat to the university. The reason is that the new demand for knowledge in the corporate and other spheres is seen by science policy and education administrators as evidence that universities need to be more oriented towards meeting these needs. A reorientation of the knowledge production in the university towards providing for corporate and public institutions would also ease the burden of the university on the public purse. The global trend of reduced public funding of university research, particularly exploratory or blue sky research may, therefore, be seen as a concerted policy initiative to foster industry—public sector-university partnership. Having achieved a critical mass of educated people in their respective population, industrialized countries now feel it is time to employ this resource as a capital good for the development of other kinds of products. For the limited purposes of this discussion, however, it is sufficient to note that the present public policies have had a number of negative side-effects on the University. Myths such as academic freedom that have contributed to making the relatively low levels of remuneration in university reflectively acceptable are also becoming harder to swallow with the rise of contract research. The present day academic discourse is literally drowning in a beluga of symposia, workshops, seminars, conferences, etc. In an effort to grapple with the turbulence in which they find themselves scholars have turned to examining the idea of the university with respect to the nature of knowledge as well as the nature of the institution. Much of this debate seems to take the view that constant recitation of the traditional values of academic, such as its function as a critical voice from within society or its role as a disinterested seeker of front-line knowledge would be enough to break whatever evil spell the policy and corporate sectors have been placed under[1].

The following scenario assumes that this particular approach will achieve no positive gains for the university and that the present trends will continue well into the future. The trends are identified and need to be explained with the factors like (1) For Knowledge—the University of the future (2) The role of teachers in the changing scenario, (3) Repositioning of Higher Education, (4) Leadership of Comparison, (5) Strategy, Policy and Planning.

For Knowledge : The University of the Future

It is the year 2010 and after several years of non-productive debates about the role of academic freedom and knowledge in society, the university has divided into two rival fractions. One fraction comprised mainly of contract researchers has—after years of unsuccessful negotiation for better conditions within the public university—decided to build an alternative institution. FORKNOW (FOR KNOWLEDGE) is the product of this struggle to create an alternative. It is the result of an alliance between contract researchers and a consortium of corporate and public sponsors. These actors are all-round by a common concern that the public university's capacity to resist change is greater than its ability to innovate. Their argument is evidenced in its insistence that the creation of knowledge should be confined within the narrow bounds of disciplines. They further stated that the criteria for production and evaluation of knowledge are time independent and potential for the future growth and development of nations.

(a) Organizational Structure

Having drawn the experiences from the traditional universities, the designers of FORKNOW understood that if the institutions were going to be able to implement their three guiding principles, its organizational structure would have better agile and provide the opportunity for continuous renewal. This implied low levels of bureaucratic organization and a high dependence on structured networks for the performance of tasks. The organizations had to be one which was easily intelligible to all members and management routines had to be developed in such a way that they would not compete with core functions such as teaching and research. A second important overall consideration in the design of the organizational structure of FORKNOW was that the institution had to be able to keep on top of developments within the communities it served.

Flexi-sitting of Education and Research

Teaching and research at FORKNOW are flexi-sited, wherein the traditional campus-based classroom education is expanded to include both the virtual classroom and the contextual. Flexi-sitting of education has several advantages for students as well as for the institution as a whole. Some of the more important of these are :

- It challenges teachers to find new methods of communicating and brings students together in a variety of different learning contexts.

- Students from outside the area in which the campus is located find flexi-sitting advantageous, since it leads to some reduction in the actual costs of the degree to the student.
- FORKNOW can offer certain short-term courses for professional development, which can be delivered on the site of the corporation for which the course is developed.
- Students have the opportunity very early in their education to familiarize themselves with workplace routine, network with potential employers and learn how to use their knowledge in the context of application.

Within FORKNOW, teaching is regarded as a profession and teaching staff are evaluated based on special criteria developed for this purpose. It is also recognized that effective teaching entails keeping abreast with the research front as well as methods of pedagogy. For this reason, theme networks have a rotating system of a one-year mandatory sabbatical period in which each lecturer is entitled to the full-time equivalent of one fully paid year during this period, they may spent on a range of activities, including developing course materials and pursuing research related to improving the theme's pedagogy[2].

FORKNOW and other Knowledge-producing Organizations

FORKNOW's structure and approach to the task of knowledge production has meant that in rélation to consultant companies it possesses certain advantages. The more important of these is core staffs who are dedicated to the production of knowledge in a particular area, backed up by an orientation to seeking out problems that are of interest to users outside the academy. This has in turn created a preference for contracting FORKNOW researchers rather than traditional consultant companies to perform certain tasks. The initial impact of this has been to create a rivalry between FORKNOW researchers and some consultant companies. In response to this, some companies have made strategic alliances with theme networks in FORKNOW in order to retain access to certain areas of world. A more difficult problem posed by FORKNOW has been that of competition for labour, which would have chosen consultant companies[3].

Role of Teachers in Changing Scenario

The system of higher education in India is often criticized on the ground that it lacks relevance and significance and has not been able to contribute adequately to national development. To some extent, the present situation can be ascribed to certain extraneous circumstances such as the unplanned proliferation of institutions, lack of infrastructural facilities, incidence of educated unemployment, growing social imbalance, a slow pace of economic development and erosion of values. Even so, the academic community cannot altogether escape the blame for this situation as some of the shortcomings also stem from dysfunctional ties within the university system, weakening of student motivation, tone and tenor of discipline and a certain degree of indifference on the part of the teaching community. A nation-wide effort for a simultaneous break-through on the social and educational planes is an urgent necessity. For this the teachers and students have to carry out their part of the existing system, *e.g.* by initiating examination reforms, restructuring of courses etc. and to make education responsive to the needs of the society and the nation.

"The most urgent and significant reform needed in the field of education is to transform the value system, to make it flexible and dynamic and to move in the direction of providing opportunities for life long learning to every individual. This transformation will emphasize ethical values and human welfare enriched by science and technology. It will also imply the shifting of emphasis from teaching to learning, from the individual to social objectives and from mere acquisition of information to the development of skills and character formation based knowledge."

The role of the teacher in the context of this philosophy of education is not going to be easy and smooth. The teacher should have a genuine interest in youth and an understanding of psychology. He should be able to contribute to scholarship and advancement of the frontiers of knowledge. A part from these traditional functions which continue to be as valid as ever before, today's teacher has to perform two functions.

Firstly, he has to play an important role in the transformation of the education system through active participation in such programmes as restructuring of courses, examination reforms, faculty improvement, and employment orientation, practical and relevant education.

Secondly, he should have commitment to a society based on justice and should, therefore, strive for the inculcation of these values and extension of knowledge and skills to the society at large. In effect, the teacher should become effective instruments in the process of development and social changes. He should be a key factor in the transformation of our value-system.

The universities and colleges are national institutions supported by the resources of the society. In both the developing and developed countries, the resources required for the maintenance and growth of the education system, especially at the tertiary level, constitute a significant portion of the total budgetary resources. It is only right the university system is responsive to the needs of the society and fulfils its social obligation and responsibility towards various social groups and especially the deprived groups like basic philosophy of extension to be developed as a new significant area on the basis of priority.

Extension work is not merely adult education and literacy; its scope is much wider. Accordingly, teachers may take up adult literacy/education of community service or educational extension depending upon their interests and aptitude. The details of adult education are spelt out in the Government of India's policy statement on Adult Education and in the UGC document on Adult Education. These programmes have to be related to environment and local needs. Community service involves close interaction with the society in programmes of rural development, inculcation of scientific temper and awareness of the impact of science in every day life and proper utilization of products of science and technology extension lectures etc. It also includes non-formal education programmes including use of mass-media and educational technology, science education centres for creative work by all sections of the society and action-oriented research programmes for solving local problems. The measures discussed below would, to some extent, strengthen the motivating of teachers in both the short and long periods.

(a) ***Participation by Teachers :*** Participation by teachers has two aspects—firstly in bringing about interaction with the community on a continuing basis; and secondly, in becoming fully involved in the functioning of the department. The essential component of education is the interaction of teachers with the community. For this purpose, teachers have to interpret recent trends in their respective fields, to create scientific awareness and to participate in the programme of adult education and non-formal education of youth, women and the weaker sections of the society. Teachers should also help in the preparation of development projects for the community in their neighbourhood, especially the rural community. The basic structure of the system of higher education in our country leads to concentration of responsibility in a few hands, at one hand, and a mood of passivity on the part of the teachers on the other.

(b) ***Academic Freedom :*** While the issue of university autonomy is a wider issue, which is more important from the point of view of university and college teachers. However, freedom in academic matters, *viz.*, selection of students, appointment and promotion of teachers, determination of course structure, methods of teaching, areas of research, etc, does not mean that universities and their teachers have no responsibility in the exercise of this freedom or no accountability with regard to financial matters. The Education Commission (1964-66) has rightly observed : "The universities should also realize that it would be unwise to expect that autonomy would descend as a gift from above : it has to be continuously earned and deserved. The universities derive their right to autonomy from their dedication to the pursuit and service of truth." In recent years there have been attempts to make inroads into the functioning of universities. A provision was sought to be made in some universities regarding the premature retirement of teachers. The question of transfer of university teachers has also been raised on several occasions. Public opinion will have to be built up so that the proper functioning of universities within framework of autonomy can be ensured.

(c) *Teacher as an Agent of Change* : It is no mere rhetoric to mention that the destiny of the country is being made in the classrooms and the teacher has an important and vital role to play in the total programme of national development and social change. The first and foremost responsibility of the teacher is in relation to his students. His job cannot remain confined to delivering a set of lectures or mere 'coverage of syllabus'. What is called for is a revolution, in education "changes in objectives, content, teaching methods, academic programmes, size and composition of student body, selection and professional preparation of teachers and organization." The primary objective should be to treat each individual student as an end in himself and to give him the widest opportunity to develop his skills, abilities and potentialities to the full. He should go out of the institution with a sense of values and purpose and fully equipped to play his role not only as a 'professionally trained person', but as an enlightened and dedicated member of the society.

The teacher has also an important role to play in the acceptance and adoption of various educational innovations *e.g.* restructuring of courses, autonomous colleges, examination reforms, practical orientation to courses, making studies relevant and so on. In the past, many of the reforms reached a dead end because of the apathy of the teacher. The teacher should also accept his responsibility in the realization of our social objectives, which implies that education should relate to the 'life, needs and aspirations of the people'. From this point of view, it becomes important that the teacher becomes an active participant in (i) programmes of community development, (ii) adult education and extension, (iii) social and national services, (iv) Co-curricular and extra-curricular activities, (v) programmes of non-formal education, and (vi) social and national integration.

(d) *Evaluation* : If the objectives have to be realized, it becomes important to consider questions relating to working days, examination schedules and workload of teachers, keeping in view the expectations of the society on the one hand and the realities of the situation on the other. It is also important to recognize the fact that many of the measures being suggested here would require a spontaneous and ready acceptance by the academic community and not merely their concurrence. These cannot be laid down by way of the code of conduct or as part of the conditions of service and have to be in the nature of something which is self-imposed or comes from within. It is in this sense that a code of professional ethics has to be evolved in our country, as in many developed countries of the world.

Serious concern has been expressed over the fact in many universities the number of working days during an academic session is less than the stipulated 180 which by no means is high often; examinations were held far behind the schedule in a number of universities. There is also the growing phenomena of cheating and use of unfair means at examinations, thus eroding the confidence of people in teaching, learning and evaluation.

(e) *Workload of Teachers/Vacation/Leave* : It would be desirable to prescribe and follow the minimum workload for all university and college teachers as stipulated in the report of the Sen Committee. The precise mix of various activities on the part of a teacher in regard to teaching, research and extension will vary from time to time and will be distributed by the university/college concerned.

It has been recommended that the minimum workload of a teacher should be forty hours per week of which twenty hours should be by way of formal classroom work. It is to be considered whether universities and colleges be asked to maintain a proper record of the formal classroom work including tutorials and seminars done by a teacher and the time spent by him in study, research, consultation, extension work, writing of papers, participation in conferences, faculty improvement programmes, etc.

(f) ***Assessment of the Teachers :*** At present there is no inbuilt device for the proper assessment of the work of a teacher. Any definition of the role and responsibility of a teacher would remain on paper unless there is a system of continuing assessment of the teacher which can best be done by one's peers in the discipline concerned. A suggestion that merits serious consideration is assessment of the work of a teacher by his students. While such assessment should, in the nature of things, be a guide to the teacher and should, therefore, remain in his custody, it is necessary to ensure that there is a minimum response, say from 50 per cent of the students.

(g) ***Norms of Professional Ethics :*** The Committee on Governance of Universities and Colleges in Part II of its report on Teachers (Sen Committee) made the following pertinent observations on professional standards for teachers. "Every profession is expected to maintain certain standards and society has a right to demand those standards from the teaching community. A teacher's research publications, his writings and their impact on society, his skills and his behaviour pattern with his students, etc. are some of the professional activities, which are indication of the acquisition and contribution to the understanding and growth of accumulated knowledge."

The University Grants Commission is of the view that the norms of professional ethics should be evolved by the Teachers Associations and followed in a voluntary sense rather than as part of conditions of service. Amongst its essential features, it may be suggested that a teacher is expected to :

(i) Uphold the dignity of the university and work towards the realization of its aims and objectives and keep the interest of students uppermost in his mind *i.e., espirit de corps.*

(ii) Conscientiously perform his academic duties such as preparation of lectures and demonstrations, assessment, guidance, invigilation, extension and research.

(iii) Participation in adult education and extension programmes, NSS, Physical education and other extra-curricular and co-curricular activities, in keeping with his interest and aptitude.

(iv) Assess the work of the students impartially.

(v) Avoid inciting students against other students, colleagues or administration.

(vi) Express his free and frank opinion seminars, conferences etc., towards the contribution of knowledge.[4]

Repositioning of Higher Education in the Changing Scenario

(a) Challenges to attain Peaks : The Dearing Committee of Inquiry into higher education at Britain succeeded by resolving number of issues. The conclusions of lifelong learning, part-time degrees, student financial support and quality control can well be imagined, and if they are formulated clearly and backed up with appropriate resources, they will help enormously in strengthening progressive high education and the long-term competitiveness of the British economy. The problems can be drawn up into our picture and can be addressed as following: primarily, the planning process; secondly, nature of democratic citizenship; and finally the management values and institutional flexibility of university institutions themselves in the West, especially in the United Kingdom[5].

(b) Changing Models : The discourse is none which limits what can be achieved in education by myopic short-term calculations of its cost and which institutionalizes the assumption that higher education is essentially the preserve to clever stratum of the younger generation. Dearing is asked explicitly to consider the needs of mature students and lifelong hearing, but he will do so against a climate in which such developments will be read as additional demands on universities and not something which they should be engaged in as part of their central mission. Progress in the past decade about widened access to higher education has had to be achieved through struggle against these assumptions. Even when they have been actively promoted by the University Grants Committee or the Department for Education and Science, the rationale for change has always been couched in terms of increasing the number of students to a system which was expected to retain its form despite growth in numbers.

Institutions are expected to improve their resources in competition with others. The use of a bidding process to allocate resources to institutions is a device to impose uniformity of resource on a system while claiming to celebrate the diversity of different missions. Resources follow students, but student choice is something of a myth when the Government and its bodies place restrictions at institutions through the tight control of maximum aggregate student numbers. This is top-down dependent model of educational planning dependent on expert advice which can be relied upon to be pragmatic and responsible. The task facing people in higher education is to think beyond the constraints of conventional wisdom. If universities are to respond to the challenges and uncertainties of the new century, they must find fresh ways to do so. It is better to imagine a society whose higher education institutions contribute to these wider goals within the public realm and whose own systems of management reflect the values of a civilized and democratic society. Current political discourse about higher education has barely touched on these questions. The result is that universities in the world face the future with considerable uncertainty and precarious public support.

The purposes of higher education cannot be separated from debate about the kind of society it is part of and is expected to contribute to. Too much of debate about higher education in the past two decades has been narrowly focused on issues of resources and management. In the new millennium, it is time to life the sights and transform out vision of what the future could be like. The twenty-first century is an age of extremes; the twenty-first will be no less challenging or threatening. The relationship between higher educational institutions and the society has been changed with students and employers who are ready to support.

The thrust of the analysis developed here is that the new bargain needs extensive, open debate and those universities themselves should inform that debate and be much more prepared than they have so far been to articulate their own missions along with wider public goals. Sir Ron Dearing on the future of higher education will make some headlines for a while; it may even bring about some welcome changes in current policies. Beyond Dearing a more fundamental task will still remain that of articulating and defending a vision of higher education which promotes world-class teaching and research and the democratic values without which such achievements are meaningless. If there is one lesson to be critic, sustainable and productive society, a higher education worth the name has no future[6].

Comparison of Indian and Western Ethos

The terms organizational culture and managerial culture are used very frequently in discussions and theories on management. Culture is used to refer to customs, traditions and codes of behaviour by an organization. When applied to a group it implies the same thing expert that the period over which these traits or characteristics are acquired and ingrained is much longer than in an industry or similar social organization. According to Lewis, Hofstede defines culture as "the collective programming of the mind which distinguishes the members of one category of people from another". In this definition, the word programming implies a conscious setting of the rules and regulations which create a core of disciplined group behaviour, with inevitable deviations Lewis further adds organizations are usually created by leaders, whether the leadership is despotic, individual, or collective leadership functions in two modes : one networking and the other of task orientation.

Lewis goes on to make distinctions between cultures and identifies three types : linear active, multi-active, and reactive. Managers in linear active cultures seek technical competence, put logical before emotion and are always concerned about the immediate achievement of results. Managers in a multi-active culture are extroverts, use persuasion, use human face as an inspirational factor and often engage in human transactions emotionally. On the other hand leaders—Lewis uses the word managers and leaders interchangeable—in reactive cultures are people-oriented knowledge dominated, patient, modest, courteous and respect seniority and on the whole they are paternalistic.

The foregoing discussion points to an emerging interest in understanding group behaviour at various levels of aggregation. There seems to be a distinct, discernible pattern in the behaviour of any social groups existing as a unit for a reasonably long period of time. Among all these studies, Indian ethos and leadership styles seem to be the least understood or investigated. Recently, several significant studies have been done by Chakraborty in this area of leadership. This chapter attempts to understand leadership in the Indian ethos and its distinctive features in contrast with western concepts.

(a) A Great Leader—Mahatma Gandhi

Mahatma Gandhi was a remarkable leader who moved men to action and continues to inspire them. He made men out of mud. How many such leaders have emerged who have entered the world's memory and national psyche and culture? It is little wonder that his book on *My Experiment with Truth* is to be read again and again.

(b) Leaders and Leaders

But there are leaders and leaders. With explosion in activity in every walk and arena of life there are leaders in every profession: business, academics, art, culinary arts, management, etc. what distinguishes them from the likes of Gandhi? Western writers and researchers have laid down some ways of grooming leaders and have developed benchmarks for identifying leaders in action. There are leaders of hour, leaders of the year, leaders of the decade, leaders of the age, leaders of the era, etc. in all professions. A manager on the shop floor, a manager leading a group, a head of a marketing group, a head of division, a head of an institution, a head of a government are all leaders, that is , persons who influence the pattern of work, the pace of activity, the productivity from activity, the quality of the product, etc. All these people lead or influence of groups by allocating assignments as in a power hierarchy, by choice as in a political or social activity, by attainment as in an artistic or academic pursuit. According to Peter Drucker, 'management is doing things right; leadership is doing the right things'. 'Management is efficiency in climbing the leader of success; leadership determines whether the ladder is against the right wall.'[7]

(c) Stephen Covey's Seven Habits

Stephen R. Covey analyses the various recognized role models who set up industries and managed governments and identifies seven habits which are common to these leaders. They are :

- Be proactive.
- Being with the end in mind.
- Put first things first.
- Think win/win.
- Seek first to understand, then to be understood.
- Synergize.
- Sharpen the saw.

It is obvious that the basic motivation is success in terms of effectiveness and efficiency and attainment of the goal with which one started and acted. For this purpose, habit is defined as there instruction of knowledge. Skill and desire knowledge is the theoretical framework : what to do and why. Skill is how to do and desire is the motivation[8].

(d) Indian Ethos

The principles are natural laws and that God, the creator is the source of them and also the source of our conscience. This is the beginning of the Indian concept of leadership. Unfortunately, this is not as practiced now but as practiced and established by the epochal and infinitely endowed role models of ancient Indian saga. One can read their life stories again and again and perhaps future generations will also do so.

(e) Ethos of an Ordinary Indian

The ethos of an ordinary Indian is always supposed to maintain his link with the mystic, and consider life as part of the Divine action and creation with no end or beginning. According to the Indian philosophical works, man is a spark of the Divine. The life of a human being is guided by the four *Pursharthas : Dharma, Artha, Kama* and *Moksha*. In this, an Indian is influenced very deeply by the holy texts of his religion: the Christian by the *Bible*, the Muslim by the *Quran* and the Hindu largely by the *Bhagavad Gita* among a host of texts like the *Upanishads*, the *Vedas* and the *Puranas*. The essence is that the higher truth, seek resolution and liberation from the problems of life through the many prescribed and tested techniques like meditation. The ultimate goal is to be a *sthita prajna*, a man who is established in peace and acts in life without desire.

(f) Indian Ethos—The Basic Triad on which the Indian Ethos Stands

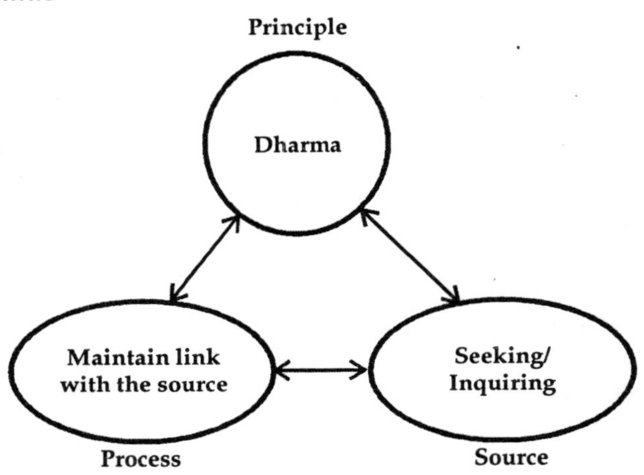

(g) Leadership in the Indian Ethos

The concept is rooted in the basic source, the primordial *Satchitananda,* which is consciousness or bliss. A leader must preserve his link with the source; act rigorously, vibrantly and pervasively as an agent of the Supreme to create blissful and happy conditions for all beings, unmindful of the obstacles in the way[9].

Leadership in the Indian ethos is a very exacting role if seen from the viewpoint of highly pragmatic result-oriented action. The leader is the divine worker performing actions in a mood of a *yatha prapta karyam,* that is, an unintended, undesired and unexpected action conditioned, controlled and regulated by the *dharma* of the leader in harmony with the *dharma* of the land and the natural law of becoming, that is, *swabhava* of the leader. The difference between the leader and others lies only in the *swabhava,* which in ordinary people is generally regenerated, and in the *swadharma,* which is chiefly conditioned by the lower *gunas* and the level of evolution of the self.

(h) Traditional Role Model

These role models are Rama, Krishna, Bharata, Harischandra, Sibi, Bali, Manu, Ikshavaku, Janaka, Prahlada, Bhishma, Dhramaja, Arjuna, and Buddha. Indian tradition is replete with stories of kings who had extraordinary personalities and led very austere life. Spiritually-oriented lives never swerving from the path even under very trying conditions. All of them in one way or another kept their minds alert to inquire about and be aware of their spiritual origins.

(i) The Famous Rama

Rama developed a deep disgust for worldly life at an early age and questioned the very existence, the creation and all that is called life. Over a period of 18 days Vasishtha patiently taught him all about the manifest world, the primordial source, and the relation of the human being with the source. He convinced

Rama not to wean himself from action in the world but act in it with detachment to elevate him and protect that which is placed in his hands. He acts without any desire in the interests of the world with detachment, without likes and dislikes, and without concern for happiness or unhappiness, without indulging in small discussions about right or wrong, with an attitude of witness, with an equal mind, without any self will, without excitement, behaving in an appropriate manner doing works as they come, and is by nature peaceful[10].

(j) Characteristics of Leadership

It can be seen that the Indian model of leadership starts at the source of all existence which is diametrically opposite to the western approach which begins at the other end, which is desire for the result of action as the motivation. One is the spiritual source leading to human action and the other is the human source trying to embellish itself with some spiritual training and gloss.

On Indian ethos, a leader should have the following characteristics :

- A deep, enduring and continuous inquiry into self.
- Inspired by a great idea, with no desire for personal benefit.
- Sharing without hesitation.
- Action for *Lokasamgraha.*
- Doing all actions in the spirit of *yatha prapta karma,* with detachment.
- Enjoy action, renounce all ownership of action.

(k) Characteristics of Leaders of the Hour

Only leaders of all time can fit this bill and for other leaders of the hour and year, the following characteristics apply :

- Engage in continuous learning.
- Pursue a vision with perseverance.
- Carry the group with you.

Perform all action to benefit the group at least without causing any harm to anyone and act without concern for the result in the best interest of all concerned. Even if the action is motivated by the desire for a particular end, do not grieve if the outcome is not as expected. Vivekananda wrote about many of these principles nearly a century ago, especially in his numerous letters to his *gurubhais*[11].

Self-Regulation is the Key for Leadership and Institution Building

(a) Self-discipline and Responsibilities of Committees

Stress was placed on maintaining the autonomy of the institute, developing the culture of professional and non-hierarchical relationships, with an emphasis on a matrix type of organization in which people performed various roles and their significance depended on the roles they performed in the institute rather than on a hierarchical status. A deliberate attempt was made to build a culture of self-reliant and competent creativity in diverse roles.

The weight of the faculty opinion influenced a faculty member's priorities and as to how he should behave. Again, as far as consulting was concerned, it was not that rules mattered so much as the fact the members of the faculty did exercise their own sense of responsibility in regulating the time to be spent on consulting. Self-regulation was also developed through the way in which committees functioned the way in which individuals took responsibility without authority. This made the committees' job and the job of the Decision-makers doubly difficult. Unless there was a very strong sense of self-discipline the faculty member could easily have regarded the job as much too difficult for him, and also a waste of time. In fact, a few faculty members did protest against responsibility without authority. People in the various roles acted because of such norms, rather than the imposed regulation of the decision-maker. Self-regulations are necessary for any organization that is intended to grow over the period of time.

Role of Self-regulating Mechanisms

Self-regulating mechanisms meant for sense of responsibility which every faculty member felt for the institutional, organizational and individual task that everybody undertook academic, administrative or whatever they may be. This sense of responsibility must be hoped that would evolve only with a very high sense of autonomy to develop the individual faculty member's initiative, ability and confidence to satisfy one's own creative expression without losing sight of the difference between the freedom implied in autonomy and license.

Factors of Self-confidence and True Autonomy

Most of the institutions are not used to a high degree of free self-expression, discrimination lacking, freedom and license, frankness and rudeness, autonomy and the implicit freedom requires a great deal of interpersonal sensitivity, understanding and consideration. Insensitivity and intolerance vitiates the culture. It was hoped that the organizational and institutional points of view and regard for others would be brought about to some degree by the shared experiences of group work through committees and other task teams. At the meetings, discussions of personal issues must avoid in order to create mutual respect in the organizations. This would enhance the processes of the organization that also creates 'academic entrepreneurship' among the faculty members. Building Self-confidence consist two factors : they are both internal factors and external factors. Having regular meetings that would develop a very strong self-respect can solve these factors. The second aspect was that whenever the responsibility for a task was given to a committee, which should solve the problems that are faced, going back to the decision-maker of the organization would result waste of time and efforts.

Factor of Intrinsic Quality

Intrinsic quality refers in the organization to search, to determine, to define some problems that are faced over the period of time. Here, planning is necessary in each and every aspect of activities and their implementation. Most of the organizations are failure in this aspect because of the reason unable to provide quality of autonomy to the people who are pursuing the activities in the organization. If the employees in the organization are not self-reliant, rationalistic then building the institutions is impossible.

Factor of Attitudinal Biases : Attitudinal biases are another important factor in creating Future Education Enterprise. This is required freedom of views and expression again which is required self-discipline, which required self-confidence again which required self-esteem and mutual respect among colleagues and so on.

Factor of Emotional Involvement

In the changing scenario, the higher education systems that are required greater diversities in terms of attitudes, directions, skills and activities. The Indian higher education institutions should not follow any foreign culture. The joint ventures and memorandum of understandings could not influence our own culture instead they will become barriers for successful education enterprise. Therefore, the question is how much diversity used rather than as a dissipating or divisive aspect of our functioning. A wide range of general, functional and sectoral programmes is necessary to have the changes in recruiting and development patterns of faculty.

Planning and Development of Institution

Institutional building process is another important area which needs to be considered. Here, stress is required on building of people, their relationships, attitudes and behavioural norms, which is conducive to the development of individual, self-esteem, autonomy and creativity that is itself a characteristic to the institutions. Each individual in the organization should be able to carry and should not vulnerable by being dependent on the job. Another important aspect is thinking about the institution far beyond the period for which an individual might be the head of it and, therefore, beyond his own commitment. The fact would remain that the individual had thought of himself as only a part of a very, every long process[12].

Strategy, Policy and Planning for Educational Institutions

In order to integrate best practice principles, the following guidelines provide a list of key points to address and a checklist for each for assessing compliance. Guidelines are best developed at the instructional level. However, faculties, divisions and operational units should interpret the criteria within their own structure and context to work through the guide.

(a) Top Decision-Makers **:** The decision-makers should provide clear strategic directions, communicate the vision, inspire and influence staff. Create an environment for quality practices and management, such as ethical decision-making processes. Reinforce the values of the institution, because without values it is very difficult to implement any process or strategy. In another scenario, promoting improvement and facilitate change by putting in place approaches, systems and structures, including reward mechanisms which are necessary process in the organization.

(b) The Leadership **:** The leaders of any institution or university need pose some of the following questions :

(i) What training do senior executives have in quality management principles?

(ii) Do Senior executives promote quality management principles?

(iii) How are institutional values introduced and reinforced through leadership at the executive level?

(iv) How are senior executives involved in managing change and implementing a quality culture?

(v) What initiatives do senior executives take to promote unity of purpose and eliminate departmental barriers within the institution?

(vi) What key strategies for involving all levels of management and supervision in quality principles, management, practices and procedures are taken?

(vii) How is the quality principles integrated into day-to-day management activities, including meetings, decision-making and planning?

(viii) What steps are taken by management to assess the effectiveness of its approaches and to improve or change its approaches to integrate quality into day-to-day management?

(c) Education and Training : There is requirements to have an approach and rationale used to decide the education and training needed by staff link directly to the institution's strategic directions and plans including skills training, multi-skilling, process of control and improvement and general education future needs. Further, statistics and cost maintained on staff education and training necessarily recorded to acknowledge the activities. There must be some processes in place to improve and to assess the effectiveness of the institution's education and training to activate.

(d) Ethics and Morale : Institutions must measure key indicators and trends in staff well-being. There must be actions to be identified to resolve problems and weaknesses in matters such as absenteeism, staff turnover, satisfaction, grievances, strikes and compensation matters. The staff mobility, flexibility and retraining, support the transition to new technologies and lead to improved productivity or changes in work process. Some special facilities, services and opportunities exist at the institution for the sake of staff, like, counseling, child care, health services, and financial services, recreational and cultural facilities. There are issues need to discuss like safety and health, staff satisfaction and egronomics included in improvement activities; where goals, methods and trends are identified and resolved[13].

Conclusion

The foregoing discussion has tried to anticipate some of the challenges such an institution would face both internally and in its relations to other similar organizations.

The arguments outlined above, although based on a hypothetical scenario, provide insight into some of the potential obstacles to be faced as the academy becomes more and more integrated into the productive force of the economy. At the present time, the essential tension is that of academic knowledge as common property resource *versus* academic knowledge as intellectual property. The impact of the increasing commercialization of knowledge production in the academy on issues such as the position of academic labour, sharing of knowledge and individual scholars' traditional right to ownership of knowledge *vis-à-vis* fenders' rights need to be brought to centre stage.

In another aspect, the Indian ethos laid down a spiritual basis for all action by leadership. The leader is one, who consciously lives and acts from this base of humanness. All his actions germinate and flow out of this idea or vision. He is a divine worker performing divine action without being attached to the outcome. On the other hand, the need to achieve big ends and all action is guided by that purpose. It is seen that a kind of personal mastery is essential to achieve such ends.

A further contrast between the two approaches is the manner in which benchmarks have been determined. In the Western approach, the characteristics of leadership have been derived from the practice of the successful. The rules and practices of leadership have been derived for the leader by realizing their origin or the supreme who is *ekamev adwitiym*[14].

NOTES

1. Beare, H. and Slaughter, R. (1993) '*Education for the Twenty-first Century*'. London, Rutledge.
2. Gibbons, M. *et al.* (1994), '*The New Production of Knowledge: The Dynamics of Science and Research in Contemporary Societies*'. London, Sage Publication.
3. Elliott, J. *et al.* (1996), '*Communities and their Universities: The Challenge of Lifelong Learning*' London, Lawrence and Wishart.
4. Keep, E. and Mayhew, K. (1995), 'The Economic Demand for Higher Education and Investing in People: Two Aspects of Sustainable Development in British Higher Education', in F.

Coffield (ed.), *Higher Education in Learning Society*, Durham, Durham University School of Education.

5. Kogan, M. and Kogan, D. (1983), *The Attack on Higher Education*, London, Kegan Paul.
6. Mohan, J. (1996), 'Re-connecting the Academy Community Involvement in American and British Universities' in J. Elliott *et al.* (ed.) *Communities and their Universities: The Challenge of Lifelong Learning*, London. Lawrence and Wishart Searle,
7. *Intentionality* (1983), *'The Rediscovery of the Mind'* (1992) chapter 8.
8. Stephen R. Covey, *The Seven Habits of highly Effective People.* (New York: Simon & E. Schuster, 1989), 101.
9. *Ibid.*
10. *Bhagavad Gita* [S.S. Jhunjhunwala, (Ed.)] Pondicherry: Sri Aurobindo Ashram Trust, 1974.
11. Ramsden, P. and Entwistle, N.J. Effects of Academic Departments on Students' Approaches to Studying, *British Journal of Educational Psychology*, 1981, 51,368-383.
12. Scott, P. (1995), *The Meanings of Mass Higher Education*. Buckingham, Open University Press.
13. *Ibid.*
14. S.K. Chakraborty, 'Wisdom Leadership: Leading from the Self', *Perspectives on Business and Global Change*, 1977, 10(2).

17

Bilateral Relation with Myanmar

Its Influence on Rural Development in Nagaland

SUDIPTA SARKAR and PRIYAM KUMAR ROY

In Asia, political boundaries have separated peoples who have cultural, historical, racial and ethnic affinities and they share the socio-economic condition of this sub-continent. The Nagas are one of them. There are lots of views regarding the original homeland of the Nagas. Someone says that the Nagas belong to the Mongoloid race. They migrated and settled in the North-East India. But, according to ancient Sanskrit scripture *Kiratas*, the golden-skinned people of the sub-Himalayan region with distinct culture, migrated to the mountains of the East. Sixteen major tribes along with a number of sub-tribes (Angami, Chang, Konvak, Lotha Phom, Sangtam, Kuki, etc.) inhabit Nagaland. Each tribe and sub-tribe is distinct from each other in respect of culture. Therefore, the concept of "Unity in Diversity" is being embodied here. But according to the post-modern writers, there is a probability of division of India on the basis of ethnicity. The main reasons behind this are illiteracy, exploitation and marginalization and the aspiration of the concerned people to be in the better position through the formation of a separate State and environmental isolation from the rest of India. The chain of the Himalaya stretches nearly 2400 km. from north-eastern border of India with China and Burma to the Hindukush. For thousands of year the extraordinary variety of micro-environment, extreme of climate have accommodated the variety of populations of diverse origin. Each has developed its own adaptive strategies for subsistence production and systems of social, political and religious organization. This diversity of settlement is combined with the isolating tendencies of the natural environment.[1] This environmental and settlement diversification of the people of the North-East India hindered the cultural amalgamation that give birth to the tendencies of isolation along with the natural environment. In this respect there are a number of terrorist groups whose activities took place in that region including Nagaland. As Nagaland and other North-Eastern provinces border Myanmar, Bhutan, Bangladesh and China. These terrorist groups take shelter in those countries (China?).[2] We cannot deny that the most of the separatists belong to the youth who face the problem of unemployment and poverty. Therefore, we should be careful enough to pay the attention for the welfare of the people of the concerned area.

After the end of the cold war, India took the policy of "Look East" in 1992 to strengthen its relation in respect of economic cooperation with the South-East Asian countries and in this respect the centre and our Prime Minister Dr. Manmohan Singh also referred the North-East as the gateway for India for ASEAN and the sub-regional grouping BIMST-EC (Bangladesh, India, Myanmar, Sri Lanka, Thailand-Economic Cooperation). It was proposed that a serious stress would be given on trade, commerce and tourism of the North-East India and it will play as an "Economic Bridge".

The economy of Nagaland is primarily forest-based and agricultural. It has very rich forest resources. Nagaland is also rich in mineral resources including coal, limestone, iron, nickel, cobalt, chromium, and marble. The economy of Nagaland is highly agrarian. About 68 per cent of total working populations are involved in agriculture. Nagas are blessed with the skill of making beautiful decorative materials also. Cottage industries such as weaving, woodwork and pottery are also an important source of revenue. Tourism is important, but largely limited owing to the State's geographic isolation and political instability in recent years. The major possibilities of industrial development of the State lies in food processing, bio-tech industries, tourism, floriculture, agro-forest based industries, handloom and handicrafts, mineral-based industries, electronics and IT, sericulture and petrochemicals.

Therefore, we should capitalize the "Look-East" policy of the Central Government for upliftment of rural people of Nagaland and thereby detached them from involvement in terrorism or other anti-social element activities. In this respect, we should focus on several sectors like tourism, information and technology, communication and small-scale industry. While North, West and South India attract 49 per cent, 29 per cent and 18 per cent respectively of total volume of tourism of the country. North-East India gets just 4 per cent despite of its huge natural resources and natural beauty. If properly explores, Nagaland can be one of the ideal tourist destinations for rest of the world. Nagaland Tribal Tourism, Tribal Festival tourism can be easily marketed throughout the world and thereby increase the earning potential of rural people of the State. Prior to the North-Northeast Business Summit, 14 giant companies of the world have shown interest in investing in the tourism sector. In the IT sector in the country although 20 per cent of workforce in the country comes from the North-East only, still one IT company has approached to invest. In case of heavy or large scale industry, we can refer Nagaland Pulp and Paper Company. This enterprise is also going through a hazardous way. It is struggling for survival now. There was the proposal of fresh investment and were several recommendations on behalf of operating agencies (IDBI, HPC). The other industries belong to rice mill, furniture making, woollen industry, printing, automobile, etc. Therefore, no heavy or large scale profitable industry takes place in Nagaland till now (even after 61 years of Independence) that can create employment. Poor infrastructure is responsible largely.

It is said that Air connectivity has improved dramatically but it is not sufficient when the total area measures 16,579 sq. km. because road journeys are arduous.[3] Besides, limitation of rail and road transportation hinders the proper economic development. There is a trend in all over India to revive the small scale and agro-based industries which need a strong transport system but when we look at the transport system of Nagaland the situation is really disappointing, only 12 km of railway has been built while in Darjeeling (88 km), Kangra Valley (164 km), Nilgiri (46 km.) or Kalka-Simla (96 km.) railway run kilometres after kilometres. Even the total distance of rail line connecting Jammu and Udhampur is 54 km and for these Rs. 1300 crore has been spent so far. The road connecting villages goes only 1092 km. Therefore, the proper movement of rural production cannot take place, which caused obstruction in economic mobilization and thereby giving birth to economic distress of local people. This economic backwardness may create terror prone mentality among the rural society. Therefore, the government should focus on the infrastructural development for economic and social mobilization. Small-scale industries and handicrafts industries should be brought to light through exhibition, showroom, internet marketing, within the State and outside the State and the country. Nagaland's Handloom and Handicrafts Development Corporation (NHHDC) has a vital role to scatter the domestic products outside the State. Agro-based industry like food processing and others should be encouraged by providing bank loan on easy terms and conditions. Nagaland State Cooperative Bank, NEDFI, NICON, SISI has to be more dynamic in this respect.

For the engagement of local people in economic activities we should think of international trade of domestic productions which is of great viability due to short distance of transportation through the international trade stations in Mon, Tuensang, and Phek on the Indo-Myanmar border. The bilateral border trade agreement of 1994 provides framework facilities by which trade is carried out between India and Myanmar. Under the agreement, trade is currently carried out through three designated border points one each in Manipur, Mizoram and Nagaland.

A report published in *Assam Tribune* in July 24, 2008 states that, "for over half a dozen villages, scattered on a mountainous terrain and cut off from the rest of the world in the absence of motorable road, villages in Myanmar just across the international border have come as a saviour, reports PTI. The villagers belonging to Yimchunger Naga tribe inhabiting the Kiphire district of Nagaland, sustain themselves through barter trade with their counterparts in Myanmar." Thus border trade facilitates the rural people to earn their livelihood. We can hope that by means of proper infrastructure the whole North-East India can take part in international trade through Nathula in near future. To promote the international trade in north-east region we should strengthen the bi-or tri-lateral relations with China, Myanmar or Bangladesh. Though *Arthasastra* says that two nations on a common border are hostile to each other naturally and it is at least true to India. However, in the age of super technology we must have to overcome it following a neutral foreign policy.

It is believed that the cold war is ended after the fall of the U.S.S.R. but it is true that there is a underlying tension between the two ideology-based blocks (capitalist and communist/socialist). Till today, the communist countries are not supporting the penetration of market economy like the USA. Therefore, the capitalist block try to invest in non-communist countries at their own sweet will. Here, we shall discuss the nature of underlying conflict between the two blocks, which influences the bilateral relation between India and China, and no one can deny the influence of it on the development of North-East Region of India.

In West Bengal, when a chemical hub was proposed to take place in Nandigram, the local people opposed it and the State Government cancelled that project. Nevertheless, the movement was going on under the leadership of "SUSHIL SAMAJ" which identified itself as non-political. The American Embassy in Kolkata was very much active in support of Sushil Samaj, which is suspicious enough. Because within last two decades a number of non-political movements (Solidarity Movement of Poland, Tulip Revolution in Kirghizstan, Rose Revolution in Georgia, etc.) caused the downfall of the governments of the concerned countries. The source of the idea of Colored Revolution is the book "A Force More Powerful" of Peter Ackermann. When the Western Capitalist power intends to establish the westernized democracy in any country, they depend on those people (addicted to western culture and value) who have no responsibility to the tradition, culture, and value of the concerned nation. In this respect, the embassy, intelligence department and the NGOs take the responsibility of organizing the movement and help the westernized culture/ yanki culture addicted people to organize the movement. Economically and strategically, several agencies like York Zimmerman and Brickaway Limited (USA agencies), National Endowment for Democracy, the International Republican Institution, the National Democratic Institution (USA), and Westminster Foundation (U.K), etc. prepare stimulating games regarding the strategies to organize this movement. Besides Indo-US military relation are always sensitive to political and strategic shifts. Therefore, the communist countries are very much aware of the sabotage prone activities of the western powers.

Myanmar is now viewed as a critical area of interest to China and India. It is of special interest to the U.S. which would like to check the overriding influence of China in this region while cruising on its journey to the status of a contending global power. While China has developed close political, military and economic relations with Myanmar, India is in the process of following suite. Sudha Ramachandran, a Bangalore based researcher shows that India estimated in 2005 more than one million Chinese infiltration to Myanmar over the past decade, and "the influx is believed to have changed the demographic makeup of northern Myanmar"[4]. A further study of India-Myanmar and Sino-Myanmar relations offer some interesting aspects of how they are adopting the geo-strategic setting and political environment of the region to their advantage.[5] Myanmar shares common border with India 1,463 km. India dominates Myanmar's western borders, just as China dominates its north-eastern borders. And this makes Myanmar a strategic land bridge linking South, and South-East Asia. As a littoral of the Indian Ocean, Myanmar's strategic value further increases. Its 1930 km. long coastline dominates the eastern arch of the Bay of Bengal, leaning on to the Malacca Strait China has also set up listing post in Sittwe Zedetkyi Kyun Island enabling them to monitor traffic in the strait of Malacca [6] Thus, Myanmar provides China the shortest land and sea access to South Asia, just as it provides convenient external land and sea communication options to India's landlocked North-Eastern States. Myanmar's ocean boundaries are barely 30 km from the Andaman Islands increasing its maritime security potential. Both sides of the regions bordering Myanmar are mostly populated by ethnic communities with their own distinct ethnic, religious and linguistic identities from the rest of the countries. However, the majority Burmese population, who are Buddhists, lives in the fertile and more developed southern Myanmar with easier access from China. Thus the northern tribal regions of Myanmar have suffered, neglected and remain underdeveloped. This has given rise to a sense of alienation among ethnic tribes; many of them had waged relentless wars for their independence. Thus ethnic militancy has always affected Myanmar's democratic governance, destabilizing the country.

Most of Myanmar's mountain ranges and major river systems run north-south. This makes construction of road communication and movement from India's east to Myanmar against the grain of the country difficult. At the same time, it facilitates easier movement from the Chinese border in the north-east, and provides for natural flow of traffic. The Chinese have used this favourable terrain configuration to build road from the Chinese border to Mandalay in the heart of Myanmar and onward to the coast. As Myanmar provides the shortest access from mainland China to India's eastern borders, these developments have special strategic significance. India's north-eastern States bordering Myanmar are not as well developed as Yunnan province of China bordering Myanmar in the north-east. China has found it useful to link the development of Yunnan region jointly with Myanmar and Laos. Thus the two-way border trade and commerce is qualitatively and quantitatively better with China than with India.

India-Myanmar relations have a long history of substantive political, cultural, religious and social interaction. Pandit Jawaharlal Nehru and Aung San, spearheaded the freedom struggle. After Independence, India's reservations about the Myanmar military regime's violent suppression of the peoples' movement for democracy from 1988 onwards and the incarceration of Aung San Suu Kyi soured the relationship between 1989 and 1992. India also provided sanctuary and financial assistance to fleeing pro-democracy activists. In a marked departure from the past, India's Myanmar policy had been undergoing a radical change since 1992. The new policy focused purely on India's strategic and economic considerations based on pragmatic grounds. It is a vital area of influence for India's security.

After economic liberalization, *i.e.* 1991, India started looking at the lucrative markets of ASEAN region as part of the 'Look East Policy'. Following the admission of Myanmar as a member of the ASEAN in 1996 its importance in furthering India's trade with ASEAN increased. Development of the seven north-eastern States has remained stagnant resulting in the alienation of sections of society and encouraging the growth of insurgency. Development of land and sea links through Myanmar could end their isolation and wean them away from insurgency. Some of the insurgent groups like the National Socialist Council of Nagaland (NSCN) and the United Liberation Front of Assam (ULFA) operate from sanctuaries in Myanmar. Better relations and coordination with the regime in Myanmar could put an end to the operation of such insurgencies. Myanmar's abundant reserves of natural gas waiting to be exploited, could help India in meeting its ever-increasing demand for energy resources as the economy keeps growing at a fast pace.

In keeping with these considerations, India has been focusing on giving substance to India-Myanmar relationship with specific actions. There have been a number of high level visits between the leaders of the two countries. Gen. Than Shwe, Myanmar's head of State, visited India in October 2004. President APJ Abdul Kalam visited Yangon in March 2006.

Visits of Ministers and Chiefs of armed forces from both countries have also taken place. There had been regular meetings at the ministerial level to monitor the progress of various projects involving India and Myanmar. To improve connectivity with Myanmar, India has taken up a number of road and port construction projects. India has constructed the 160-km Tamu-Kalewa-Kalemyo road in Myanmar from Manipur border. It is also assisting in the proposed trilateral highway project to connect Moreh in Manipur to Mae Sot in Thailand *via* Bagan in Myanmar. India's Kaladan multi-modal transit transport facility is aimed at improving linkage between Indian ports on the eastern seaboard and Sittwe port in Myanmar. This would enable transportation by river transport and road to Mizoram providing an alternate route for transport of goods to north-east India. A proposal to build a rail link from Jiribaum in Assam to Hanoi in Vietnam through Myanmar is also on the cards.

India's trade with Myanmar is growing at a fast clip. India and Myanmar are considering series of initiatives for expansion of border trade between the two countries. India has given its approval for the signing of a proposed agreement with Myanmar for the avoidance of double taxation and prevention of fiscal evasion with respect to Income taxe. The agreement once comes into effect will stimulate the flow of investment, technology and personnel from India to Myanmar and *vice versa*. It is also expected to provide tax stability and facilitate mutual economic cooperation between the two countries. The Government has approved the linking of United Bank of India (UBI) at Moreh post in Manipur with Myanmar Economic Bank at the Tamu town in Myanmar. The two banks would avail the letter of credit (LoC) facilities and under this system Indian rupees and Myanmarese Kyat can be legally converted into foreign currency at these banks. Once this facility becomes operational, the exchange of cash would not only become legal but much easier. It is also expected that the volume of trade will automatically increase as well. Better communication between trading partners is the key to increasing bilateral trade. The importance of business delegations, special promotion campaigns would create awareness between the two countries. The business communities would definitely come forward to take a lead and help in increasing the volume of the trade.

Myanmar is fourth largest trading partner with its investment reaching $ 35.08 million last year. In 2006-2007, India-Myanmar trade was estimated at $ 650 million falling short of the target of $ one billion. In 2004-2005, China-Myanmar trade was $ 1.145 billion as against India's figure of $ 341.40 million in 2004-05. India is taking steps such as extending airlines, land and sea routes to strengthen trade links with Myanmar. It is also cooperating with Myanmar in areas like agriculture, telecommunications, and oil and gas sectors, etc. India's policy of building closer relations with the military regime in Myanmar has drawn criticism both at home and abroad. This was considered a betrayal of India's ethos. During a recent visit to Myanmar on January 19, 2007, India's External Affairs Minister Pranab Mukherjee made clear the country's "hands off" policy on the struggle for restoration of democracy going on in Myanmar. He said that India had to deal with governments as they exist. We are not interested in exporting our own ideology. We are a democracy and we would like democracy to flourish everywhere. But this is for every country to decide for itself.

Thus to conclude, it is worth-mentioning that improvement in bilateral relation of India-Myanmar can be an important initiative for improvement in living standard of the rural people of Nagaland. Through bilateral relation with Myanmar, border trade can be improved to a large extent which can easily be a way out improving the earning potential of local Naga people. There are so many products in Nagaland which can easily be exported to the neighbouring countries. Look East Policy can be a boon to the people of Nagaland if besides improving the bilateral relation with neighbouring countries, Government takes proper initiative for industrial development along with the development of transport and other infrastructure of this hilly area. It is expected that improvement in bilateral relation and consequent development will open up many avenues of employment of local people and more specifically, rural and tribal people of Nagaland. If it is so, they will not be involved in terrorism or other social crime in future.

NOTES

1. Himalayan State *vs.* Formation and the Impact of British Rule in the Nineteenth Century—Richard English.
2. According to the Intelligence Dept. of Government of India there are several centres of terrorist (*Muzahidin*) on the border area in Bangladesh and Myanmar. The religion biased terrorist groups give the Indian terrorist in other word separatist.
3. Bezbaruah said that "Infrastructure is a big handicap in the north-east. Air connectivity in the region has improved dramatically, but looks at the roads shows road journeys are arduous.
4. Sudha Ramchandran, "Yangon still under Beijing's thumb", *Asia Times,* Online February 11, 2005.
5. [Col. R. Hariharan (Retd.), AT] [Presentation made at an interaction on "Emerging India-China-Myanmar Relations", jointly organized by the Chennai Centre for China Studies and the Department of International Relations of Stella Maris College, Chennai, at the college on July 19, 2007].
6. Shee Poon Kim, "the Political Economy of China-Myanmar Relation : Strategic and Economic Dimension", Retsumeikan Annual Review of International Studies, 2002, Vol. 1.

18

English Education and Rural Development

A North-East Perspective

KOMOL SINGHA

Introduction

Education is the backbone of any society. It is the long-term continuous process, involves value and ethics. Development of a community or society is not possible overnight, it requires time. In this regard, Chinese proverb says, *if you want to plan for one year—plant paddy; if you want to plan for ten years—plant tree; and if you want to plan for hundred years—plant Education.* So, education is the cornerstone of socio-economic and cultural development of a country. It has emerged as the most important single input in promoting human resource development, in achieving rapid economic development and technological progress, and creating a social order based on the virtues of freedom, social justice and equal opportunities in the country. An appropriate education system cultivates knowledge, better skills, positive values and attitudes among the people, especially those who acquire it (Gill *et al.*, 2005). In today's world, the wealth or property of a nation is shaped by the quality of higher education of the people. In the opinion of Reddy (2008), education is universally recognized as an important investment in building human capital, which is the driver for technological innovation and economic growth. Similar observation was also given by many scholars (*e.g.*

Chattopadhyay 2005; Kumar and Kumari 2008; and others). Education is the basic requirements and 'Fundamental Right' of the citizens of a nation, so in our Constitution, it is made free and compulsory education to all the children up to 14 years of age. While higher education is important in building up a quality human resource base for the nation, the basic or elementary education system holds much more significance[1]. In fact, since the inputs of the higher education system are nothing but the inputs of the elementary education system, the latter serves as the base over which the super-structure of the whole education system is built (Mukherjee 2005).

A country can reach a stage in its economic and technical development when a major effort is made to derive the maximum benefit from the resources available, assets already created and to ensure that the fruits of change reach all sections. Education is the medium to reach that goal. Higher education provides people with an opportunity to reflect on the critical social, economic, cultural, moral and spiritual issues facing in humanity. It contributes to national development through dissemination of specialised knowledge and skills. Higher education creates a huge magnitude of positive externalities (Tilak 2005), which are very much necessary for sustainable economic development. So, the investment in this sector is very significant. It is, therefore, a crucial factor for a nation to survive in this globalised era.

Even the India's successive Five Year Plans have given due recognition to education. The Eleventh Five Year Plan (2007-12) is quite distinct from other plans. It is basically a knowledge investment plan and Government's effort has been to create the next big wave of investment in higher education. The knowledge industry is driven by innovation and that innovation is inculcated in institutions of higher learning and research[2]. Higher Education plays the fundamental role in the construction of knowledge society and knowledge base economy (Kumar and Kumari 2008).

The well-known feature of the education sector is complementarily of three levels of education, which are sequentially connected namely, elementary, high/higher secondary, and College and University education (higher education). In the research findings of Shah (2006), that the working of whole education system gets crippled when one level, especially elementary education which is the base/ foundation of the whole system, is kept weak. The cycle of low access, equity and quality starts from here affecting in turn the other two higher levels and *vice versa*. The same idea was also reflected in the studies of some other scholars in the past (*e.g.* Dreze and Sen 1996; Gill *et al.* 2005; Kumar *et al.* 2003; Mukherjee 2005; Tilak 2004; etc.). The secondary education cannot be strengthened without strengthening the primary education from where the students enter the secondary education system (Gill *et al.*, 2005). The remarkable neglect of elementary education in India is all the more striking given the widespread recognition, in the contemporary world, of the importance of basic education for economic development (Dreze and Sen 1996:13).

It is increasingly being advocated that global wealth today is concentrated less in the factories and machinery and that knowledge and skills are increasingly becoming critical to the world economy (D'souza 2004), and they emanate from the sound higher education. In the findings of Tilak (2003), only those countries that have developed their higher education system, and attained a gross enrolment ratio of at least twenty per cent, could achieve economic miracles, and not the others. The growth of higher education depends mainly upon the sound primary and secondary education. In this context, the role of English education is very significant and it is the base for sound higher education. Through this chapter, the researcher tried to analyse the defects of education system in the North-East India (NEI) and the possible suggestions to overcome them.

Objectives of the Study

This research article is a modest attempt to analyse the English education and its impact on rural development on the one hand, and the defects of the education imparted through regional languages in the valley areas on the other in North-East India. The specific objectives are identified as follows :

1. to review the need and genesis of English education in NEI.
2. to specify reasons for the emergence of private education and its failure to provide quality,
3. to analyse the importance of English education in attaining higher education and its impact on rural/village economy,
4. to pinpoint the defects of regional medium of education system[3] in NEI, and
5. to recommend some possible suggestions of education system in attaining sustainable economic development in NEI, especially for rural development.

Methodology and Plan of the Study

The present study is both descriptive as well as analytical one and based on primary data. The primary data were obtained by conducting a field survey. For the purpose, a well-structured questionnaire was designed and administered accordingly from the respondent of the villages selected on the random basis. The survey was conducted at eleven villages in five North-Eastern States. They are five villages from Assam, two from Nagaland, two from Manipur and one each from Mizoram and Tripura. The villages were selected on the basis of their medium of education. The medium of education for the tribal villages was in English, while for the non-tribal villages was in regional language (*i.e.* Manipuri). The data so collected were processed and analyzed as per the requirement of the study to draw important inferences and conclusion. Personal experience and knowledge in the field also helped the researcher to make meaningful interpretation. A comparison was made between tribal and non-tribal villages (hill and valley) on the basis of medium of education and its impact on their economies. Due to practical inconveniences and vastness of the population, the survey could not be conducted in all the villages of the seven

North-Eastern States. Very often, the word English education may be interchangeably used with higher education throughout this chapter.

In order to provide an objective and concrete view points, the entire study (excluding Introduction and Conclusion) is divided into five sections, *viz.* Need and Genesis of English Education, Market *versus* Quality Education, Reasons for Poor Quality Private Education, North-East India and Higher Education, Observations of the study followed by the suggestions and conclusion.

Need and Genesis of English Education

Mankind uses hundreds of languages. Some languages do not have sufficient number of words. Some languages have no script, as it is happening in the tribal communities of North-East India (NEI). Some languages are spoken by millions of persons. But English is the universal language. Due to the process of history, this language has spread to almost all parts of the world. It is used as a link language for international business and diplomacy (Rao 2005). Anyone who aspires to excel today in any professional field must possess a reasonably good command over English language. As the world moves faster and, therefore, communication skills have become most important these days, whether we like it or not, English has become the decider of fate of future generations in job market (Azim 2007). In this regard, nine renowned economists[4], together wrote a paper in 2002, entitled 'Strategy for Economic Reform in West Bengal' and it says that the policies such as abolishing English as a language of instruction in public schools at the primary level has disastrous implications for essential skill formation in a globalized economy in West Bengal. Even countries poorer than India, such as Ghana have been able to attract a lot of data transcription and operator services from the United States on a sub-contracting basis just by virtue of having low wage workers who know English and have basic computer skills (Banarjee *et al.*, 2002). The research result of Singh and Sridhar (2002), says that desire of English taught in private schools were making these children turn away from government schools. This same idea was also observed by De *et al.* (2002), that the demand for English education has been stimulated by the widespread understanding that it is linked with higher education and employment opportunities. Knowing this opportunities, some schools in valley areas in NEI (non-tribal region) have started imposing even fine on students for not speaking English in the school campuses.

Colonial Education[5]: In terms of its historical context, the education system of India owes little to the traditional Hindu or Muslim systems of education that prevailed before the advent of Europeans on the sub-continent. As a matter of fact, the colonial education system was not a modernized transformation of any traditional system of Indian education. It was established outside the traditional system and without any relationship to them. During British rule, the Charter Act of 1813 had permitted missionaries to go to India in order to educate and proselytize, while the East India Company had accepted responsibility to educate Indians in Western knowledge. In 1823, a General Committee on public instruction was set up to give shape to an education policy that the Government of India needed to pursue. This Committee consisted of Orientalists and Anglicists, and the ideas of both groups were put before Lord Macaulay who at the time was Law Member of India. Macaulay rejected the ideas of Orientalists and, through a forceful and now well-known Minute, made a vigorous plea for Western learning taught through the English language.

In 1837, English was made the language of administration, and a Government Resolution 1844 threw subordinate positions open to Indians. The result was that the institutions of oriental learning declined as English was made the main language of study and the medium of instruction after the primary stage. Rapid expansion occurred of schools and colleges that taught English education, with the higher stratum of society adopting and patronizing it. The system of English education had taken root. Concentration, since 1835, on the urbanized upper and middle classes led to the neglect of mass education[6]. Education system emerged from the needs of the colonial power. It was this restrictive system of education that India inherited at the time of Independence. The post-colonial history of reform has been a struggle to unshackle the system from its past by making it accessible to all sections of society and correcting its bias of emphasizing the study of language and humanities. Mahatma Gandhi whose vision sharply differed from the one that was offered in the modern and industrial societies of the West has been a powerful influence on the nationalist reformers. There has been a continuous struggle between the modernizers and Gandhians and the modernizers have usually won.

English Education in NEI: The foundation of English education in NEI was laid when American Baptist Mission established an English School at Guwahati in June 1835 under the Headmastership of Mr. Singer (Barpujari 1994). The demand for English education in NEI cropped up with the spread of Christianity. The earliest known Christian contacts with this region were made by the Catholic Missionaries in the seventh and eighth centuries (Jeyaseelan 1996). Further, study of the same scholar advocated that the speed of English education was first shown by the Capt. Gordon when he organized a Primary Education Centre at Imphal in the beginning of the nineteenth Century. Due to the untimely death of Capt. Gordon, the seed could not germinate. In 1872, Major General W. E. Nuthall, the then Political Agent opened a school at Imphal with English language as the medium of instruction. But the school did not function properly due to lack of local cooperation.

As the days had gone by, circumstances changed. The deep feeling of untouchability slowly disappeared (mainly from the *Meitei* society). Side by side, the English Missionaries became active and made the people feel the necessity of English education. Sir James Johnstone established an English school in 1885 at Imphal which is now known as Johnstone Higher Secondary School. With the resolution taken at the Synod of Allahabad in 1887 to create the Prefecture Apostolic of Assam, the seed of Catholic Christianity was sown. The entire North

East was designated as the province of Assam. Fr. Otto Hoffenmuller was chosen to be the first Mission Superior. He, together with Fr. Angelus Muenzloher and two Brothers, Marianus Schumm from Bavaria and Joseph Baechle from Beden reached Dhubri, Assam on 1st March 1890. St. Anthony's School in Shilong was opened on 1st May 1908, mainly to cater to the education of Catholic children. Later the Loreto Sisters also joined the Mission on 8th May 1909 to educate the girls. St. Edmund's College was inaugurated at the beginning of 1916. It was no wonder that upto 1941 high schools were conspicuous by Missionary institutions in the Naga Hills (now Nagaland). In the Khasi and Jayantia Hills (now Meghalaya), there was only one high school which was established in 1878. The Christian Missionary Societies at Shillong made attempts to impart collegiate education after 1930s (Barpujari 1994). However, in spite of the opposition, Christianity has emerged as the religion of the hill people of NEI. Consequently, English education is booming in the hill region of NEI[7]. The influence of Christianity had little impact in valley and non-tribal region of NEI. As a result of which, the Missionary work had intensified in the hilly and tribal region.

According to the scholar like, Barpujari (1994), in the hills of NEI until the appointment of the Education Commission (1882), education received only a step-motherly attention of the British administration. The Commission while appreciating the role of Christian Mission laid stress on the need of private agencies for undertaking educational activities amongst the backward people. It did not object the policy of the government of giving grants-in-aid to the Missionary Institutions, but suggested that the institutions run by the Missionaries should be brought under the general supervision of the government. In the opinion of Barpujari (1994), the spread of education of a secular nature was not the primary objective of the Christian Missionaries. But, in totality, North Easterners particularly the hill tribal communities are greatly indebted to the Christian Missionary Institutions for their contribution in the field of education and religion.

Now, in India we have almost reached a stage where mere education is not important, rather the intelligence of a person is measured by his/her ability to speak English. If he/she communicates in English, then he/she will be considered fit to deliver goods in the market. There are many evidences where most of the rural students were failed to impress the interviewers at the time of selection for a job (Azim 2007). The very English education excluding University Education (Post-Graduate and above) is imparted especially by the private institutions in the tribal areas of NEI, but not so in the non-tribal rural regions.

Market versus *Quality Education*

Education had been one of the important sectors in which the role of the State had been recognized widely (Tilak 2005). In the last few decades, mushrooming of private educational institutions and the poor performance of government institutions have become very serious concern not only for the NEI but also for the country as a whole. About one-third of students globally are in the private sector (Levy 2008). In the study of Tiwary (2008), reveals that earlier the higher education was considered as public good that provides valuable contribution to the society, State and the nation and, therefore worthy of support of any welfare State. But, today the same higher education is being seen as private goods as benefiting those who have higher professional studies or do research, so the users have to pay and the State is unwilling to fund it. This is the general phenomenon for an economy, which is in transition; transition from Keynesianism to a Neo-liberal paradigm (*e.g.* Tilak 2005).

A research finding of Kumar and Reddy (2008), the case of privatization of economic activity is based on two grounds. Firstly, the state exchequer can no longer bear the burden of public enterprises. Secondly, the operation of public sector enterprises left much to be desired; they turned out to be failures in competitive efficiency. The reasons for higher education coming under the grip of privatization or market manifest these two grounds. According to Levy (2008), the basic causes of private expansion remain religion, social advantage, and absorption of the accelerated demand for higher education. De (2002) also observes, private institutions are often looked more inviting students than government because maintenance was better. Naturally, well-to-do parents send their children to private institutions. This may probably be due to regular homework (Singh and Sridhar 2002) given to the students, while it is found to be absent in the government institutions. According to Amartya Sen, primary education in India suffers not only from inadequate allocation of resources, but often enough also from terrible management and organization[8]. English education, especially the elementary education is basically imparted by private agents.

The education style inherited from the colonial rulers still flourishes and the dream that education will be a system that promotes equality and national integration in society continues to be elusive (Mathur 2007). There is also a theoretical underpinning in the neo-classical thinking that when market fails to cope with externalities as it happens in cases of many quasi-public goods like, basic education, governments have to fund it appropriate to support activities that are felt to generate external benefits. Moreover, the recent endogenous growth theories also identify that *ceteris peribus*, education alone can generate substantial growth augmenting dynamics (Muhamad *et al.*, 2004). Despite these, the entering of private agents in this sector cannot be resisted in the country. A study by Goel and Goel (2008) found that Indian higher education is being governed by neo-liberalism, neo-capitalism, and neo-colonialism and *vice versa*. English education day by day is being governed by the private sector, which has more of commercial motive than educational. This education has been made commodity and commerce. Those who have power to purchase English as well as higher education of any kind, from anywhere, at any time can purchase it.

The quality issue is concerned (whether it is lower or higher education), teachers' qualification and infrastructural facilities are the important components (Dreze and Sen 2006).

Many scholars in the past had blamed the private institutions in regard to impart quality education (*e.g.* Azim 2007; Goel and Goel 2008; Kumar and Reddy 2008; Levy 2008; Singh 2008; Singh and Sridhar 2002; De *et al.* 2002; Tilak 2003; 2004; 2005; 2007 etc.). Now, the schools are run like companies (Singh and Sridhar 2002). In the opinion of Tilak (2007), higher education in developing countries is more privatized than in many advanced countries. The economies with predominant private higher education systems[9] have not developed much economically, educationally, socially/politically. Only those countries with strong public higher education systems could prosper economically, socially, culturally or educationally. The situation is not different in the case of elementary education too. In a slight different opinion, Kumar and Reddy (2008) advocated that privatization may be useful in the case of school level education. But as far as higher education is concerned, rich students and parents are more interested in borrowing the degree instead of being quality conscious. Further, they said the students who obtained their entry into higher educational institutions on the basis of money power show less interest in their studies.

According to Singh (2006), India is facing the problem of degree devaluation in higher education. It is mainly due to the employment has occurred within the private sector was mostly in the semi-skilled or low skilled areas. This shows the liberal education policy adopted by the States in opening colleges for general education. Dreze and Sen (2002) observed poor educational outcomes and educational deprivation can be on account of lack of accessibility, affordability and the poor quality of school services. Research by Singh (2006), revealed that a large number of young unemployed have poor and unsuitable qualifications for employment. Here the poor qualification refers to the inefficiency in executing job, not poor performance in examinations. In the opinion of Shah (2006), it is due to the long cherished ideology of education is being replaced by the entire corporate and entrepreneurial ideologies of free market and competition, permitting education to be treated as a commodity available in the provision store from which profit can be earned.

Reasons for Poor Quality Private Education

In this world of competition, market is expected to deliver quality in the real sense. In practice, measuring quality education is not an easy task and there is no definite yardstick to measure quality education. Though the measurement of quality in the service sector is based on customer's perceptions[10], Vachhrajani (2008) argued the difference between students and customers lies in the freedom of choice, responsibility for paying the price and requirements to provide merit and eligibility.

As Tilak (2005), observes that markets cannot ensure optimum supply of education and that left to the individuals or the market mechanism, social investment would be below optimum or socially desirable levels. Education cannot be treated like any other commodities available in the provisional store. It is public goods or merit goods and it creates huge magnitudes of positive externalities which cannot be quantified easily. Many scholars (*e.g.* De *et al.* 2002; Gill *et al.* 2005; Goel and Goel 2008; Levy 2008; Singh 2006; Shah 2006; Singh and Sridhar 2002; Tilak 2005, 2007; etc.) have proved the inability of the private institutions in providing quality education.

According to Fernandes (2008), the quality education fails to make in India due to the lack of infrastructure, shortage of quality teaching faculties. Goel and Goel (2008) also observe the devaluation of higher education in India is now because of being excessive market oriented in nature. Still, in the study of Levy (2008) found the private institutions continue to be more hierarchical than public counterparts, limiting faculty and student participation. It further stressed that even the serious institutions rarely pursue academic research or graduate education and rarely have ample full-time faculties. Teachers in the private institutions are paid substantially lower than those in government institutions. On an average, they get only 20 per cent, even worse, the average salary of the unrecognized institutions is only 14 per cent of government teachers' salary (Singh and Sridhar 2002), and more importantly, job security in the private institutions is also a worrying factor. Quite contrary to the ideal Teacher-Pupil ratio of 1 : 40 (Singh and Sridhar 2002; Yesaiah 2008), 1 : 30 (Kumar *et al.* 2003), it is found that the teacher-pupil ratio is about 1 : 85 in the private institutions particularly in NEI. As far as teacher training is concerned, private institutions lag behind drastically. Teachers in the private institutions are young and usually join as a temporary arrangement while they look for better alternatives and other careers. This probably explains inexperience and fresh, lack of training for many private institutions (Singh and Sridhar 2002; De *et al.* 2002). It is also found that, apart from the normal class, average 4-5 periods (50 minutes in a period) in NEI, workload especially other co-curricular activities is very heavy in these institutions and which directly or indirectly compromises with quality.

There is a general practice in NEI that a graduate joins teaching profession primarily not by choice but by chance. Reason for this is numerable. Few of them are, the inability to get a government job in the fast or successive attempts. This is why, in many cases teaching job in the private institutions becomes a last resort for many educated youths. This makes the teaching profession especially in private institutions very cheap, as a result of which quality of output becomes very poor. One most commonly found practice in the private institutions is that the teachers simply dictate notes in the class. Therefore, they have become only 'dictators' in the class. Students often mug up what is being dictated in the class and teaching has been restricted to pass the examination only (Azim 2007). It is very much demanded by the private institutions. Both the students and institution want short cut method, because the objective of private institutions is to maximize profit while students want exam passed. This may probably be the reason why large number of well-to-do students could not get admission in the good government institutions (Kumar and Kumari 2008). Now, the question that poses in front of us is whether the situation is same or different in NEI is being dealt in the next section.

North-East India and Higher Education

North-east India (NEI) comprising of eight States *viz.*, Assam, Arunachal Pradesh, Meghalaya, Mizoram, Manipur, Nagaland, Sikkim and Tripura is situated in the outskirts of the country. Though the entire north-eastern region constitutes *7.98* per cent of Indian geographical area (an area of 262,179 km), its population is only *3.91* per cent of the country's population (40.2 million of population) as per the 2001 Census. Despite being rich in natural resources with fertile land, rich forests and mineral deposits, the region is still very poor. At the national level, the forest constitutes about *19.39* per cent of the geographical area of the country; whereas *64* per cent of the total geographical areas of the north-east is covered by the forest (Ao and Kharmawphlang, 2002)[11]. The entire NE region except Sikkim is connected to the rest of the country through a narrow 20 km wide Chicken's neck corridor near Siliguri (West Bengal). Sikkim is also connected with the Indian mainland *via* West Bengal but it remains at a distance from other NE States. Out of six international boundaries touch the whole of India (*i.e.* China, Pakistan, Bangladesh, Nepal, Bhutan and Myanmar) five of them with about 5000 km touch North-East India (namely, China, Nepal, Bhutan, Myanmar and Bangladesh). The bio-diversity of NEI is considered as one of the 19 identified bio-diversity *"hot spots"* of the world. Around three-fourth of NEI is filled with hills and mountains where mainly the tribal people of various races, especially the different mongoloid stock are found. The Indo-Aryan population is concentrated mainly in the Brahmaputra and Barak Valley of Assam, and the plain areas of Tripura. On an average, the density of population is very low in the hill areas as compared to the plains or valleys. The entire NEI is called a *"melting pot"* because of the people from varied religious sects, linguistic groups and cultures live there. While Hindu religious groups and Muslims dominate the plains or valleys, Christian religious groups followed by marginal number of Buddhists/Hindus dominate the hill areas. The North-East is composed of numerous linguistic and dialectical groups like Assamese, Nagamese, Tripuri, Mizo, Manipuri, Khasi, Garo, Bengali, Nepali etc.

After Independence, the establishment of few Universities in NEI gave a real boost to the expansion of higher education. The first University, Guwahati University at Guwahati was set up in January 1948 in this region. It was followed by North Eastern Hill University (NEHU) at Shillong, the first Central University in the region in 1973 with campuses in Nagaland and Mizoram. Later on, few more Universities like, Dibrugarh University, Manipur University, Assam University, Arunachal University (Rajiv Gandhi University), Tezpur University, Tripura University, Nagaland University, and Mizoram University were set up in this region. The growth of higher education is accelerated in the hill areas of NEI due to the advent of English education.

Tables 18.1 and Table 18.2 give a comparative view point of the educated people attaining higher education and their employment rates from the elementary level in tribal and non-tribal areas respectively. A comparison is also made between these two areas with regard to the socio-economic condition of the people. Table 18.1 depicts socio-economic conditions of the villages perusing education in English language, while Table 18.2 depicts the socio-economic conditions of the villages pursuing education in regional languages. On an average, the percentage of higher educated persons employed in the tribal community is 52.00; whereas it is 26.00 per cent in the non-tribal villages. The overall percentage of educated people attained higher education (graduate and above) in this tribal villages is 26.00 as against 16 per cent in the non-tribal villages. On an average the percentage of Post Graduates of the total higher educated people is about 24 per cent, while it is only about 10 per cent in the non-tribal areas. It is evident from the above description that the level of education and employability in tribal areas with English as a medium of study is much higher than that of the non-tribal areas where regional language (Manipuri) is the medium of study. Thus, it is inferred that education in English language has better job opportunities as compared to the type of education in regional language. Also, it can be said that the number of higher educated people is comparatively more in tribal areas than non-tribal areas because of imparting education in English language.

Table 18.1 : Population, Education and Employment in Tribal Villages

Name of the Village	No. of House-holds	Popula-tion (Ex-cluding below 5 Years)	Educated Persons			% of educated people attained Higher Edu-cation*	No. of Em-ployee (Both private and Govt.)	% of Higher educated persons employ-ed**
			Matric	Gra-duate	PG			
1. Noagang	311	1560	800	195	66	25.00	357	59.77
2. Chheihlu	83	467	101	13	5	15.00	40	61.11
3. Ziumi	105	657	147	48	6	27.00	59	68.51
4. Maram	432	2174	378	89	18	22.00	200	45.36
5. Thizama	120	665	166	66	26	36.00	97	50.00
6. Sunglup	140	795	128	50	27	38.00	115	74.02
Average	—	—	287	77	25	26.00 %	868	52.00%

Source: Field Survey

* Graduate and above and it is calculated from the number of educated persons (Matric+Graduate+PG)

** Calculated from the number of Graduate and P G and including employment in Private Sector

Table 18.2 : Population, Education and Employment in Non-Tribal Villages

Name of the Village	No. of House-holds	Popula-tion (Ex-cluding below 5 Years)	Educated Persons			% of educated people attained Higher Edu-cation*	No. of Em-ployee (Both private and Govt.)	% of Higher educated persons employ-ed**
			Matric	Gra-duate	PG			
1. Moinarband	64	293	96	18	-	16	11	27.77
2. Seramkhul	44	226	55	13	-	19	12	30.76
3. Koroikandi	86	438	143	23	2	15	16	32.00
4. Lupabari	84	448	140	29	1	18	18	10.00
5. Rongpur	172	840	277	44	8	16	36	30.76
Average	—	—	143	26	3	16.25%	93	26.00%

Source: Field Survey.

* Graduate and above and it is calculated from the number of educated persons (Matric+Graduate+PG).

** Calculated from the number of Graduate and P G and including employment in Private Sector.

Observations of the Study

Union HRD Minister, Arjun Singh has expressed concerned over 'quite a number' of private higher educational institutions in the country becoming 'Teaching Shops' and misleading students (*The Morung Express* 12/07/08). In the private institutions, employers are pretending to pay the faculty members are pretending to teach and students are pretending to be known. By this process, parroting and call-centre quality manpower is produced by the private institutions. Philanthropies turned commercial system of education in NEI as well as in the country as a whole are not a new history. Still, the present survey result says that the English education or private education has transformed the tribal communities of NEI into a new life in this globalized world. As a result of which they are developing much faster than the non-tribal communities within the NEI.

Despite a sea change in the field of education in the last one-two decades in tribal areas of NEI, the ***opportunity cost*** of quality education, which was supposed to be provided at the subsidies rate by the State has become very high. It is perhaps due to the emergence of private institutions in this sector. On the one hand, general masses of tribal in NEI cannot buy quality education at the reasonable prices and this pulls down the hill economy into a subsistence level. On the other hand, public institutions cannot do justice on the face of globalization in the non-tribal (valley) region of NEI. It is because of non-compatibility and regional medium of public education. All the non-tribal villages which are studied in this chapter are basically very close to the city/town, infrastructural condition is better than the hill villages. Still they are much behind the tribal community in regard to the education. It is a paradox as to why the highly qualified faculties in highly paid public institutions are not being able to deliver the right types of goods, whereas the private institutions with unskilled and marginally paid faculties are performing well. Government's control over the public educational institutions has been ineffective and lacks adequate supervision while it is reverse in case of private educational institutions having strict management control and supervision. In fact, none of the institutions, whether public or private, are perfect in all respects. In government institutions, quality of education is deteriorating due to poor management control and supervision, whereas quality of education in the private institutions is comparatively better despite having abnormal teacher-student ratio, overwork load, unskilled and inexperience teachers, especially in NEI. It is, therefore, proved beyond doubt that private institutions are able to produce better results only because of effective supervision and control as well disciplines and routine exercises. This is mainly because of English education and rest comes afterwards. It helps in further economic development in the tribal villages in NEI.

Suggestions and Conclusion

Quality education is the engine of growth in any economy. To bring quality, many scholars have given different opinions. The role of quality teacher was highly emphasized by many scholars in the past (*e.g.* Banerjee *et al.* 2002; Dreze and Sen 1996 etc.). Others suggested like, educational voucher (Kumar *et al.* 2003); community participation and community pressure (Mythili 2002); inter-regional exchanges of faculties, etc. are some of the approaches for enhancing quality education. One may not enjoy the dividend of investment on education immediately; it is a long-term investment with a certain percentage of dividends. Education is thus *a priori* variable and income/ poverty a consequential variable (Lynden and Khonglah 2004). It cannot be bought and sold any time in the daily market. Teaching learning is a long-term and continuous process. It is not like any other production process in the factory or industry, in which some definite quantity of labour and capital will produce some corresponding output.

Since the public institutions are inefficient due to uncontrolled on the one hand and private institutions are below the required quality due to over controlled, a system of

Public-Private Partnership will be suitable for the NEI. Prime Minister, Manmohon Singh has also said that the need for facilitating creative partnership between the public and private sectors in the field of education. This system is very much successful in the southern States and even in Meghalaya. In these States, many colleges are being run by the Christian Missionaries but the salaries are paid by the Government. In the global context, many eminent educational institutions all over the world were partnering with industry to set up collaborative knowledge partnerships in campuses and they were to the mutual advantage of both industry and academia.

Singh (2008) suggested that in order to be able to impart quality education, education system has to acquire the following qualities—quality syllabus, quality faculty, quality teaching and evaluation, quality research and quality character. Exploitation of teachers in the private institutions needs to be checked (Gill *et al.* 2005). Job security is to be protected for smooth functioning and retaining quality teachers especially in the higher educational institutions. Teaching faculties must be enthused by good salaries and better infrastructures are to be improved and the objective of the educational institutions should be student-centred (Fernandes 2008). If the existing institutions lose their best faculty and students to the newly emerging ones so be it—nothing else will shake up the system better (Banerjee 2002).

For the valley region of NEI, there should be compulsory English education in the regional medium school, if not completely ignore regional medium. From the above analysis, it has been cleared that the English education is one of the most important factors for the development of rural region. English education should be emphasized and all the regional medium schools in the villages should be converted into English medium in the step-wise manner, if not instantly. Inter-village transfer of teachers should be considered to make the school effective and maintain regularity of the teachers. Special English classes should be arranged for the weaker students to cope up with the market competition.

NOTES

1. The two, *i.e.* Higher and Primary education will be used interchangeably throughout this chapter, but the ultimate objective is to get quality higher education.
2. Hon'ble Prime Minister Dr. Manmohan Singh delivered a lecture at IIT, Guwahati on 26th August 2008.
3. Some of the regional medium of education system in NEI is Assamese, Bengali, and Manipuri etc. For the present study, we have selected the areas where education upto class X is imparted through Manipuri medium only.
4. Nine of them are: namely, Abhijit Banarjee, Pranab Bardhan, Kaushik Basu, Mrinal Dutta Chaudhuri, Maitresh Ghatak, Ashok Sanjay Guha, Mukul Mazumdar, Dilip Mukherjee and Debraj Ray.
5. This part is excerpted from Kuldip Mathur's text on 'Does Performance Matter? Policy Struggles in Education' delivered on 16/01/07 at ASC, JNU, New Delhi.
6. For the argument, see Basu, A. (1982): Essays in the History of Education, Concept Publishing Co. New Delhi.
7. For more elaboration, see Jeyaseelan (1996).
8. As quoted by Kumar (2003).
9. Tilak (2007) advocated that countries with large private higher education system cannot prosper except few countries like, Japan and Korea.
10. See Lovelock (1983), quoted by Vachhrajani (2008).
11. As quoted by Basantia and Singha (2008) in Singha, K. (ed), *Village Development in NEI: New Approaches*, Concept Publication, New Delhi.

REFERENCES

Azim, Shaukath (2007): *Higher Education in Rural India*, University News, Vol. 45 (45): 4-7.

Banarjee, A. (2002): 'Strategy for Economic Reform in West Bengal', *Economic and Political Weekly*, XXXVII (4): 4203-18.

Chattopadhyay, A. *et al.* (2005): 'Scenario of Primary School Attendance: A Study of Less Developed States in India', *Journal of Educational Planning and Administration*, XIX (1): 111-30.

De, Anuradha *et al.* (2002): 'Private Schools for Less Privileged: Some Insights from a Case Study', *Economic and Political Weekly*, XXXVII (52): 5230-36.

D'Souza, E. (2004): 'Contractual Arrangements in Academia: Implications for Performance', *Economic and Political Weekly*, XXXIX (21): 2165-68.

Dreze, J. and Sen, A. (1996): *India—Economic Development and Social Opportunity*, Oxford University Press.

Fernandes, L. M. (2008): 'Focus on Higher Education', *Indian Currents*, XX (33): 37-38.

Government of India (1998): *National Policy on Education* 1986 (*As modified in 1992) with National Policy on Education, 1968* Department of Education, Ministry of Human Resource Development, New Delhi.

Gill, S.S. *et al.* (2005): 'Educational Development, Public Expenditure and Financing of Secondary Education in Punjab', *Journal of Educational Planning and Administration*, XIX (3): 335-74.

Kumar, C.D. and Reddy, M.V. (2008): 'Indian Education System: Past and Future', *University News*, 46 (6): 1-7.

Kumar, K. and Kumari, K. (2008): 'Shift in Financing and Mode of Higher Education in India', *New Frontiers in Education*, 41 (1): 16-22.

Kumar, S. *et al.* (2003): 'Primary Education in Rural Areas: An Alternative Model', *Economic and Political Weekly*, XXXVIII (34): 3533-36.

Levy, D.C. (2008): 'Private Higher Education: Patterns and Trends', *New Frontiers in Education*, 41 (1): 3-4.

Lynden, B. and Khonglah, M.P. (2004): 'Rural Development: An Educational Perspective' in Ray, B.D. and Das, G. (eds.), *Dimensions of Rural Development in NEI*, Akansha Publishing House.

Mathur, Kuldip (2007): *Does Performance Matter? Policy Struggles in Education*, Text of the lecture delivered in the UGC Orientation Course on 16/01/07 at the ASC, JNU, and New Delhi.

Muhammad, A. *et al.* (2004): 'Opening Black Box of Education System in Bangladesh: Analysis of University Admission Test Results and Background Performances', *Economic and Political Weekly*, XXXIX (28): 3131-37.

Mukherjee, Dipa (2005): 'Educational Attainment in India: Trends, Patterns and Policy Issues', *Journal of Educational Planning and Administration*, XIX (4): 523-41.

Mythili, N. (2002): 'Community Pressure for Higher Quality of Education: Rural Primary Schools in Karnataka', *Economic and Political Weekly*, XXXVII (24): 2349-55.

Rao, M.V.S. (2005): 'English for International Career', *New Frontiers in Education*, XXXV (2): 127-29.

Reddy, C.Y. (2008): '*Privatization of Higher Education*', Southern Economist, 46 (23 and 24): 31-32.

Singh, A.K. (2006): 'Degree Devaluation in Higher Education: Unemployment and Unemployability among the Graduates in India', *Journal of Educational Planning and Administration*, XX (4): 411-28.

Singh, S. and Sridhar, K.S. (2002): 'Government and Private Schools: Trends in Enrolment and Retention', *Economic and Political Weekly*, XXXVII (41):4229-38.

Shah, K.R. (2006): 'State Inaction in Education in India', *Journal Educational Planning and Administration*, XX (4): 465-72.

Singha, Komol (2008 ed.): *Development of Villages in NEI: New Approaches*, Concept Publication, New Delhi.

Tilak, J.B.G. (2003): 'Higher Education and Development' in Kleeves, J.P. and Watanabe, R. (eds.) *The Handbook on Educational Research in the Asia Pacific Region*, Kluwer Academic Publishers, Dordrecht. pp. 809-26.

—— (2004): Absence of Policy and Perspective in Higher Education', *Economic and Political Weekly*, XXXIX (21): 2159-64. 27.

—— (2005): 'Higher Education in Trishanku: Hanging between State and Market', *Economic and Political Weekly*, XXXX (37): 429-37.28.

—— (2007): *Private Sector in Higher Education: Some Stylized Facts*, National University of Educational Planning and Administration, New Delhi.

Tiwary, H.V. (2008): 'Perspectives of Privatization of University Education in New Indian States', *University News*, 46 (17): 1-8.

Vachhrajani, Hardik (2008): Who Our Customers Are and What Do They Expect?—A Review Literature from Higher Education Perspective, *University News*, 46(34): 14-17.

19

Inter-District Disparities in Socio-Economic Development in Nagaland

D.S. DHAKRE and AMOD SHARMA

Introduction

Development has been appropriately conceptualized as a process, which improves the quality of life. The programmers of development have been taken up in the country in a planned way through various Five Years Plans. The main objective of this programme is to enhance the quality of people's life as well as effecting improvement in their social and economic well-being. The economic growth and uniform regional development are the basic development of the programme. The Green Revolution in agricultural sector and commendable progress in the industrial front have certainly increased the overall total production in the country, but there is no indication that these achievements have been able to reduce substantially the regional inequality in the level of development. It is found that the entire areas of the low developed districts are not backward but some parts are middle level or high level developed. Keeping this in view, a study was made for evaluating the socio-economic development in Nagaland.

For the purpose of this chapter a survey had been conducted on the evaluation of economic development of Nagaland. The data incorporated in this study covers a period from 1991-2005 in respect of 8 districts, and had been critically analysed and wide disparities in the level of development were found in different stages. It was, therefore, felt necessary to make a deeper analysis using the district level data for socio-economic indicators for evaluating the imbalances of development in the State.

Nagaland, the 16th State of Indian Union inaugurated on the 1st December 1963.The people of Nagaland is almost tribal and agrarian in character. There are several tribes and sub-tribes amongst the Nagas, with their own distinctive language and cultural features. About 82.26 per cent population of the State reside in rural areas. As per 2001 population census, the total population of the State was 19,88,636. This was about 0.19 per cent of the total all-India population. The percentage of workers to total population was about 42.74 per cent. The population density of population is 120 per square kilometre and the annual growth of the population is about 64.41 per cent. The literacy rate in the State is about 67.11 per cent, which is higher than the all-India rate of 65.18 per cent. Agriculture is an important and primary sector in the State. It provides food to the growing population, raw materials to the agro-based industries and various other products to fulfil the basic needs. The State's economy is largely depending upon agricultural sector. Major food crops are rice, jowar, wheat, bajra, barley, maize and pulses. Important commercial crops grown in the State are sugarcane, cotton, jute, potato, coffee, tea, cardamom, etc. The total forest area in the State is about 11.68 per cent and the major forest produces are basically, teak, oak, bamboo, pulpwood and firewood, etc.

Knowledge of the level of development will help in identifying where a given State stands in relation to others. The study also throws light on the relationship of socio-economic development with the agricultural development and infrastructural facilities. Improvements required in the development indicators of the low developed States have been suggested. The regions and the population under different stages of development have been evaluated and the model districts have been identified for fixing up the potential targets of different indicators for low developed districts so that these districts or the State may make improvement in the present level of development

Methodology of the Study

Development is a multi-dimensional continuous process. Its impact cannot be evaluated fully by any single indicator. Moreover, a number of indicators when analyzed individually do not provide an integrated and easily comprehensible picture of reality. Hence, there is a need for building up of a composite index of development based on various indicators combined in an optimum manner. For this study, the districts have been taken as the unit of analysis. 8 districts of the State are included in the study .The data on twenty development indicators for the year (2000-2001) are utilized in the analysis.

Developmental Indicators

Each district faces situational factors of development unique to it as well as common administrative and financial factors. Indicators which are common to all the States have been included in the analysis for evaluating the level of development. The composite indices of development have been calculated for different districts by using the data on the following indicators :

Agricultural Sector

1. Productivity of total cereals,
2. Productivity of pulses,
3. Productivity of oilseeds,
4. Productivity of commercial crops,
5. Per capita cereal production,
6. Number of farms,
7. Number of Beneficiaries under IRDP,
8. Percentage of net area irrigated, and
9. Number of veterinary hospitals and dispensaries.

Infrastructural Facilities

1. Number of banks per lakh population,
2. Credit/Deposit ratio,
3. Decadal growth rate of population,
4. Population density,
5. Sex ratio,
6. Literacy rate (male),
7. Literacy rate (female),
8. Total literacy rate,
9. Birth rate,
10. Death rate, and
11. Infant mortality rate.

These indicators may not form an all inclusive list but these are the major interacting components of development in the State. Out of these indicators, nine indicators are depicting the progress of agricultural development and the eleven are concerned with the infrastructural facilities.

Estimation of Composite Index of Level of Development

Variables in respect of different indicators are taken from various population distributions and these are recorded in different levels of measurement. The values of these development indicators are not quite suitable for simple addition in combined analysis. For obtaining the composite index of development, the values of indicators are transformed as follows.

Let X_{ij} be the value of j=th indicator for i=th unit, $i = 1, 2, \ldots, n$ and $j = 1, 2, \ldots, k$. X_{ij} is transformed to Z_{ij} as follows:

$$Z_{ij} = \left(X_{ij} - \overline{X}_j\right) / S_j$$

where $\overline{X}_j$ = mean of the j=th indicator; S_j = S.D. of j=th indicator

The best value of the transformed variables for different indicators (with maximum value depending upon the direction of the impact of indicator on development) is identified and the squares of the deviations of the transformed variables from best values are obtained. The inverse of the coefficient of variation of the original variables is used as weight for obtaining the pattern of development. The statistical technique given by Narain *et al.* (1991, 1999) is applied to construct the composite index of development for different district. The composite indices have been worked out separately for agricultural, infrastructural and overall socio-economic fields. The value of the composite index lies between 0 and 1. A value close to 0 indicates high level of development and a value near to 1 indicates poor level of development. The association between the levels of development of different sectors of economy has been worked out. For low districts, improvements needed in various indicators are also presented.

Results and Discussions

The composite indices of development have been worked out separately for agricultural sector, infrastructural sector and overall socio-economic sector for different districts are given in Table 19.1. The sectors have also been ranked on the basis of level of development.

It may be seen from the Table 19.1 that in case of agricultural development, the district Kohima is ranked first and the district Zunheboto is ranked last. The composite indices of development vary from 0.59 to 0.89 in case of infrastructural facilities. The district Dimapur is found to be on the first position and the district Mon is ranked last. The composite index varies from 0.20 to 0.75. In overall socio-economic development, the district of Kohima is ranked first and the district Zunheboto is ranked last. The composite indices of development vary from 0.39 to 0.81.

Table 19.1 : Composite Index of Development

Sl. No.	Districts	Agriculture		Infrastructure		Socio-economic	
		C.I.	Rank	C.I.	Rank	C.I.	Rank
1.	Kohima	0.59	1	0.55	6	0.39	1
2.	Dimapur	0.79	6	0.20	1	0.62	6
3.	Phek	0.76	4	0.54	3	0.61	5
4.	Mokokchung	0.76	5	0.52	2	0.61	4
5.	Zunheboto	0.89	8	0.55	5	0.81	8
6.	Wokha	0.82	7	0.54	4	0.71	7
7.	Tuensang	0.72	3	0.64	7	0.58	3
8.	Mon	0.66	2	0.75	8	0.50	2

Different Stages of Development

For relatives comparisons among the districts with regard to the level of development, it appears appropriate to assume that the district having the composite indices less than or equal to (Mean–SD) are highly developed whereas the district having the composite indices greater than or equal to (Mean + SD) are low developed. Districts with composite index lying between (Mean–SD) and Mean are medium level developed and the district having the composite index between lying (Mean) and (Mean + SD) are at developing district. On the basis of this classification, districts are put in four categories of development, high, medium, low and developing. Table 19.2 present the classification of districts lying in different levels of development along with percentage area and population.

In case of agricultural development, the districts Kohima and Mon are found to be better developed as compared to other districts of Nagaland. These two better developed districts occupy about 30 per cent area and 29 per cent population of Nagaland districts covered under the study. The district Tuensang is middle level developed covering about 26 per cent area and 21 per cent population. The districts Phek, Wokha, Mokokchung and Dimapur are in the developing stage. These districts cover about 36 per cent area and 42 per cent population. The district Zunheboto is observed to be in the low developed category. This district covers about 8 per cent area and 8 per cent population.

Table 19.2 : Area and Production in Different Levels of Development

	AGRICULTURE		
Level of Development	*Name of Districts*	*Area %*	*Population %*
High	Kohima, Mon	30	29
Middle	Tuensang	26	21
Developing	Phek, Wokha, Mokokchung, Dimapur	36	42
Low	Zunheboto	8	8
	INFRASTRUCTURE		
Level of Development	*Name of Districts*	*Area %*	*Population %*
High	Dimapur	6	16
Middle	Mokokchung, Phek, Wokha	32	27
Developing	Kohima, Zunheboto, Tuensang	51	44
Low	Mon	11	13
	SOCIO-ECONOMIC		
Level of Development	*Name of Districts*	*Area %*	*Population %*
High	Kohima	19	16
Middle	Tuensang, Mon	36	34
Developing	Mokokchung, Wokha, Phek, Dimapur	37	42
Low	Zunheboto	8	8

Infrastructure facilities include medical, banking and overall economic enterprises available to the people in Nagaland districts. The position of various districts regarding the availability and use of the above facilities for the people is assessed by the composite index. It may be seen from the Table 19.2 that the district Dimapur is found to be better developed as compared to the rest of the Nagaland districts. This better developed district occupies about 6 per cent area and 16 per cent population of Nagaland. The districts Mokokchung, Phek and Wokha are middle level developed covering about 32 per cent area and 27 per cent population. The districts Kohima, Zunheboto and Tuensang are in the developing stage. These districts cover about 51 per cent area and 44 per cent population. The district Mon is observed to be in the low developed category. This district covers about 11 per cent area and 13 per cent population.

Regarding overall Socio-economic development, the district Kohima is found to be better developed as compared to the rest of the Nagaland districts. This better developed district occupies about 19 per cent area and 16 per cent population of Nagaland. The districts Tuensang and Mon are middle level developed covering about 36 per cent area and 34 per cent population. The districts Wokha, Mokokchung, Phek and Dimapur are in the developing stage. These districts cover about 37 per cent area and 42 per cent population. The district Zunheboto is observed to be in the low developed category. This district covers about 8 per cent area and 8 per cent population.

Inter-relationships among different Sectors

To examine the relationship among development of agriculture, infrastructure, overall socio-economic sectors and total literacy, pair-wise correlations have been worked out and presented in Table 19.3.

Table 19.3 : Pair-wise Correlation Coefficient

Sl. No.	*Pair of Sectors*	*Correlation Coefficient*
1.	Agriculture and Infrastructure	-0.35
2.	Agriculture and socio-economic	0.99*
3.	Agriculture and total literacy	0.46
4.	Infrastructure and socio-economic	-0.22
5.	Infrastructure and total literacy	-0.66
6.	Socio-economic and total literacy	0.38

* Significant at 1% level.

The correlation coefficient between the developments in agriculture and socio-economic sectors is found to be significantly at 0.05 probability level. However, the correlation coefficient between the developments in agriculture and infrastructural facilities is not significant. The correlation coefficient between the development in infrastructural facilities and socio-economic sectors is also not significant.

Infrastructural facilities in respect of banking, medical and other economic enterprises are also not found to be associated with the agricultural development.

Literacy rate is also not associated with the agricultural, infrastructural and socio-economic development.

Potential Targets for Low Developed Districts

For bringing out uniform regional development among the Nagaland districts, it is important to examine the nature of improvement required in different indicators of low developed districts for enhancing the level of development. This information is useful for readjusting the resources in reducing inequalities in levels of disparities in development among different districts. It would also provide avenues to bring about uniform regional development in State. Potential targets of various developmental indicators for the low developed districts have been determined by taking the best value among the Nagaland districts. Table 19.4 gives the value of various important developmental indicators along with the potential targets in respect of these two districts.

The district Zunheboto is found to be low developed in agricultural and overall socio-economic sectors. The district Mon is found to be low developed in infrastructural facilities.

Table 19.4: Potential Targets of Low Developed Districts

	Developmental Indicators	*Zuneboto*	*Mon*	*Potential Target*
1.	Productivity of total cereals	0.8	8.7	23.7
2.	Productivity of pulses	8.5	22.5	22.5
3.	Productivity of oilseeds	15.2	8.2	37.91
4.	Per capita cereal production	0.01	0.12	0.36
5.	Productivity of commercial crops	1.3	62.7	62.69
6.	No. of farms	2	2	7
7.	Percentage of net area irrigated	5.2	7.7	26.4
8.	No. of banks/lakh population	4.51	1.54	7.13
9.	Decadal growth rate	61	73.42	95.01
10.	Total literacy	81.28	42.25	84.27
11.	Birth rate	21.42	14	35.31
12.	Death rate	2.75	1.86	4.23
13.	Infant mortality rate	1.24	1.35	2.77

It may be seen from Table 19.4 that the values of such developmental indicators are very low as compared to the potential targets. In case of those indicators which are related to agricultural development like productivity of total cereals, pulses, oilseeds, commercial crops, farms, net irrigated area and per capita cereal production are very low in comparison to the corresponding potential targets. In Mon district the total literacy rate is very poor. Improvements needed in the level of development in these two districts are as follows :

Zunheboto

This district is low developed in agricultural and socio-economic fields. Improvement in forest production should be made. Road transport is not very satisfactory which may be improved. This district is backward in agricultural development. For ensuring per capita food production, measure improvements are required in creating more irrigation facilities.

Mon

Mon district is the home of *konyaks.* These people also chiefly practice *jhum* cultivation. An adoption of the terraced cultivation is now encouraged in these areas also by the State Government. Whereas, on the other hand this district is low developed in infrastructural and educational field. Welfare developmental programmes may be enhanced for the required development.

Conclusions

The broad conclusions emerging from the study are as follows :

- With respect to overall socio-economic development, the district of Kohima is found to be highly developed. The district of Tuensang and Mon are middle level developed. The district Mokokchung, Wokha, Phek and Dimapur are at the developing stages. These districts are making fast improvement in their level of development. The district of Zunheboto is found to be low developed. This district requires a care in implementation of developmental programmes.

- In agricultural field, the district of Kohima and Mon are found to be better developed and the district of Zunheboto is low developed.
- Agricultural development is highly associated with socio-economic development.
- Wide disparities in the level of development have been observed between different districts.

REFERENCES

Narain, P. *et al.* (2000a): "Regional Disparities in socio-economic Development in Tamil Nadu", *Journal of Indian Social and Agricultural Statistics,* (53): 35-46.

— (2000 b): "Regional Dimension of Disparities in Crop Productivity in Uttar Pradesh", *Journal of Indian Social and Agricultural Statistics,* (54): 62-79.

Narain, P. *et al.* (2002): "Dimensions of Regional Disparities in Socio-economic Development in Madhya Pradesh", *Journal of Indian Social and Agricultural Statistics,* (55): 88-107.

Narain, P. *et al.* (2003): "Evaluation of Economic Development at Micro Level in Karnataka", *Journal of Indian Social and Agricultural Statistics,* (56): 52-63.

Narain, P. *et al.* (2004): "Estimation of Socio-economic Development in Hilly States", *Journal of Indian Social and Agricultural Statistics,* (58): 126-135.

Statistical Hand Book—Nagaland (2006), Directorate of Economics and Statistics, Nagaland, Kohima.

20

Rural Transport Development in Nagaland

GAUTAM PATIKAR

Introduction

India lives in the villages. It is no mere rhetoric, and has been proved by the latest (2001) census, which shows 70 percentage of country's total population are in the villages. The last fifty years of industrialization concentrated in and around the cities or urban centres, and succeeded in drawing the resourceful youths and talent of the villages to the urban centres. The 100 per cent increase in the population of the country during the last three decades has not been matched by a proportional increase in the means of transportation. If we were to add the effect of industrial and agricultural growth which requires their imperative of mobility, we would get a picturesque of transportation system of the country.

The country has an extensive rail networks, which has doubtlessly succeeded in linking up important cities and towns. Even so, having regard to the wide dispersion of the human habitat in the country, it cannot provide the necessary links between the thousands of villages, which constitute rural India. Air transport is mostly confined to metropolitan cities and has no impact whatsoever on rural transportation and the rural sector. Still, it has priced itself beyond the reach of the villagers.

The inability of these two modes of transport system, the rural masses meaningfully and adequately have placed the road transport in unique position of being a primary and in some cases, the only mode of transport system of the thousands of villages in the country. Road and road transport are, therefore, the prerequisites for the effort to open up rural hinterland to the outside world. In the absence of adequate rail and air connectivity, road transport is being widely used as a principal mode of transport system in Nagaland. Roads are the veins of the State in uplifting the rural sector. It is, therefore, envisaged to study the rural transport system in Nagaland with reference to *Pradhan Mantri Gram Sadak Yojana* (PMGSY).

The overall objective of this study is to provide a window into the scenario of rural transport system and its development potentials in Nagaland. The specific objectives are identified as follows:

- to review the development of road transport in Nagaland,
- to identify the problems with rural roads development,
- to highlight the development potentials of rural roads, and
- to evaluate the achievement of PMGSY in Nagaland.

Historical Status of Rural Roads

The means of transport is not new to the mankind. It grows along with the civilization. From the very beginning of civilization, the human and the beast of burden have been the most primitive means of transport since they lived in jungle. As population expanded couple with the shrinking of resources around them, they had to cover many kilometres everyday for collecting necessary foods for living. Gradually, the activities of human being increased and the animals such as dogs, horses, camels, bullocks, elephants, etc. came to be in use as vehicles of transporting goods from one place to another.

The invention and the use of *wheel cart* was a significant development to the transport system. It was possible for man to drag more than what he could carry with their head-loads. It is believed that the introduction of *wheel cart* as a vehicle of transportation was first used in China. The Greek historian

Herodotus noted that the Egyptians made wide stone roads along with the huge building blocks and were transported to the construction site. Modern research suggests that the Egyptian probably used sledges, scattering sand in front of the runners when necessary to assist progress.

In the fifth century B.C., the Persians built an extensive road network. The Romans proved to have a real talent for building roads, it was no accident that all roads were said to lead to Rome. It was built at the end of the fourth century B.C., *"the great road builders"*—Netcalf and Telfore, brought about phenomenal progress in road in the nineteenth century.

In India, the rural development was kicked off during the early nineteenth century. The roads are the principal means of carrying agricultural produces from villages to the marketing centres and for the social and cultural uplift of the villages. According to the Indian Road Development Committee, the total length of roads in India in 1927 was 1,99,140 of which 30 per cent were surfaced and the rest were unsurfaced roads.

India has a Rural Road Network of about 2.70 million km. with Rs. 35,000 crore investment (Rs. 180,000 crore of replacement value), which constitutes over 80 per cent of total road network. More than 10,00,000 km is tracks and roads not meeting technical standard. Rural roads sector suffered from lack of systematic planning, quality and sustained maintenance. It was a myth that rural roads do not require planning/design/ quality assurance. More than 45 per cent of the habitation is still to have All-Weather Road connectivity at the beginning of PMGSY Programme. As per Rural Development Ministry's statistics, by the end of March 2008, under PMGSY a total number of 71,090 roads have been cleared, 52,828 new connectivity have been made, 18,258 number of roads have been upgraded while 41,806 km. of roads construction have been completed. The 29,125 km. length of roads construction is still in progress (Chandrasekhar 2005).

Development of Roads during the Plan Periods

Coming to Nagaland, over the years, there has been a steady progress of the road connectivity. Beginning with 1955-56, when Nagaland had only a road of about 322 km., the roads were principally meant to connect the main administrative centres with points on the arterial links in the Assam Valley. Thus, the National Highway No. 39, which is the most important road and connects the rail-head at Dimapur with Imphal in Manipur *via* Kohima passed through Nagaland for a distance of 102 km. The Amguri (in Assam) to Mokokchung road of 103 km. was connecting central Nagaland with Amguri rail head in Assam. The road connecting Kohima and Amguri *via* Wokha and Mokokchung district is now converted to National Highway No. 61. The other two important roads were, Mokokchung-Tuensang of 84 km. and Namtila-Mon of 37 km. There were a few bridle tracks and mule paths connecting the villages to the arterial roads, but there were no feeder roads.

During the Second Plan, a large scale programme for strengthening and expanding the road system was taken up. It was proposed to build 41 minor bridges, construction, widen and improve the existing roads in the State. At the end of the Second Five Year Plan, the road position (in miles) of Nagaland stood at a total of 1012 miles. The break up of it is as follows, 64 National Highway, Surfaced Roads 09, and Unsurfaced Roads 939.

During the beginning of Third Five Year Plan (1961-62), an expenditure of Rs. 343.01 lakh were incurred for the construction, widening and improvement of roads. At the end of the Plan, the road position (in miles) was 1,739 miles. It consists of Surfaced Roads (other than National Highway) 76, Gravelled Roads 256 and the *Kutcha* Roads 1,407.

As it increased, at the end of the Fifth Five Year Plan, the total road length increased to 4,466 km. in the State. During this period, *i.e.*, 1974-78, the expenditure was Rs. 1904.41 lakh against the outlay of Rs. 2071.00 lakh. The achievement during the Fifth Plan period is as follows :

	Surfaced	*Unsurfaced*	*Total*
State Highway (km.)	1070	44	1114
Major District Roads (km.)	—	262	262
Other District Roads (km.)	112	516	628
Rural Roads (km.)	18	2444	2462
Total	1200	3266	4466

At the end of the Fifth Five Year Plan a total of 579 villages in the State were connected with motorable roads. And at the end of the *ad hoc* (1978-80) plan, a total of 628 villages of Nagaland were connected by roads.

At the end of 1980 the road position was as follows :

	Surfaced	*Unsurfaced*	*Total*
State Highway (km.)	1114	—	1114
Major District Roads (km.)	—	276	276
Other District Roads (km.)	131	547	678
Rural Roads (km.)	31	2784	2815
Total	1276	3607	4883

The physical achievements during the Sixth Plan in the State were stood at the level of where construction of new roads 220 km.; Widening and improvement 225 km.; Surfacing 20 km.; Bridges 6 Nos., etc. Thus, the total road length by the end of Sixth Plan was as follows :

	Surfaced	*Unsurfaced*	*Total*
State Highway (km.)	1114	—	1114
Major District Roads (km.)	—	282	283
Other District Roads (km.)	152	567	719
Rural Roads (km.)	53	3151	3204
Total	1319	4001	5320

During the Seventh Plan, drastic measures were taken to extend and improve the existing road length. Thus, at the end of the Seventh Plan, the total surfaced roads increased to 1948 km., while unsurfaced roads increased to 6,708 km. making surfaced roads at 22.50 per cent of the total road length.

At the end of the Eighth Plan, the total road length went upto 13,732 km. The surfaced roads increased by 567 km. and unsurfaced roads to 4,509 km. The percentage of surfaced roads to total road length stood at 18.31 per cent.

At the beginning of the Ninth Plan, surfaced roads increased by more than hundred per cent at 5,241 km. which was 28.55 per cent of the total road length in the State. The unsurfaced roads were 13,115 km. By the end of the Plan, the total road length increased to 19,860 km., and 98 per cent of the villages in Nagaland have now been connected with approach roads.

During the Tenth Plan, additional roads of length 1,428 km. have been in pipeline, of which 903 km. were targeted for major district roads, 236 km. for other district roads and 289 km. for rural roads. While under Eleventh Plan in the State, an additional road length of 604 km. has been proposed.

Extension of roads in Nagaland has gone on since the Chinese aggression in 1962. Both the Public Works Department (PWD) and the Border Roads Organization (BRO) have participated in this task. The road density in Nagaland is measured either in terms of per 100 sq. km. of area or per 1,00,000 of population, compared well with similar areas in the country.

Table 20.1 a depicts the district-wise classification of roads in Nagaland during 1999-2000. It is observed from the Table 20.1 that Wokha District shares the longest of National Highway of 137 kilometres out of a total of 361 kilometres throughout the State followed by Mokokchung with 113 kilometres and the Kohima with 90 kilometres. Out of a total of 277 kilometres of State Highways, Mon accounts for the largest share with 233 kilometres, followed by 44 kilometres in Tuensang. The Major District Roads totalling of 855 kilometres, of which 66 kilometres surfaced roads and 789 unsurfaced roads. 332 kilometres of Major District Roads run through the district of Tuensang, followed by 145 kilometres in Kohima.

Table 20.1a: District-wise Classification and Length of Roads in Nagaland (As on 1999-2000 in km.)

Districts	*National Highway*		*State Highway*		*Major Dist. Road*		*Other Dist. Road*	
	Sur-faced	*Un-sur-faced*	*Sur-faced*	*Un-sur-faced*	*Sur-faced*	*Un-sur-faced*	*Sur-faced*	*Un-sur-faced*
Kohima	90	—	—	—	15	130	95	318
Mokokchung	113	—		—	14	126	70	160
Tuensang	—	—	44	—	12	320	84	507
Phek	—	—	—	—	8	103	40	165
Mon	—	—	233	—	—	—	105	376
Wokha	137	—	—	—	9	75	40	157
Zunheboto	21	—	—	—	8	35	40	250
Total	361	—	277	—	66	789	474	1933

Table 20.1b : Road under Village and Border Road Organization

Districts	*Village Road*		*Road under Border Road Organization*	
	Surfaced	*Unsurfaced*	*Surfaced*	*Unsurfaced*
Kohima	395	443	65	—
Mokokchung	383	440	188	—
Tuensang	411	798	298	—
Phek	209	451	150	—
Mon	310	287	—	—
Wokha	208	291	60	—
Zunheboto	213	311	49	—
Total	2129	3021	810	—

Source: Statistical Handbook of Nagaland, 2001.

Problems with Rural Roads Development

Rural roads construction and maintenance is difficult. The State being in the tropical region and hilly, receives highest amount of rainfall with prolonged monsoon. This affects the roads and causes landslides very often during the rainy season. The construction and maintenance cost of roads here is comparatively very high. Apart from this, rural roads in Nagaland suffers from the number of problems like :

- Rural roads sector suffered from lack of systematic planning.
- Decisions on construction were *ad hoc* and not need-based.
- Multiple agencies involved in the development of rural roads.
- Technical standards and quality assurance was lacking.
- Government concentrates more on employment generation.

Development Potential of Rural Roads in Nagaland

Rural transport or village road transport is considered as the mirror of the area and it links the villages with urban areas. There is no better single yardstick than road transport to measure the stage of development in the rural areas. Roads are the veins of the rural regions, especially Nagaland. The transport is the *de facto* barometer of economic, social and commercial progress.

Impacts of Rural Roads on Agriculture

Agriculture is the life of rural masses, and commercialization of it determines the development of the region. The role of rural roads in the sphere of agriculture cannot be ignored. It increases production and periodicity by providing facilities like chemical fertilizer, market and other resources. These can be channelled through proper road and transport system. Companies find it easier to market improved seeds, pesticides, weedicides, etc. Agricultural machinery becomes available for agricultural operations. Technical services are readily available on agricultural and veterinary matters. Agricultural produce can be transported quickly and economically to market centres, reducing wastage and fetching better prices. Assured of all-weather access to his village, a farmer can plan value addition to his operations including land development, irrigation, multiple cropping, switch over to more remunerative crops like fruits and vegetables, improving breed of cattle.

Impacts of Rural Roads on Employment

Rural transport has opened a number of employment avenues. Road connectivity provides both ingress and egress of resources and has multiple impacts on employment opportunities. New employment opportunities arise due to ingress of better agricultural inputs since agricultural tempo picks up due to increasing on-farm and off-farm employment potential. Minor forest produce or other raw materials can be made available to cottage and local industries. Rural roads provide access to larger catchments area for milk and other outputs in the villages. New techniques and improved rural technologies can come into being in the newly connected villages creating additional opportunities. Improved machines for small-scale and village industries can be brought into the villages through proper road, and reduced cost of production and improved competitiveness. New employment opportunities also arise because rural roads permit outward movement particularly to market centres and thus help to create jobs in agricultural markets, increase supply for cottage and village industries, increase range of market for milk and dairy products, enables transportation of goods produced by local units. It allows for daily commutation of surplus labour to nearby market centres to find work new avenues.

Impact of Rural Roads on Socio-Economic Services

Newly connected villages have assured access to better social infrastructure—schools, health facilities, banks, post office, polling centres, bus stops, markets, etc. Rural roads enable better social infrastructure investments in improving quality of existing rural social infrastructure as well as rationalizing on its expansion. Road connectivity improve programme outreach of mobile social services particularly health, policing, etc. Road connectivity improves maintenance levels of basic infrastructural services like telephones, electricity, water supply, etc. Rural roads, because of their multi-dimensional effect, have the highest positive impact on the rural poor in terms of employment opportunities and sustained income generation. Tribal and other socially disadvantaged sections are able to join the mainstream as a result of assured connectivity. Rural roads by increasing mobility empower the disadvantaged, including women who earlier found limited opportunity, educationally, socially, economically, etc.

Impact of Rural Roads on General Area Development

Rural road provides access not merely to villages, but to an entire rural hinterland. In addition to the human resources, material resources including forest produce and mineral wealth can be developed for the economic growth of the area. If Area Development is planned along with the road connectivity programme, it enables to achieve government/individual oriented development programmes, like planned growth of market centres and common facilities, planning and regulation of public and Intermediate Public Transport (IPT) services.

Pradhan Mantri Gram Sadak Yojana (PMGSY)

PMGSY is a centrally sponsored scheme and began on December 25, 2000 on the birthday of the then Prime Minister Atal Bihari Vajpayee during the NDA regime. Rural Roads is a State subject and for effective implementation, responsibility is given to Panchayat System. Central Government funding under this scheme is an important element for the poverty reduction of the rural sector. The effective and execution responsibility of PMGSY is retained with State Governments where Panchayati Raj Institutions is involved in network planning and road works selection. Objectives and Targets of PMGSY are as follows :

- To provide farm to market All-Weather connectivity for all the habitations of 500 and above population (250 and above in case of Hill States, Desert and Tribal Areas).
- Network Augmentation and Modernization, both have been provided in the programme.
- New Connectivity being provided to about 60,000 Habitations of 1000+ population, 81,000 Habitations of 500+ population, 29,000 Habitations of 250+ population.
- Upgradation of about 3,70,000 km. Rural Roads at a cost of Rs. 53,000 crore.
- Total cost of New Connectivity is about Rs. 79,000 crore.
- Total envisaged cost of the project is about Rs.1,32,000 crore.

The State of Nagaland receives regularly the periodical grants under PMGSY for construction of new and upgradation of existing rural roads. The Rural Ministry on Thursday, May 1, 2008 officially informed that the Ministry has sanctioned Rs. 20 crore to Nagaland as the second instalment of Phase-V (*Nagarealm News*, May 02, 2008) as Grant in Aid for 2007-2008 for the scheme of PMGSY to connect the rural and remote areas of the State to maintain roads.

The PMGSY is a project handled by an autonomous body of the State, *viz.* the Rural Development Authority. This body receives allocated funds directly from the Ministry of Rural Development and has the responsibility of maintaining accounts. The utilization certificate pertaining to the project has to be submitted to the Ministry by the Rural Development Authority from time to time. There exists well co-ordination between the Central funding agency and the State level implementing authority and makes PMGSY more effective. The achievement rate of the project is satisfactory in the State. Below given is a brief account of the progress of roads in Nagaland during the period from 2000-01 to 2006-07 under the PMGSY, project. Table 20.2 describes the overall State profile of PMGSY. while the remaining tables give district-wise profile of PMGSY.

It is reported (Table 20.2) that a total sum of Rs. 134.02 crore was sanctioned during 2006-07 to the State under PMGSY against Rs. 19.74 crore in 2001. The number of roads constructed were 127 in 2000-01 against 30 in 2006-07 measuring 467.00 km. The total number of habitations benefited stood at 16 in 2000-01 and 59 in 2006-07 respectively.

Table 20.2: PMGSY—State Profile (2000-01 to 2006-07)

Year	*Value of Projects cleared (Rs. in crore)*	*Total No. of road works*	*Total length of road works (Km.)*	*Total No. of Habitations benefited*
2000-01	19.74	127	870	16
2001-02	46.08	27	318.37	24
2002-03	—	—	—	—
2003-04	21.44	22	193.42	26
2004-05	37.5	9	2245	14
2005-06	70.2	23	390.38	32
2006-07	134.02	30	467.00	59

Source: Ministry of Rural Development. Government of India.

The district-wise profile of PMGSY (given in Table 20.3, 20.4, and 20.5) shows that the PMGSY project focuses on balanced development of rural roads evident from the value of project cleared each year for the eleven (11) districts of Nagaland. During the period of seven (7) years from 2000-01 to 2006-07, one of the eleven districts received highest sanction indicating the approach of improving rural connectivity on priority basis. The highest value of project cleared in 2000-01 was for the district of Mokokchung followed by Zunheboto in 2001-02, Phek in 2003-04, Tuensang in 2004-05, Dimapur in 2005-06 and Kohima in 2006-07.

Table 20.3 : Value of Projects cleared under PMGSY—District Profile

Districts	*Value of Projects cleared (Rs. in Crore)*						
	2000-2001	*2001-2002*	*2002-2003*	*2003-2004*	*2004-2005*	*2005-2006*	*2006-2007*
Dimapur	1.98	4.32	—	2.34	—	8.42	6.31
Kohima	1.90	1.47	—	2.25	—	6.40	23.16
Kiphire	0.74	2.13	—	1.16	12.90	6.21	9.21
Longleng	0.66	2.76	—	—	—	7.10	11.81
Phek	2.56	5.50	—	3.56	—	3.55	5.73
Peren	1.19	3.67	—	—	2.60	5.34	9.53
Mokokchung	3.04	5.85	—	1.87	—	5.15	16.79
Mon	2.19	4.93	—	2.12	—	7.83	17.78
Tuensang	1.36	3.82	—	2.93	17.18	8.39	8.60
Wokha	1.52	5.00	—	2.83	4.82	4.29	2.89
Zunheboto	2.60	6.63	—	2.38	—	7.52	22.22

Table 20.4 : No. of Road works under PMGSY—District Profile

Districts	*Total No. of road works*						
	2000-2001	*2001-2002*	*2002-2003*	*2003-2004*	*2004-2005*	*2005-2006*	*2006-2007*
Dimapur	9	3	—	2	—	3	4
Kohima	7	1	—	3	—	3	5
Kiphire	6	1	—	1	4	2	1
Longleng	5	1	—	—	—	2	2
Phek	14	3	—	3	—	1	1
Peren	8	2	—	—	1	2	2
Mokokchung	16	3	—	2	—	1	3
Mon	17	2	—	—	—	3	4
Tuensang	17	3	—	2	3	2	3
Wokha	13	3	—	3	1	1	1
Zunheboto	15	4	—	2	—	3	4

Table 20.5 : Length of Road Works under PMGSY—District Profile

Districts	*Total Length of roads works (km.)*						
	2000-2001	*2001-2002*	*2002-2003*	*2003-2004*	*2004-2005*	*2005-2006*	*2006-2007*
Dimapur	54.50	24.50	—	23.00	—	50.51	31.00
Kohima	41.00	9.00	—	21.00	—	38.86	73.50
Kiphire	42.00	16.87	—	10.00	8350	28.00	35.00
Longleng	39.50	20.00	—	—	—	38.00	47.00
Phek	125.50	43.00	—	33.20	—	19.00	22.00
Peren	54.14	19.00	—	—	15.00	33.00	40.00
Mokokchung	135.50	40.00	—	17.00	—	30.00	61.00
Mon	115.50	37.00	—	19.00	—	43.02	54.00
Tuensang	78.00	22.00	—	29.00	108.00	45.02	54.00
Wokha	80.00	33.00	—	26.48	18.00	25.00	12.00
Zunheboto	104.36	54.00	—	14.74	—	39.30	54.00

Table 20.6 : Number of Habitations Benefited under PMGSY—District Profile

District	*Total No. of Habitations Benefited*						
	2000-2001	*2001-2002*	*2002-2003*	*2003-2004*	*2004-2005*	*2005-2006*	*2006-2007*
Dimapur	2	4	—	2	—	4	7
Kohima	3	1	—	3	—	4	9
Kiphire	1	2	—	2	8	3	1
Longleng	0	2	—	—	—	3	3
Phek	0	2	—	3	—	1	2
Peren	1	2	—	—	1	4	2
Mokokchung	3	0	—	3	—	4	6
Mon	1	0	—	5	—	4	12
Tuensang	0	3	—	2	4	3	6
Wokha	2	3	—	4	1	7	1
Zunheboto	3	5	—	2	—	5	7

Nagaland has not fared badly in terms of providing connectivity to uncovered habitations under the flagship programme. Pradhan Mantri Gram Sadak Yojana (PMGSY) as compared to other North-Eastern States. This was revealed in the Action Plan Reports of the conference of the thematic groups (North East Region Vision 2020) held from December 3rd and 4th, 2008, at North-Eastern Council, (NEC) auditorium,

Shillong (*Nagarealm News*, December 5, 2008). Since introduction of PMGSY in December 2000, Nagaland had a total 116 eligible unconnected habitations, including 24 with 1000 plus population; 44 with 500-999 population; and 44 habitations with 250-499 population. The State has still 25 habitations (three habitations of 500-999 population and 22 habitations of 250-4999 population) to be connected by roads. To connect the 25 habitations, a total of 289 km. road works would be required. Average cost of construction of roads per km. is about Rs. 26 lakh for Stage 1 and the total requirement of fund would be Rs. 75.14 crore.

Of the total 248 road works in the State spanning 2668.87 kms. 108 (2636.78 km.) have been completed at an expenditure of Rs. 212.71 crore. The remaining 632.08 km with estimated cost of Rs. 162.02 crore, is likely to be completed by 2009-10. At present, work on 632 km. road length would be completed. The average cost of Stage II work is estimated to be Rs. 30 lakh and total requirement of funds for this is likely to be Rs. 129 crore. It may be mentioned that the State has already 805 km. long through routes and 6,003 link routes and proposal in on to upgrade 25 per cent of through routes and 5 per cent of link routes.

Conclusion

In the absence of adequate rail and air connectivity in Nagaland, road transport plays a crucial role in providing connectivity between towns and villages. Since, roads are the veins of Nagaland; the movement of both goods and people is possible only through good network of roads, particularly rural roads. Considering the pivotal role of rural roads in the State's economy, greater attention is required towards the development of rural roads with technical standard and quality assurance. PMGSY being a centre-sponsored project provides funds to the State for construction and upgradation of rural roads. It would not be a problem for developing rural roads in the State. Nagaland is basically a State characterized by rural areas. Obviously it will derive maximum benefit from PMGSY.

What requires is the proper implementation of the schemes with transparency and accountability.

REFERENCES

Basic Statistics of NER, 2007, NEC, Shillong.

Chandrasekhar, B.P. (2005): *Rural Transport Planning and Development—A Case Study of PMGSY,* Paper presented at All India Commerce Association Conference, Andhra University, Andhra Pradesh, 9-11 August.

Jain, J.K. (1990): *Transport Economics,* Chaitinya Publishing House, Allahabad.

Patikar, Gautam (2006): *Role of Infrastructure in the Socio-Economic Development of Nagaland,* Paper presented at All India Commerce Association Conference, Andhra University, Andhra Pradesh, 9-11 August.

Statistical Handbook (various issues) , Government of Nagaland, Kohima.

Index